MATT WAGNER'S
GRENDEL TALES

FOUR DEVILS, ONE HELL

Written by
JAMES ROBINSON

Art, lettering, and collection cover art by
TEDDY H. KRISTIANSEN

Creative direction by
MATT WAGNER

Chapter cover art by
MATT WAGNER
and
TEDDY H. KRISTIANSEN

"Bixby flashback" pencils by
JAN SOLHEIM

Edited by
DIANA SCHUTZ

Collection designed by
CARY GRAZZINI

Grendel created and owned by Matt Wagner

DARK HORSE COMICS®

MIKE RICHARDSON *publisher*

NEIL HANKERSON *executive vice president*

DAVID SCROGGY *vice president of publishing*

LOU BANK *vice president of sales & marketing*

ANDY KARABATSOS *vice president of finance*

MARK ANDERSON *general counsel*

DIANA SCHUTZ *editor in chief*

RANDY STRADLEY *creative director*

CINDY MARKS *director of production & design*

MARK COX *art director*

CHRIS CREVISTON *director of accounting*

MICHAEL MARTENS *marketing director*

TOD BORLESKE *sales and licensing director*

MARK ELLINGTON *director of operations*

DALE LaFOUNTAIN *director of m.i.s.*

Published by Dark Horse Comics
10956 SE Main
Milwaukie, OR 97222

Trade paperback ISBN: 1-56971-027-9
First trade paperback edition: December 1994

10 9 8 7 6 5 4 3 2

INTRODUCTION

From the very beginning, the evolution of *Grendel* has involved a bizarre series of accidents, coincidence, and luck.

A chance meeting on an elevator during my college days led to my first publishing efforts: a Grendel story.

A routine signing on a *Mage* promotional tour introduced me to the work of two young, local artists named Arnold and Jacob Pander.

An unusual fan/hate letter caught my attention and led to my long-running friendship/collaboration with Bernie Mireault — who, in turn, later got me to look at the work of a young punk he knew, by the name of Pat McEown.

Grendel, it would seem, has developed something of a life all its own.

How fitting, then, that the long gestation of *Grendel*'s first-born, *Grendel Tales*, would also be fraught with the same sense of dramatic convergence. As I recall, the whole convoluted staging went somewhat like this . . .

— 1988 and I'm in England to attend the annual United Kingdom Comic Art Convention (UKCAC). My first time truly abroad and the jet lag is just beginning to kick in at that stage just *past* the initial exhaustion. As a featured guest of the con, I'm expected to sit for an hour-long panel/interview about me and my work hosted by someone selected by the con. Near delirious, I was nonetheless surprised at how lively and sustained the whole affair managed to become. Part of this was due to the audience, but a great part was due to the clever and structured approach of my interviewer. Some time after the panel, I was wandering through the convention hall when I heard my name called. I turned to find my slim, smart panel host handing me a copy of his own recently published first writing work in comics. I looked down at the stylish cover to *London's Dark*, drawn by Paul Johnson and written by James Robinson.

— Almost a year later and I'm back home at work when I receive a call from the author himself, to whom I had always meant to drop a note of thanks (if only I weren't, truly, the world's worst correspondent). James glowed a bit at the praise I laid out for his story and then went on to explain that he now worked for Titan Books and would I be interested in doing a cover interview for blah, blah, blah . . . I have a bad habit of interrupting people sometimes, but, at least, *some*times it's with an offer of work. See, I had been kicking around this idea of a *Grendel* spin-off series that would allow other writers to deal with the concept. I knew James was very conversant with the Grendel concept, and I thought he was an extremely promising writer who might jump at the chance to work on such a high-visibility project. He did. The story came. I loved it. James had very neatly summed up all the variation and familiarity I was hoping to achieve with this project.

— Somewhere over the space of the next four years, there falls an international move for James, a transcontinental move for me, a wedding, a birth, three artist changes, thousands of unpaid dollars, and the implosion of my former publishers. All too messy to enumerate.

— It's 1990 and I'm in Toronto to meet with another British writer to talk about possibly working on an ultimately ill-fated Superman project. A local friend comes to see me and totes along a unique item to show me — a *European* Superman album produced in Denmark, featuring the beautiful work of a young animator named Teddy H. Kristiansen. This guy and I obviously had a very similar approach to our craft, and I tried everything short of murdering the book's owner to obtain a copy for myself. No dice.

— 1992 and I'm at the Diamond Distributors cocktail party at the San Diego Con. A Danish writer/agent I know catches me by the arm and says, "I want to introduce you to Teddy Kristiansen!" By the end of the show, James, Diana, and I had all agreed that Teddy was the perfect artist to bring the multitextural world of *Grendel Tales* to life.

Now, I've been sitting at the creative helm of this book for over ten years and counting.
Just *you* try and make some sense of this lucky, beautiful mess. I've tried and I can't. You see . . .

. . . it's *alive!*

M. WAGNER

Chapter One

Four Beginnings, One Case

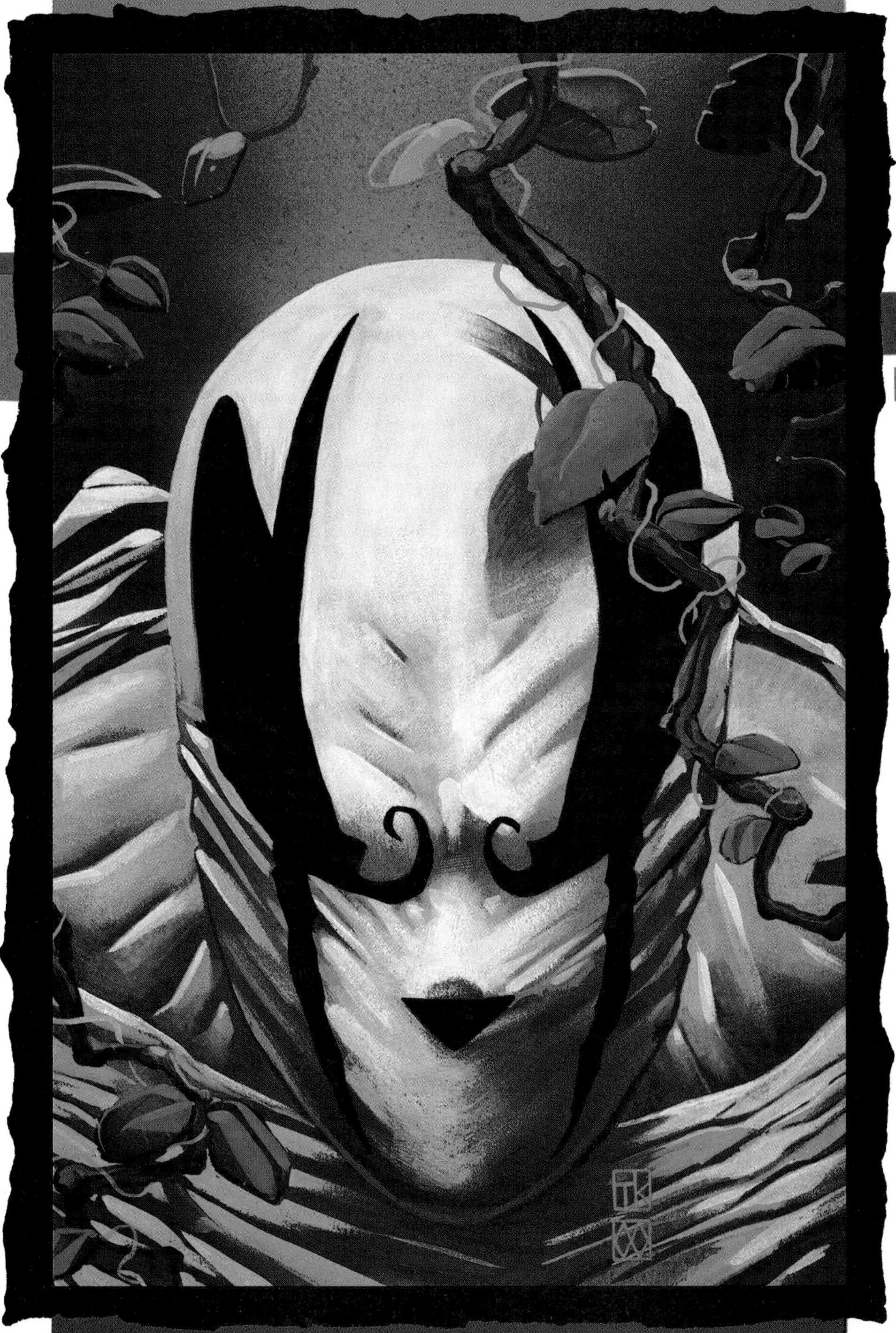

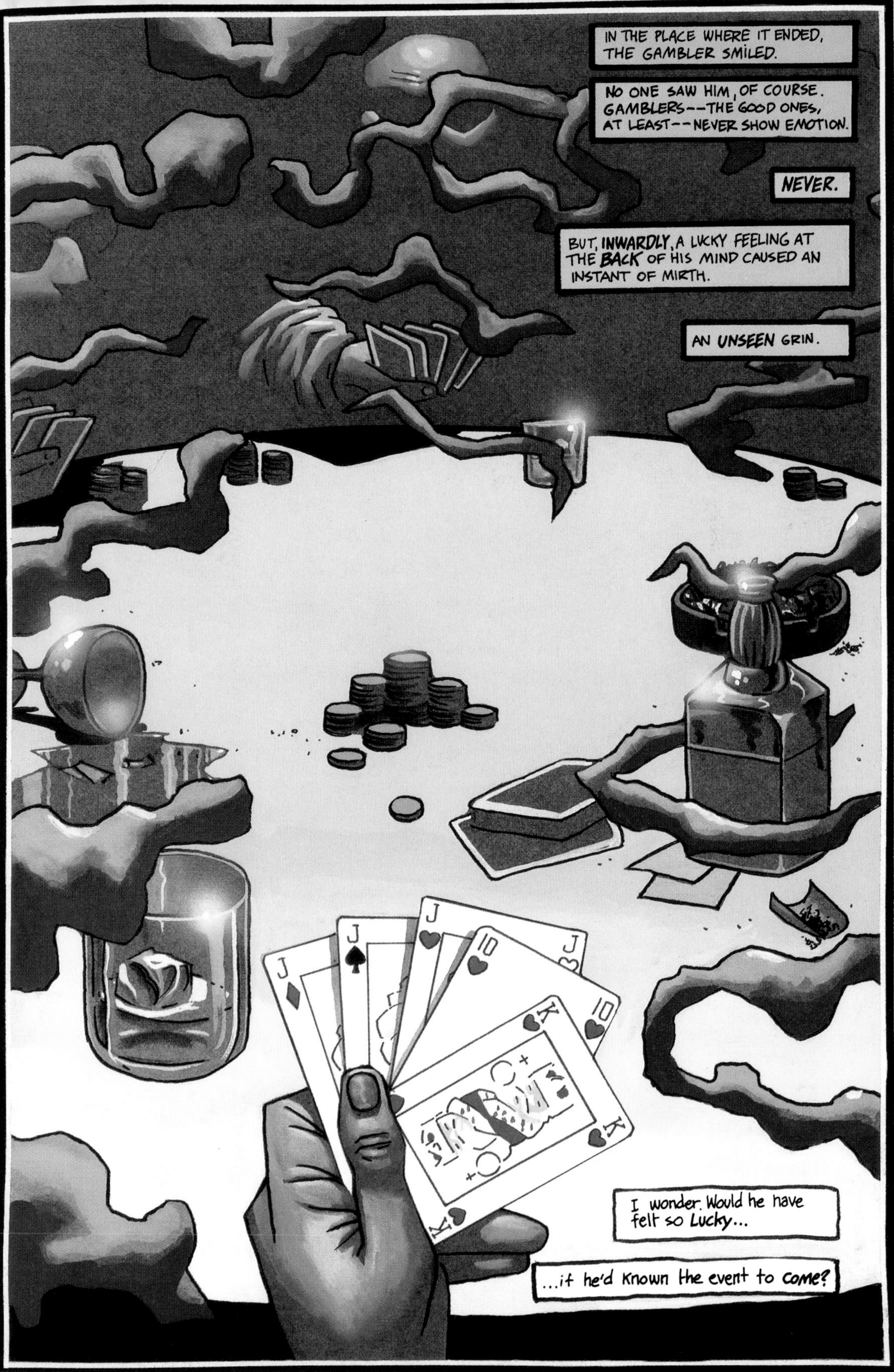
IN THE PLACE WHERE IT ENDED, THE GAMBLER SMILED.
NO ONE SAW HIM, OF COURSE. GAMBLERS--THE GOOD ONES, AT LEAST--NEVER SHOW EMOTION.
NEVER.
BUT, INWARDLY, A LUCKY FEELING AT THE BACK OF HIS MIND CAUSED AN INSTANT OF MIRTH.
AN UNSEEN GRIN.
I wonder. Would he have felt so Lucky...
...if he'd known the event to come?

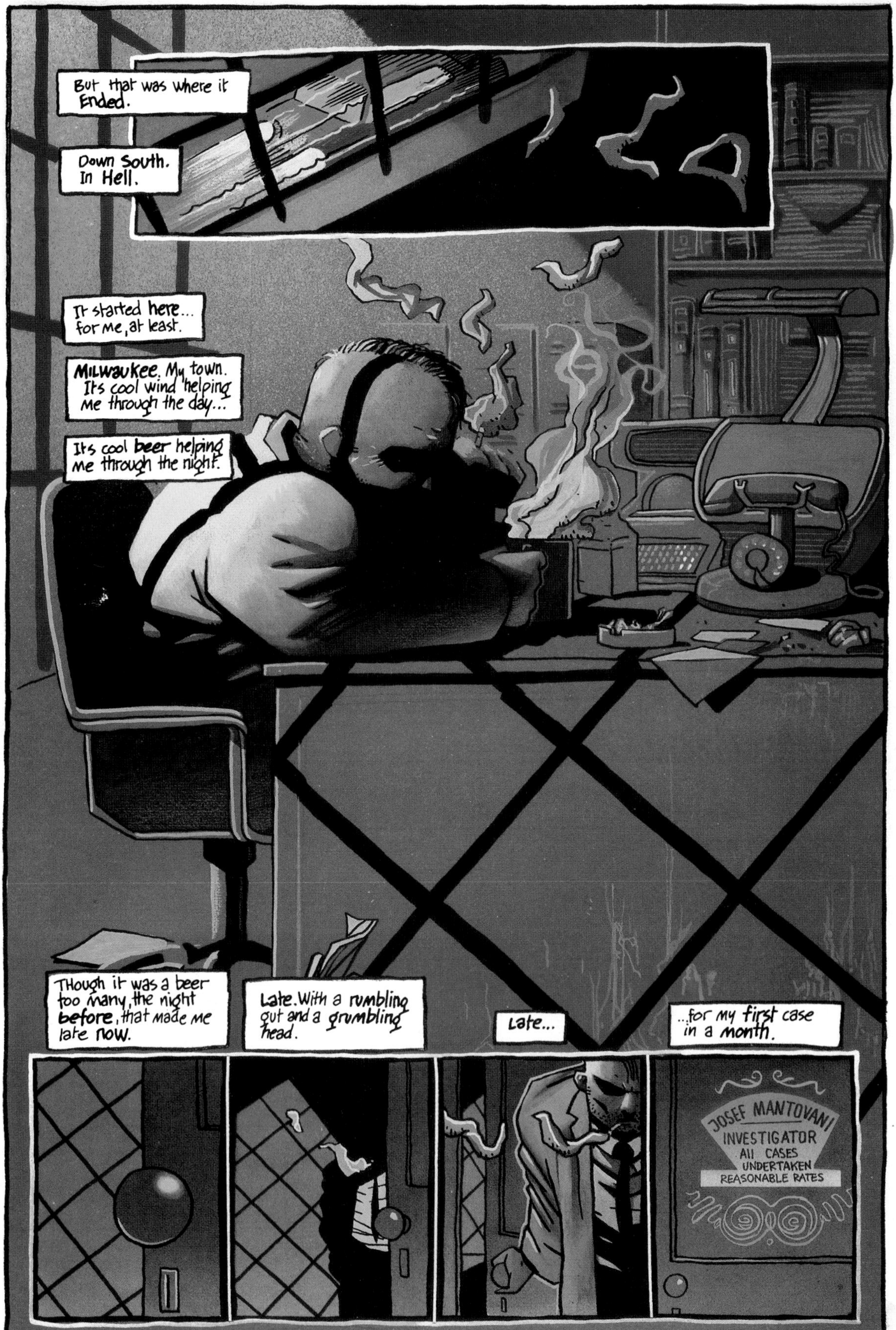
But that was where it Ended.
Down South. In Hell.
It started here... for me, at least.
Milwaukee. My town. Its cool wind helping me through the day...
Its cool beer helping me through the night.
Though it was a beer too many, the night before, that made me late now.
Late. With a rumbling gut and a grumbling head.
Late...
...for my first case in a month.
JOSEF MANTOVANI
INVESTIGATOR
All CASES
UNDERTAKEN
REASONABLE RATES

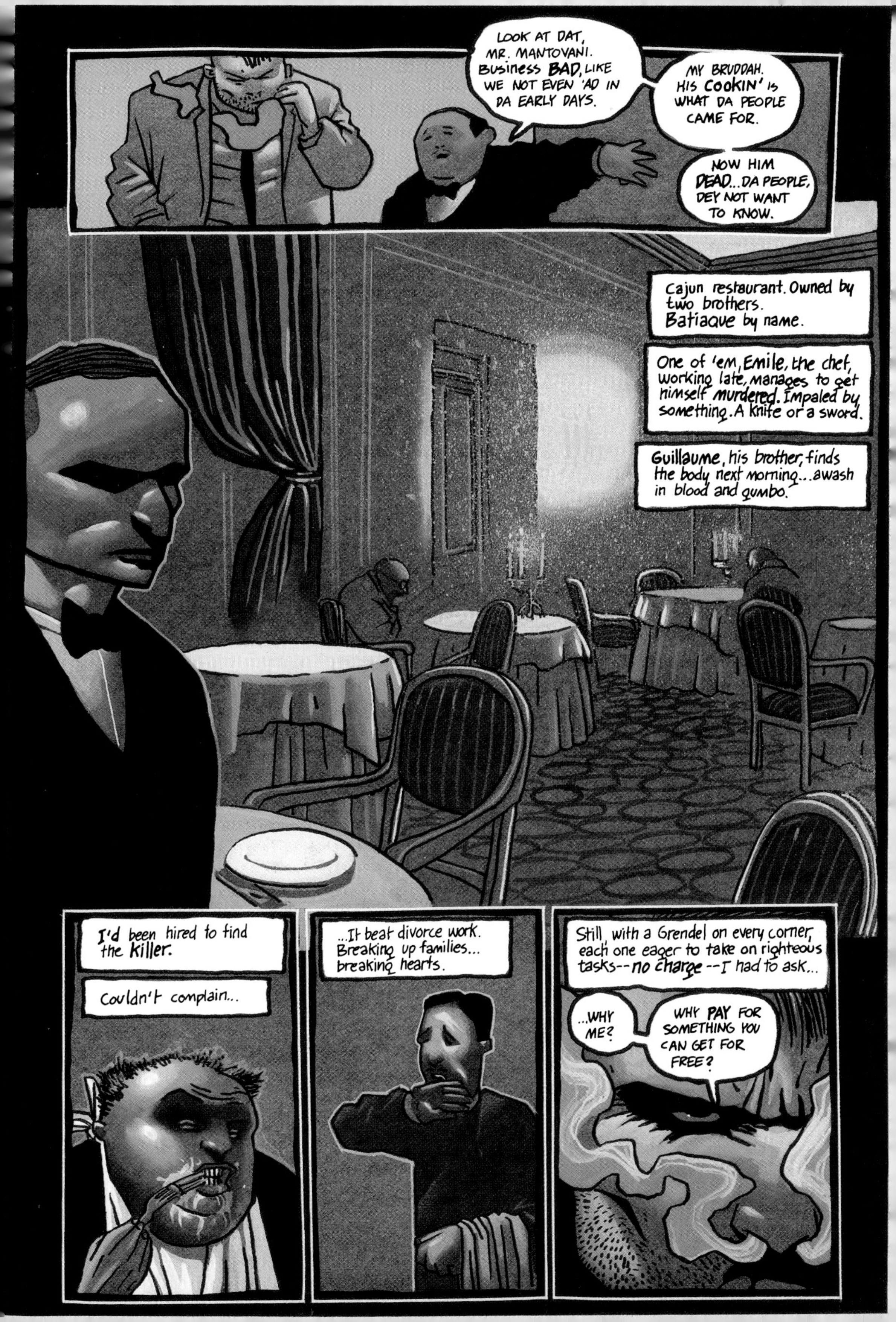
LOOK AT DAT, MR. MANTOVANI. BUSINESS BAD, LIKE WE NOT EVEN 'AD IN DA EARLY DAYS.
MY BRUDDAH. HIS COOKIN' IS WHAT DA PEOPLE CAME FOR.
NOW HIM DEAD... DA PEOPLE, DEY NOT WANT TO KNOW.
Cajun restaurant. Owned by two brothers. Batiaque by name.
One of 'em, Emile, the chef, working late, manages to get himself murdered. Impaled by something. A knife or a sword.
Guillaume, his brother, finds the body next morning... awash in blood and gumbo.
I'd been hired to find the killer.
Couldn't complain...
...It beat divorce work. Breaking up families... breaking hearts.
Still, with a Grendel on every corner, each one eager to take on righteous tasks--no charge--I had to ask...
...WHY ME?
WHY PAY FOR SOMETHING YOU CAN GET FOR FREE?

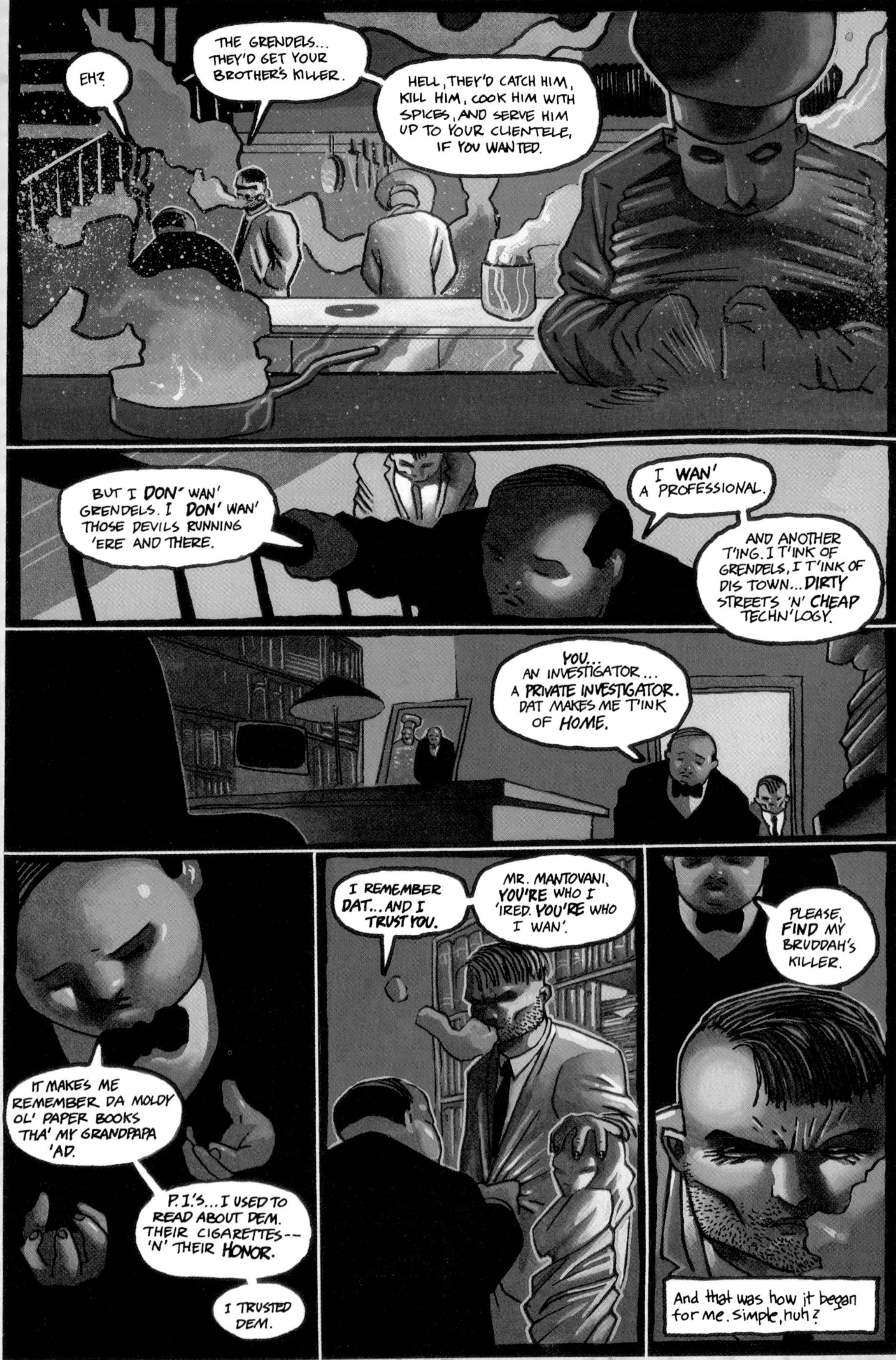
EH?
THE GRENDELS... THEY'D GET YOUR BROTHER'S KILLER.
HELL, THEY'D CATCH HIM, KILL HIM, COOK HIM WITH SPICES, AND SERVE HIM UP TO YOUR CLIENTELE, IF YOU WANTED.
BUT I DON' WAN' GRENDELS. I DON' WAN' THOSE DEVILS RUNNING 'ERE AND THERE.
I WAN' A PROFESSIONAL.
AND ANOTHER T'ING. I T'INK OF GRENDELS, I T'INK OF DIS TOWN... DIRTY STREETS 'N' CHEAP TECHN'LOGY.
YOU... AN INVESTIGATOR... A PRIVATE INVESTIGATOR. DAT MAKES ME T'INK OF HOME.
IT MAKES ME REMEMBER DA MOLDY OL' PAPER BOOKS THA' MY GRANDPAPA 'AD.
P.I.'S... I USED TO READ ABOUT DEM. THEIR CIGARETTES-- 'N' THEIR HONOR.
I TRUSTED DEM.
I REMEMBER DAT... AND I TRUST YOU.
MR. MANTOVANI, YOU'RE WHO I 'IRED. YOU'RE WHO I WAN'.
PLEASE, FIND MY BRUDDAH'S KILLER.
And that was how it began for me. Simple, huh?

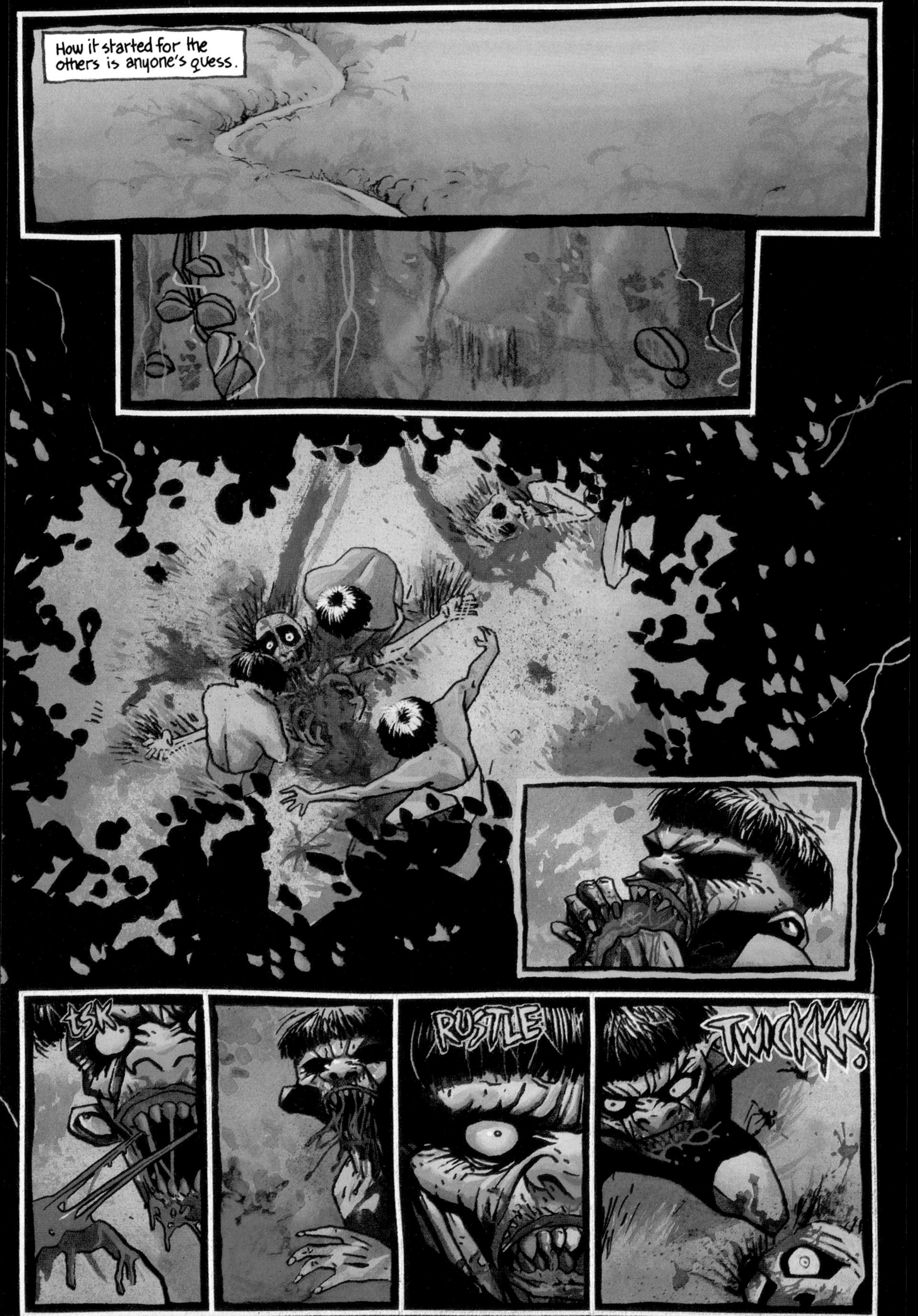
How it started for the others is anyone's guess.
TSK
RUSTLE
TWICKKK!

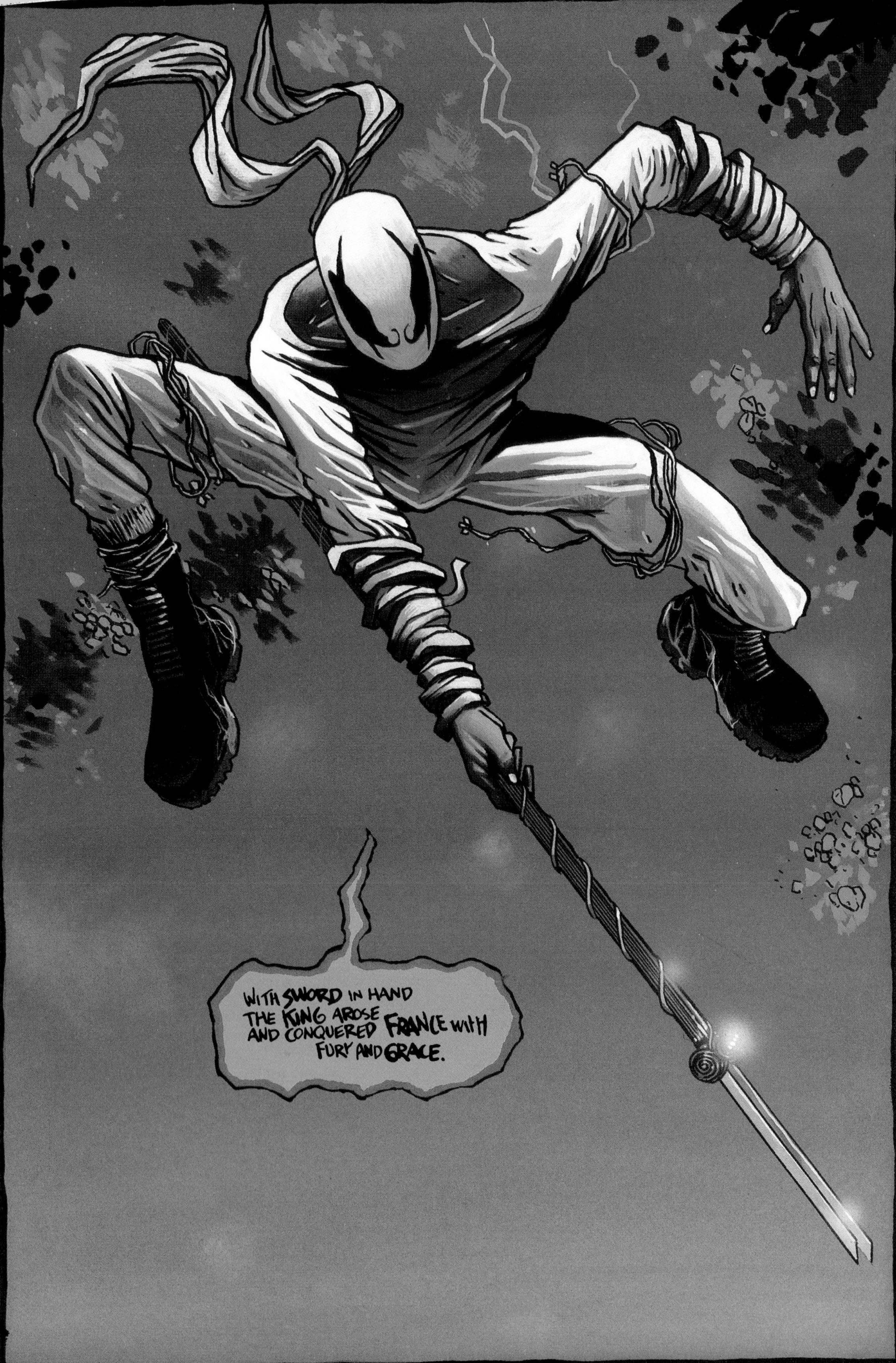
WITH SWORD IN HAND THE KING AROSE AND CONQUERED FRANCE WITH FURY AND GRACE.

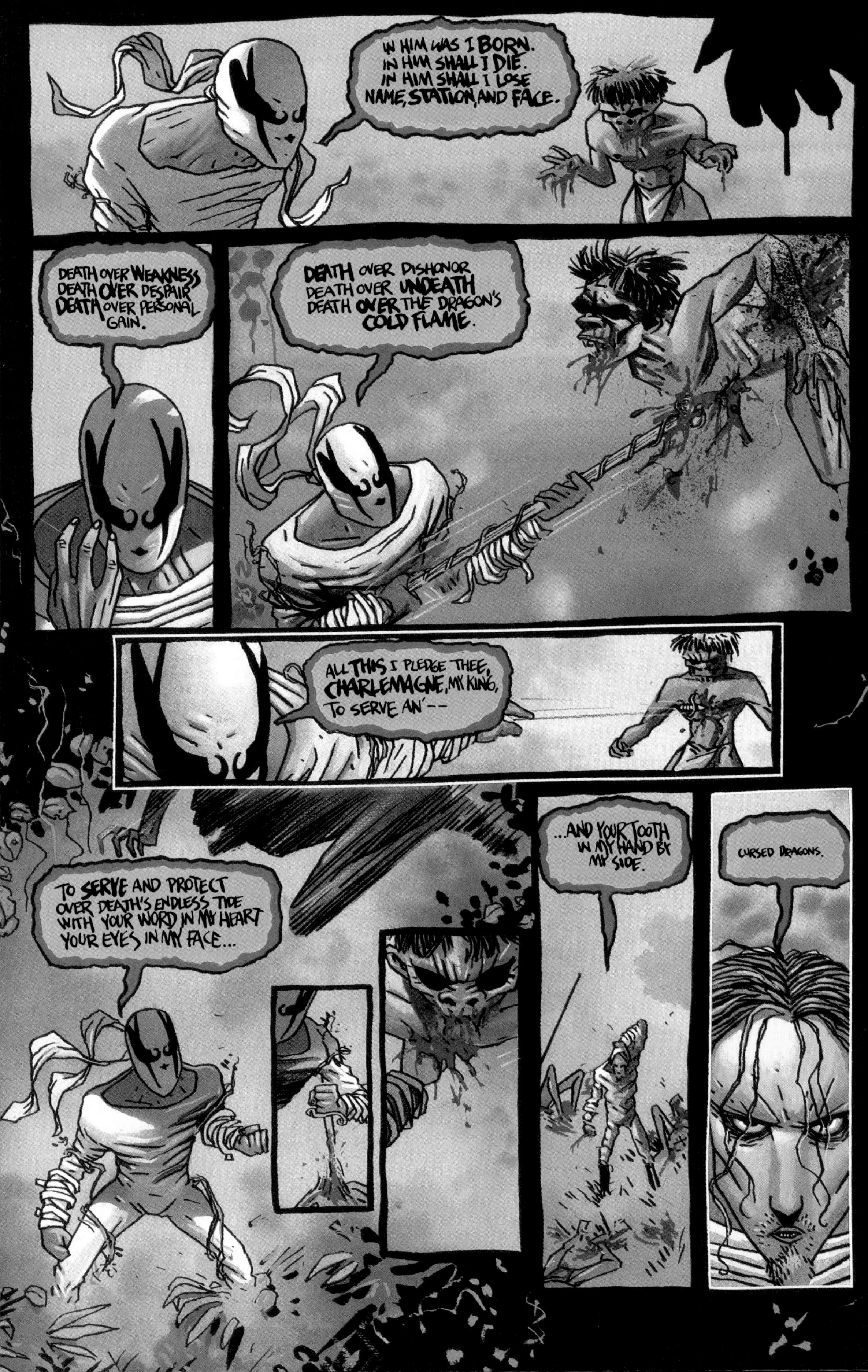
IN HIM WAS I BORN. IN HIM SHALL I DIE. IN HIM SHALL I LOSE NAME, STATION, AND FACE.
DEATH OVER WEAKNESS DEATH OVER DESPAIR DEATH OVER PERSONAL GAIN.
DEATH OVER DISHONOR DEATH OVER UNDEATH DEATH OVER THE DRAGON'S COLD FLAME.
ALL THIS I PLEDGE THEE, CHARLEMAGNE, MY KING, TO SERVE AN'--
TO SERVE AND PROTECT OVER DEATH'S ENDLESS TIDE WITH YOUR WORD IN MY HEART YOUR EYES IN MY FACE...
...AND YOUR TOOTH IN MY HAND BY MY SIDE.
CURSED DRAGONS.

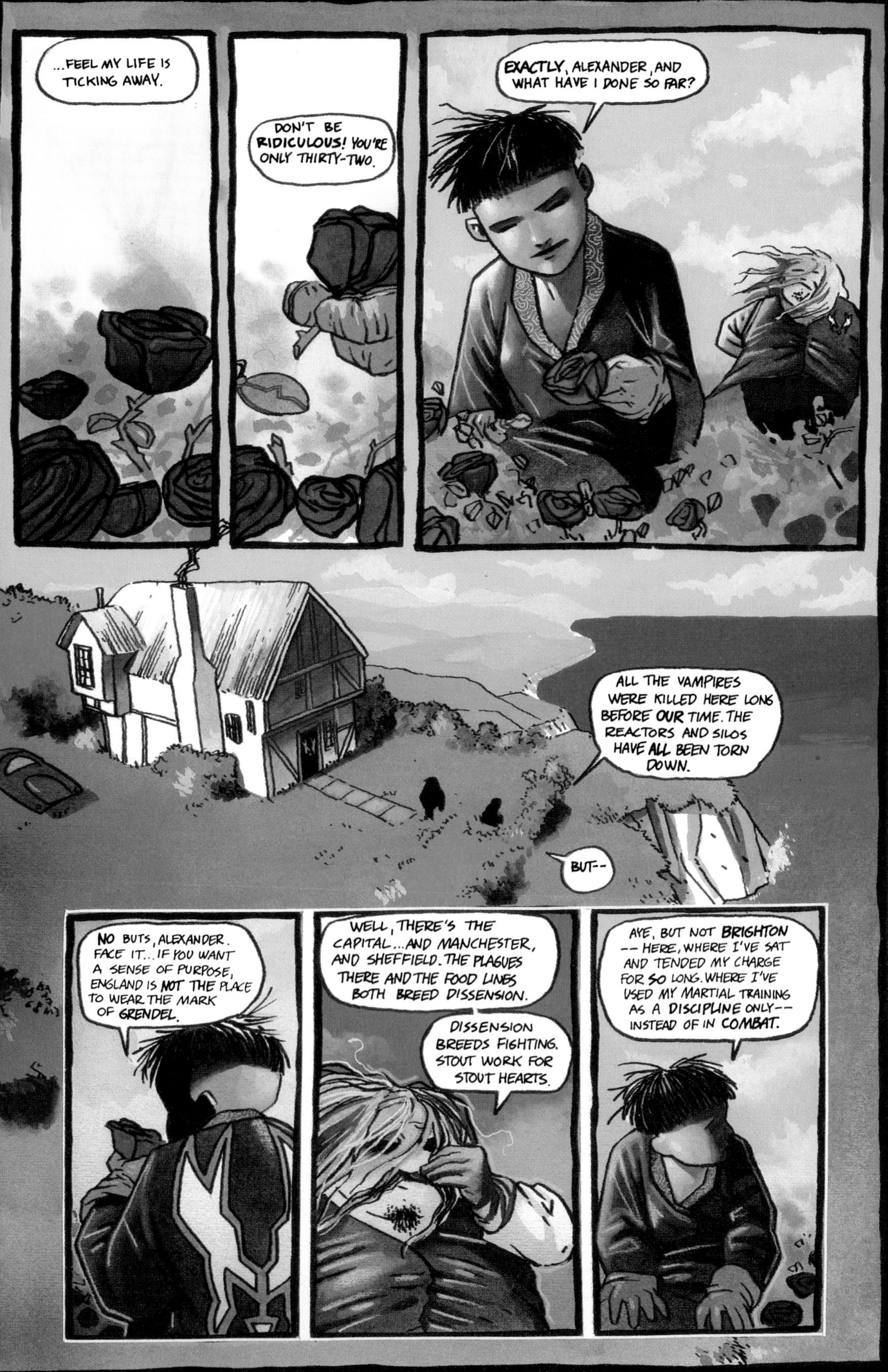
...FEEL MY LIFE IS TICKING AWAY.
DON'T BE RIDICULOUS! YOU'RE ONLY THIRTY-TWO.
EXACTLY, ALEXANDER, AND WHAT HAVE I DONE SO FAR?
ALL THE VAMPIRES WERE KILLED HERE LONG BEFORE OUR TIME. THE REACTORS AND SILOS HAVE ALL BEEN TORN DOWN.
BUT--
NO BUTS, ALEXANDER. FACE IT... IF YOU WANT A SENSE OF PURPOSE, ENGLAND IS NOT THE PLACE TO WEAR THE MARK OF GRENDEL.
WELL, THERE'S THE CAPITAL... AND MANCHESTER, AND SHEFFIELD. THE PLAGUES THERE AND THE FOOD LINES BOTH BREED DISSENSION.
DISSENSION BREEDS FIGHTING. STOUT WORK FOR STOUT HEARTS.
AYE, BUT NOT BRIGHTON -- HERE, WHERE I'VE SAT AND TENDED MY CHARGE FOR SO LONG. WHERE I'VE USED MY MARTIAL TRAINING AS A DISCIPLINE ONLY-- INSTEAD OF IN COMBAT.

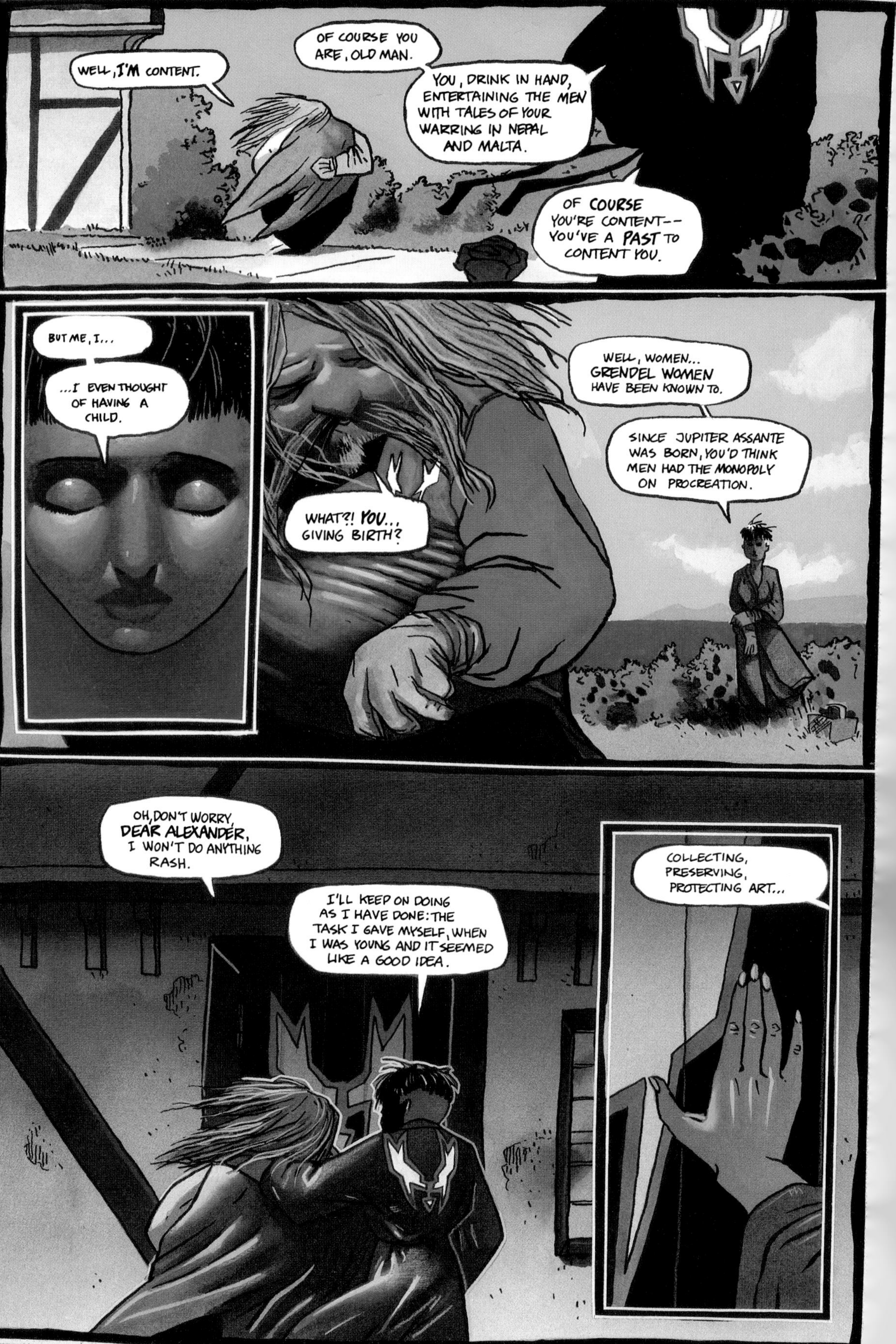
WELL, I'M CONTENT.
OF COURSE YOU ARE, OLD MAN.
YOU, DRINK IN HAND, ENTERTAINING THE MEN WITH TALES OF YOUR WARRING IN NEPAL AND MALTA.
OF COURSE YOU'RE CONTENT-- YOU'VE A PAST TO CONTENT YOU.
BUT ME, I...
...I EVEN THOUGHT OF HAVING A CHILD.
WHAT?! YOU.., GIVING BIRTH?
WELL, WOMEN... GRENDEL WOMEN HAVE BEEN KNOWN TO.
SINCE JUPITER ASSANTE WAS BORN, YOU'D THINK MEN HAD THE MONOPOLY ON PROCREATION.
OH, DON'T WORRY, DEAR ALEXANDER, I WON'T DO ANYTHING RASH.
I'LL KEEP ON DOING AS I HAVE DONE: THE TASK I GAVE MYSELF, WHEN I WAS YOUNG AND IT SEEMED LIKE A GOOD IDEA.
COLLECTING, PRESERVING, PROTECTING ART...

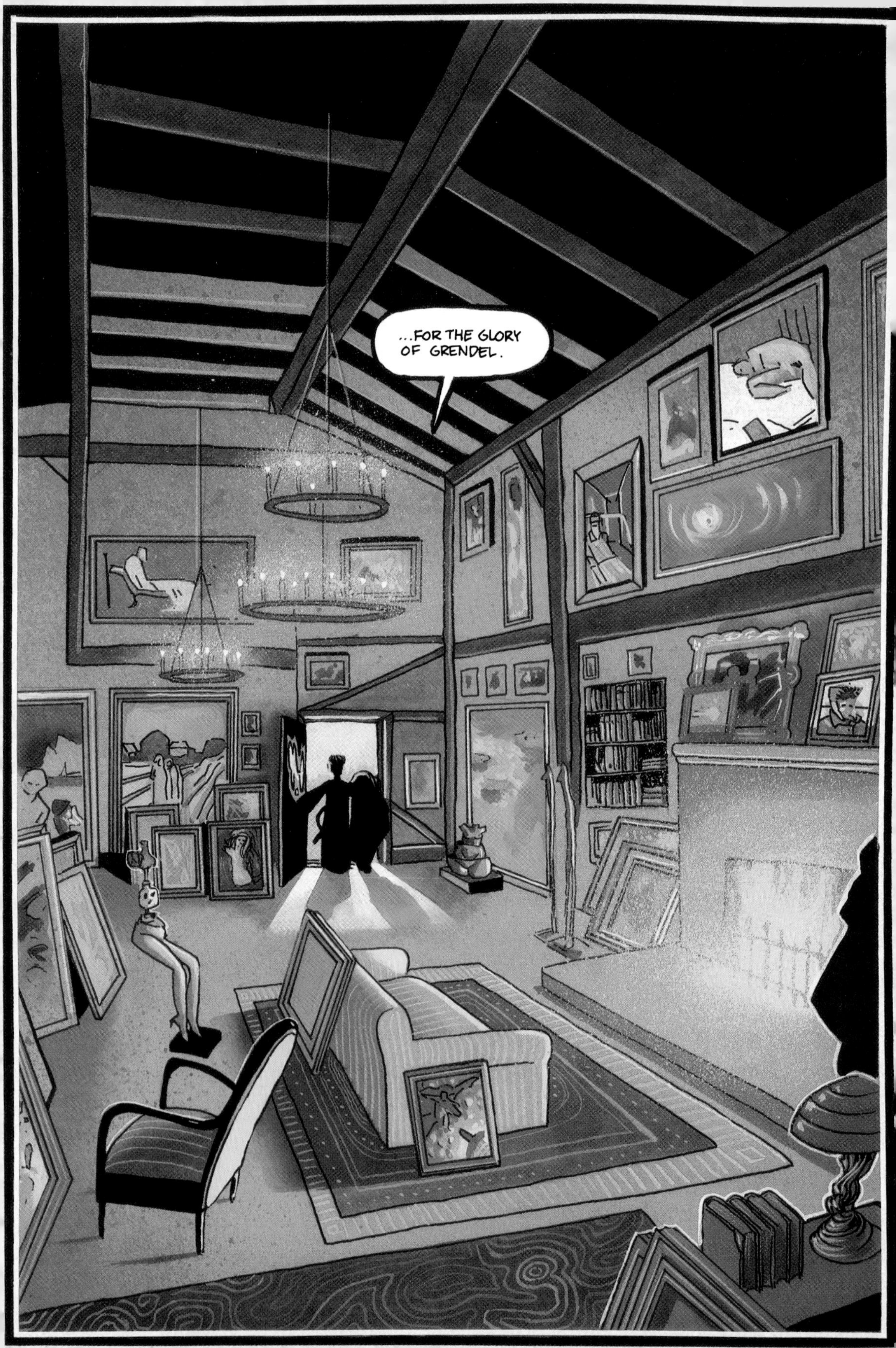
...FOR THE GLORY OF GRENDEL.

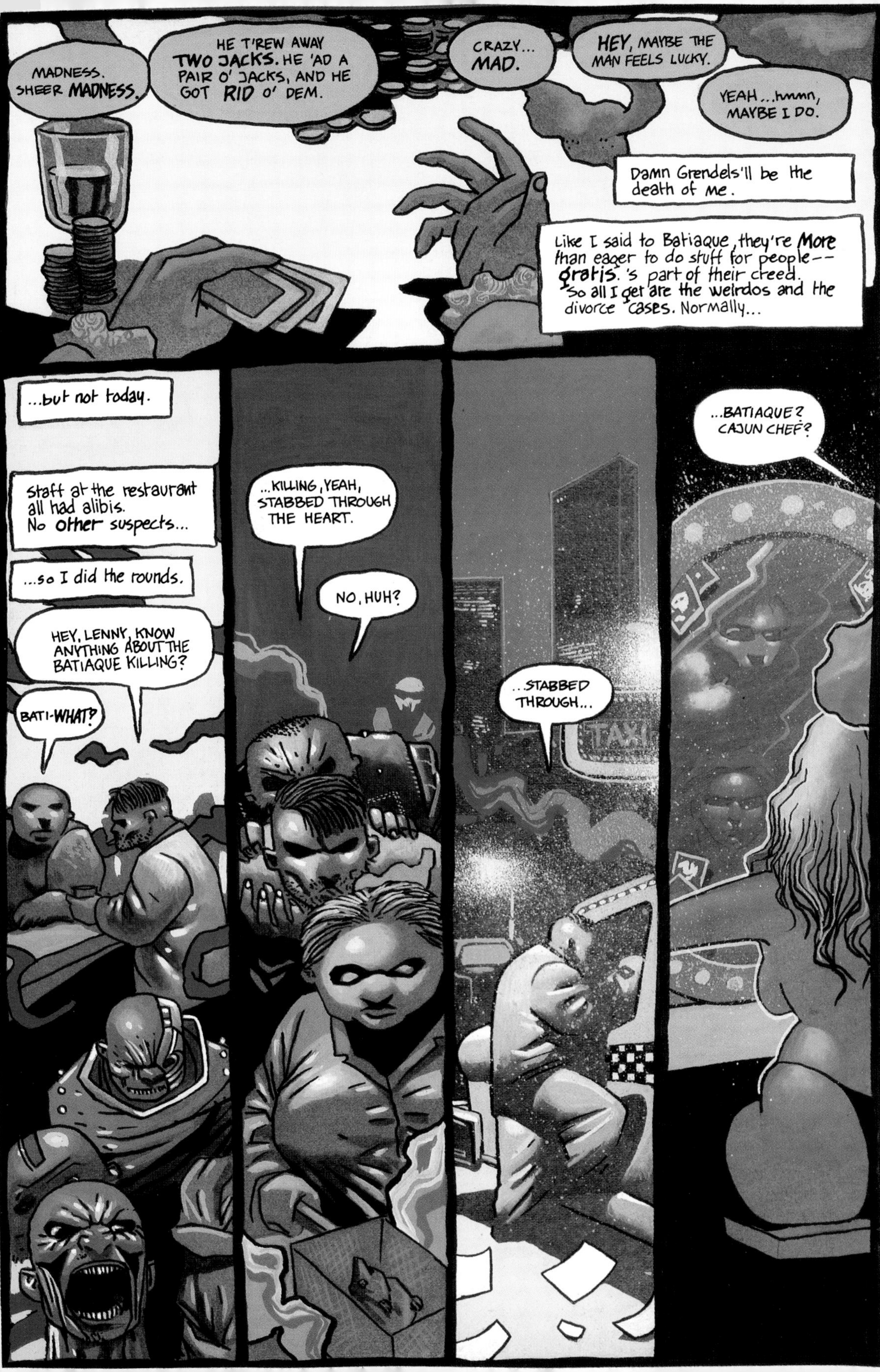
MADNESS. SHEER MADNESS.
HE T'REW AWAY TWO JACKS. HE 'AD A PAIR O' JACKS, AND HE GOT RID O' DEM.
CRAZY... MAD.
HEY, MAYBE THE MAN FEELS LUCKY.
YEAH...hmmn, MAYBE I DO.
Damn Grendels'll be the death of me.
Like I said to Batiaque, they're More than eager to do stuff for people-- gratis. 's part of their creed. So all I get are the weirdos and the divorce cases. Normally...
...but not today.
Staff at the restaurant all had alibis. No other suspects...
...so I did the rounds.
HEY, LENNY, KNOW ANYTHING ABOUT THE BATIAQUE KILLING?
BATI-WHAT?
...KILLING, YEAH, STABBED THROUGH THE HEART.
NO, HUH?
...STABBED THROUGH...
TAXI
...BATIAQUE? CAJUN CHEF?

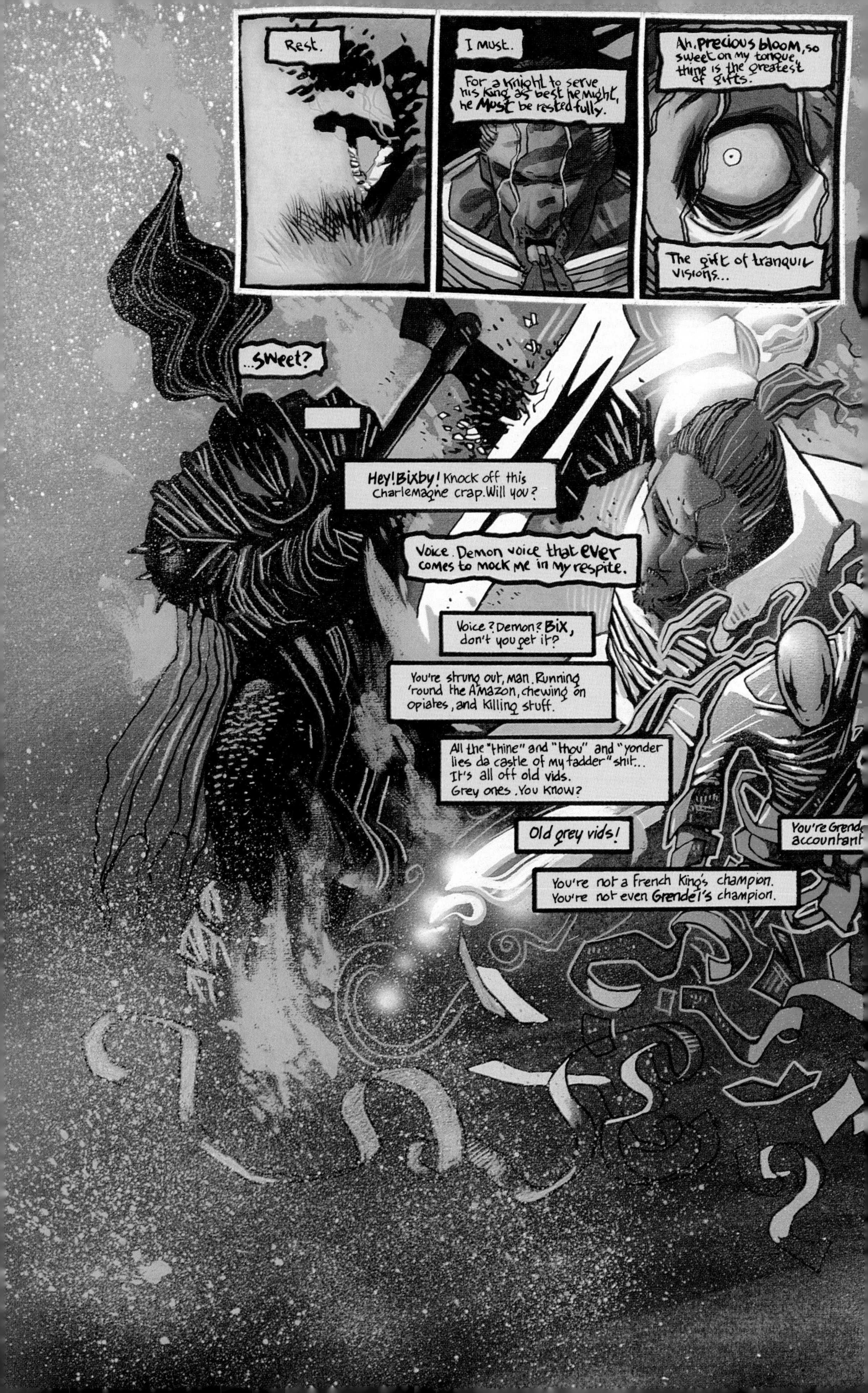
Rest.
I must.
For a knight to serve his king as best he might, he MUST be rested fully.
Ah, precious bloom, so sweet on my tongue, thine is the greatest of gifts.
The gift of tranquil visions...
...sweet?
Hey! Bixby! Knock off this Charlemagne crap. Will you?
Voice. Demon voice that ever comes to mock me in my respite.
Voice? Demon? Bix, don't you get it?
You're strung out, man. Running 'round the Amazon, chewing on opiates, and killing stuff.
All the "thine" and "thou" and "yonder lies da castle of my fadder" shit.. It's all off old vids. Grey ones. You know?
Old grey vids!
You're not a French King's champion. You're not even Grendel's champion.

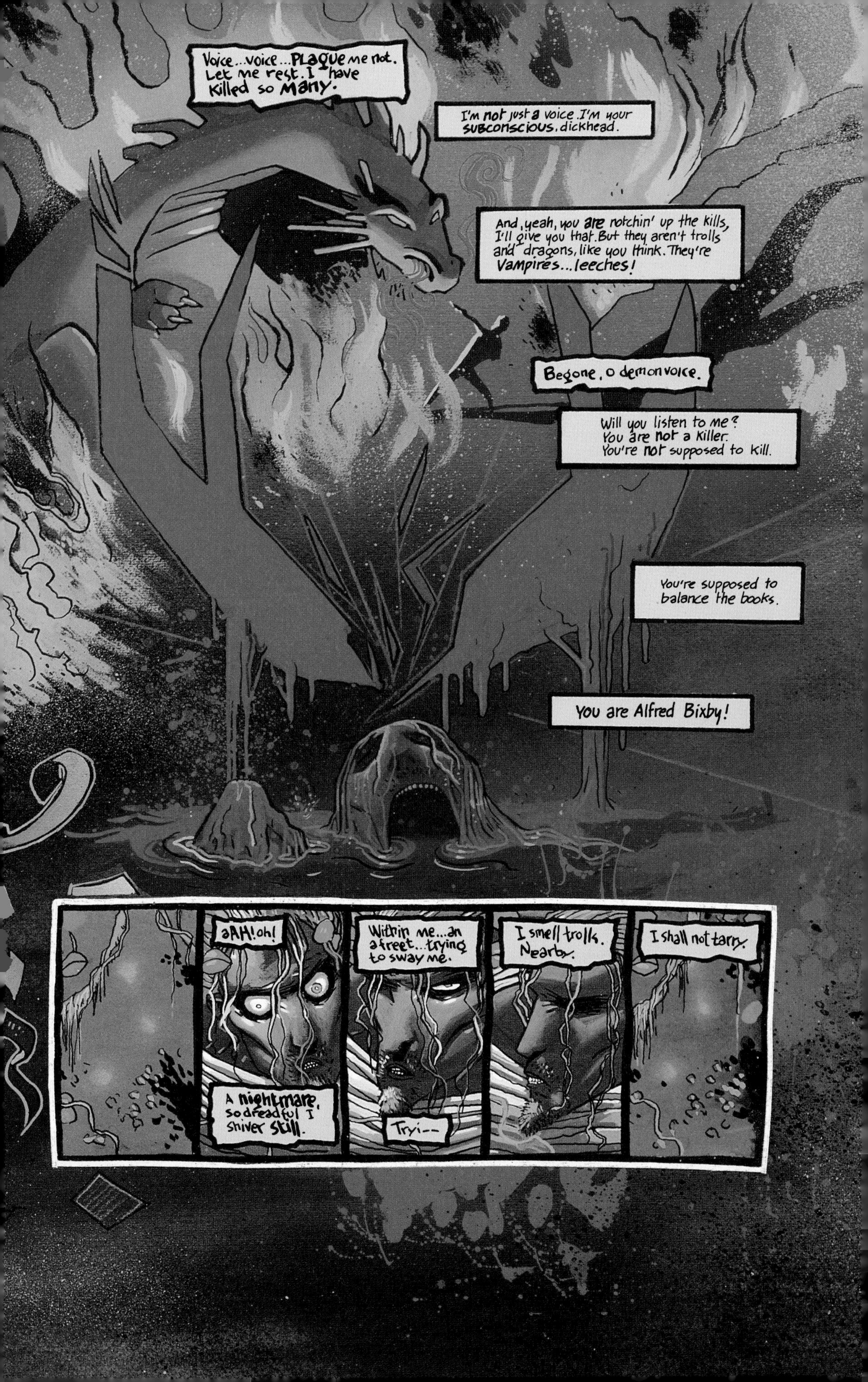

Voice...voice...PLAGUE me not. Let me rest. I have killed so many.
I'm not just a voice. I'm your subconscious, dickhead.
And, yeah, you are notchin' up the kills, I'll give you that. But they aren't trolls and dragons, like you think. They're vampires...leeches!
Begone, O demon voice.
Will you listen to me? You are not a killer. You're not supposed to kill.
You're supposed to balance the books.
You are Alfred Bixby!
aAH! oh!
A nightmare, so dreadful I shiver still.
Within me...an afreet...trying to sway me.
Tryi--
I smell trolls. Nearby.
I shall not tarry.

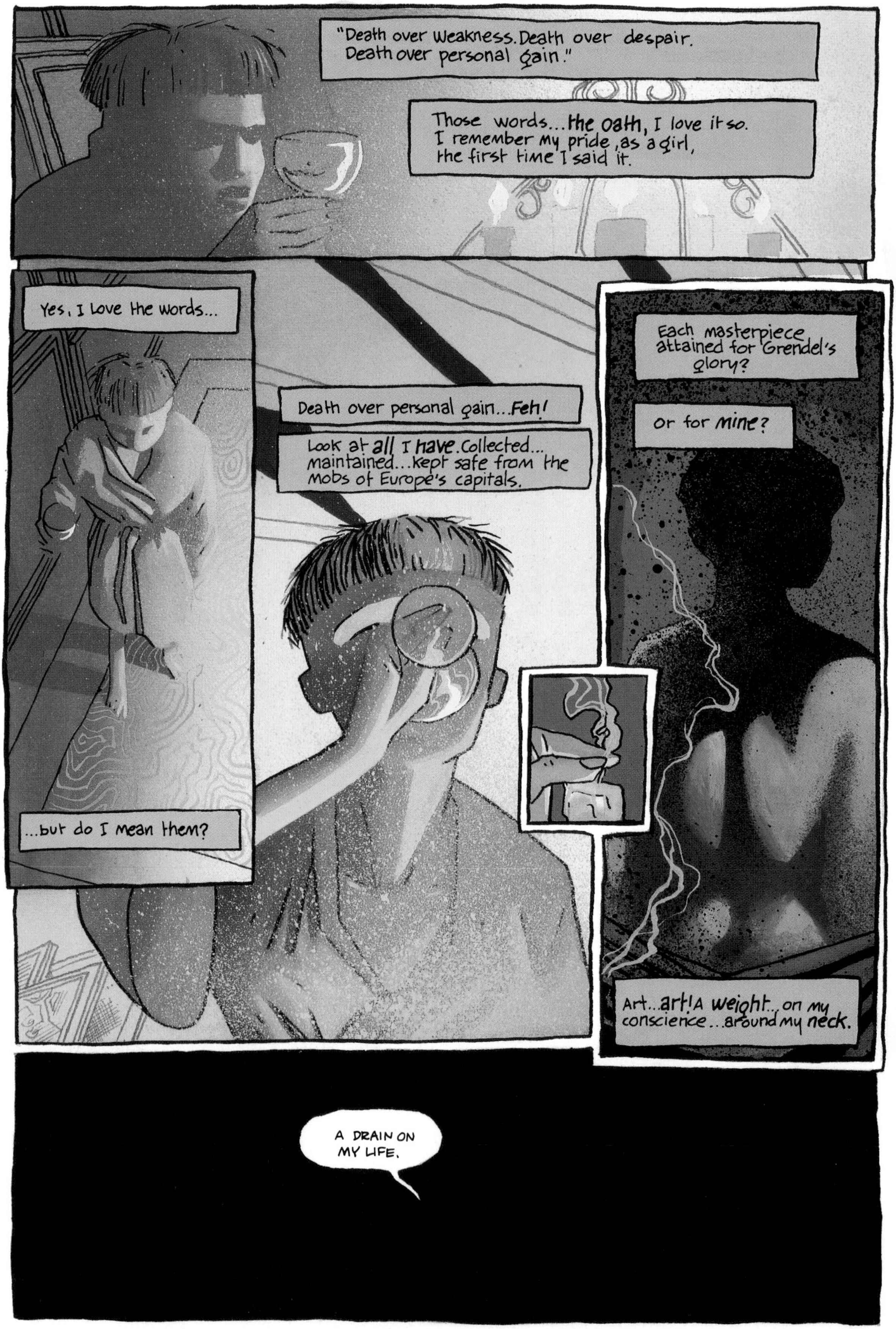
"Death over Weakness. Death over despair. Death over personal gain."
Those words...the oath, I love it so. I remember my pride, as a girl, the first time I said it.
Yes, I Love the words...
...but do I mean them?
Death over personal gain...Feh!
Look at all I have. Collected... maintained...kept safe from the mobs of Europe's capitals.
Each masterpiece attained for Grendel's glory?
Or for mine?
Art...art! A weight... on my conscience...around my neck.
A DRAIN ON MY LIFE.

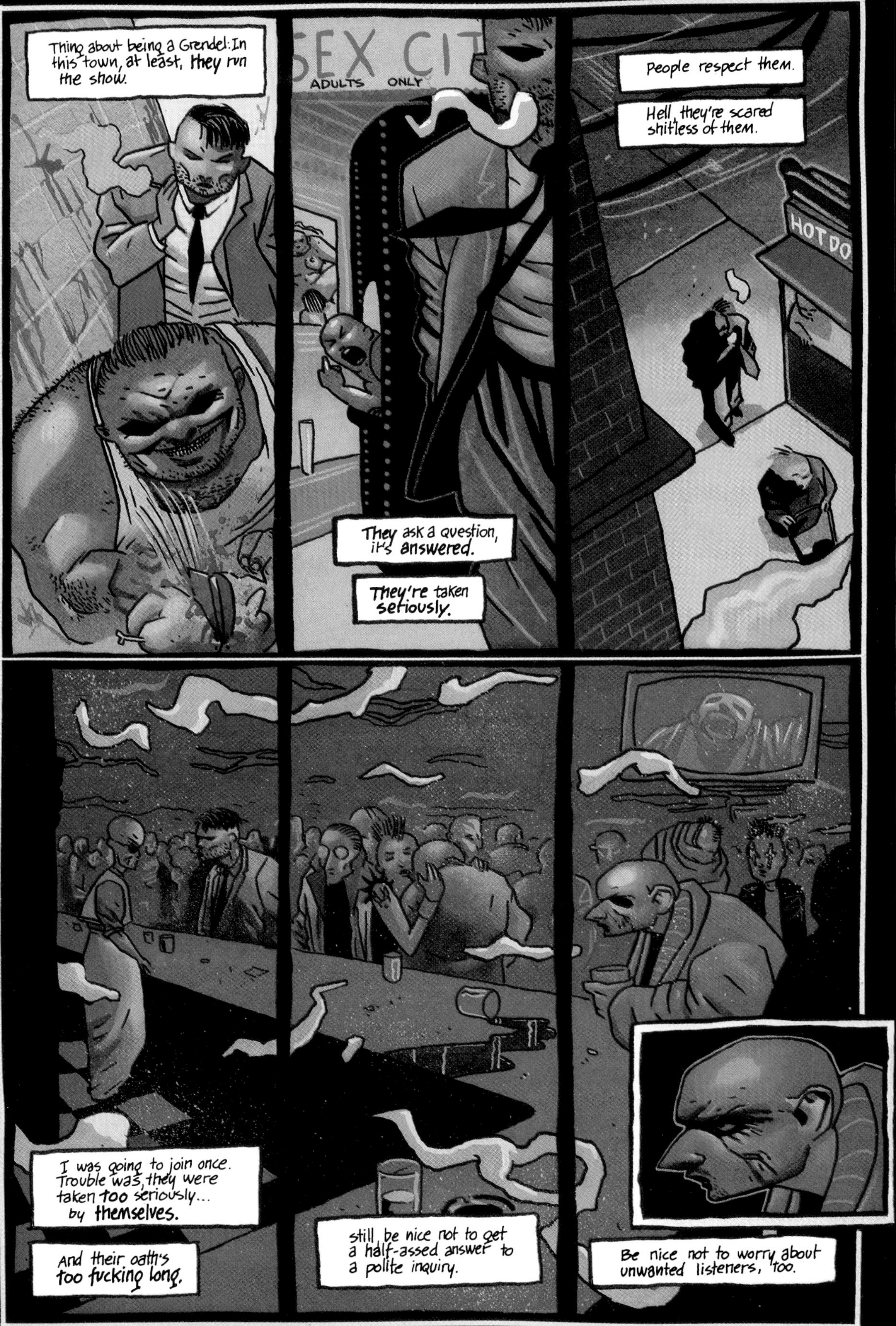
Thing about being a Grendel: In this town, at least, they run the show.
SEX CIT
ADULTS ONLY
People respect them.
Hell, they're scared shitless of them.
HOT DO
They ask a question, it's answered.
They're taken seriously.
I was going to join once. Trouble was, they were taken too seriously... by themselves.
And their oath's too fucking long.
still be nice not to get a half-assed answer to a polite inquiry.
Be nice not to worry about unwanted listeners, too.

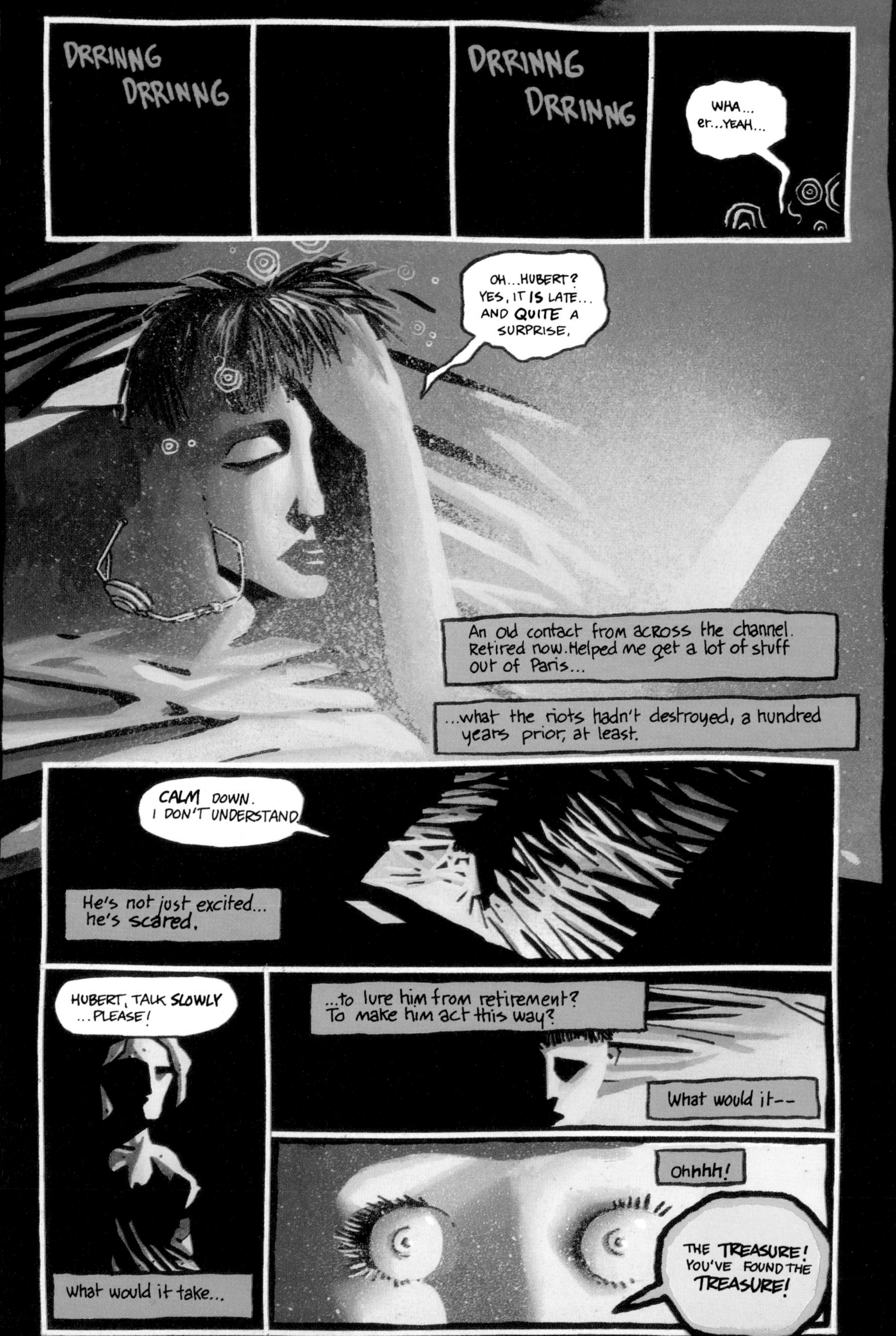
DRRINNG
DRRINNG
DRRINNG
DRRINNG
WHA... er...YEAH...
OH...HUBERT? YES, IT IS LATE... AND QUITE A SURPRISE.
An old contact from across the channel. Retired now. Helped me get a lot of stuff out of Paris...
...what the riots hadn't destroyed, a hundred years prior, at least.
CALM DOWN. I DON'T UNDERSTAND.
He's not just excited... he's scared.
HUBERT, TALK SLOWLY ...PLEASE!
What would it take...
...to lure him from retirement? To make him act this way?
What would it--
Ohhhh!
THE TREASURE! YOU'VE FOUND THE TREASURE!

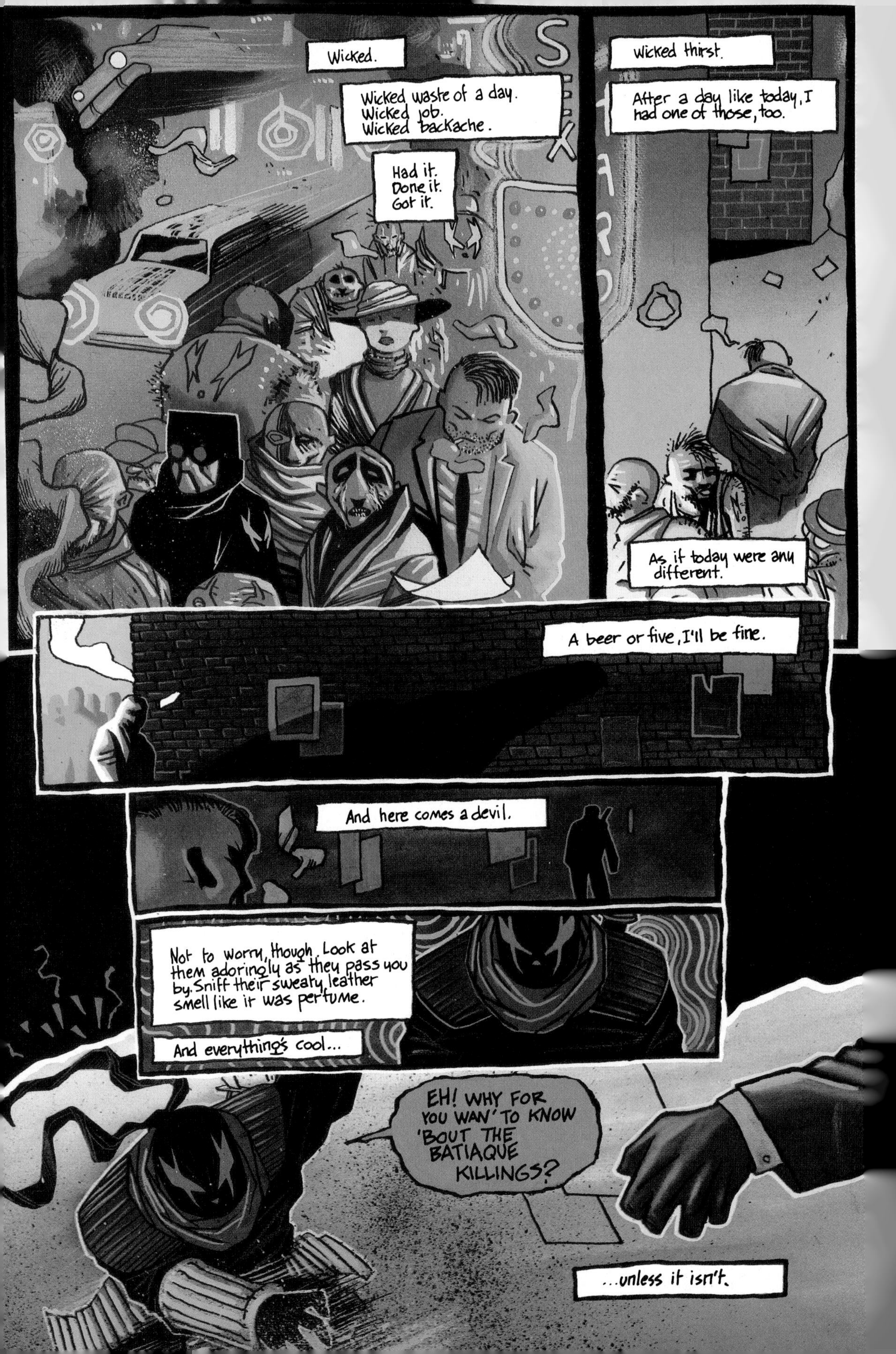
Wicked.
Wicked waste of a day.
Wicked job.
Wicked backache.
Had it.
Done it.
Got it.
Wicked thirst.
After a day like today, I had one of those, too.
As if today were any different.
A beer or five, I'll be fine.
And here comes a devil.
Not to worry, though. Look at them adoringly as they pass you by. Sniff their sweaty leather smell like it was perfume.
And everything's cool...
EH! WHY FOR YOU WAN' TO KNOW 'BOUT THE BATIAQUE KILLINGS?
...unless it isn't.

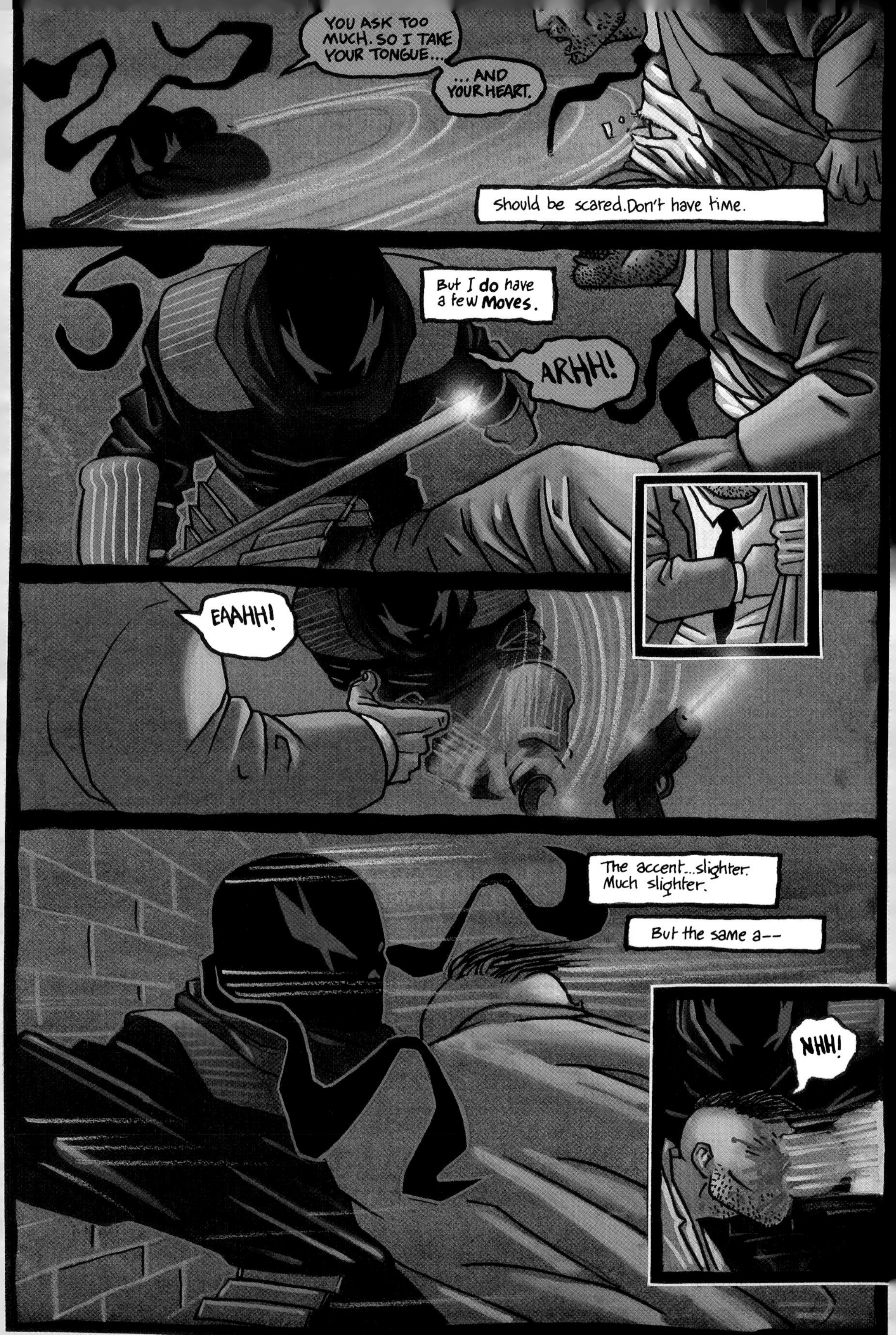
YOU ASK TOO MUCH. SO I TAKE YOUR TONGUE...
...AND YOUR HEART.
Should be scared. Don't have time.
But I do have a few Moves.
ARHH!
EAAHH!
The accent...slighter. Much slighter.
But the same a--
NHH!

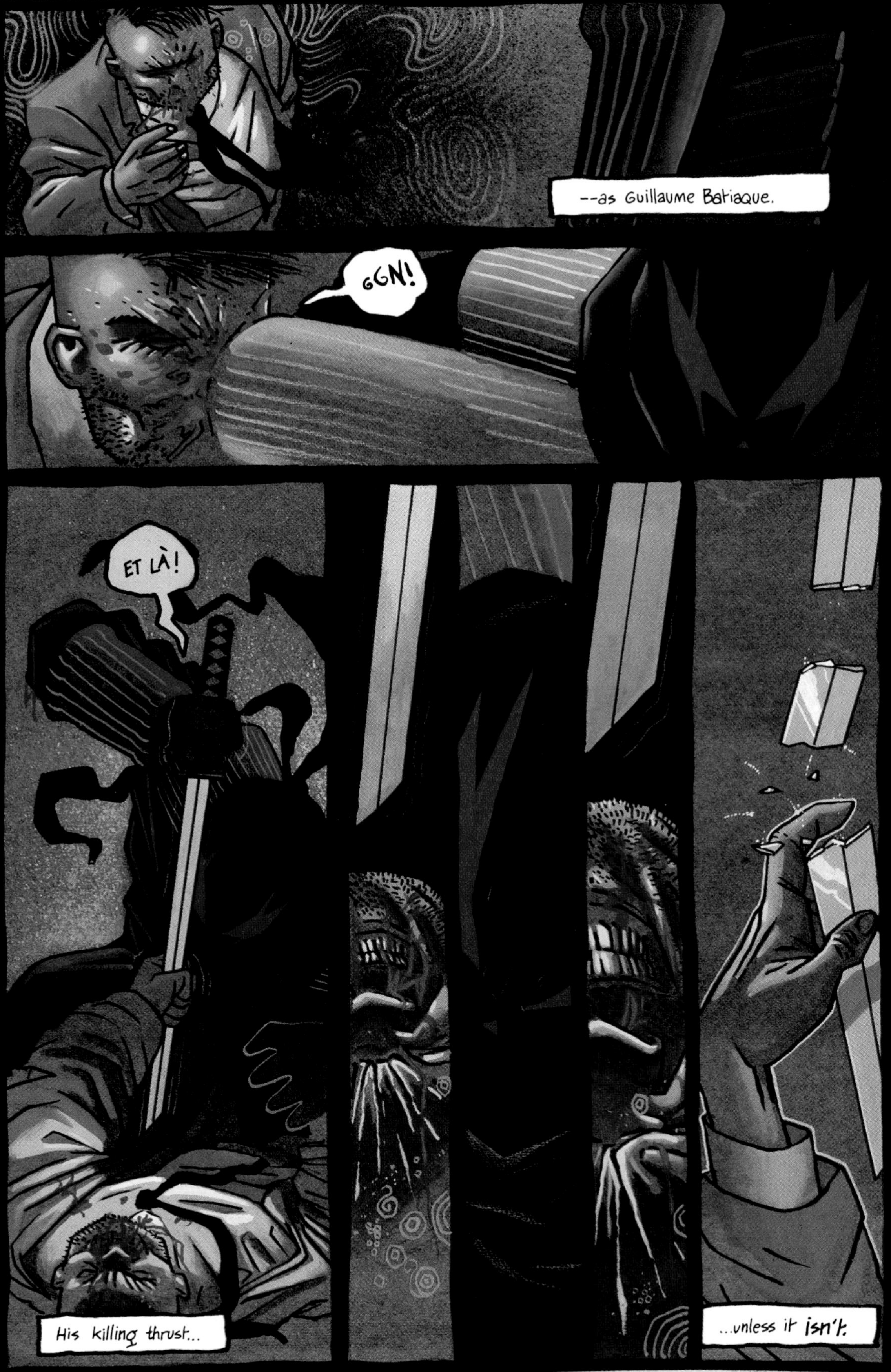
--as Guillaume Batiaque.
GGN!
ET LÀ!
His killing thrust...
...unless it isn't.

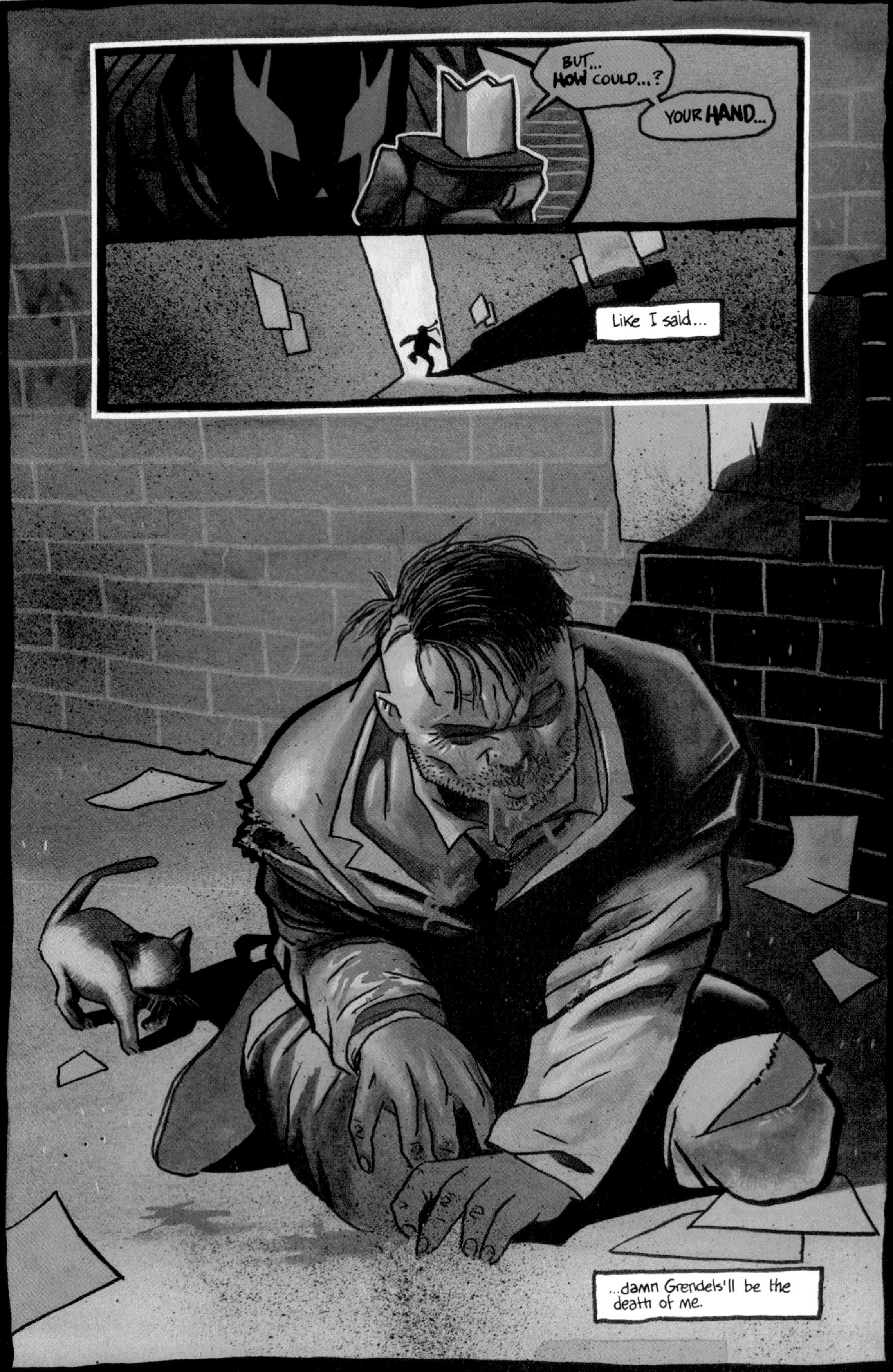
BUT... HOW COULD...?
YOUR HAND...
Like I said...
...damn Grendels'll be the death of me.

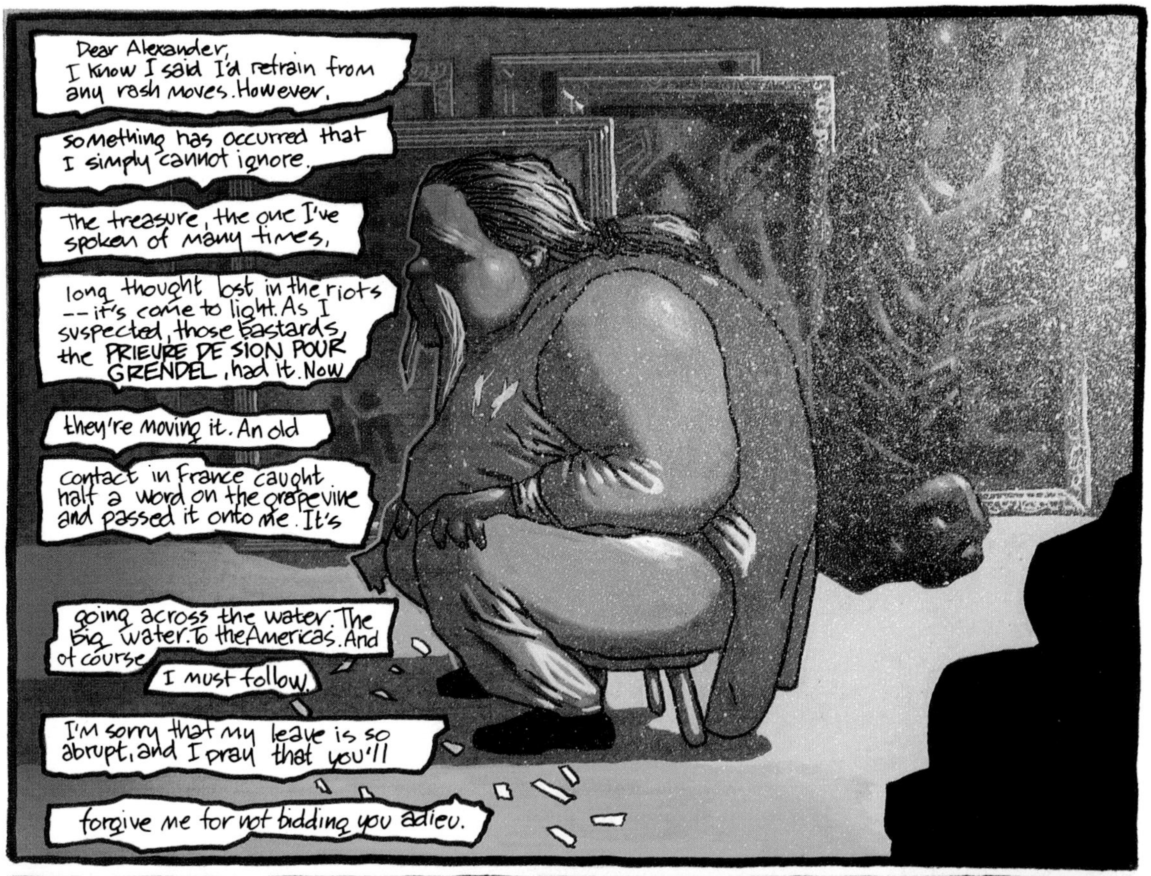
Dear Alexander,
I know I said I'd refrain from any rash moves. However,
something has occurred that I simply cannot ignore.
The treasure, the one I've spoken of many times,
long thought lost in the riots -- it's come to light. As I suspected, those bastards, the PRIEURE DE SION POUR GRENDEL, had it. Now
they're moving it. An old
contact in France caught half a word on the grapevine and passed it onto me. It's
going across the water. The big water. To the Americas. And of course
I must follow.
I'm sorry that my leave is so abrupt, and I pray that you'll
forgive me for not bidding you adieu.
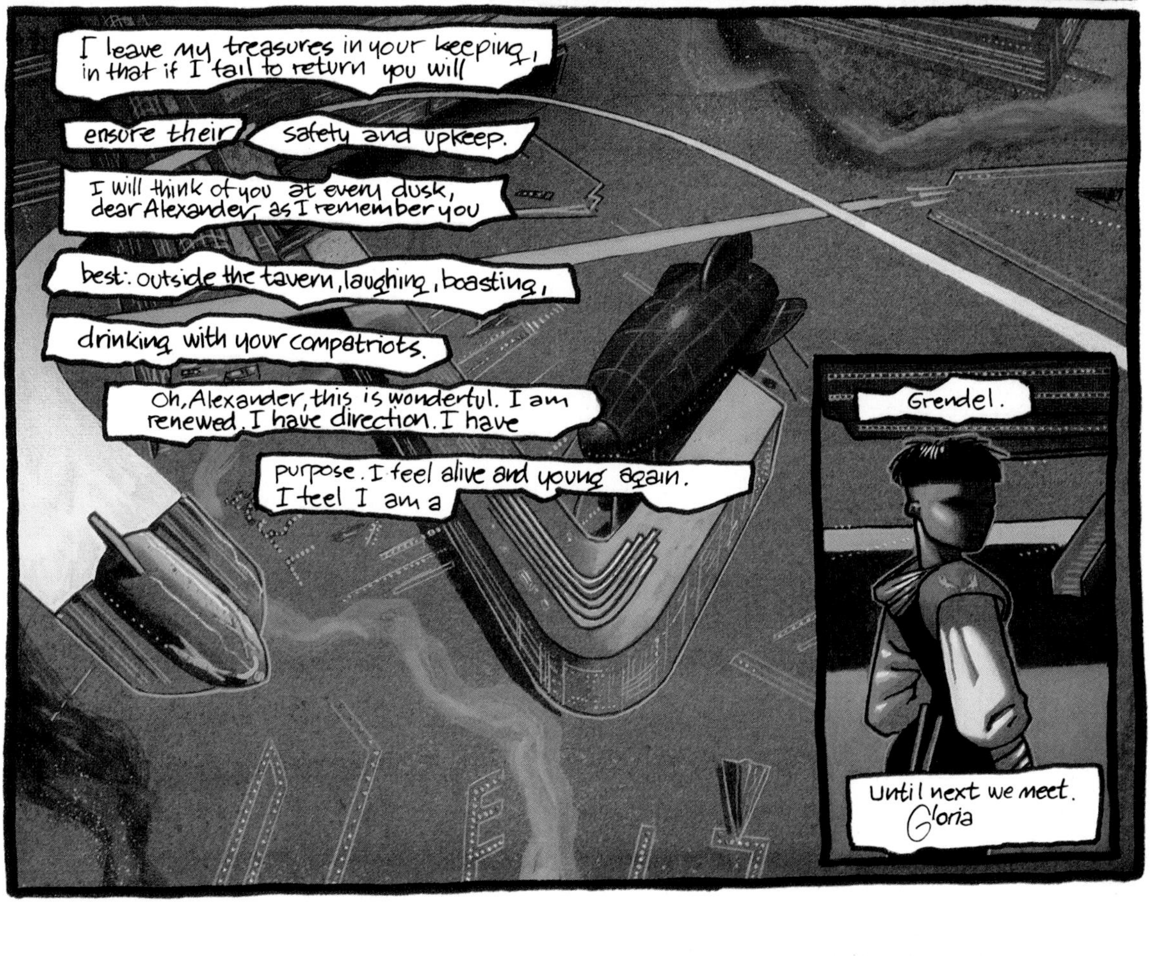
I leave my treasures in your keeping, in that if I fail to return you will
ensure their
safety and upkeep.
I will think of you at every dusk, dear Alexander, as I remember you
best: outside the tavern, laughing, boasting,
drinking with your compatriots.
Oh, Alexander, this is wonderful. I am renewed. I have direction. I have
purpose. I feel alive and young again. I feel I am a
Grendel.
Until next we meet.
Gloria

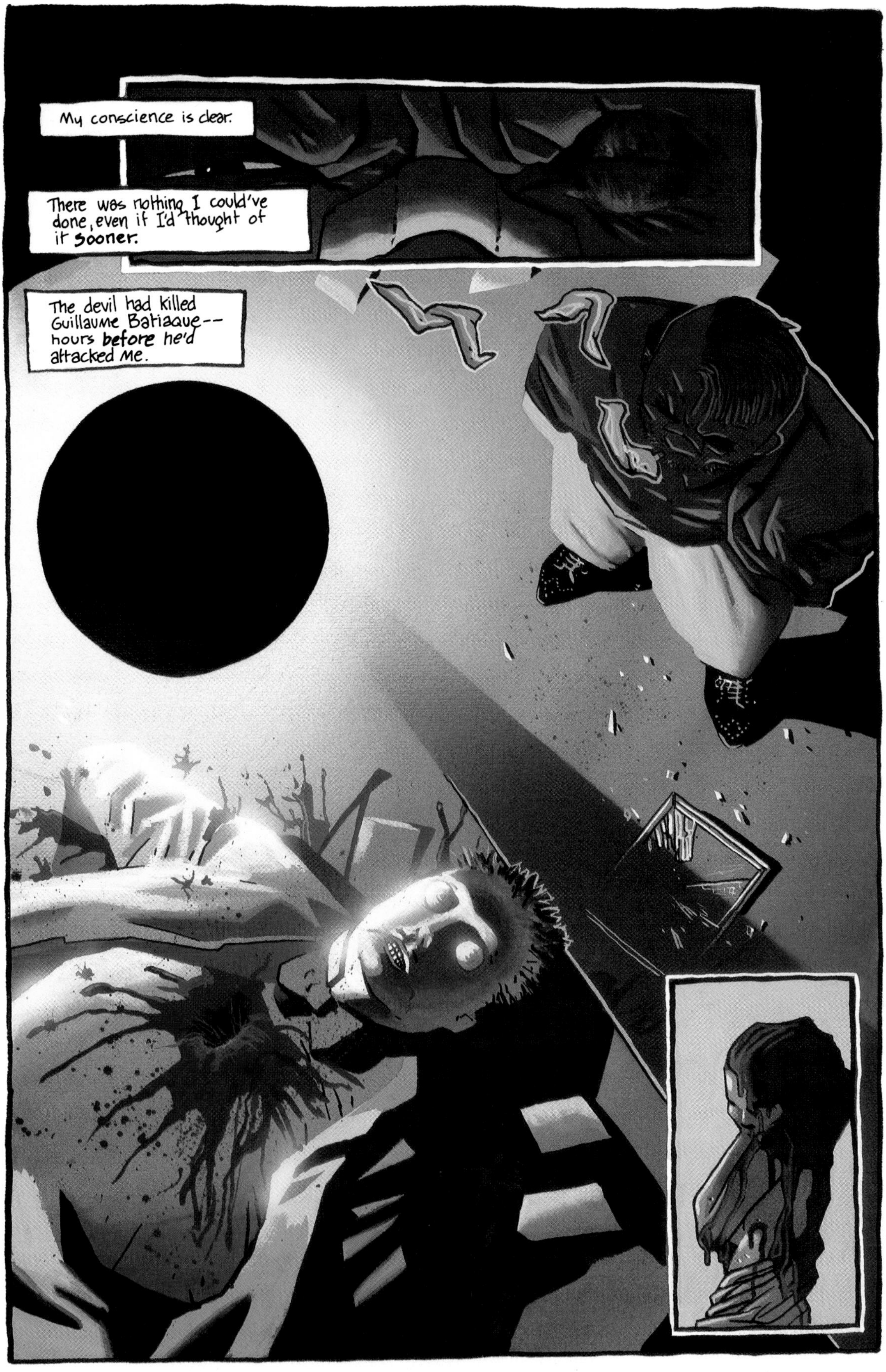
My conscience is clear.
There was nothing I could've done, even if I'd thought of it sooner.
The devil had killed Guillaume Batiaque--hours before he'd attacked me.

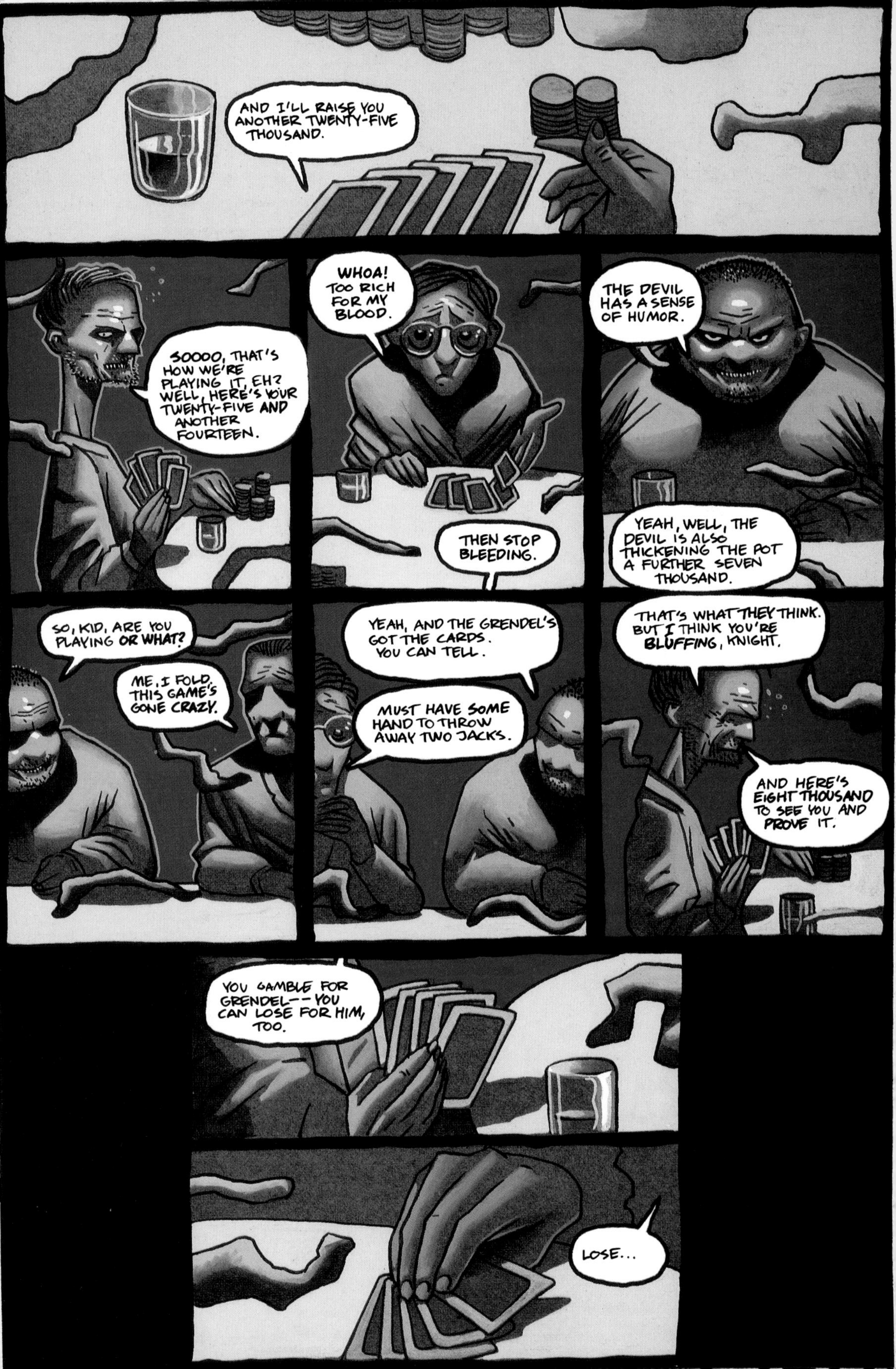
AND I'LL RAISE YOU ANOTHER TWENTY-FIVE THOUSAND.
SOOOO, THAT'S HOW WE'RE PLAYING IT, EH? WELL, HERE'S YOUR TWENTY-FIVE AND ANOTHER FOURTEEN.
WHOA! TOO RICH FOR MY BLOOD.
THEN STOP BLEEDING.
THE DEVIL HAS A SENSE OF HUMOR.
YEAH, WELL, THE DEVIL IS ALSO THICKENING THE POT A FURTHER SEVEN THOUSAND.
SO, KID, ARE YOU PLAYING OR WHAT?
ME, I FOLD. THIS GAME'S GONE CRAZY.
YEAH, AND THE GRENDEL'S GOT THE CARDS. YOU CAN TELL.
MUST HAVE SOME HAND TO THROW AWAY TWO JACKS.
THAT'S WHAT THEY THINK. BUT I THINK YOU'RE BLUFFING, KNIGHT.
AND HERE'S EIGHT THOUSAND TO SEE YOU AND PROVE IT.
YOU GAMBLE FOR GRENDEL--YOU CAN LOSE FOR HIM, TOO.
LOSE...

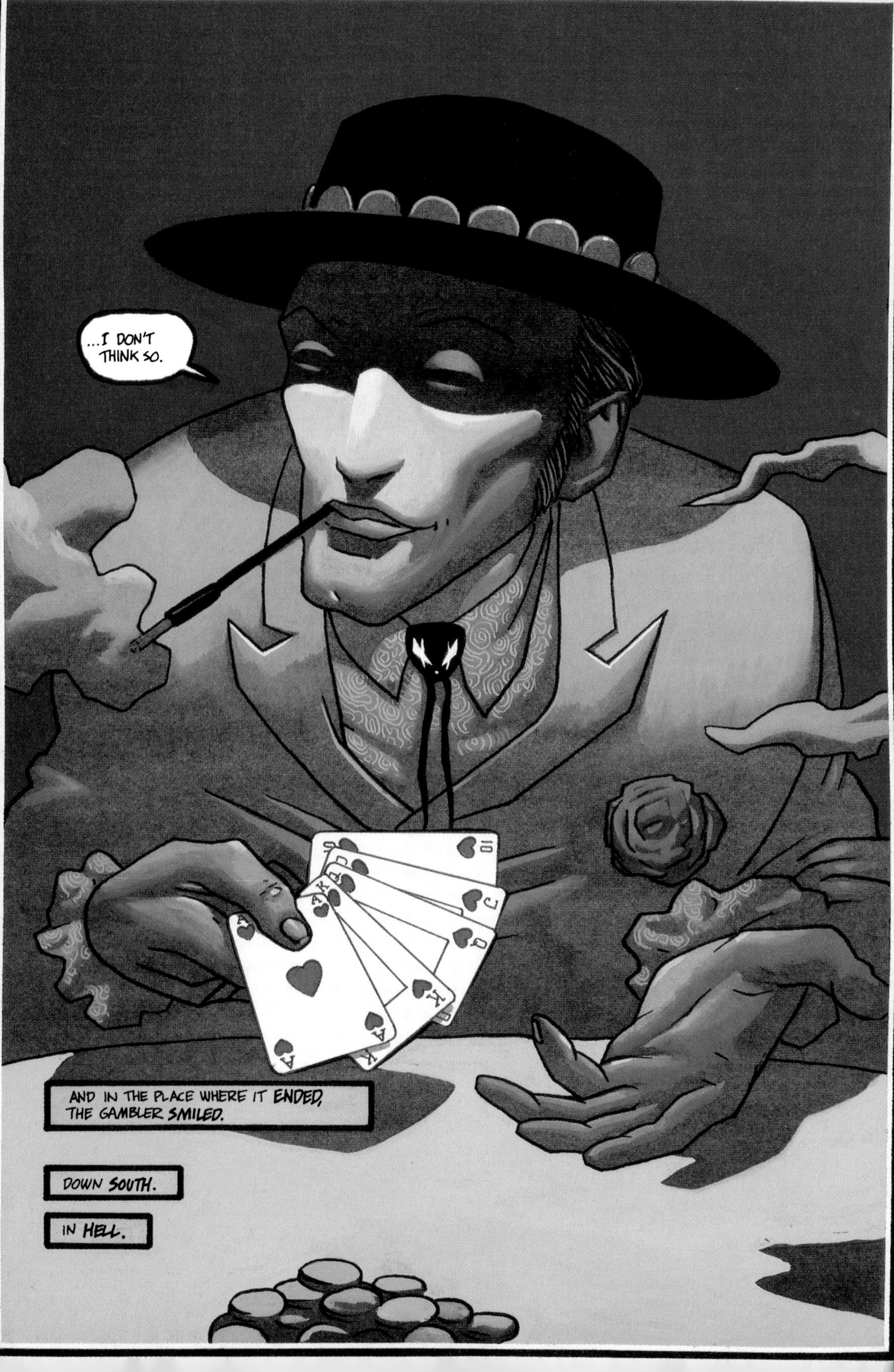
...I DON'T THINK SO.
AND IN THE PLACE WHERE IT ENDED, THE GAMBLER SMILED.
DOWN SOUTH.
IN HELL.

Chapter Two

THREE SEARCHERS, ONE LUCKY STREAK

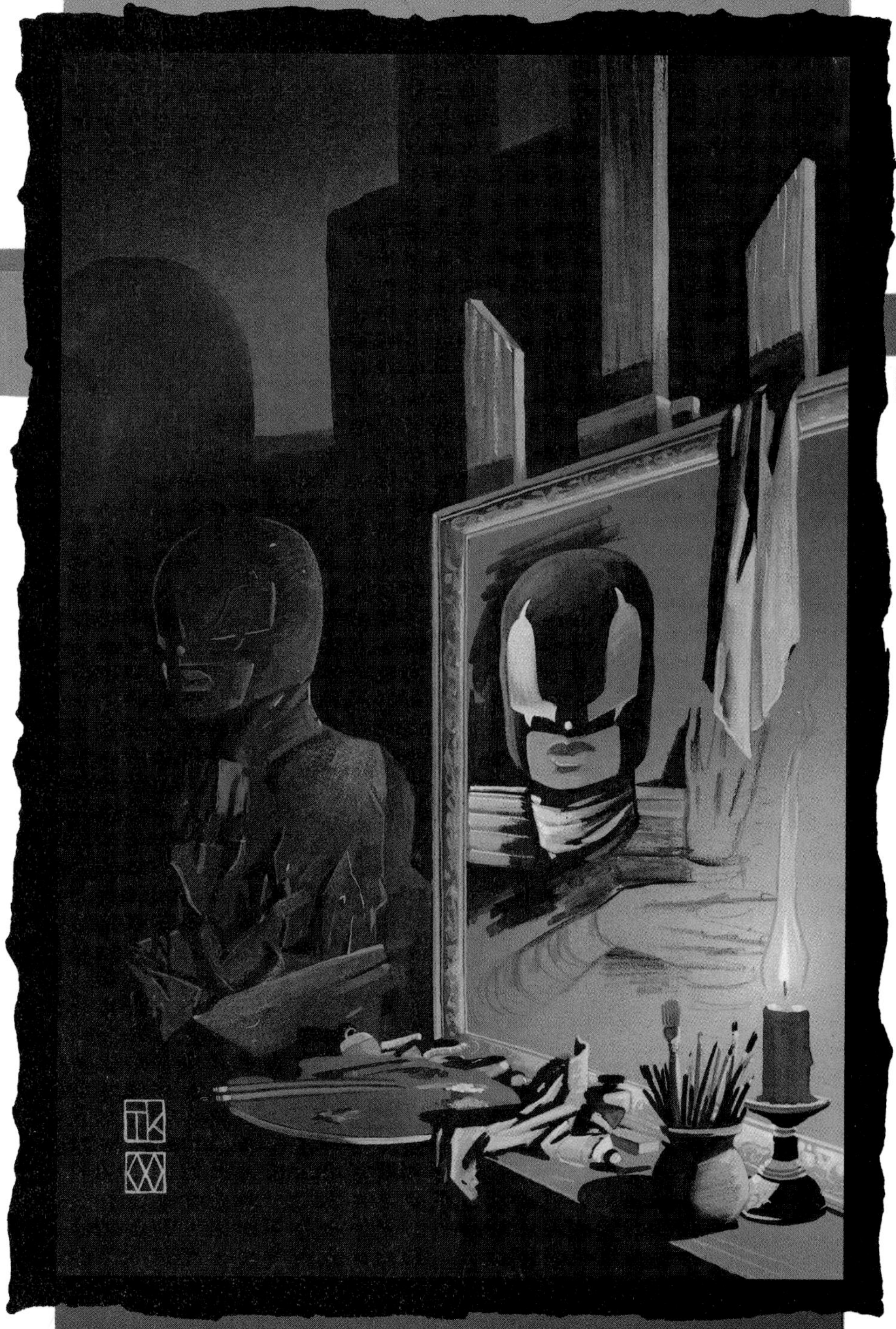

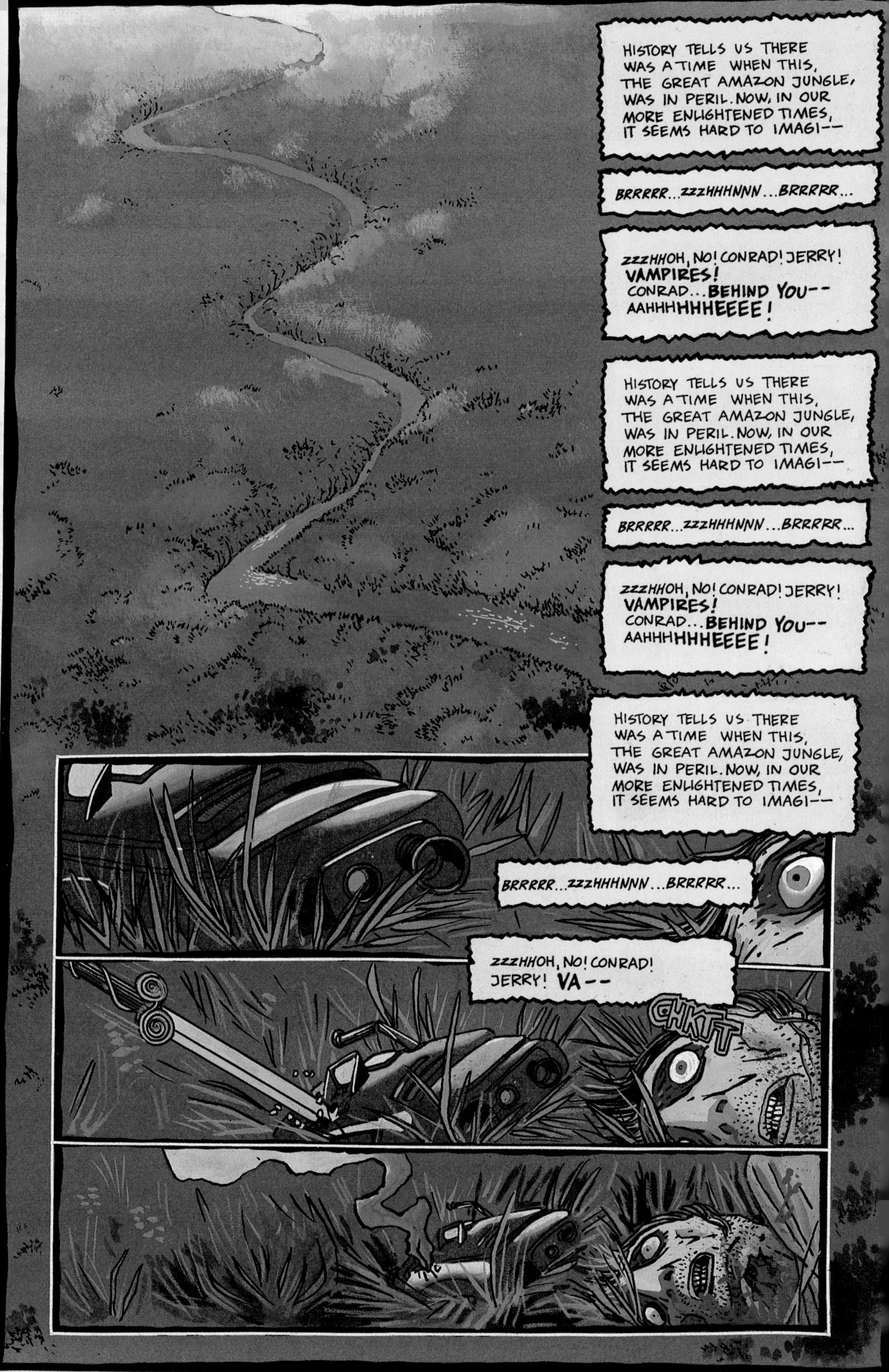
HISTORY TELLS US THERE WAS A TIME WHEN THIS, THE GREAT AMAZON JUNGLE, WAS IN PERIL. NOW, IN OUR MORE ENLIGHTENED TIMES, IT SEEMS HARD TO IMAGI--
BRRRRR...ZZZHHHNNN...BRRRRR...
ZZZHHOH, NO! CONRAD! JERRY! VAMPIRES! CONRAD... BEHIND YOU-- AAHHHHHHEEEE!
HISTORY TELLS US THERE WAS A TIME WHEN THIS, THE GREAT AMAZON JUNGLE, WAS IN PERIL. NOW, IN OUR MORE ENLIGHTENED TIMES, IT SEEMS HARD TO IMAGI--
BRRRRR...ZZZHHHNNN...BRRRRR...
ZZZHHOH, NO! CONRAD! JERRY! VAMPIRES! CONRAD... BEHIND YOU-- AAHHHHHHEEEE!
HISTORY TELLS US THERE WAS A TIME WHEN THIS, THE GREAT AMAZON JUNGLE, WAS IN PERIL. NOW, IN OUR MORE ENLIGHTENED TIMES, IT SEEMS HARD TO IMAGI--
BRRRRR...ZZZHHHNNN...BRRRRR...
ZZZHHOH, NO! CONRAD! JERRY! VA--
CHKTT

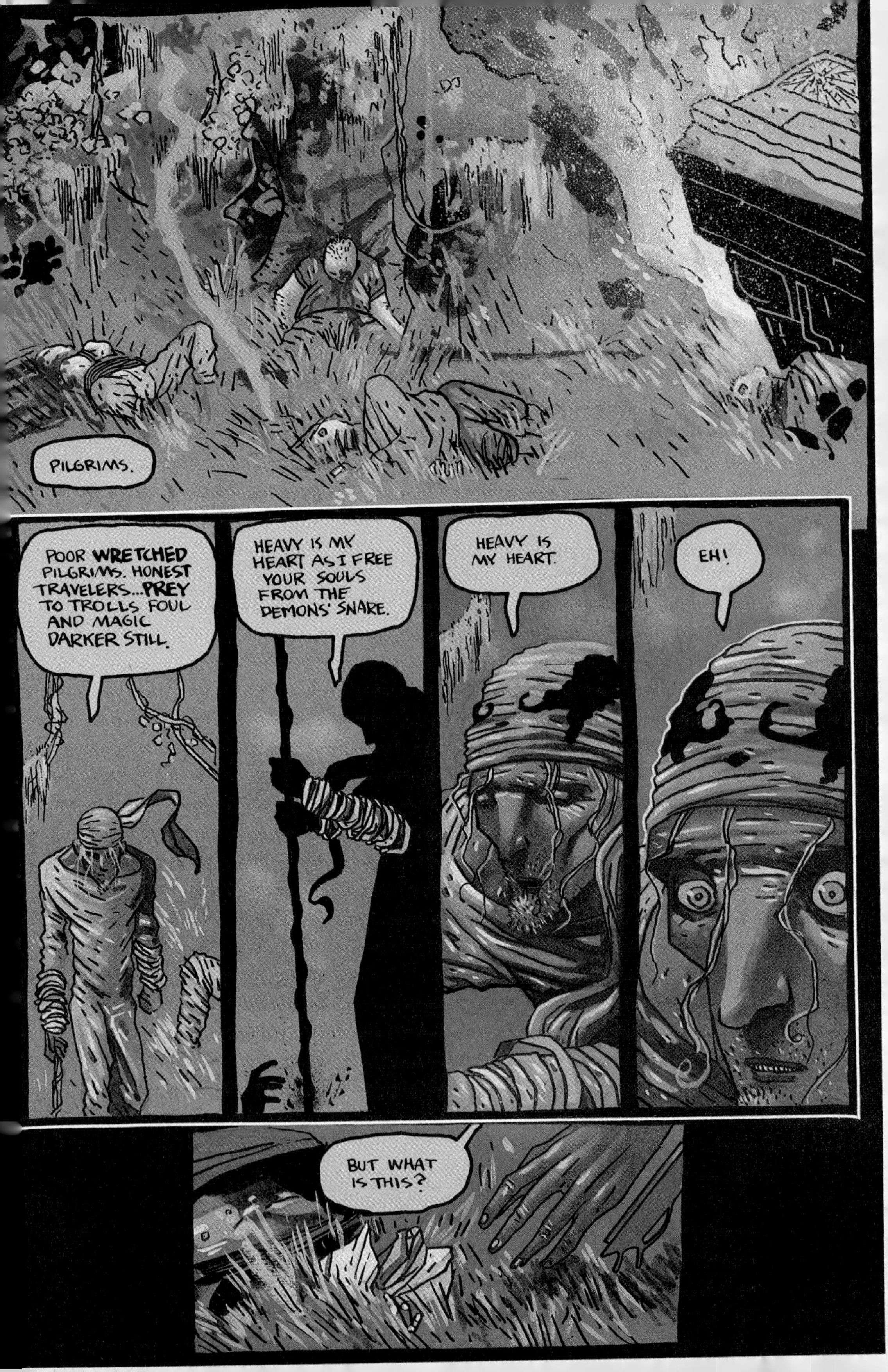
PILGRIMS.
POOR WRETCHED PILGRIMS. HONEST TRAVELERS...PREY TO TROLLS FOUL AND MAGIC DARKER STILL.
HEAVY IS MY HEART AS I FREE YOUR SOULS FROM THE DEMONS' SNARE.
HEAVY IS MY HEART.
EH!
BUT WHAT IS THIS?

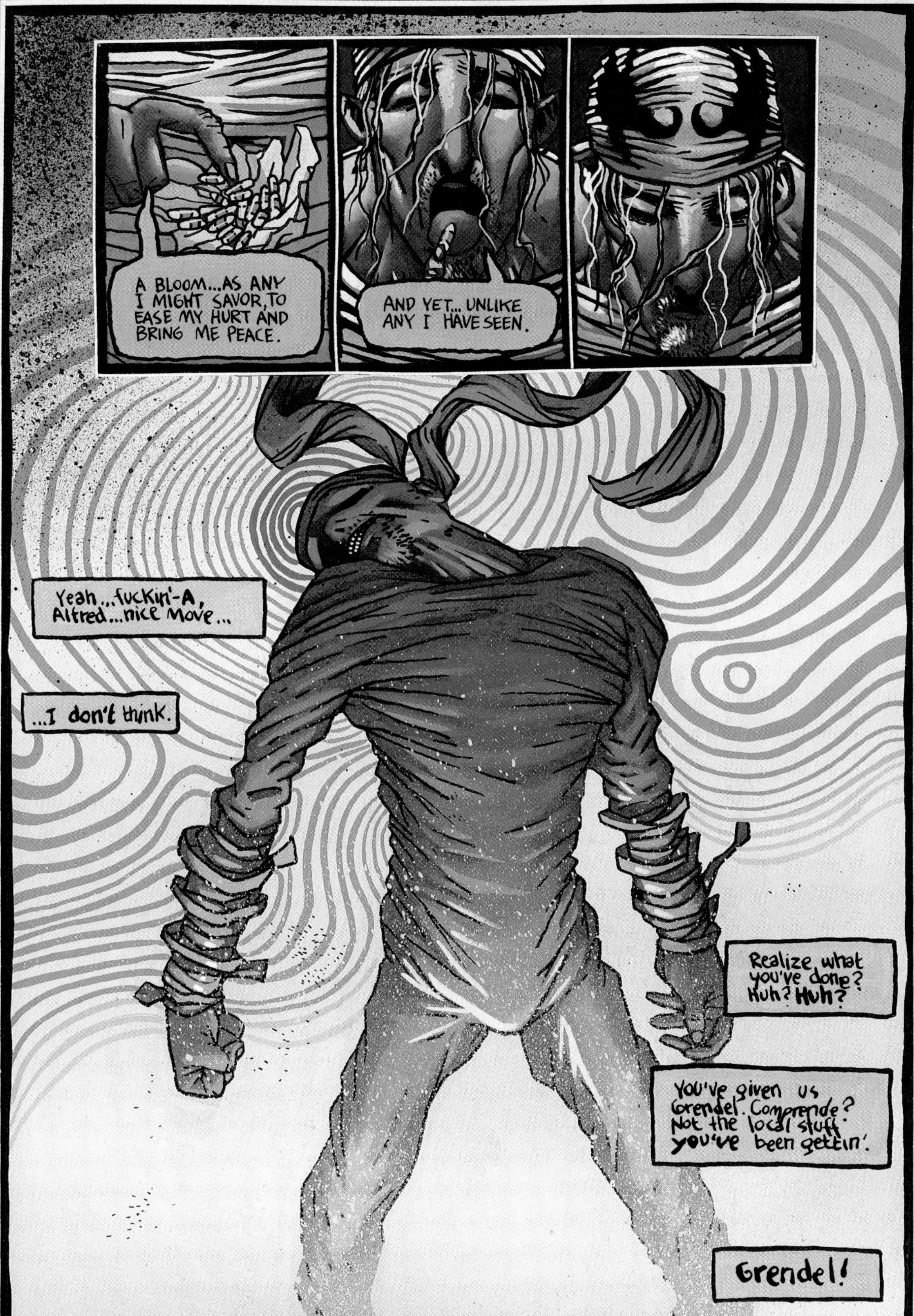
A BLOOM...AS ANY I MIGHT SAVOR, TO EASE MY HURT AND BRING ME PEACE.
AND YET... UNLIKE ANY I HAVE SEEN.
Yeah...fuckin'-A, Alfred...nice move...
...I don't think.
Realize what you've done? Huh? Huh?
You've given us Grendel. Comprende? Not the local stuff you've been gettin'.
Grendel!

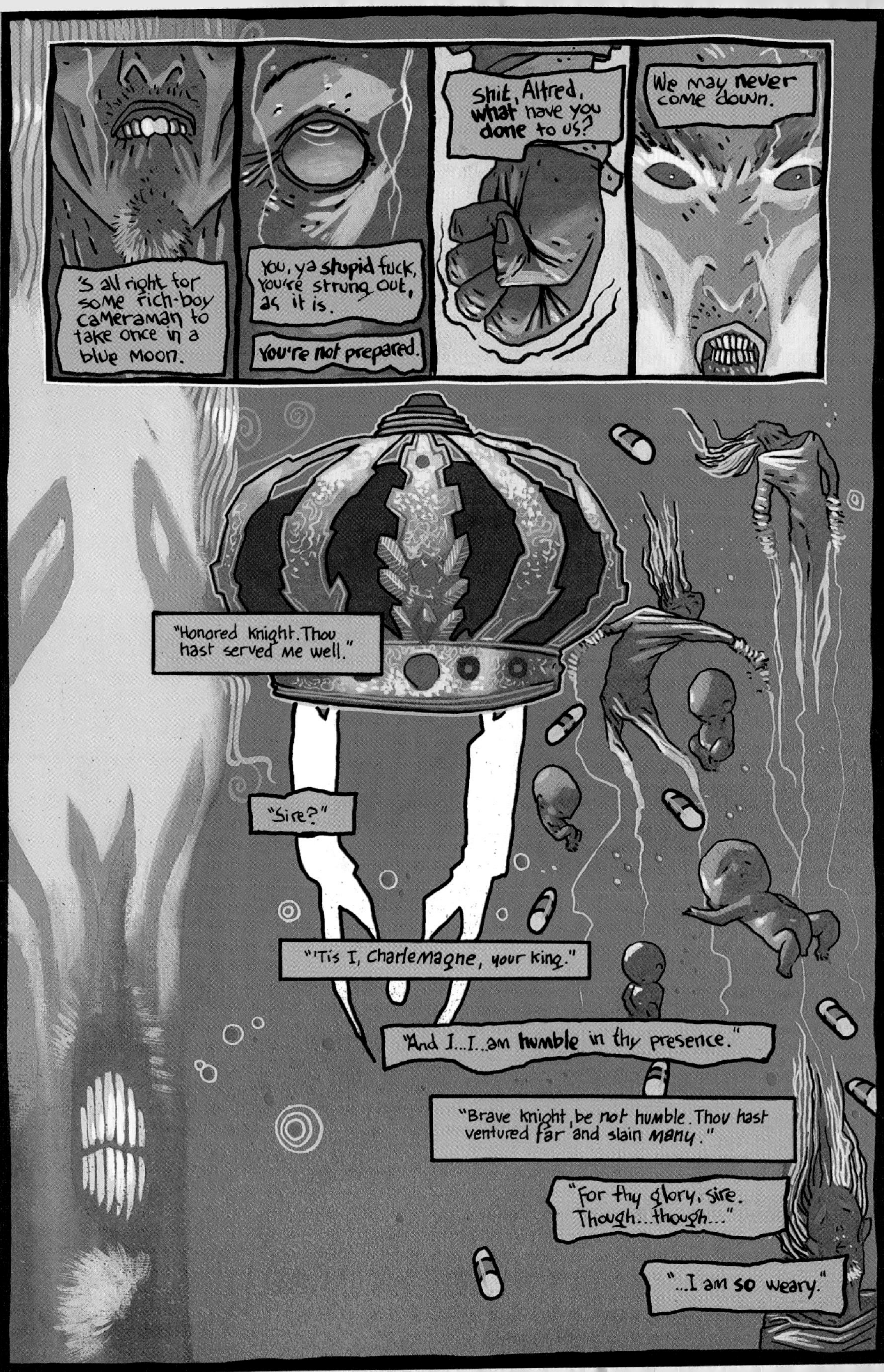
'S all right for some rich-boy cameraman to take once in a blue moon.
You, ya stupid fuck, you're strung out, as it is.
You're not prepared.
Shit, Alfred, what have you done to us?
We may never come down.
"Honored Knight. Thou hast served me well."
"Sire?"
"'Tis I, Charlemagne, your king."
"And I...I...am humble in thy presence."
"Brave knight, be not humble. Thou hast ventured far and slain many."
"For thy glory, sire. Though...though..."
"...I am so weary."

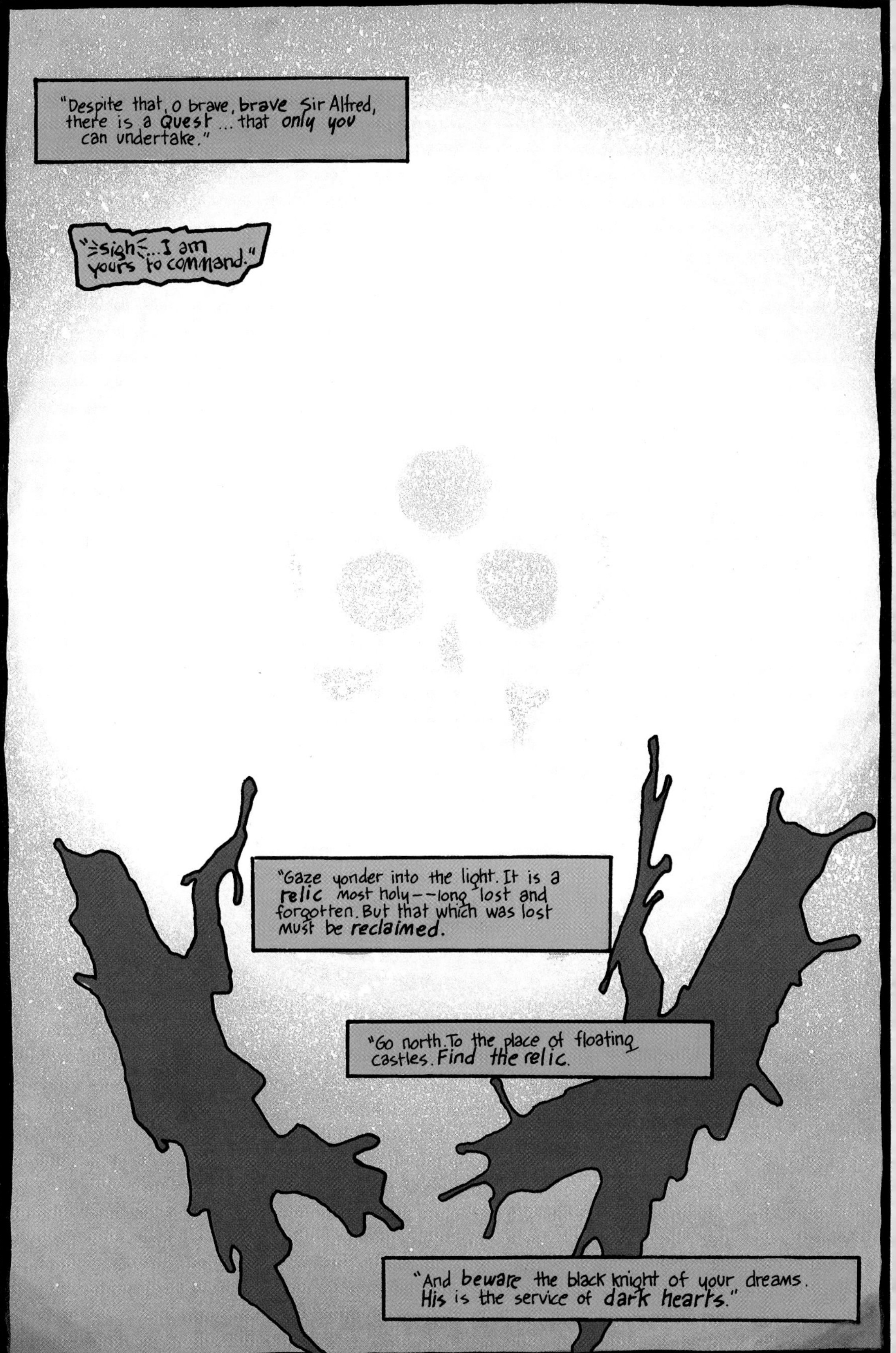
"Despite that, O brave, brave Sir Alfred, there is a Quest ... that only you can undertake."
"≥sigh≤...I am yours to command."
"Gaze yonder into the light. It is a relic most holy--long lost and forgotten. But that which was lost must be reclaimed.
"Go north. To the place of floating castles. Find the relic.
"And beware the black knight of your dreams. His is the service of dark hearts."

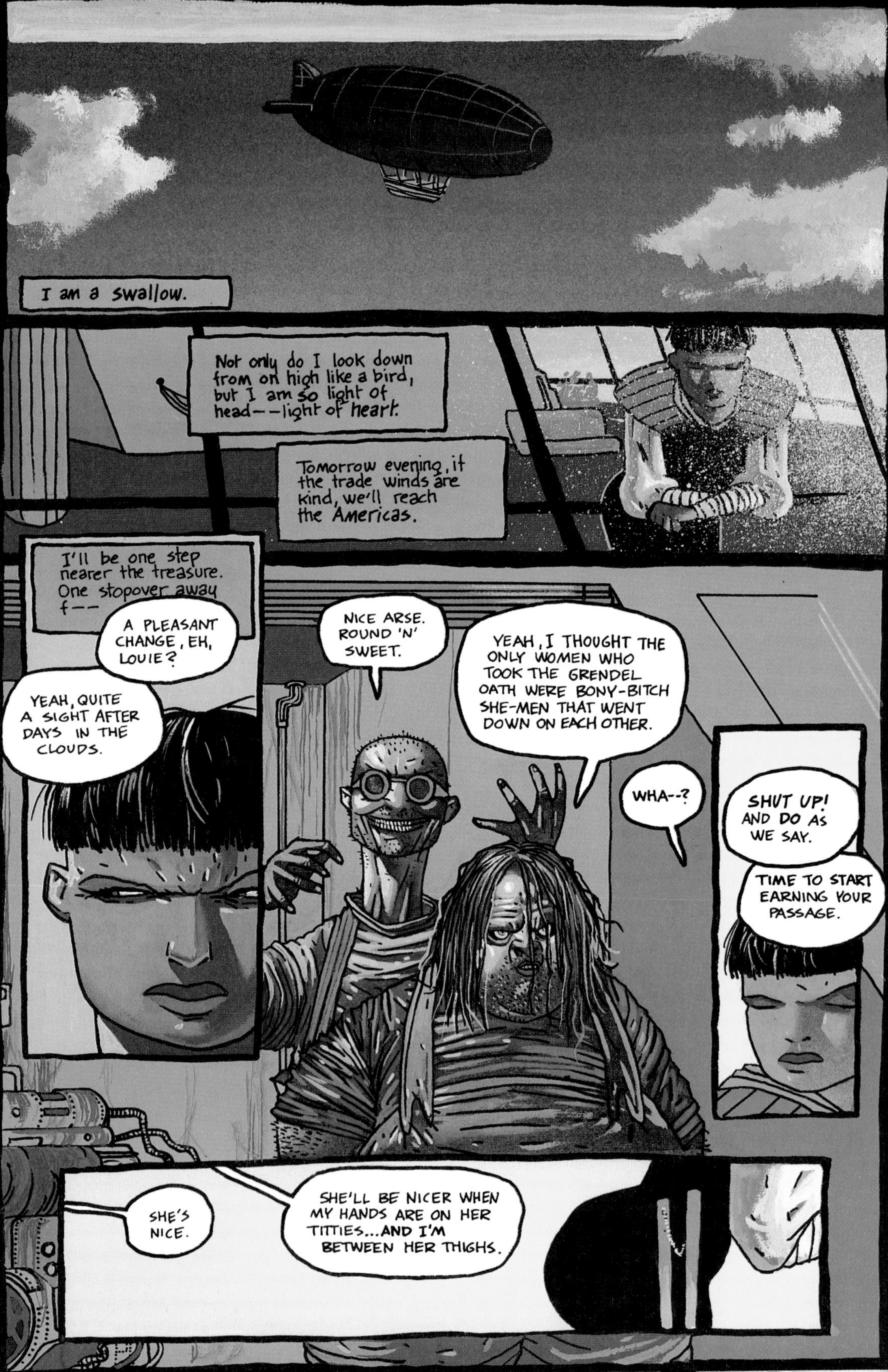

I am a swallow.
Not only do I look down from on high like a bird, but I am so light of head--light of heart.
Tomorrow evening, if the trade winds are kind, we'll reach the Americas.
I'll be one step nearer the treasure. One stopover away f--
A PLEASANT CHANGE, EH, LOUIE?
YEAH, QUITE A SIGHT AFTER DAYS IN THE CLOUDS.
NICE ARSE. ROUND 'N' SWEET.
YEAH, I THOUGHT THE ONLY WOMEN WHO TOOK THE GRENDEL OATH WERE BONY-BITCH SHE-MEN THAT WENT DOWN ON EACH OTHER.
WHA--?
SHUT UP! AND DO AS WE SAY.
TIME TO START EARNING YOUR PASSAGE.
SHE'S NICE.
SHE'LL BE NICER WHEN MY HANDS ARE ON HER TITTIES...AND I'M BETWEEN HER THIGHS.

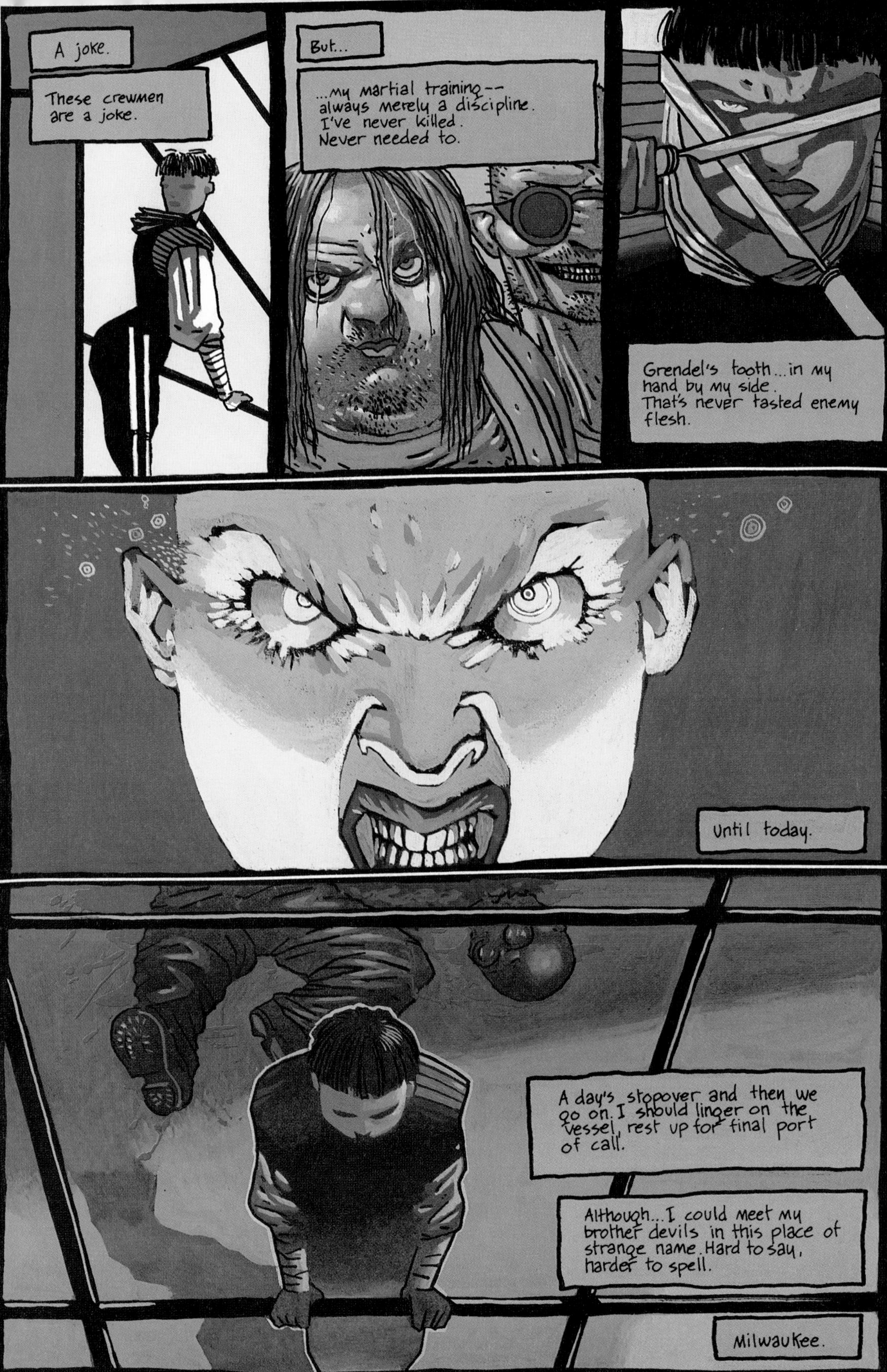
A joke.
These crewmen are a joke.
But...
...my martial training--always merely a discipline. I've never killed. Never needed to.
Grendel's tooth...in my hand by my side. That's never tasted enemy flesh.
Until today.
A day's stopover and then we go on. I should linger on the vessel, rest up for final port of call.
Although...I could meet my brother devils in this place of strange name. Hard to say, harder to spell.
Milwaukee.

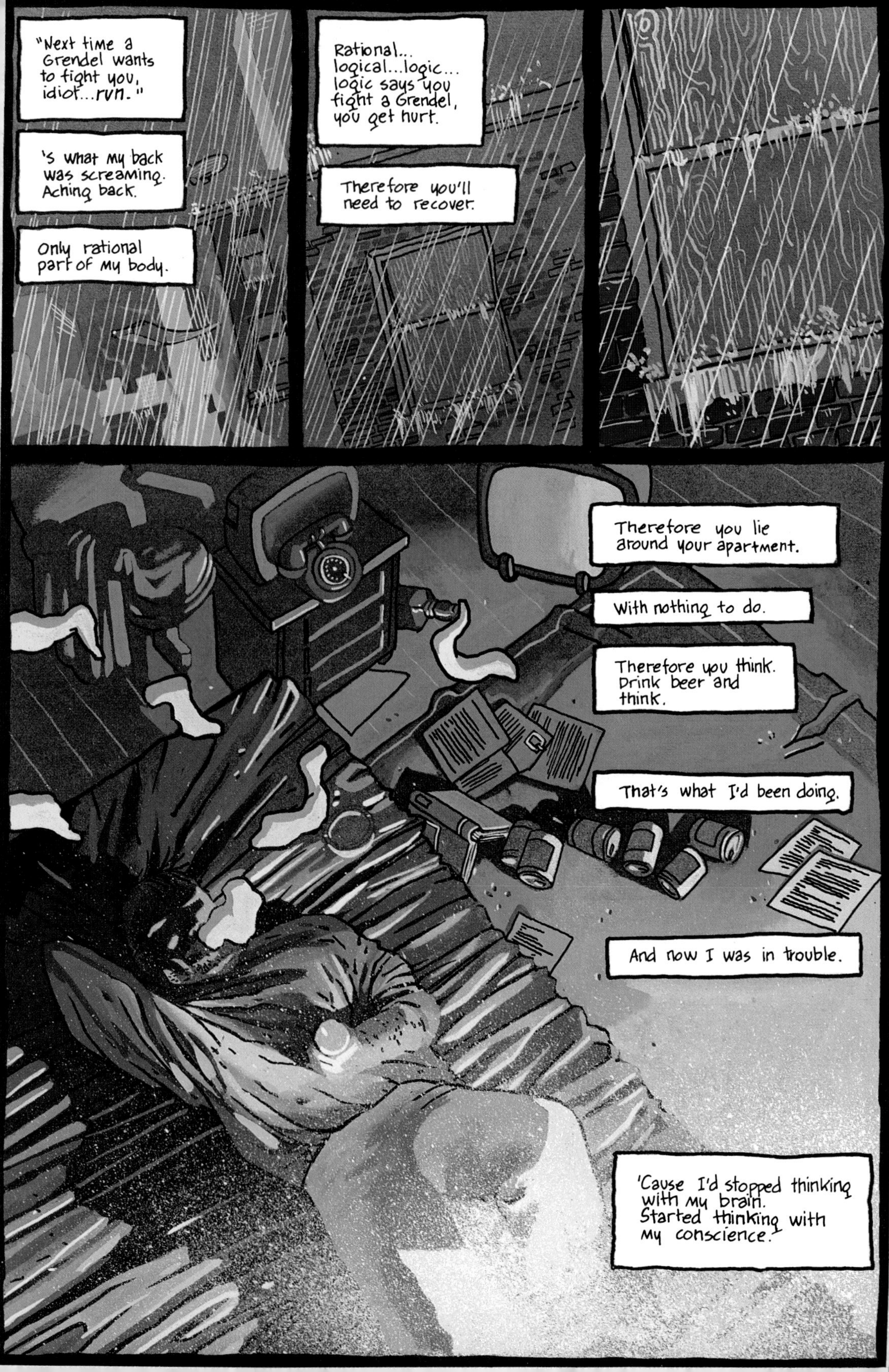
"Next time a Grendel wants to fight you, idiot...run."
's what my back was screaming. Aching back.
Only rational part of my body.
Rational... logical...logic... logic says you fight a Grendel, you get hurt.
Therefore you'll need to recover.
Therefore you lie around your apartment.
With nothing to do.
Therefore you think. Drink beer and think.
That's what I'd been doing.
And now I was in trouble.
'Cause I'd stopped thinking with my brain. Started thinking with my conscience.

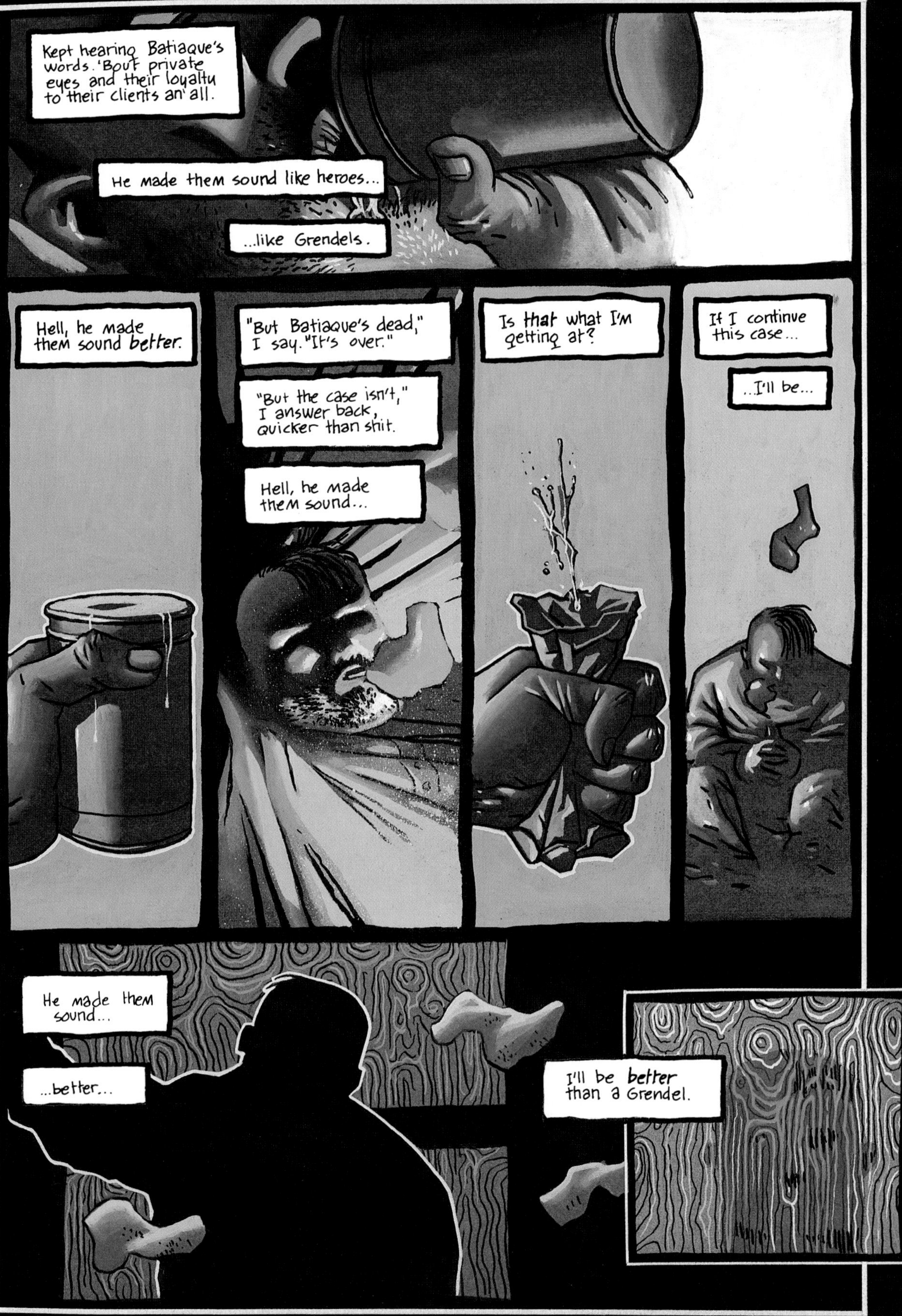
Kept hearing Batiaque's words. 'Bout private eyes and their loyalty to their clients an' all.
He made them sound like heroes...
...like Grendels.
Hell, he made them sound better.
"But Batiaque's dead," I say. "It's over."
"But the case isn't," I answer back, quicker than shit.
Hell, he made them sound...
Is that what I'm getting at?
If I continue this case...
...I'll be...
He made them sound...
...better...
I'll be better than a Grendel.

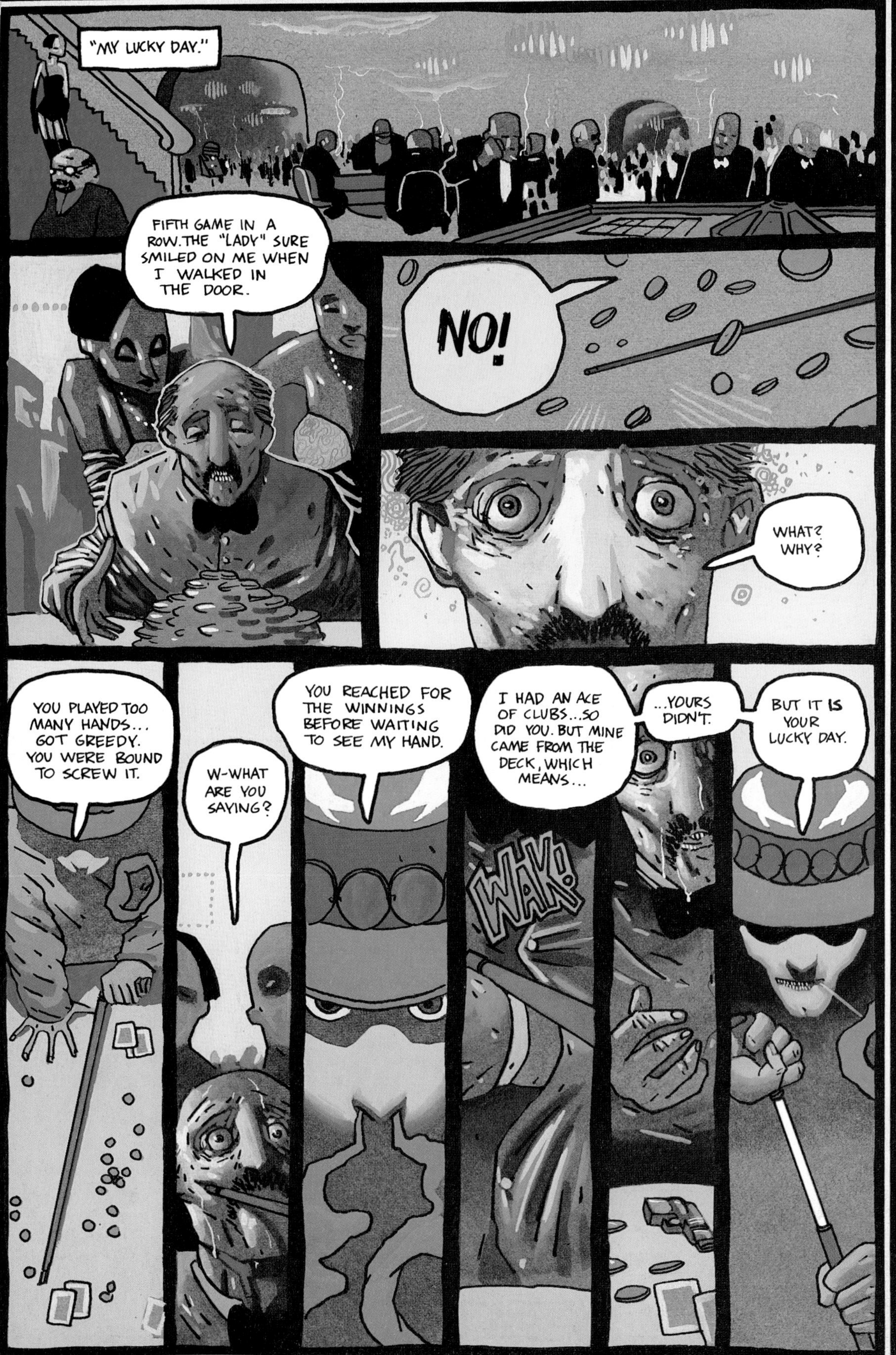
"MY LUCKY DAY."
FIFTH GAME IN A ROW. THE "LADY" SURE SMILED ON ME WHEN I WALKED IN THE DOOR.
NO!
WHAT? WHY?
YOU PLAYED TOO MANY HANDS... GOT GREEDY. YOU WERE BOUND TO SCREW IT.
W-WHAT ARE YOU SAYING?
YOU REACHED FOR THE WINNINGS BEFORE WAITING TO SEE MY HAND.
I HAD AN ACE OF CLUBS...SO DID YOU. BUT MINE CAME FROM THE DECK, WHICH MEANS...
WAK!
...YOURS DIDN'T.
BUT IT IS YOUR LUCKY DAY.

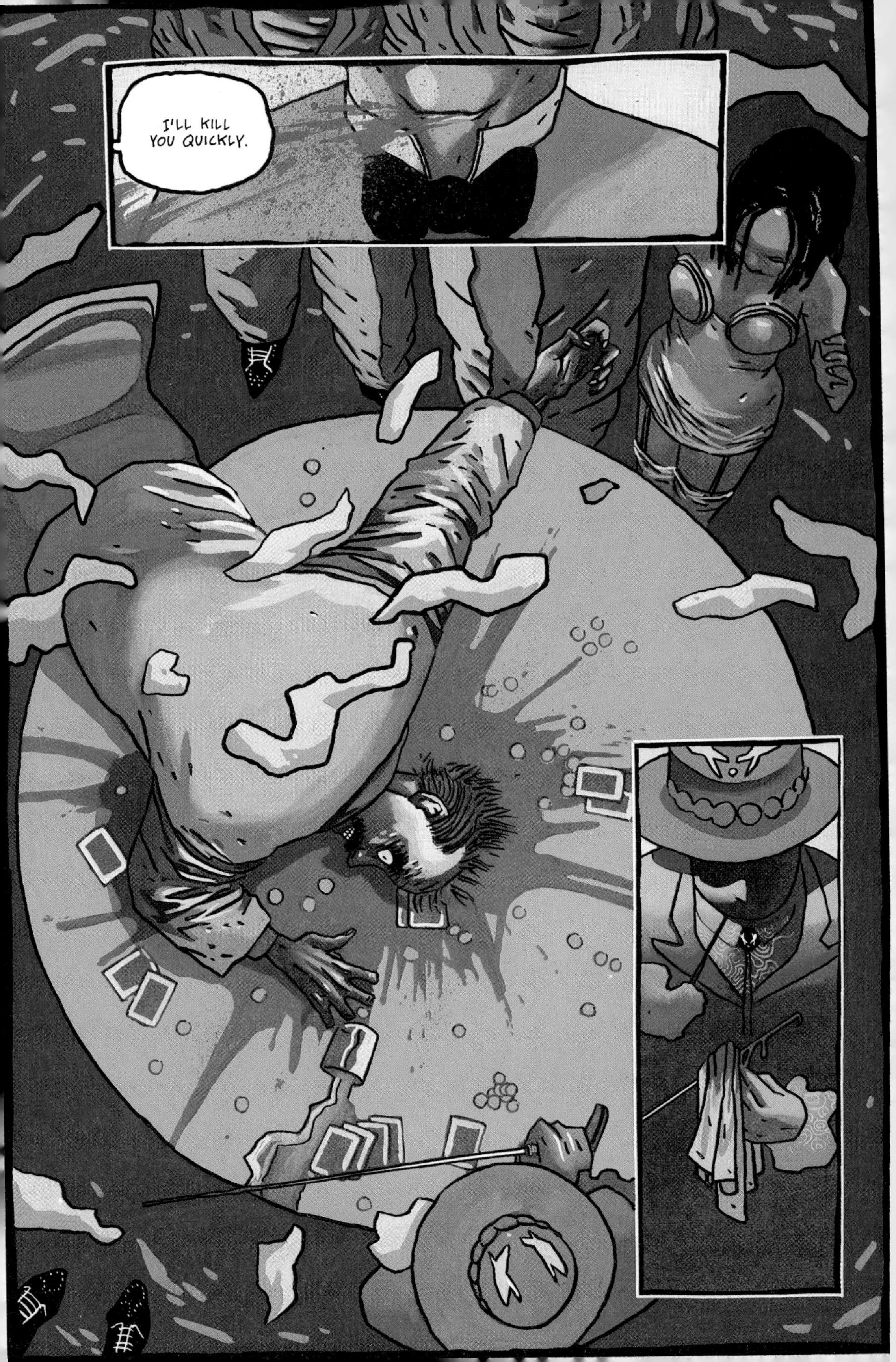
I'LL KILL
YOU QUICKLY.

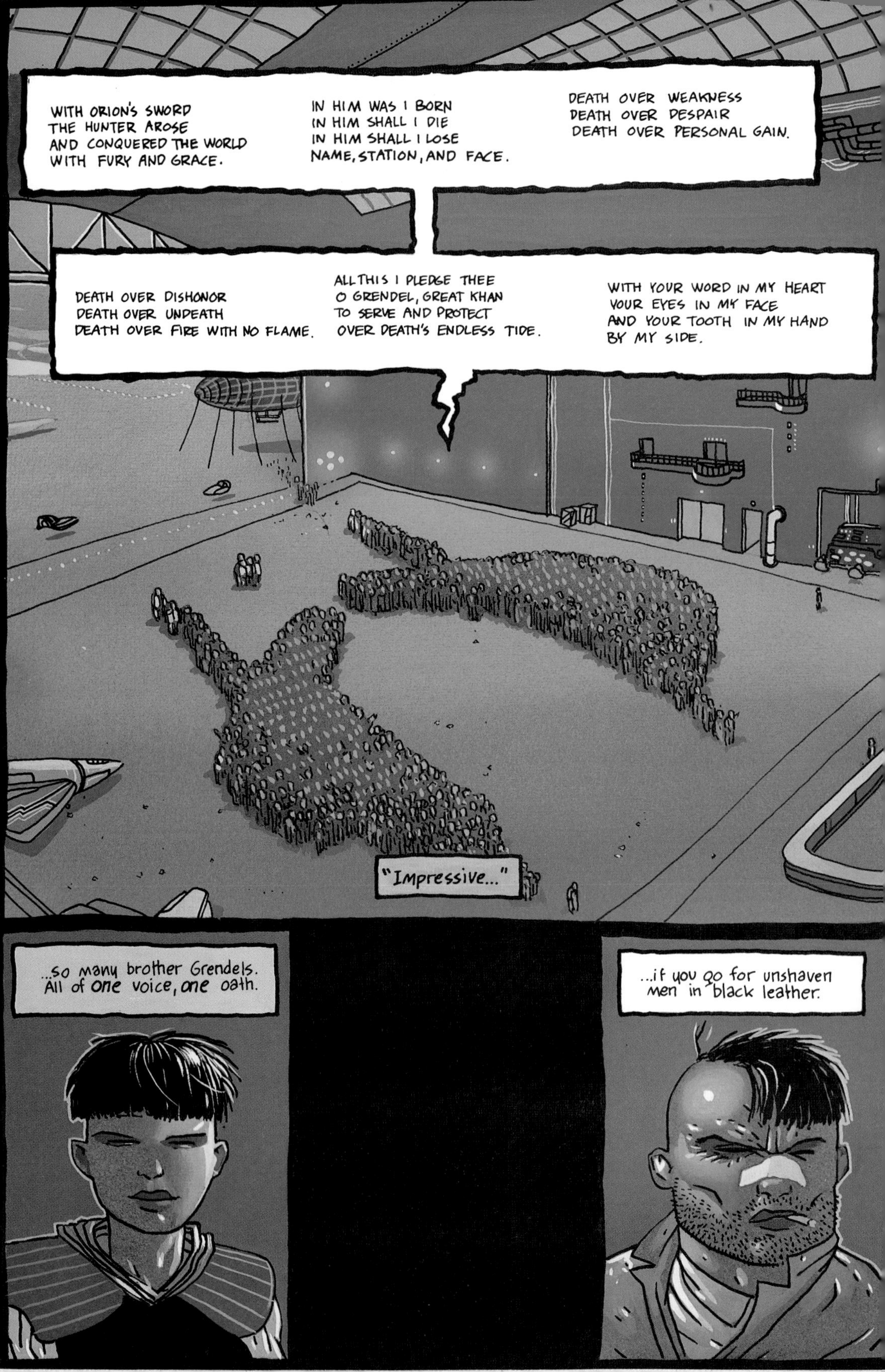
WITH ORION'S SWORD
THE HUNTER AROSE
AND CONQUERED THE WORLD
WITH FURY AND GRACE.
IN HIM WAS I BORN
IN HIM SHALL I DIE
IN HIM SHALL I LOSE
NAME, STATION, AND FACE.
DEATH OVER WEAKNESS
DEATH OVER DESPAIR
DEATH OVER PERSONAL GAIN.
DEATH OVER DISHONOR
DEATH OVER UNDEATH
DEATH OVER FIRE WITH NO FLAME.
ALL THIS I PLEDGE THEE
O GRENDEL, GREAT KHAN
TO SERVE AND PROTECT
OVER DEATH'S ENDLESS TIDE.
WITH YOUR WORD IN MY HEART
YOUR EYES IN MY FACE
AND YOUR TOOTH IN MY HAND
BY MY SIDE.
"Impressive..."
...so many brother Grendels. All of one voice, one oath.
...if you go for unshaven men in black leather.

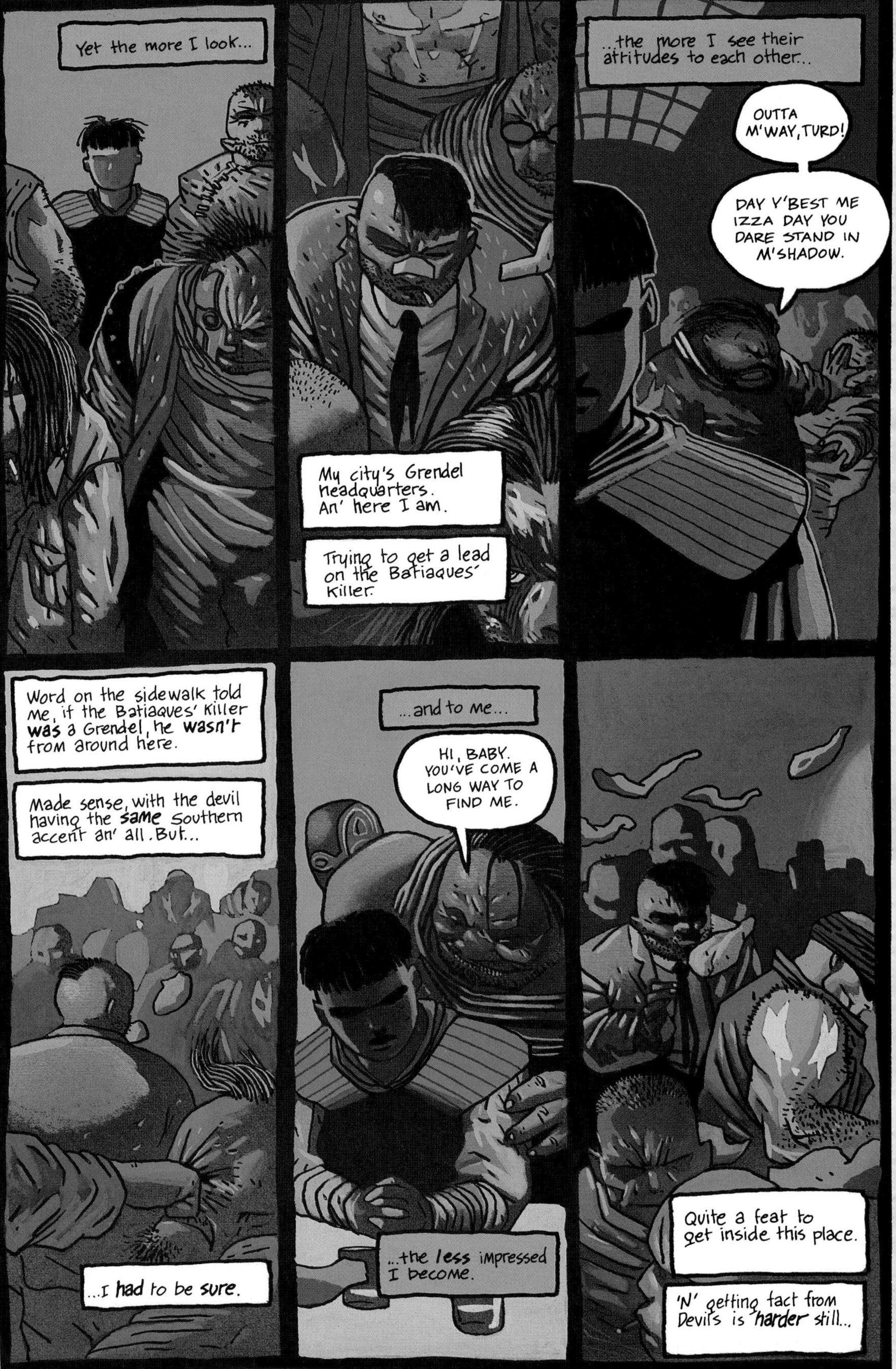
Yet the more I look...
My city's Grendel headquarters. An' here I am.
Trying to get a lead on the Batiaques' Killer.
...the more I see their attitudes to each other...
OUTTA M'WAY, TURD!
DAY Y'BEST ME IZZA DAY YOU DARE STAND IN M'SHADOW.
Word on the sidewalk told me, if the Batiaques' Killer **was** a Grendel, he **wasn't** from around here.
Made sense, with the devil having the **same** Southern accent an' all. But...
...I **had** to be **sure**.
...and to me...
HI, BABY. YOU'VE COME A LONG WAY TO FIND ME.
...the **less** impressed I become.
Quite a feat to get inside this place.
'N' getting fact from Devils is **harder** still...

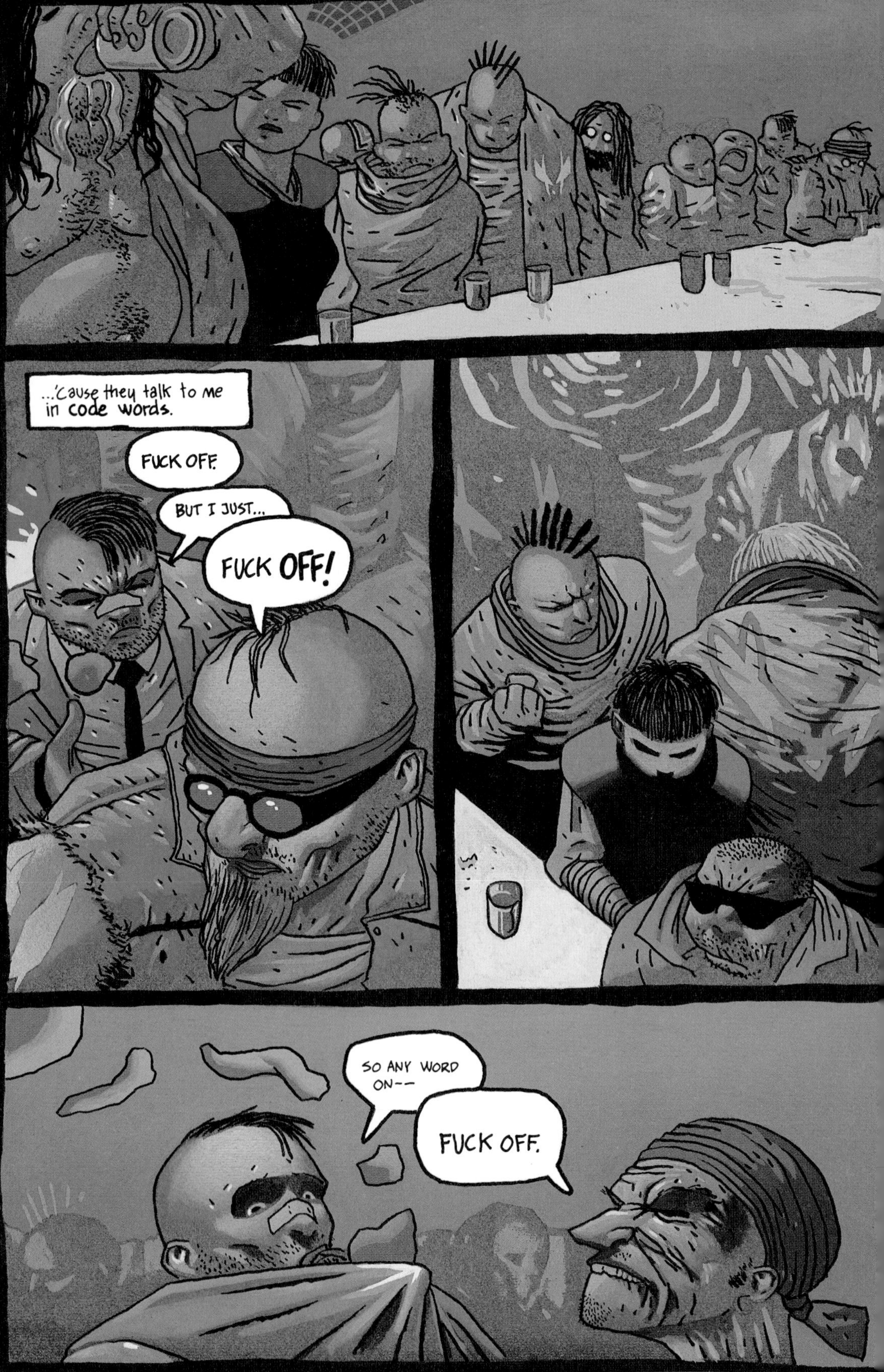
...'Cause they talk to me in code words.
FUCK OFF.
BUT I JUST...
FUCK OFF!
SO ANY WORD ON--
FUCK OFF.

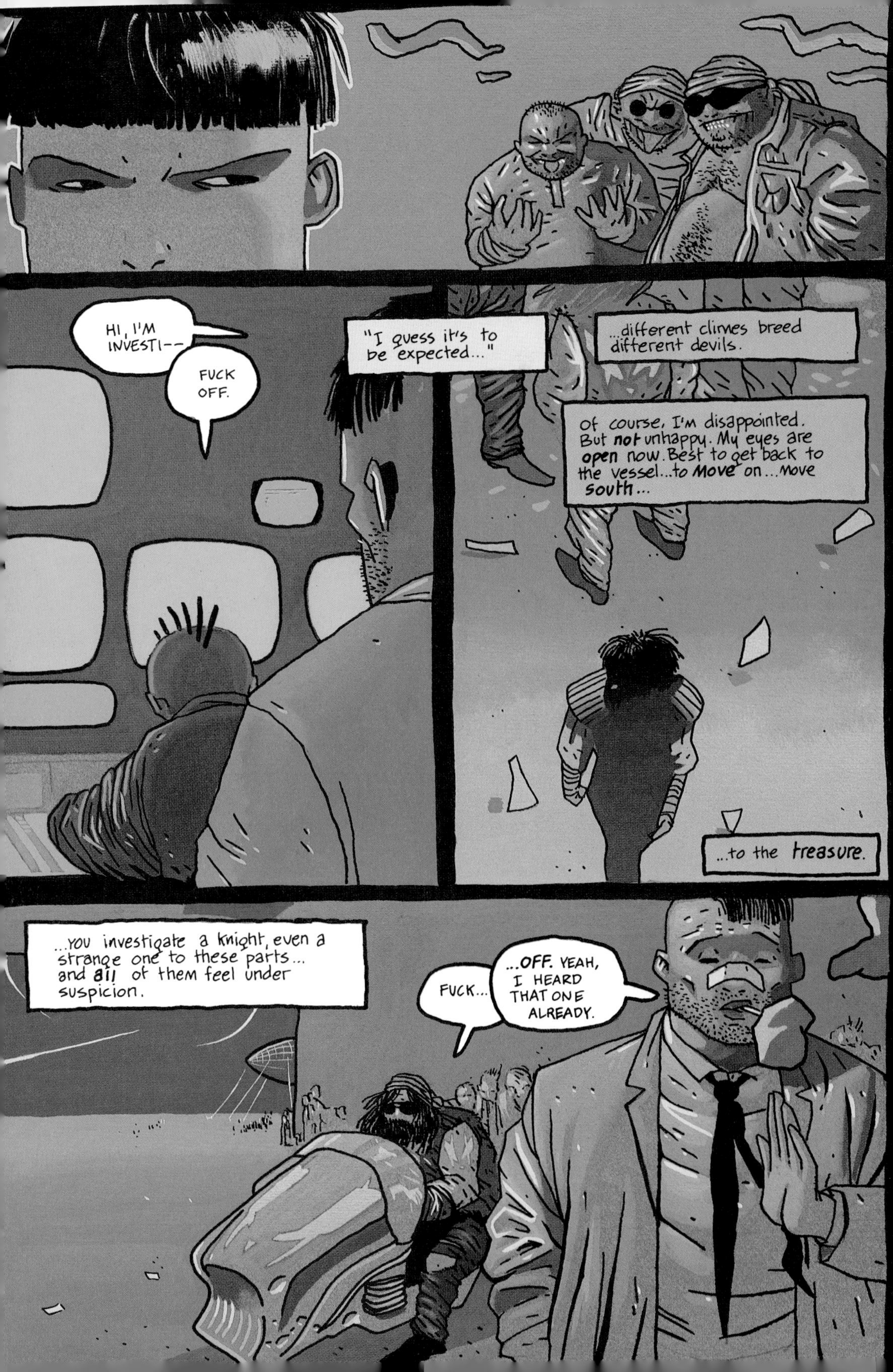
HI, I'M INVESTI--
FUCK OFF.
"I guess it's to be expected..."
...different climes breed different devils.
Of course, I'm disappointed. But **not** unhappy. My eyes are **open** now. Best to get back to the vessel...to **Move** on...move **south**...
...to the **treasure**.
...you investigate a knight, even a strange one to these parts... and **all** of them feel under suspicion.
FUCK...
...OFF. YEAH, I HEARD THAT ONE ALREADY.

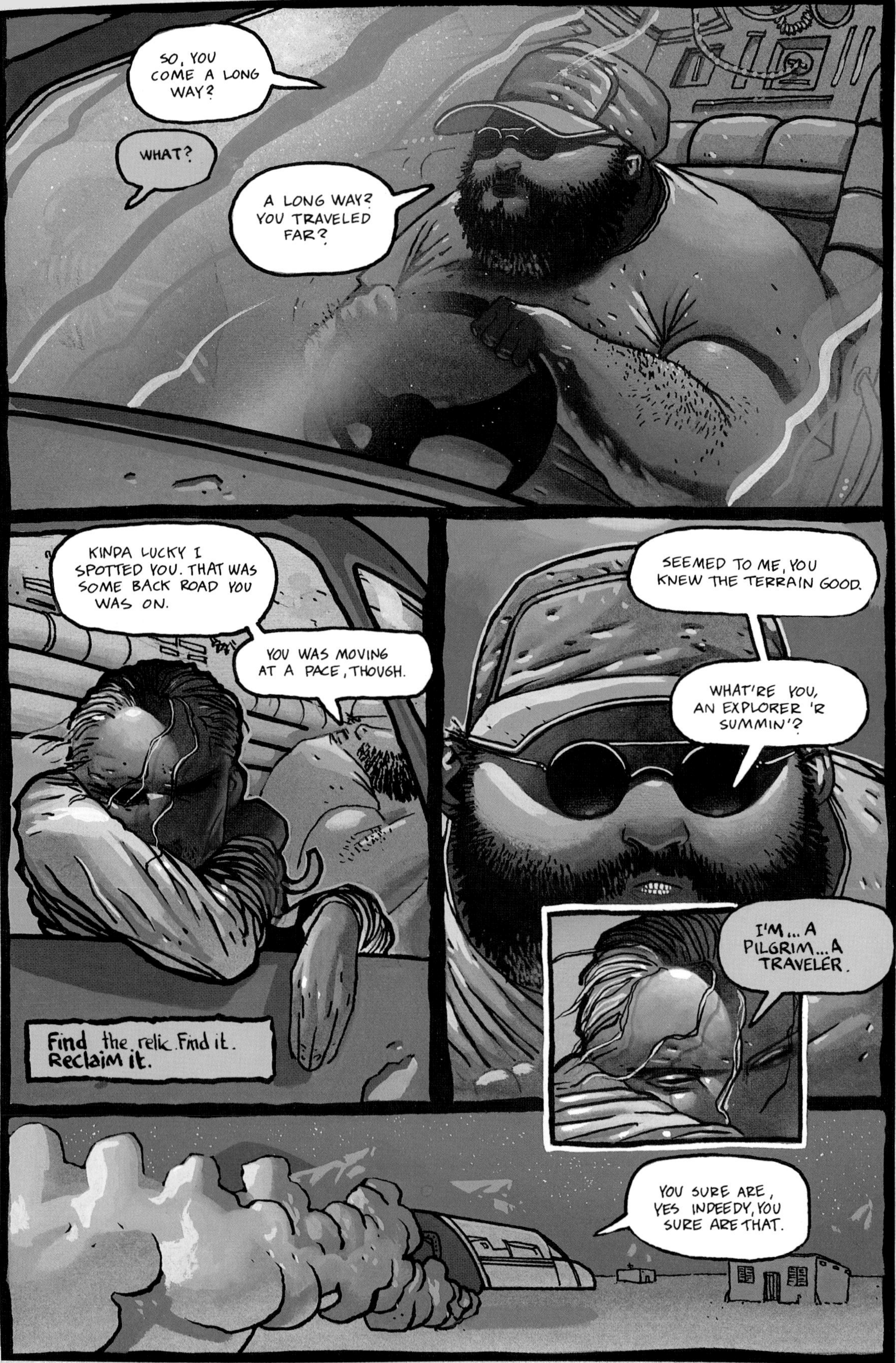
SO, YOU COME A LONG WAY?
WHAT?
A LONG WAY? YOU TRAVELED FAR?
KINDA LUCKY I SPOTTED YOU. THAT WAS SOME BACK ROAD YOU WAS ON.
YOU WAS MOVING AT A PACE, THOUGH.
Find the relik. Find it. Reclaim it.
SEEMED TO ME, YOU KNEW THE TERRAIN GOOD.
WHAT'RE YOU, AN EXPLORER 'R SUMMIN'?
I'M... A PILGRIM... A TRAVELER.
YOU SURE ARE, YES INDEEDY, YOU SURE ARE THAT.

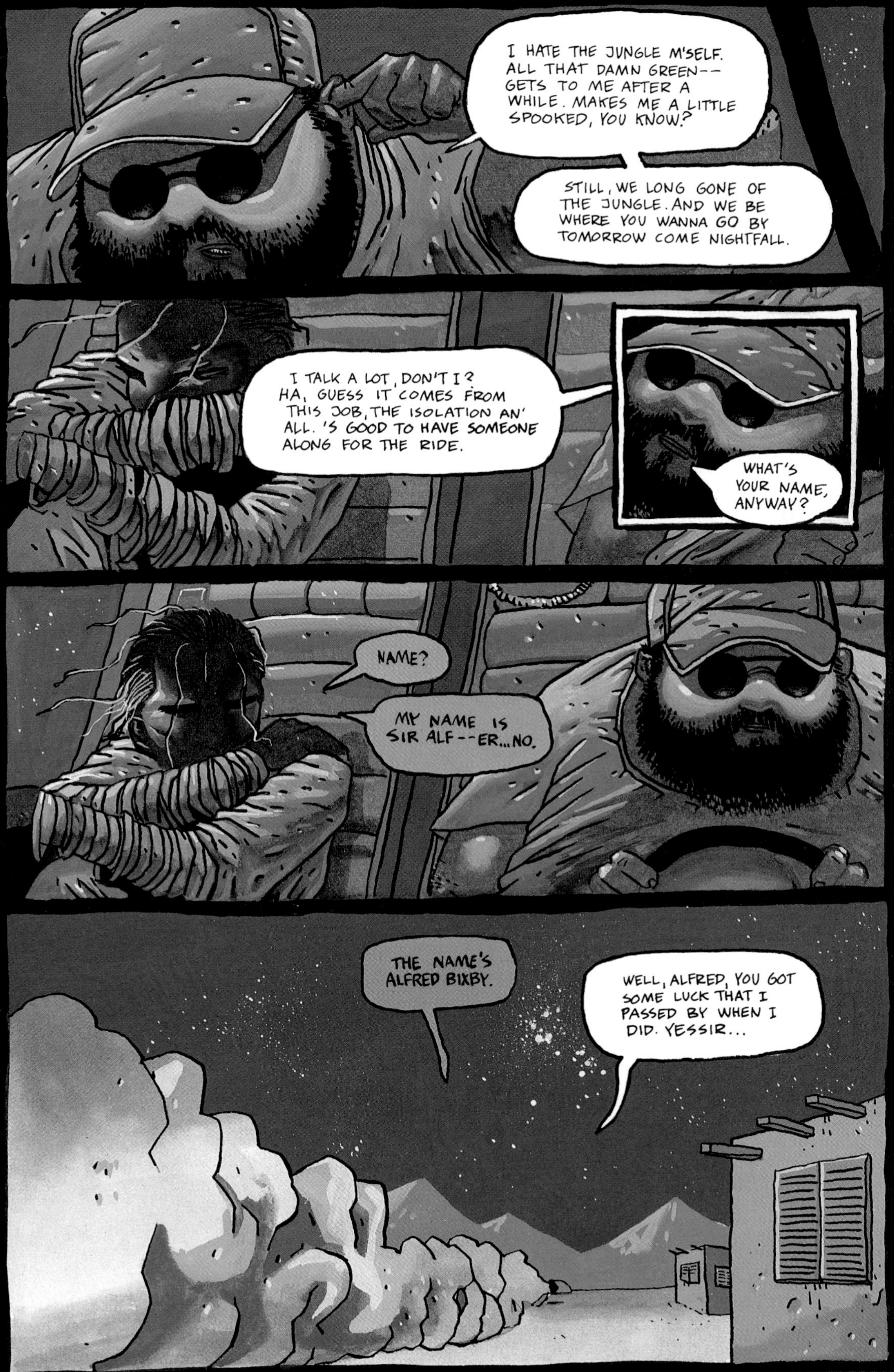

I HATE THE JUNGLE M'SELF. ALL THAT DAMN GREEN-- GETS TO ME AFTER A WHILE. MAKES ME A LITTLE SPOOKED, YOU KNOW?
STILL, WE LONG GONE OF THE JUNGLE. AND WE BE WHERE YOU WANNA GO BY TOMORROW COME NIGHTFALL.
I TALK A LOT, DON'T I? HA, GUESS IT COMES FROM THIS JOB, THE ISOLATION AN' ALL. 'S GOOD TO HAVE SOMEONE ALONG FOR THE RIDE.
WHAT'S YOUR NAME, ANYWAY?
NAME?
MY NAME IS SIR ALF--ER...NO.
THE NAME'S ALFRED BIXBY.
WELL, ALFRED, YOU GOT SOME LUCK THAT I PASSED BY WHEN I DID. YESSIR...

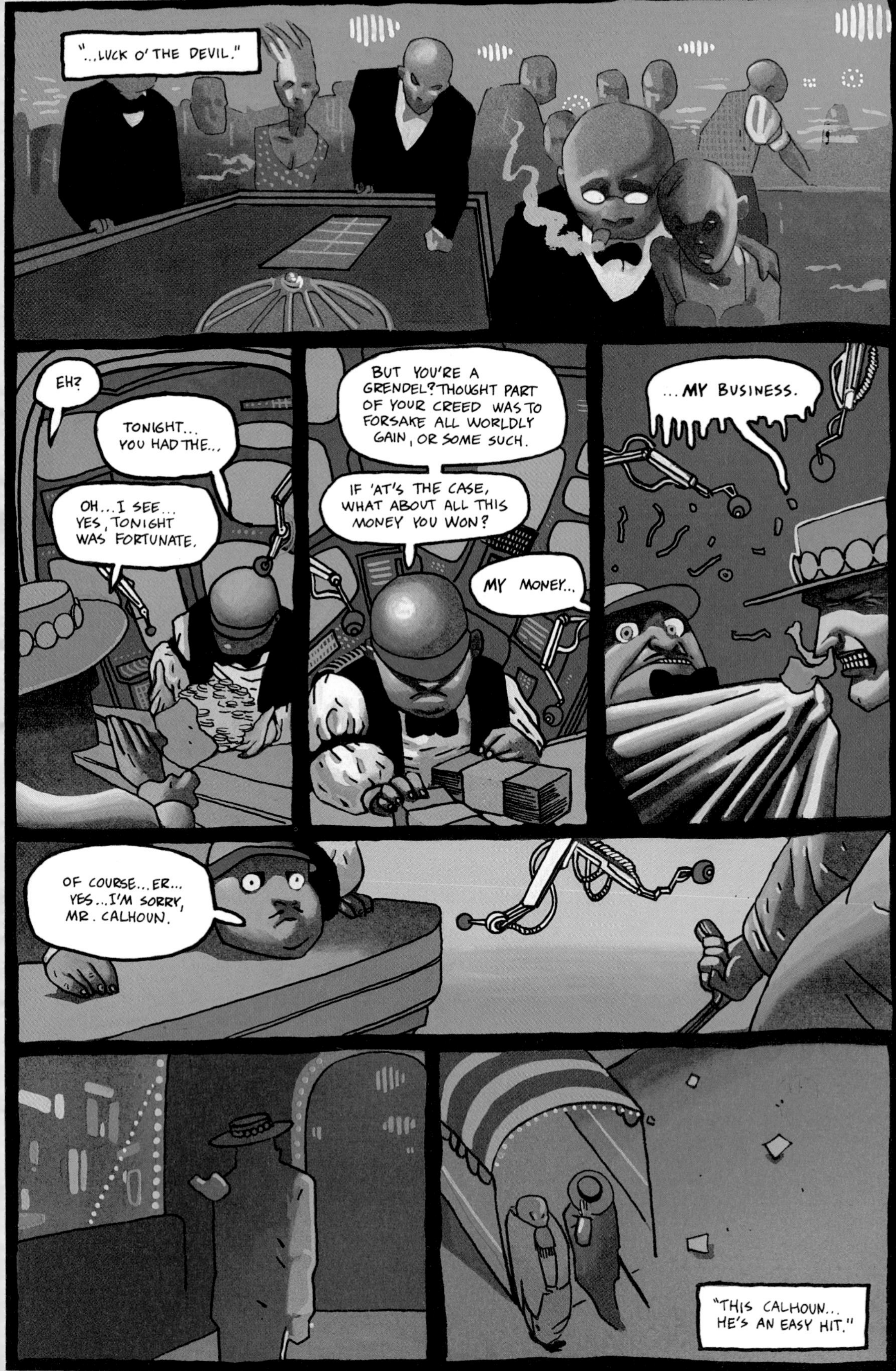
"...LUCK O' THE DEVIL."
EH?
TONIGHT... YOU HAD THE...
OH... I SEE... YES, TONIGHT WAS FORTUNATE.
BUT YOU'RE A GRENDEL? THOUGHT PART OF YOUR CREED WAS TO FORSAKE ALL WORLDLY GAIN, OR SOME SUCH.
IF 'AT'S THE CASE, WHAT ABOUT ALL THIS MONEY YOU WON?
MY MONEY...
...MY BUSINESS.
OF COURSE... ER... YES... I'M SORRY, MR. CALHOUN.
"THIS CALHOUN... HE'S AN EASY HIT."

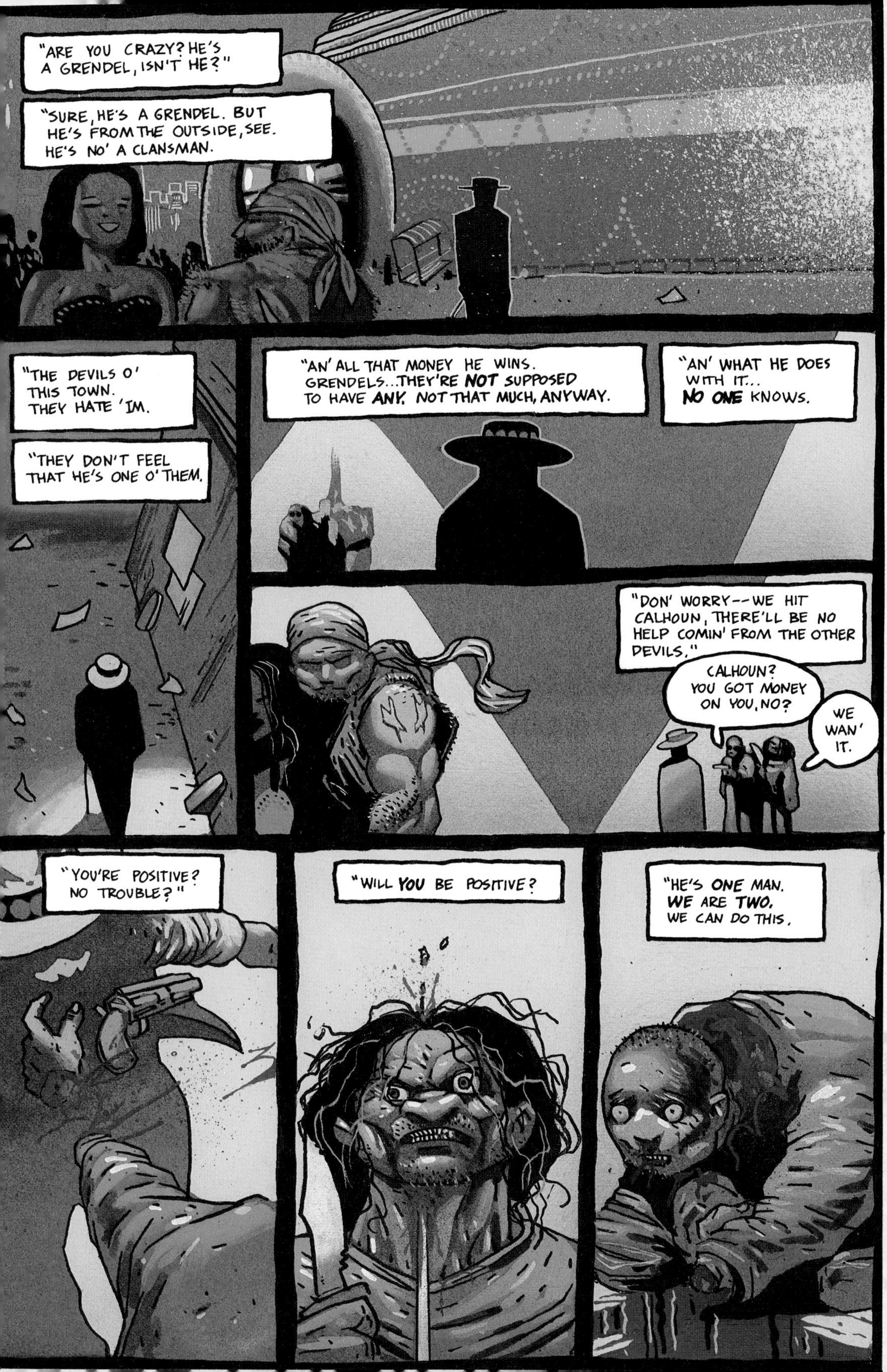
"ARE YOU CRAZY? HE'S A GRENDEL, ISN'T HE?"
"SURE, HE'S A GRENDEL. BUT HE'S FROM THE OUTSIDE, SEE. HE'S NO' A CLANSMAN.
"THE DEVILS O' THIS TOWN. THEY HATE 'IM.
"THEY DON'T FEEL THAT HE'S ONE O' THEM.
"AN' ALL THAT MONEY HE WINS. GRENDELS...THEY'RE NOT SUPPOSED TO HAVE ANY. NOT THAT MUCH, ANYWAY.
"AN' WHAT HE DOES WITH IT... NO ONE KNOWS.
"DON' WORRY--WE HIT CALHOUN, THERE'LL BE NO HELP COMIN' FROM THE OTHER DEVILS."
CALHOUN? YOU GOT MONEY ON YOU, NO?
WE WAN' IT.
"YOU'RE POSITIVE? NO TROUBLE?"
"WILL YOU BE POSITIVE?
"HE'S ONE MAN. WE ARE TWO. WE CAN DO THIS.

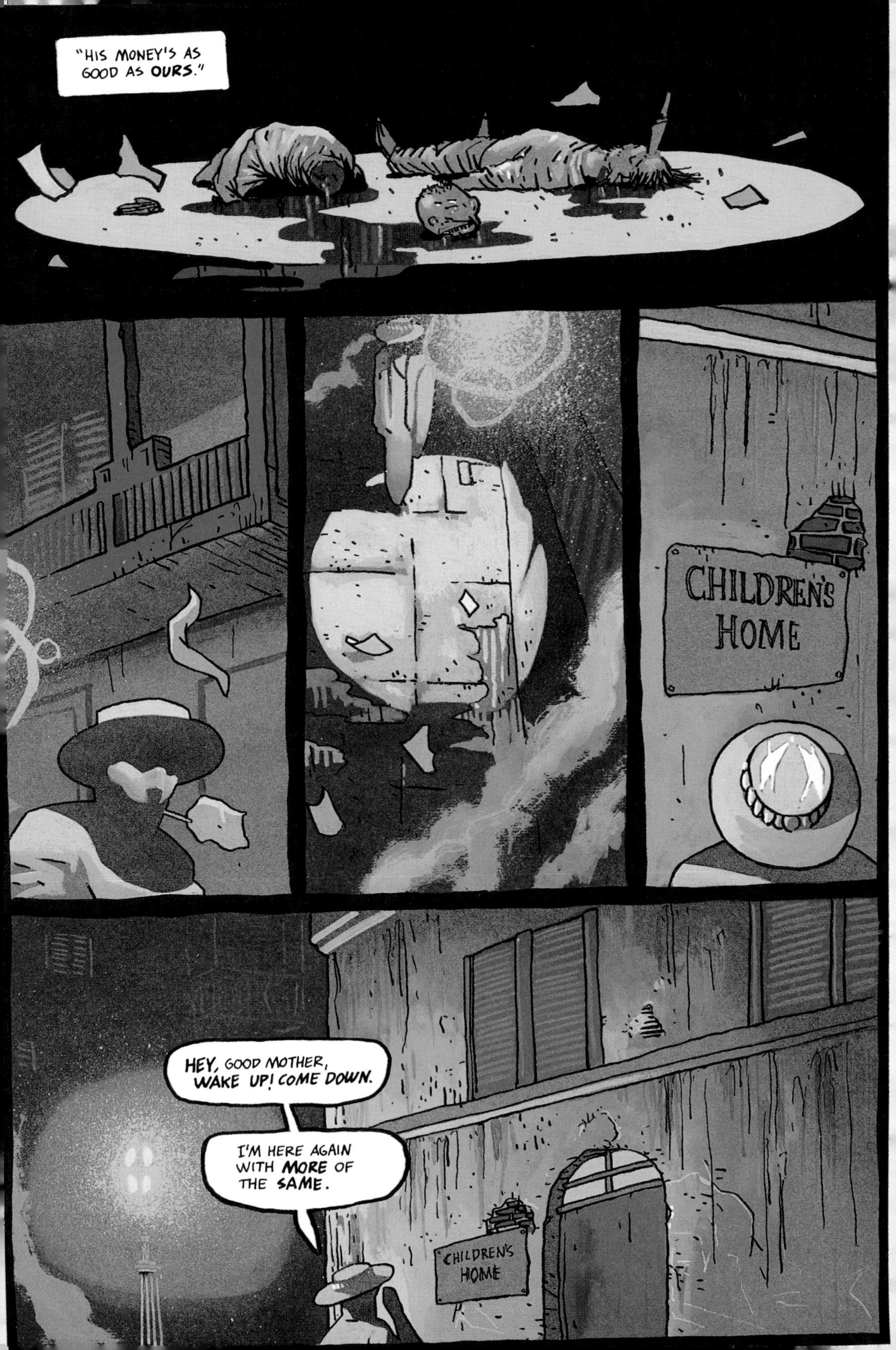
"HIS MONEY'S AS GOOD AS OURS."
CHILDREN'S HOME
HEY, GOOD MOTHER, WAKE UP! COME DOWN.
I'M HERE AGAIN WITH MORE OF THE SAME.
CHILDREN'S HOME

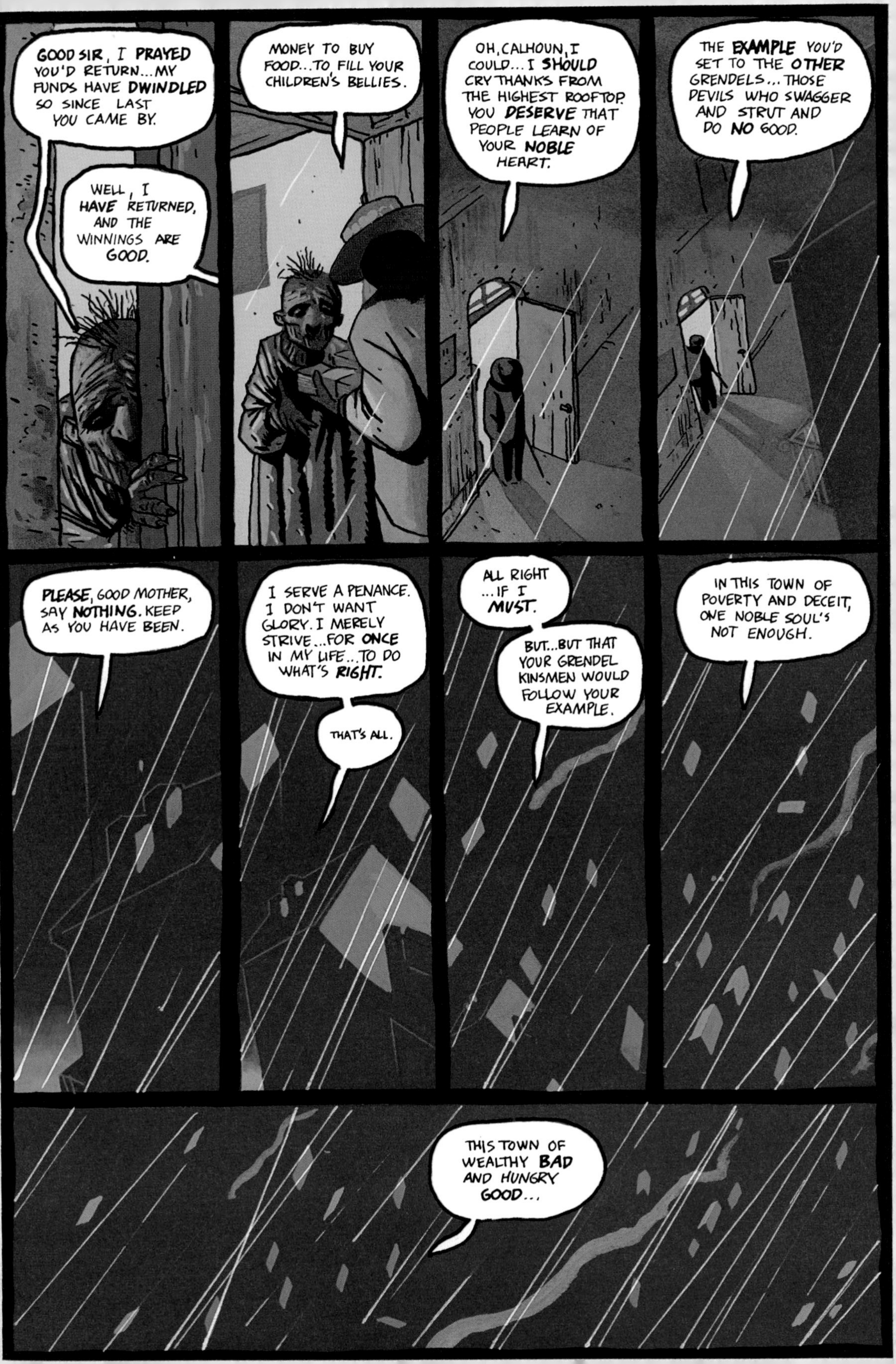
GOOD SIR, I PRAYED YOU'D RETURN... MY FUNDS HAVE DWINDLED SO SINCE LAST YOU CAME BY.
WELL, I HAVE RETURNED, AND THE WINNINGS ARE GOOD.
MONEY TO BUY FOOD... TO FILL YOUR CHILDREN'S BELLIES.
OH, CALHOUN, I COULD... I SHOULD CRY THANKS FROM THE HIGHEST ROOFTOP. YOU DESERVE THAT PEOPLE LEARN OF YOUR NOBLE HEART.
THE EXAMPLE YOU'D SET TO THE OTHER GRENDELS... THOSE DEVILS WHO SWAGGER AND STRUT AND DO NO GOOD.
PLEASE, GOOD MOTHER, SAY NOTHING. KEEP AS YOU HAVE BEEN.
I SERVE A PENANCE. I DON'T WANT GLORY. I MERELY STRIVE... FOR ONCE IN MY LIFE... TO DO WHAT'S RIGHT.
THAT'S ALL.
ALL RIGHT ...IF I MUST.
BUT... BUT THAT YOUR GRENDEL KINSMEN WOULD FOLLOW YOUR EXAMPLE.
IN THIS TOWN OF POVERTY AND DECEIT, ONE NOBLE SOUL'S NOT ENOUGH.
THIS TOWN OF WEALTHY BAD AND HUNGRY GOOD...

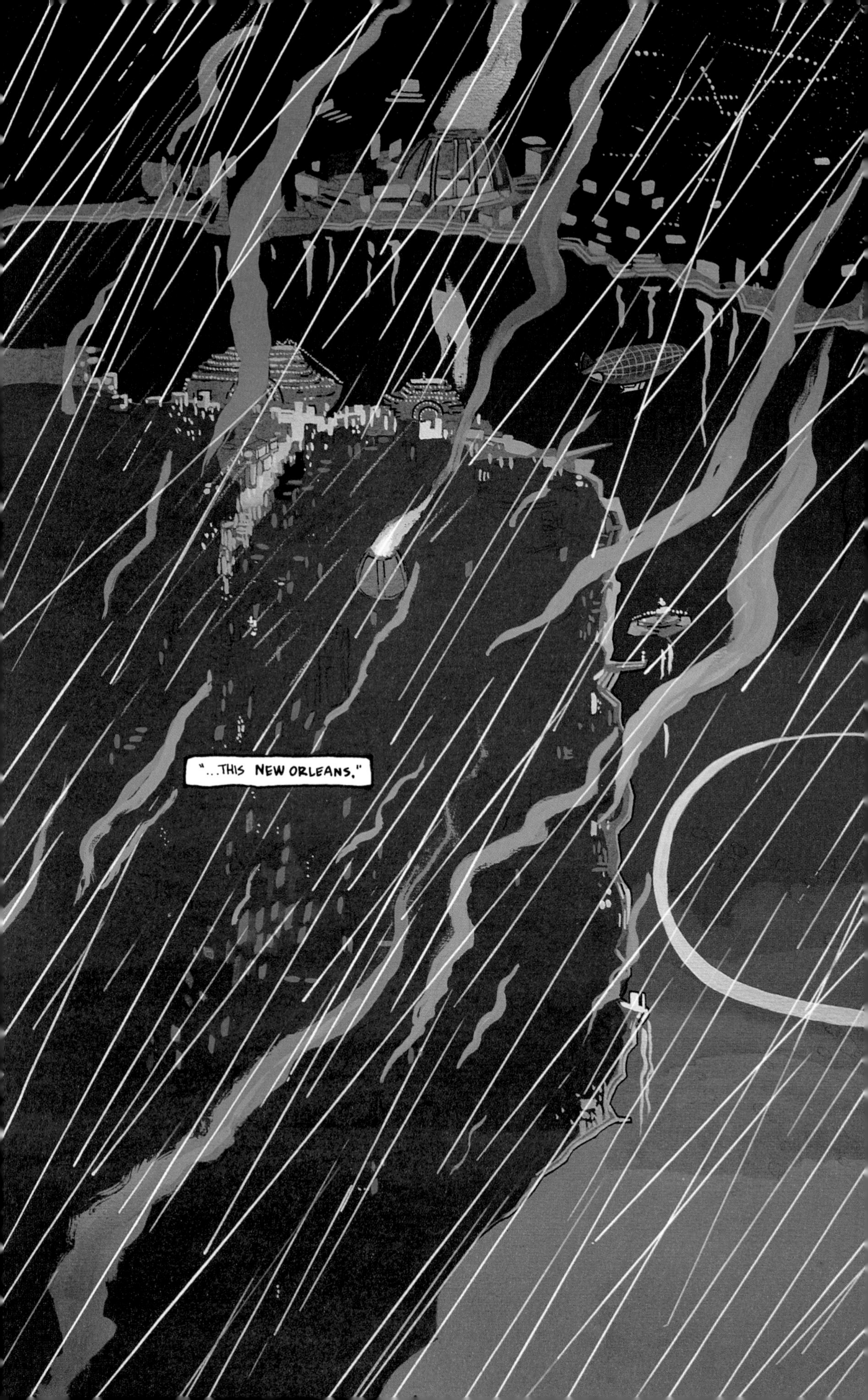
"...THIS NEW ORLEANS."

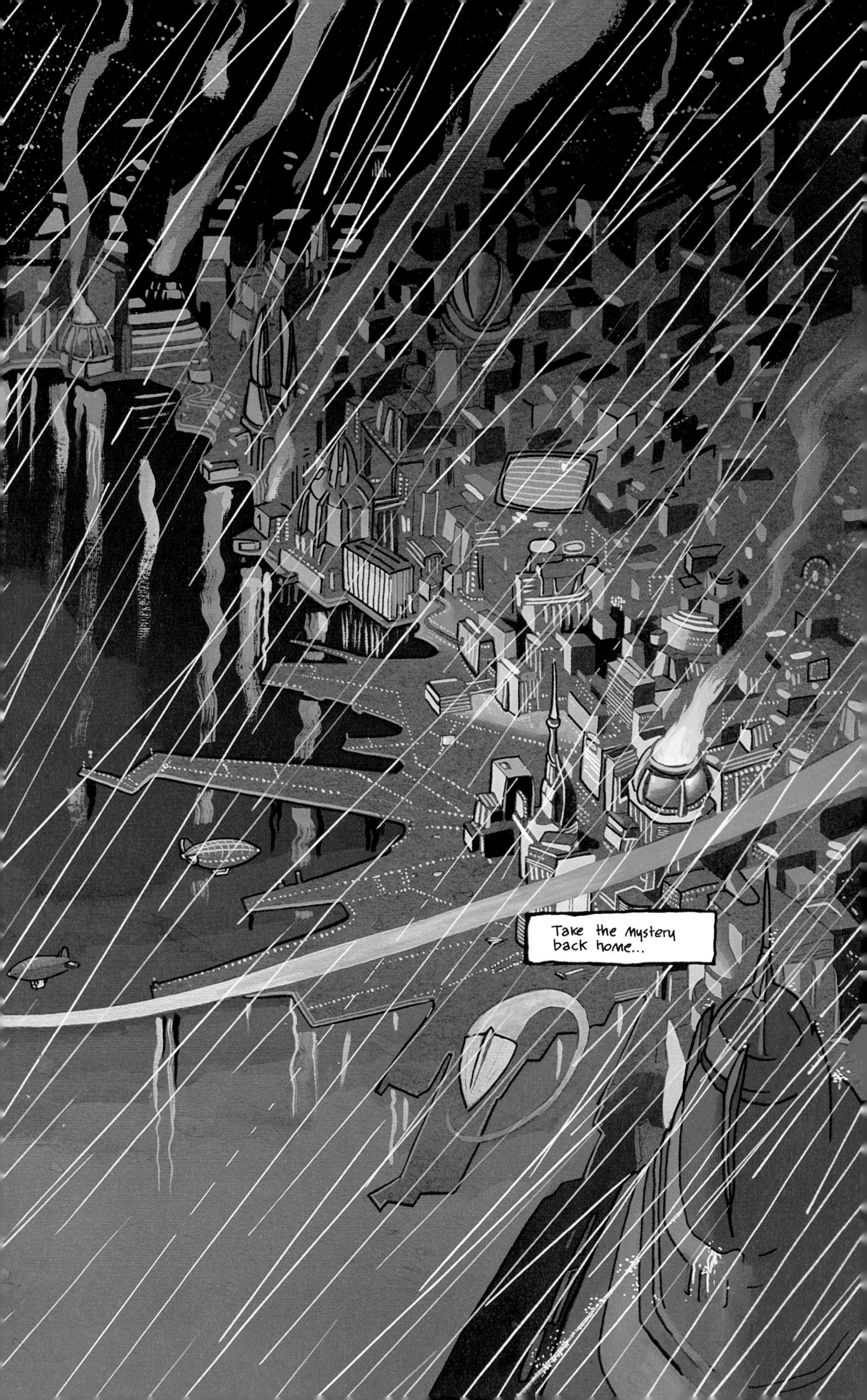
Take the mystery
back home...

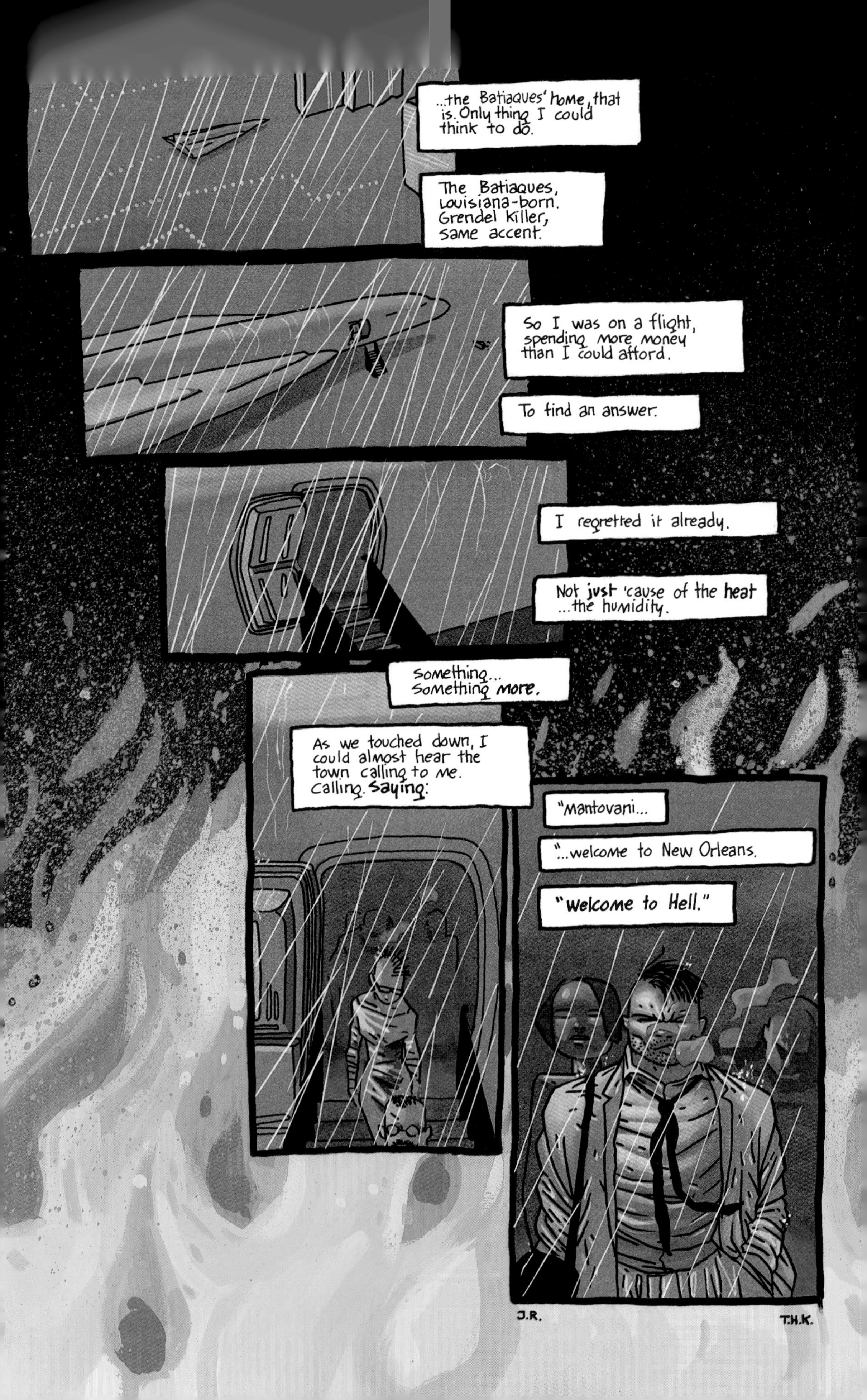
...the Batiaques' home, that is. Only thing I could think to do.
The Batiaques, Louisiana-born. Grendel killer, same accent.
So I was on a flight, spending more money than I could afford.
To find an answer.
I regretted it already.
Not just 'cause of the heat ...the humidity.
Something... Something more.
As we touched down, I could almost hear the town calling to me. Calling. Saying:
"Mantovani...
"...welcome to New Orleans.
"Welcome to Hell."
J.R.
T.H.K.

CHAPTER THREE

FOUR QUESTIONS, THREE ANSWERS

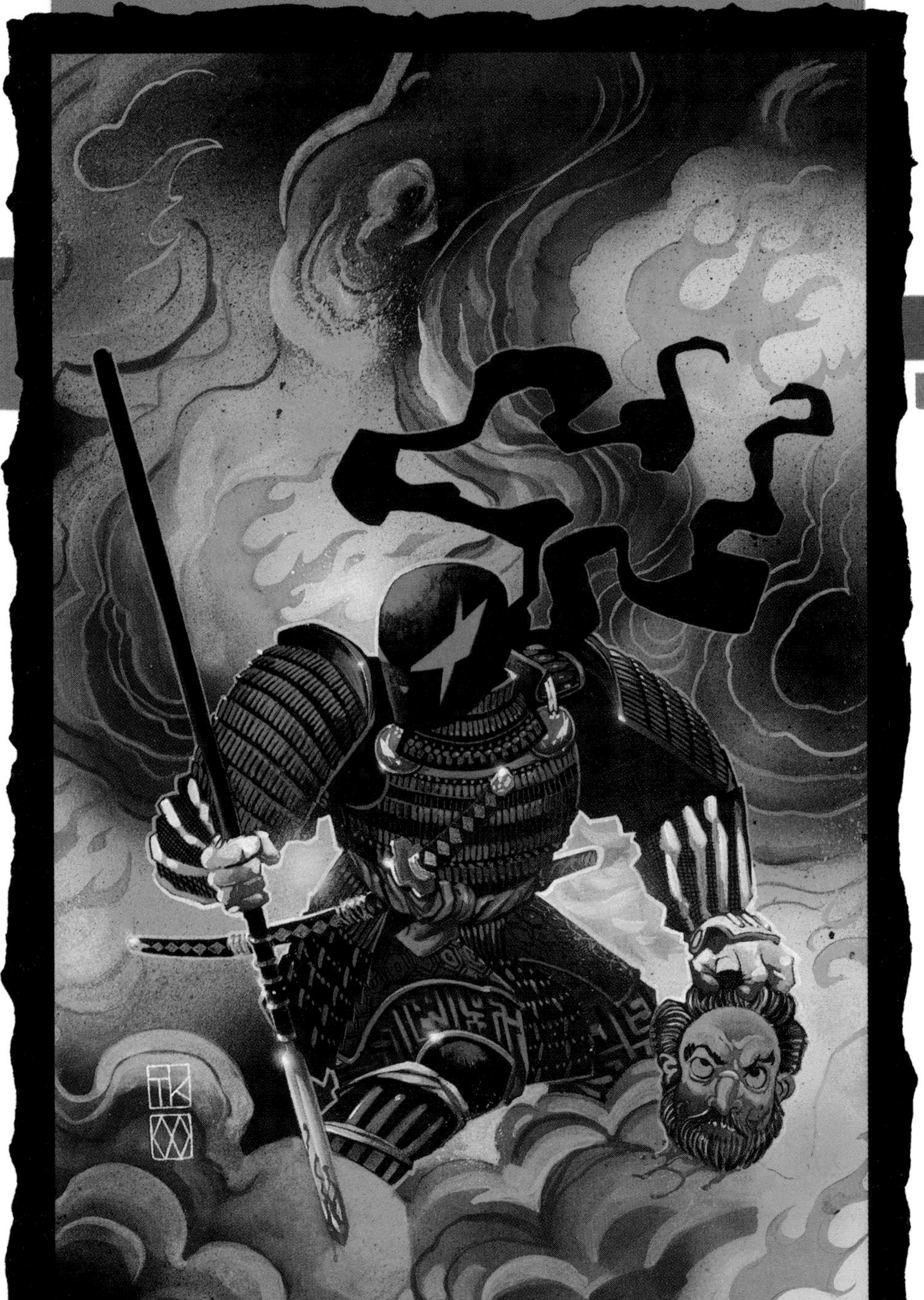

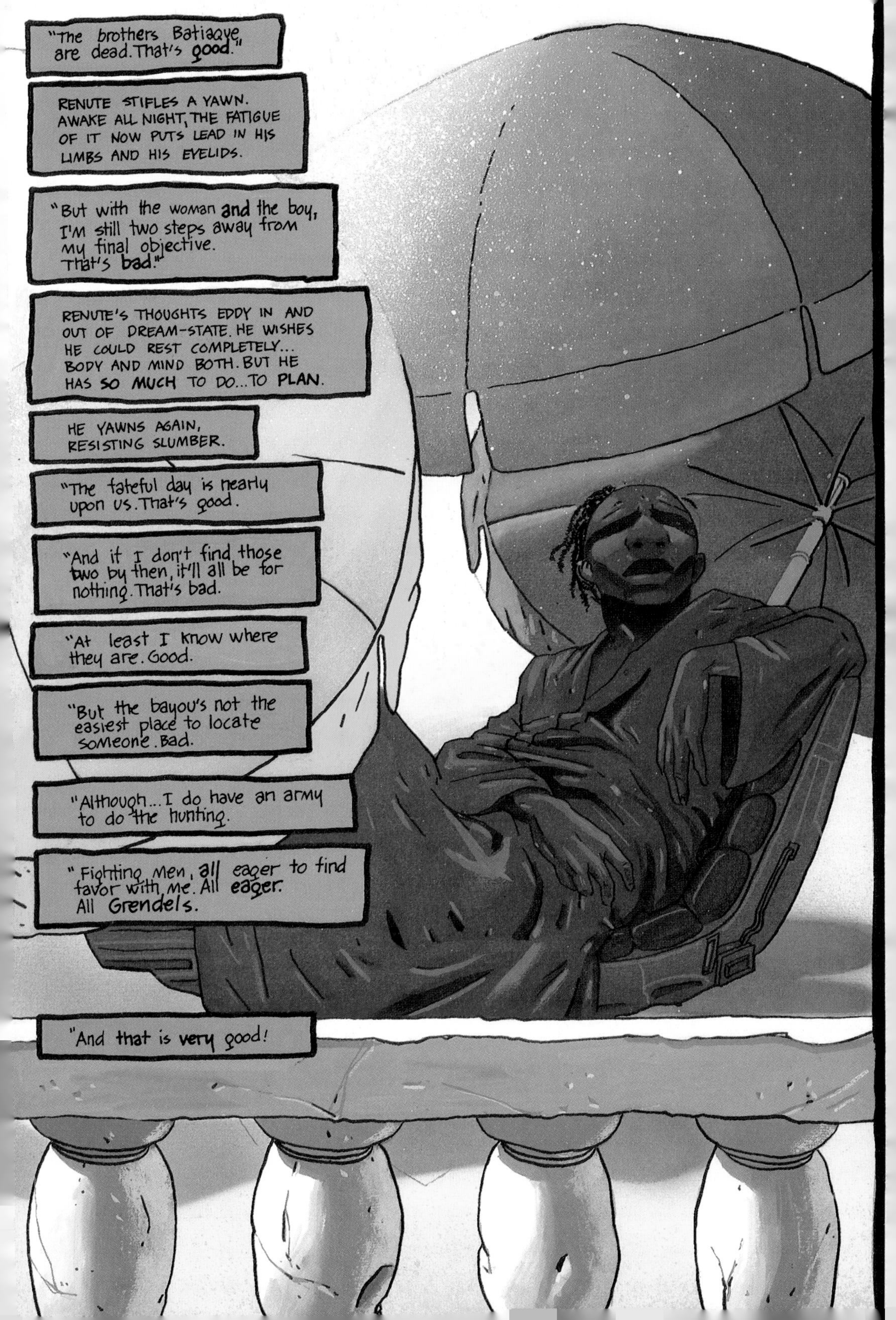
"The brothers Batiaque are dead. That's good."
RENUTE STIFLES A YAWN. AWAKE ALL NIGHT, THE FATIGUE OF IT NOW PUTS LEAD IN HIS LIMBS AND HIS EYELIDS.
"But with the woman and the boy, I'm still two steps away from my final objective. That's bad."
RENUTE'S THOUGHTS EDDY IN AND OUT OF DREAM-STATE. HE WISHES HE COULD REST COMPLETELY... BODY AND MIND BOTH. BUT HE HAS SO MUCH TO DO... TO PLAN.
HE YAWNS AGAIN, RESISTING SLUMBER.
"The fateful day is nearly upon us. That's good.
"And if I don't find those two by then, it'll all be for nothing. That's bad.
"At least I know where they are. Good.
"But the bayou's not the easiest place to locate someone. Bad.
"Although... I do have an army to do the hunting.
"Fighting men, all eager to find favor with me. All eager. All Grendels.
"And that is very good!

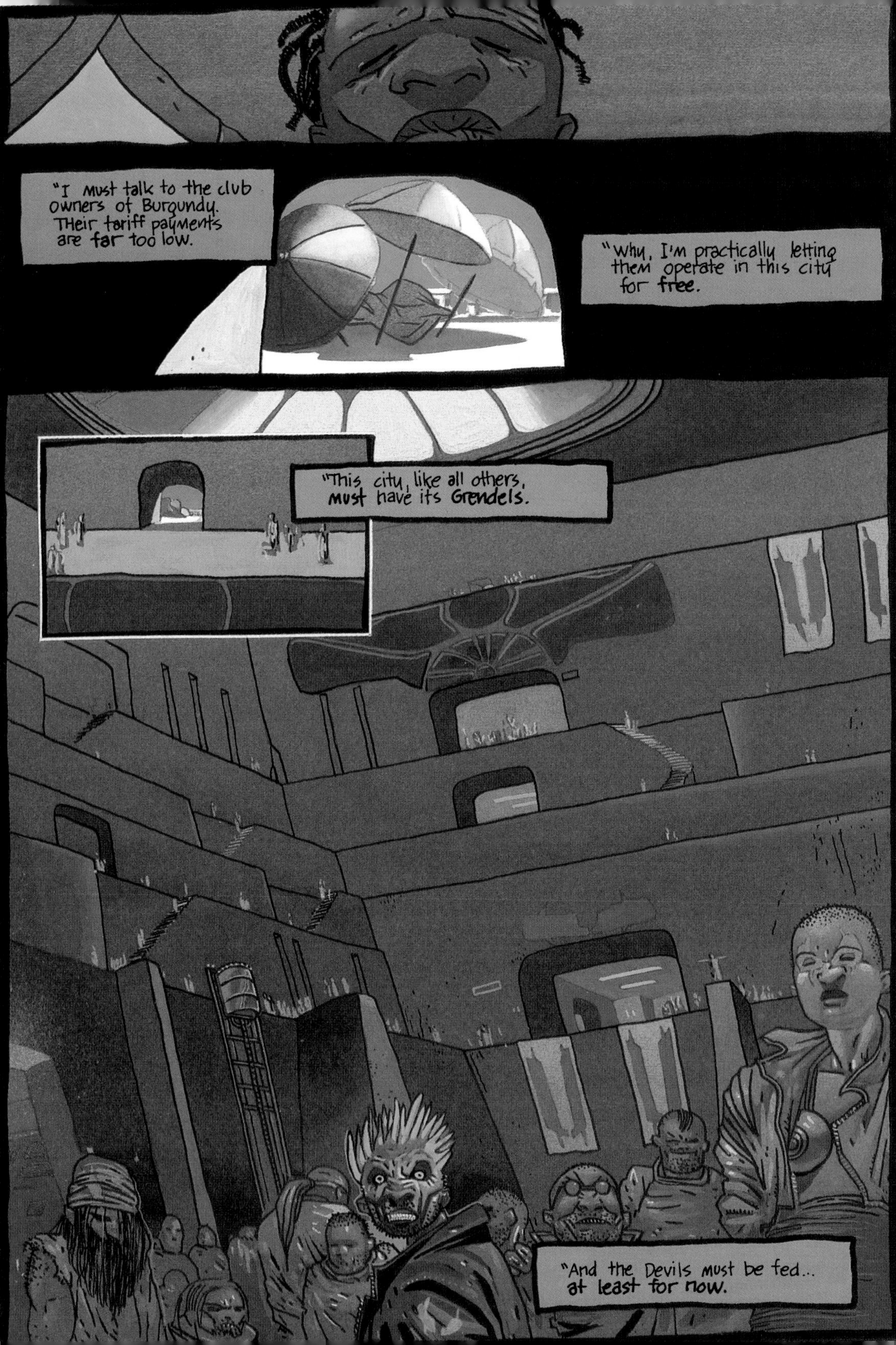
"I must talk to the club owners of Burgundy. Their tariff payments are **far** too low.
"Why, I'm practically letting them operate in this city for **free**.
"This city, like all others, **must** have its **Grendels**.
"And the Devils must be fed... **at least for now**.

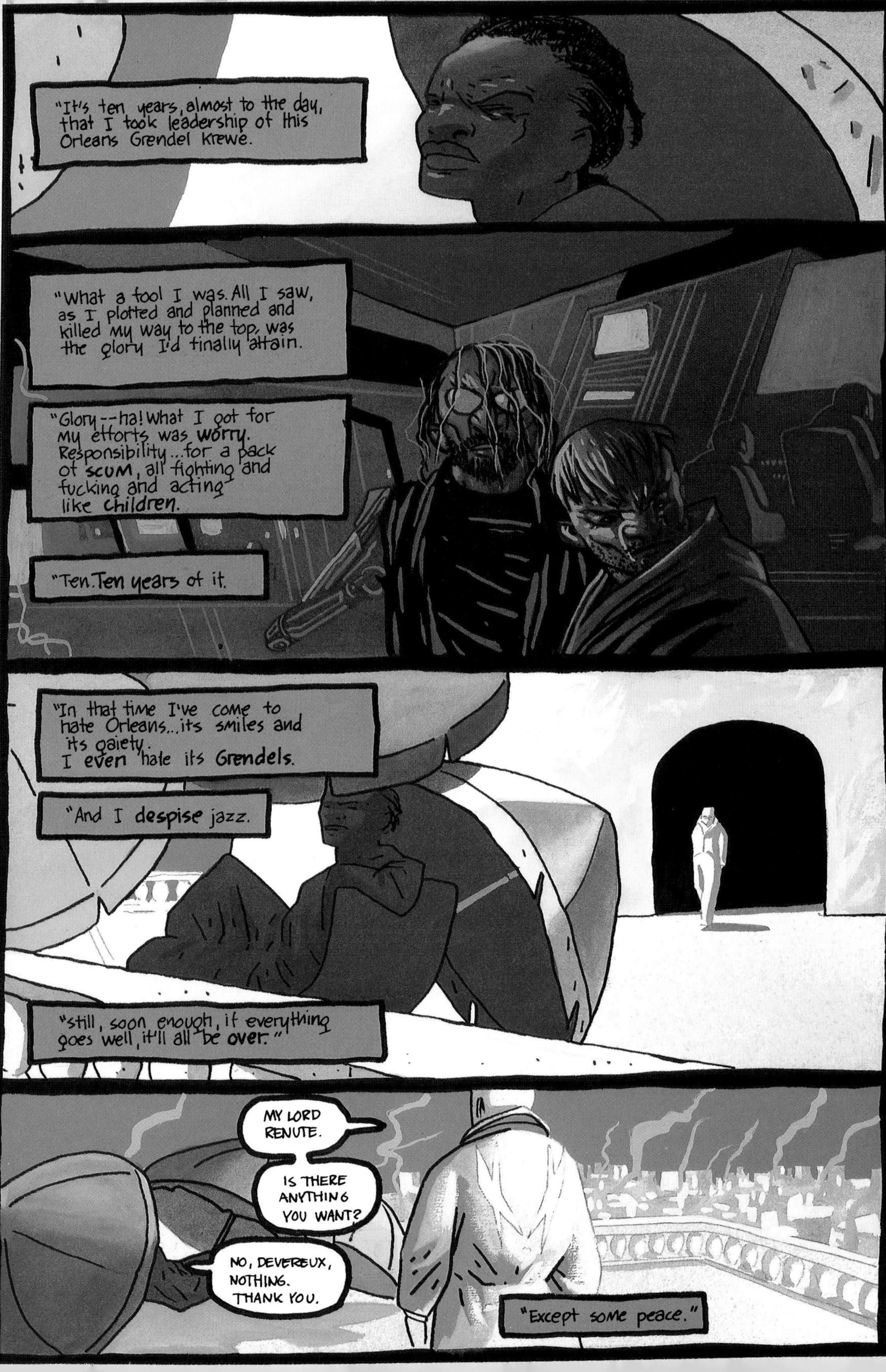
"It's ten years, almost to the day, that I took leadership of this Orleans Grendel krewe.
"What a fool I was. All I saw, as I plotted and planned and killed my way to the top, was the glory I'd finally attain.
"Glory--ha! What I got for my efforts was worry. Responsibility...for a pack of scum, all fighting and fucking and acting like children.
"Ten. Ten years of it.
"In that time I've come to hate Orleans...its smiles and its gaiety. I even hate its Grendels.
"And I despise jazz.
"Still, soon enough, if everything goes well, it'll all be over."
MY LORD RENUTE.
IS THERE ANYTHING YOU WANT?
NO, DEVEREUX, NOTHING. THANK YOU.
"Except some peace."

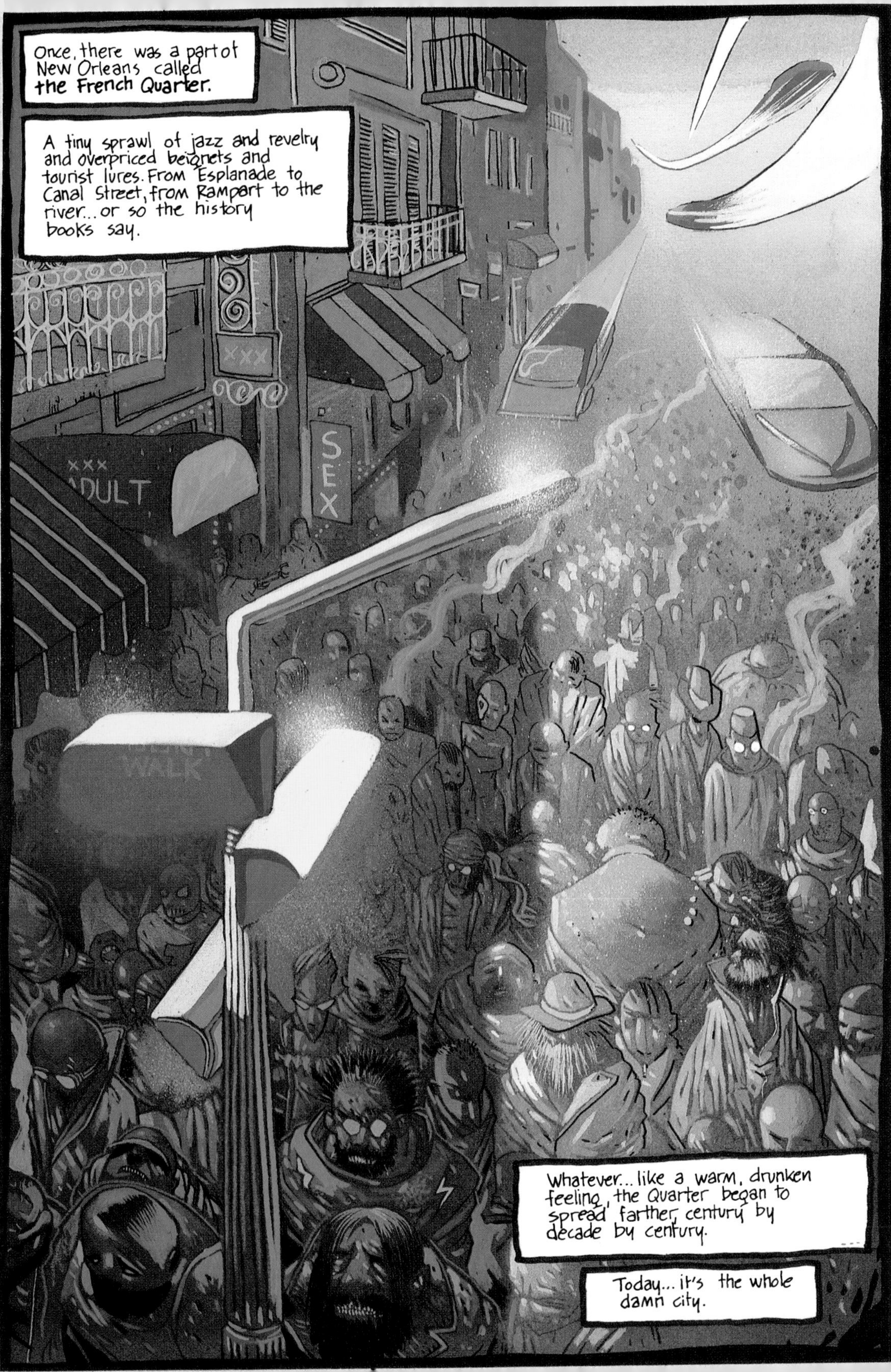
Once, there was a part of New Orleans called **the French Quarter.**
A tiny sprawl of jazz and revelry and overpriced beignets and tourist lures. From Esplanade to Canal Street, from Rampart to the river... or so the history books say.
XXX
SEX
XXX
ADULT
WALK
Whatever... like a warm, drunken feeling, the Quarter began to spread farther, century by decade by century.
Today... it's the whole damn city.

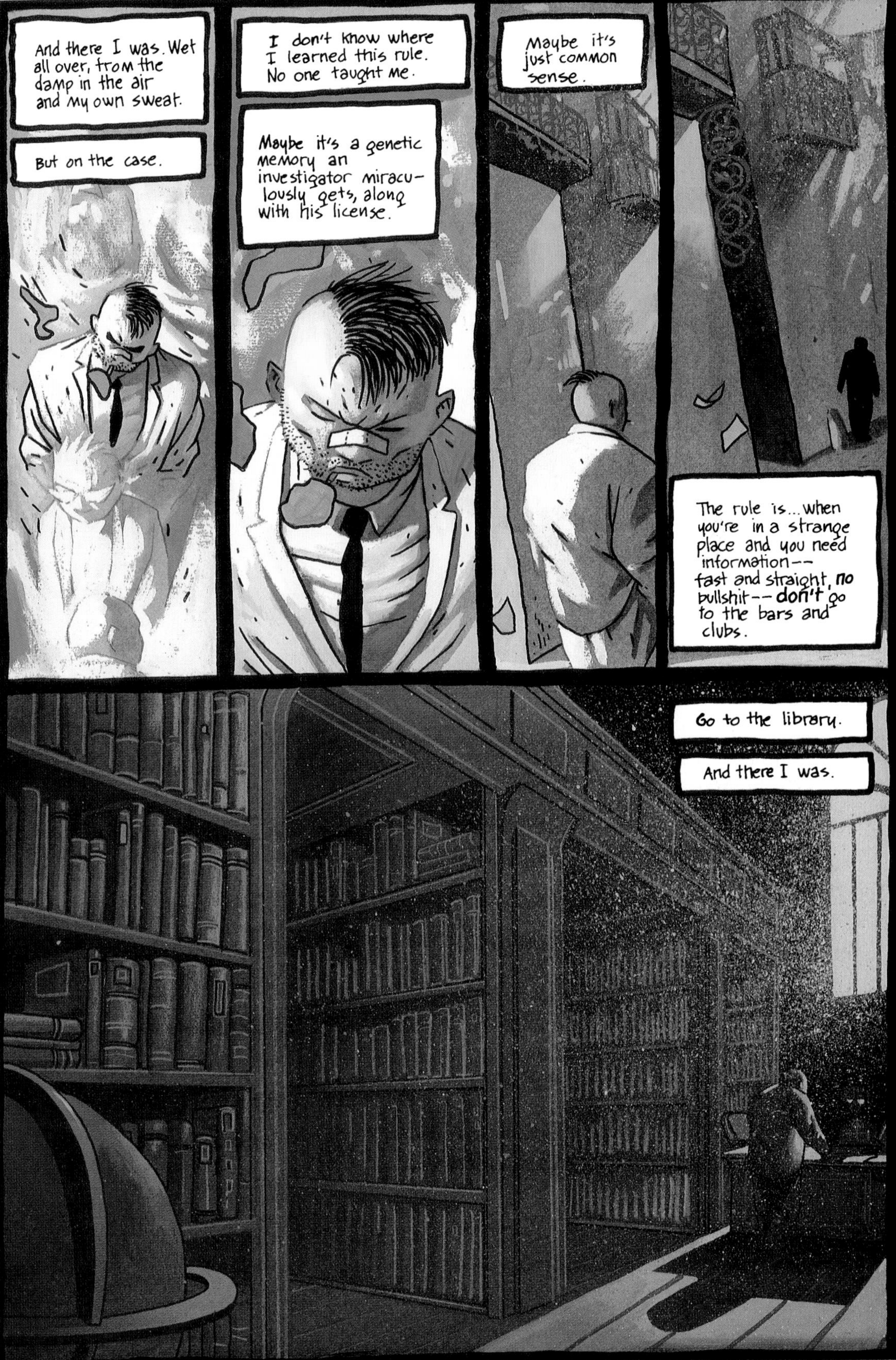
And there I was. Wet all over, from the damp in the air and my own sweat.
But on the case.
I don't know where I learned this rule. No one taught me.
Maybe it's a genetic memory an investigator miraculously gets, along with his license.
Maybe it's just common sense.
The rule is... when you're in a strange place and you need information-- fast and straight, no bullshit-- don't go to the bars and clubs.
Go to the library.
And there I was.

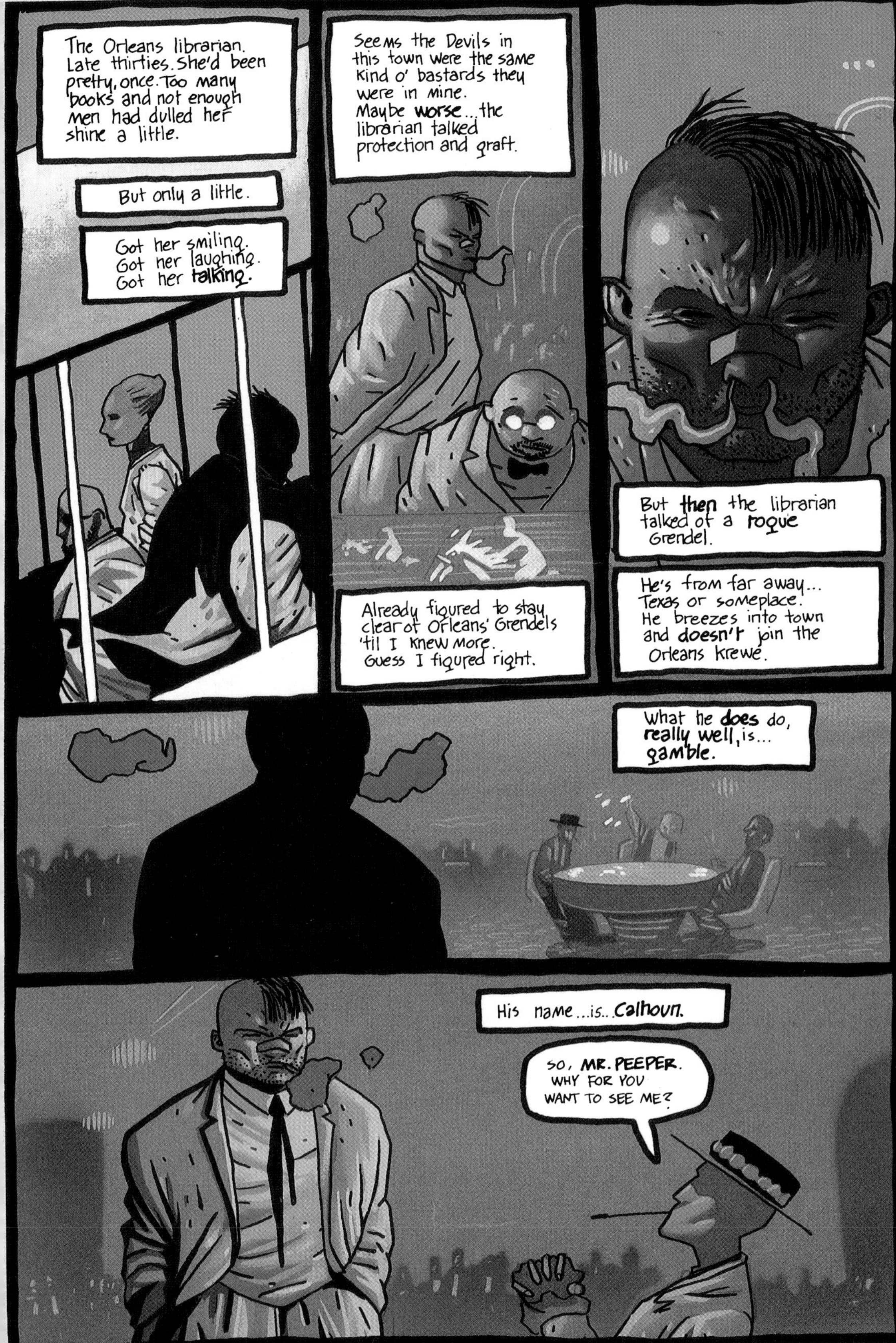

The Orleans librarian. Late thirties. She'd been pretty, once. Too many books and not enough men had dulled her shine a little.
But only a little.
Got her smiling. Got her laughing. Got her **talking.**
Seems the Devils in this town were the same kind o' bastards they were in mine. Maybe **worse**... the librarian talked protection and graft.
Already figured to stay clear of Orleans' Grendels 'til I knew more. Guess I figured right.
But **then** the librarian talked of a **rogue** Grendel.
He's from far away... Texas or someplace. He breezes into town and **doesn't** join the Orleans krewe.
What he **does** do, **really well,** is... **gamble.**
His name... is... **Calhoun.**
SO, **MR. PEEPER.** WHY FOR YOU WANT TO SEE ME?

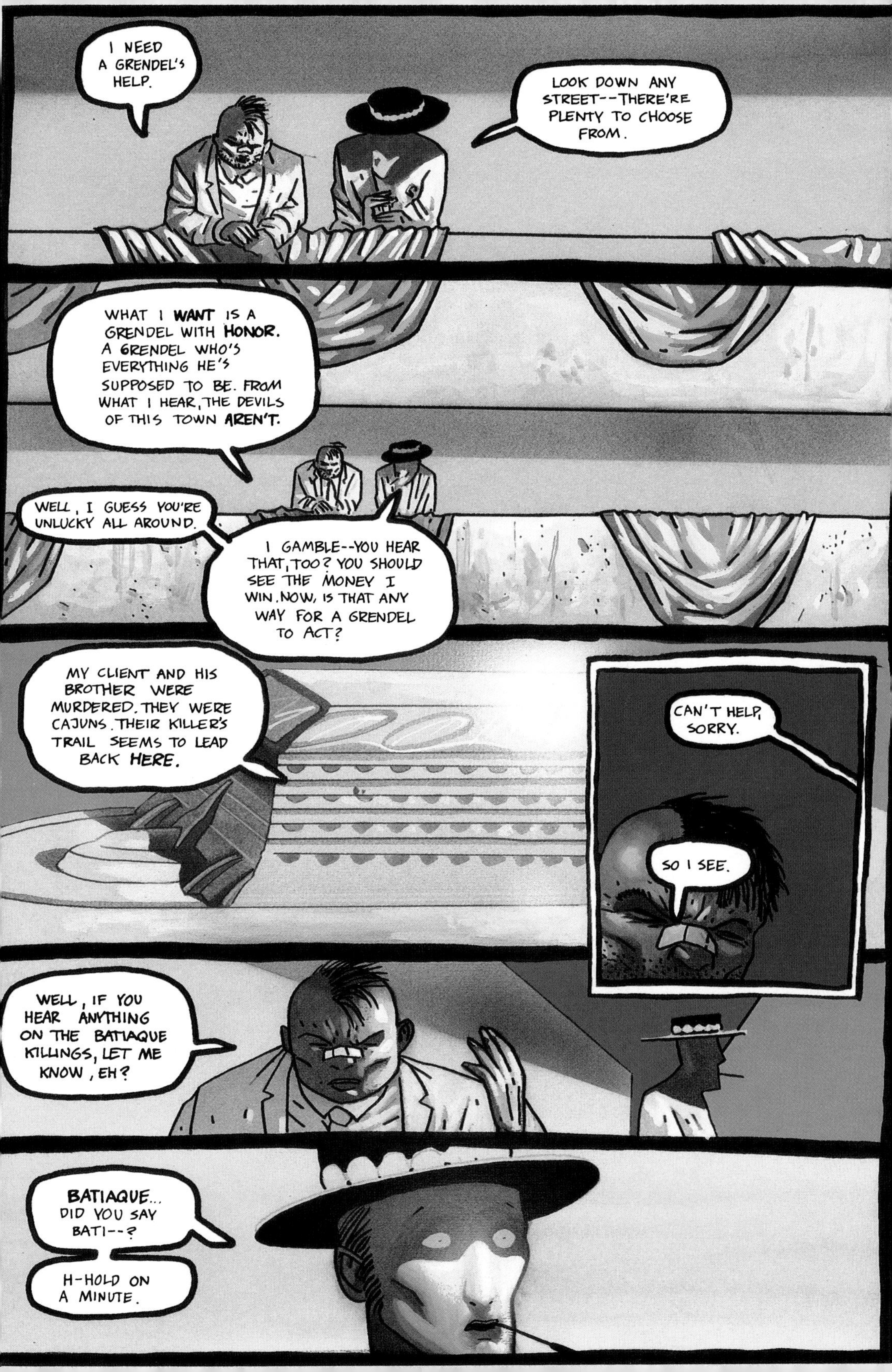
I NEED A GRENDEL'S HELP.
LOOK DOWN ANY STREET--THERE'RE PLENTY TO CHOOSE FROM.
WHAT I WANT IS A GRENDEL WITH HONOR. A GRENDEL WHO'S EVERYTHING HE'S SUPPOSED TO BE. FROM WHAT I HEAR, THE DEVILS OF THIS TOWN AREN'T.
WELL, I GUESS YOU'RE UNLUCKY ALL AROUND.
I GAMBLE--YOU HEAR THAT, TOO? YOU SHOULD SEE THE MONEY I WIN. NOW, IS THAT ANY WAY FOR A GRENDEL TO ACT?
MY CLIENT AND HIS BROTHER WERE MURDERED. THEY WERE CAJUNS. THEIR KILLER'S TRAIL SEEMS TO LEAD BACK HERE.
CAN'T HELP, SORRY.
SO I SEE.
WELL, IF YOU HEAR ANYTHING ON THE BATIAQUE KILLINGS, LET ME KNOW, EH?
BATIAQUE... DID YOU SAY BATI--?
H-HOLD ON A MINUTE.

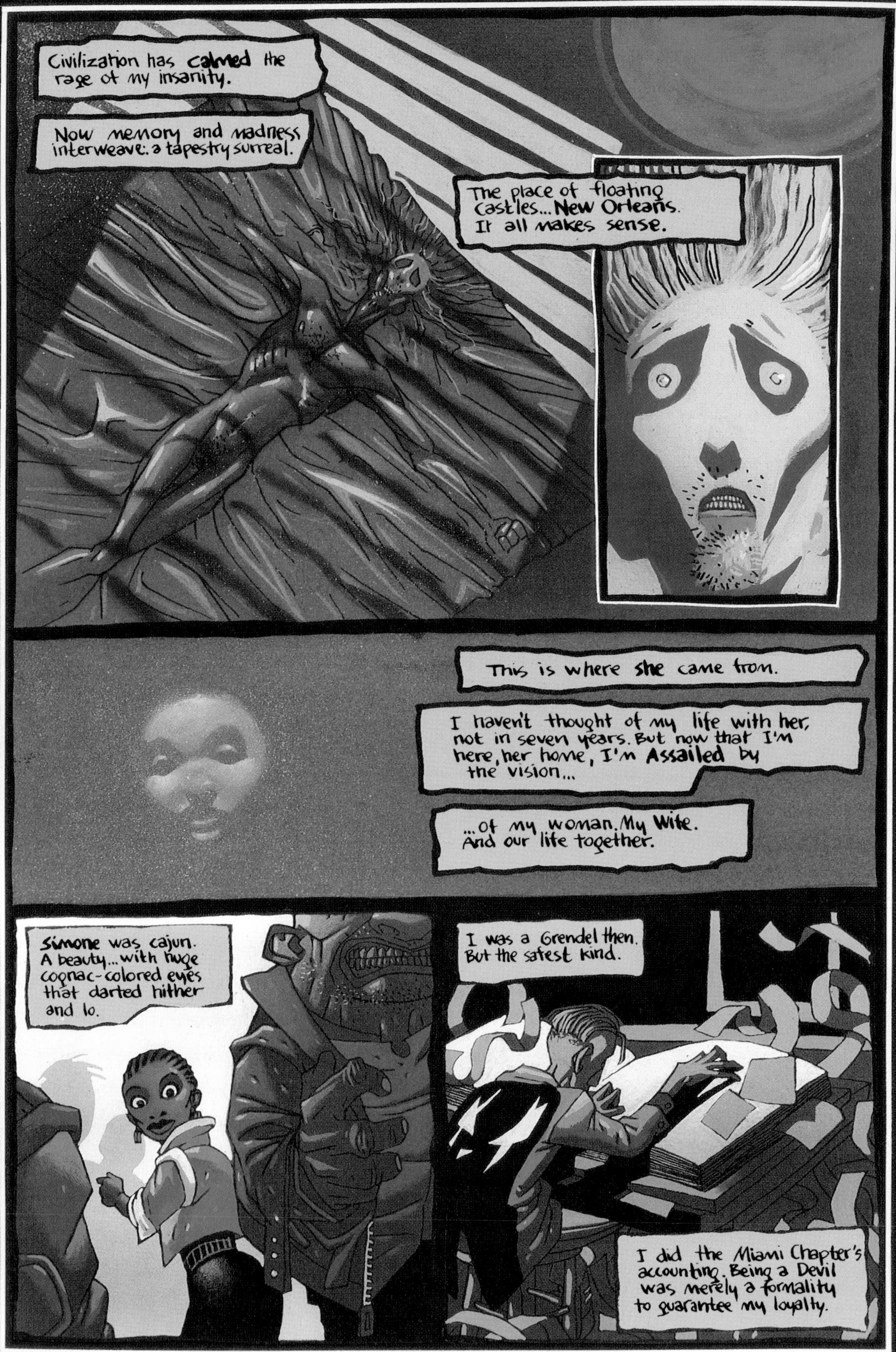
Civilization has calmed the rage of my insanity.
Now memory and madness interweave: a tapestry surreal.
The place of floating castles... New Orleans. It all makes sense.
This is where she came from.
I haven't thought of my life with her, not in seven years. But now that I'm here, her home, I'm Assailed by the vision...
...of my woman. My Wife. And our life together.
Simone was cajun. A beauty... with huge cognac-colored eyes that darted hither and lo.
I was a Grendel then. But the safest kind.
I did the Miami Chapter's accounting. Being a Devil was merely a formality to guarantee my loyalty.

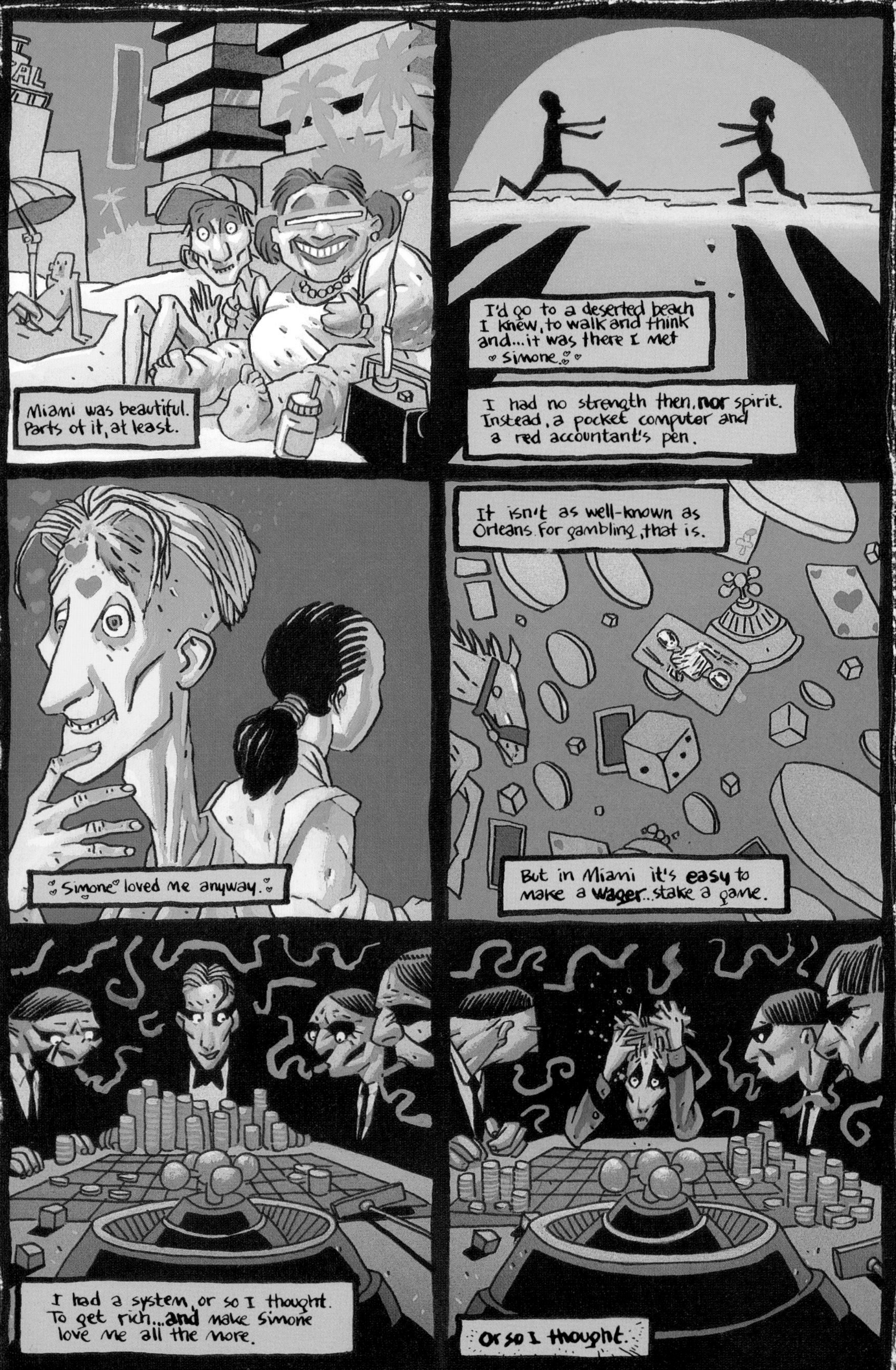
Miami was beautiful. Parts of it, at least.
I'd go to a deserted beach I knew, to walk and think and... it was there I met Simone.
I had no strength then, **nor** spirit. Instead, a pocket computer and a red accountant's pen.
Simone loved me anyway.
It isn't as well-known as Orleans. For gambling, that is.
But in Miami it's **easy** to make a **wager**... stake a game.
I had a system, or so I thought. To get rich... **and** make Simone love me all the more.
Or so I thought.

I was ruined... and addicted...

...to the royal flush, the dice, and the double-zero.

Before long, I'd bet on anything...raindrops running down windowpanes...mice crawling across tables.

Wager anything, too.

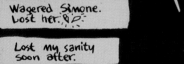

Wagered Simone. Lost her.

Lost my sanity soon after.

That Grendel. The Devil who won...who egged me on to bet Simone. He wanted her, I could tell.

Did she want him? It's hard to say.

She honored the wager quickly enough. Becoming his woman...going off with him.

I wanted a child with her.

In the end, I had to do that on my own.

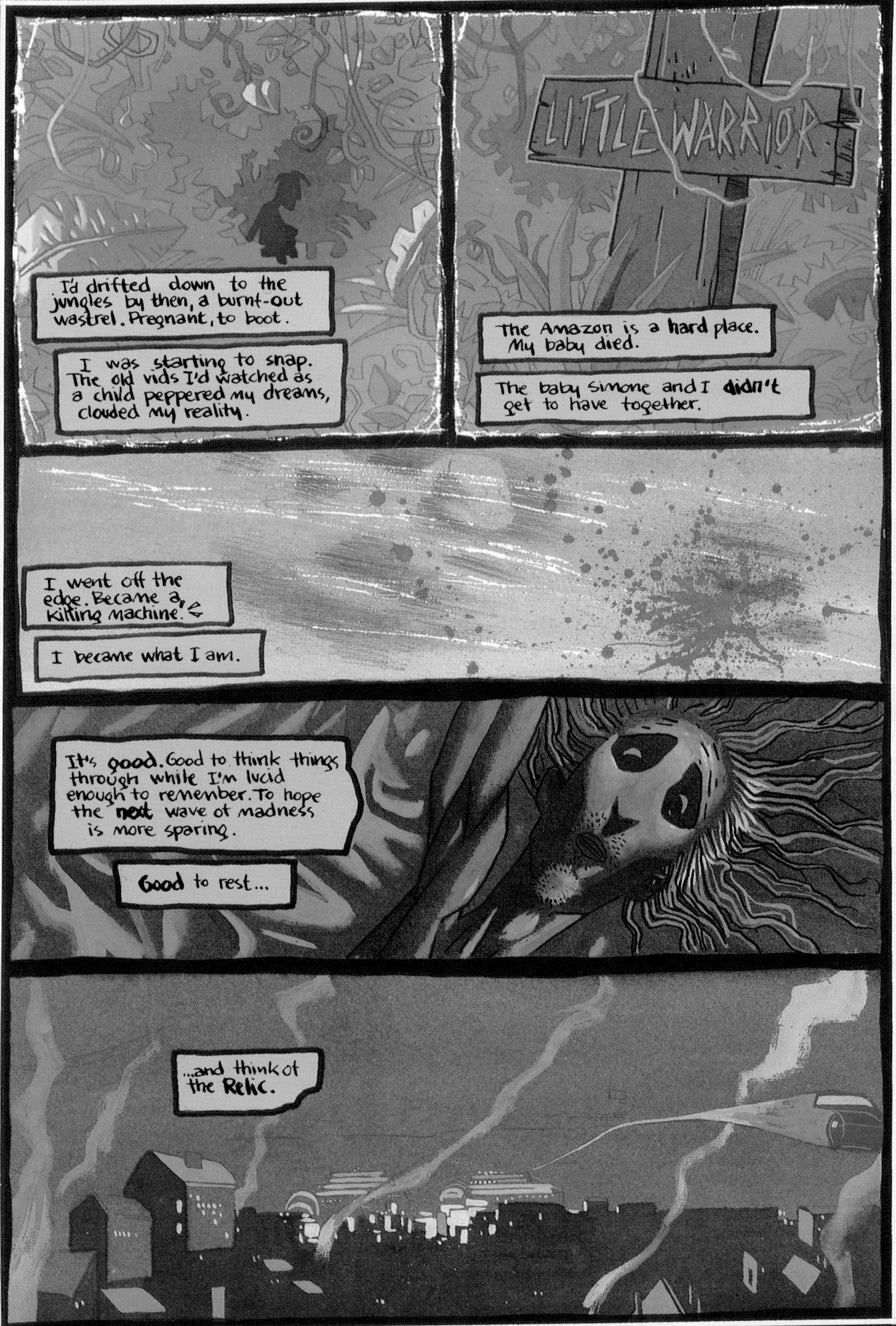
I'd drifted down to the jungles by then, a burnt-out wastrel. Pregnant, to boot.
I was starting to snap. The old vids I'd watched as a child peppered my dreams, clouded my reality.
LITTLE WARRIOR
The Amazon is a hard place. My baby died.
The baby Simone and I didn't get to have together.
I went off the edge. Became a killing machine.
I became what I am.
It's good. Good to think things through while I'm lucid enough to remember. To hope the next wave of madness is more sparing.
Good to rest...
...and think of the Relic.

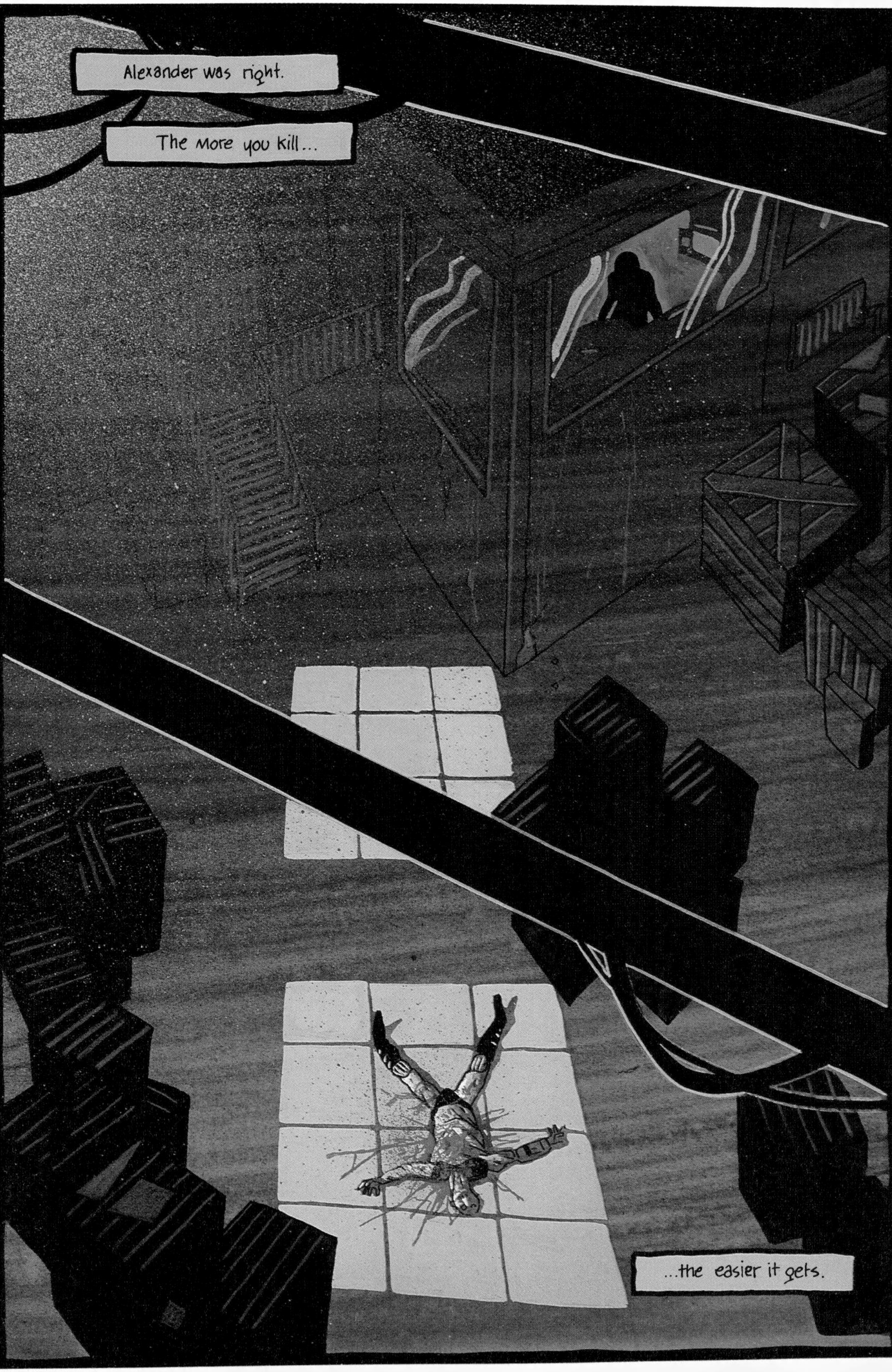

Alexander was right.
The more you kill...
...the easier it gets.

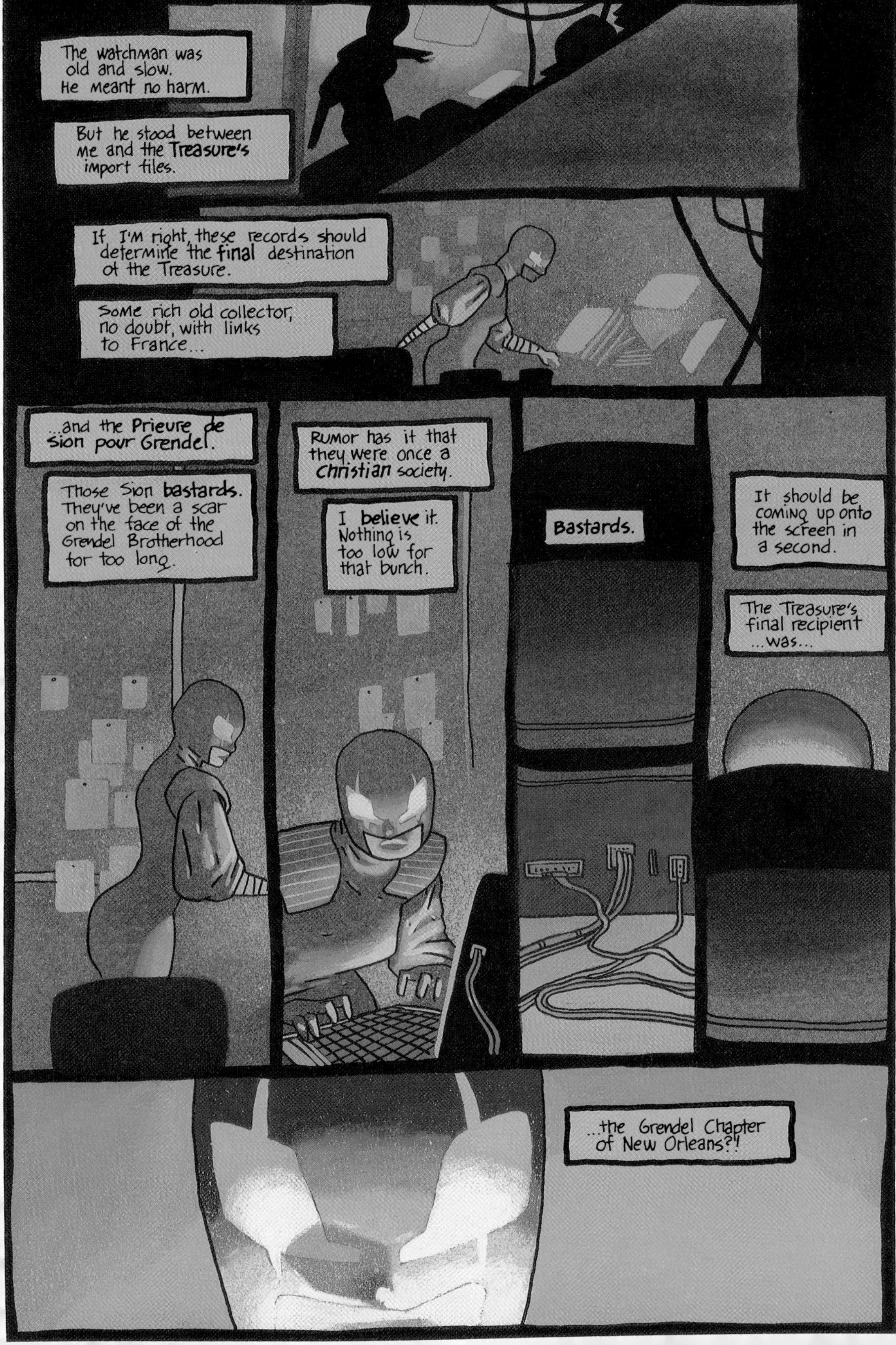
The watchman was old and slow. He meant no harm.
But he stood between me and the Treasure's import files.
If I'm right, these records should determine the final destination of the Treasure.
Some rich old collector, no doubt, with links to France...
...and the Prieure de Sion pour Grendel.
Those Sion bastards. They've been a scar on the face of the Grendel Brotherhood for too long.
Rumor has it that they were once a Christian society.
I believe it. Nothing is too low for that bunch.
Bastards.
It should be coming up onto the screen in a second.
The Treasure's final recipient ...was...
...the Grendel Chapter of New Orleans?!

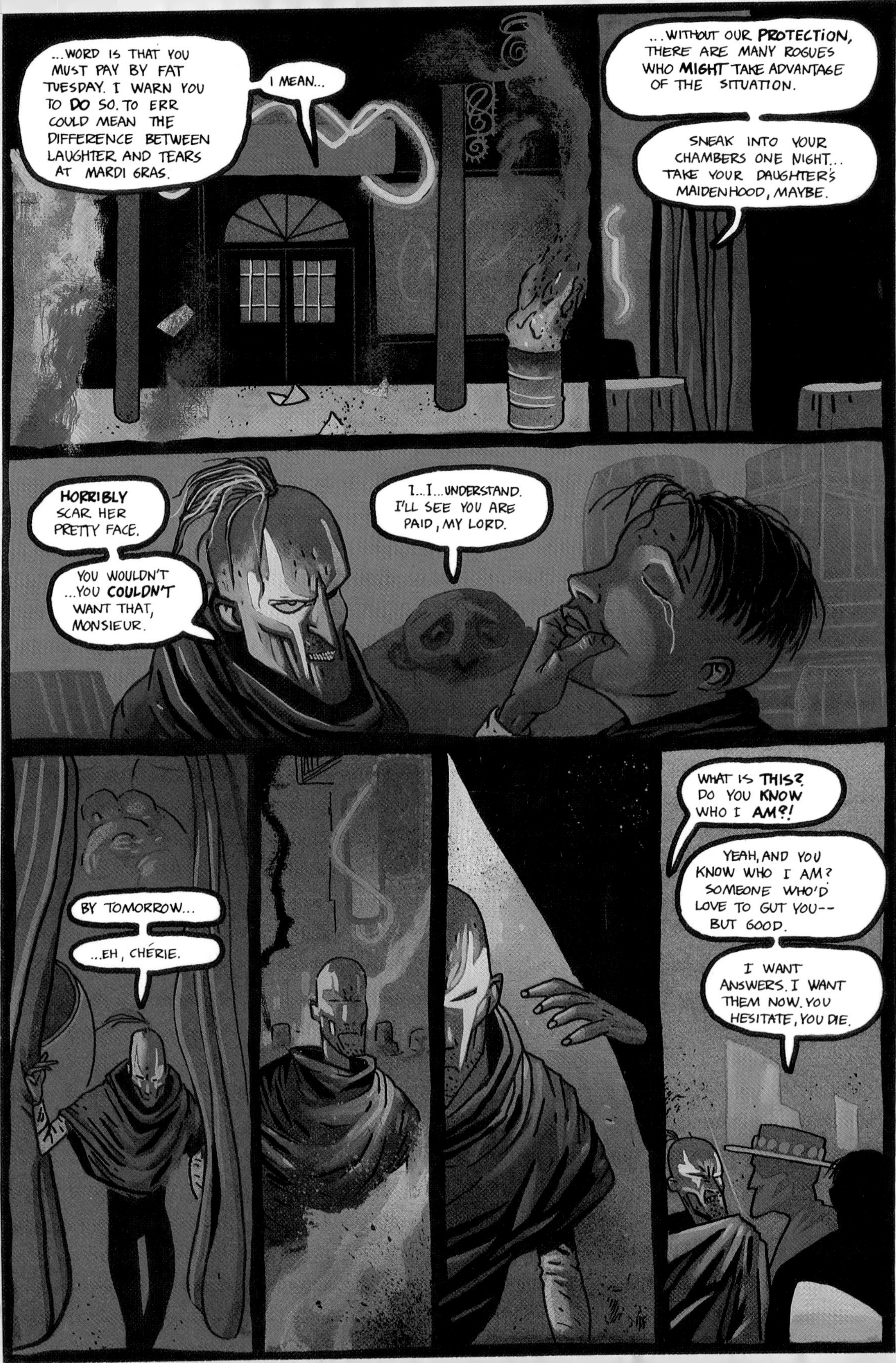
...WORD IS THAT YOU MUST PAY BY FAT TUESDAY. I WARN YOU TO DO SO. TO ERR COULD MEAN THE DIFFERENCE BETWEEN LAUGHTER AND TEARS AT MARDI GRAS.
I MEAN...
...WITHOUT OUR PROTECTION, THERE ARE MANY ROGUES WHO MIGHT TAKE ADVANTAGE OF THE SITUATION.
SNEAK INTO YOUR CHAMBERS ONE NIGHT... TAKE YOUR DAUGHTER'S MAIDENHOOD, MAYBE.
HORRIBLY SCAR HER PRETTY FACE.
YOU WOULDN'T ...YOU COULDN'T WANT THAT, MONSIEUR.
I...I...UNDERSTAND. I'LL SEE YOU ARE PAID, MY LORD.
BY TOMORROW...
...EH, CHÉRIE.
WHAT IS THIS? DO YOU KNOW WHO I AM?!
YEAH, AND YOU KNOW WHO I AM? SOMEONE WHO'D LOVE TO GUT YOU-- BUT GOOD.
I WANT ANSWERS. I WANT THEM NOW. YOU HESITATE, YOU DIE.

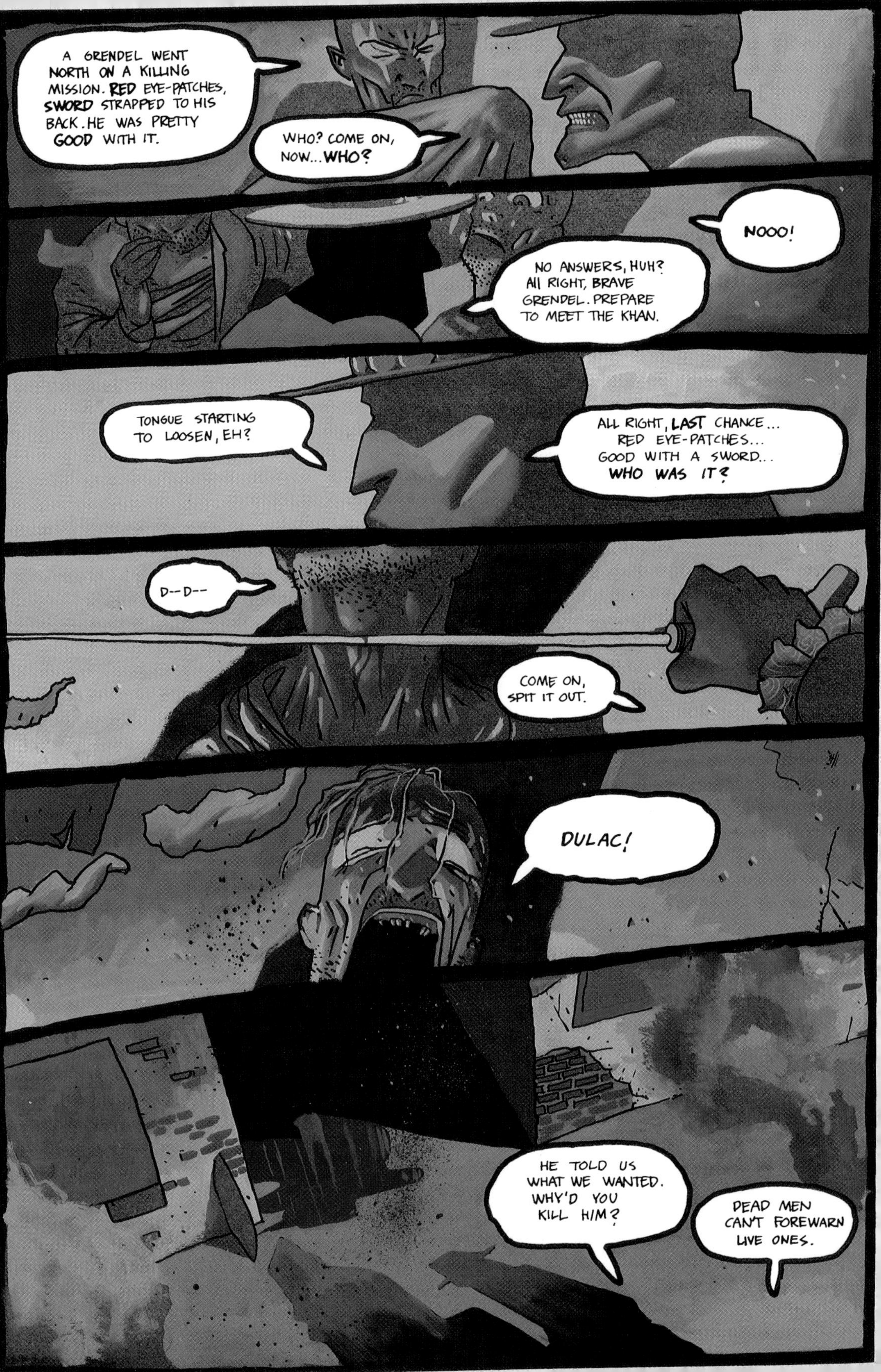

A GRENDEL WENT NORTH ON A KILLING MISSION. RED EYE-PATCHES, SWORD STRAPPED TO HIS BACK. HE WAS PRETTY GOOD WITH IT.
WHO? COME ON, NOW... WHO?
NOOO!
NO ANSWERS, HUH? All RIGHT, BRAVE GRENDEL. PREPARE TO MEET THE KHAN.
TONGUE STARTING TO LOOSEN, EH?
ALL RIGHT, LAST CHANCE... RED EYE-PATCHES... GOOD WITH A SWORD... WHO WAS IT?
D--D--
COME ON, SPIT IT OUT.
DULAC!
HE TOLD US WHAT WE WANTED. WHY'D YOU KILL HIM?
DEAD MEN CAN'T FOREWARN LIVE ONES.

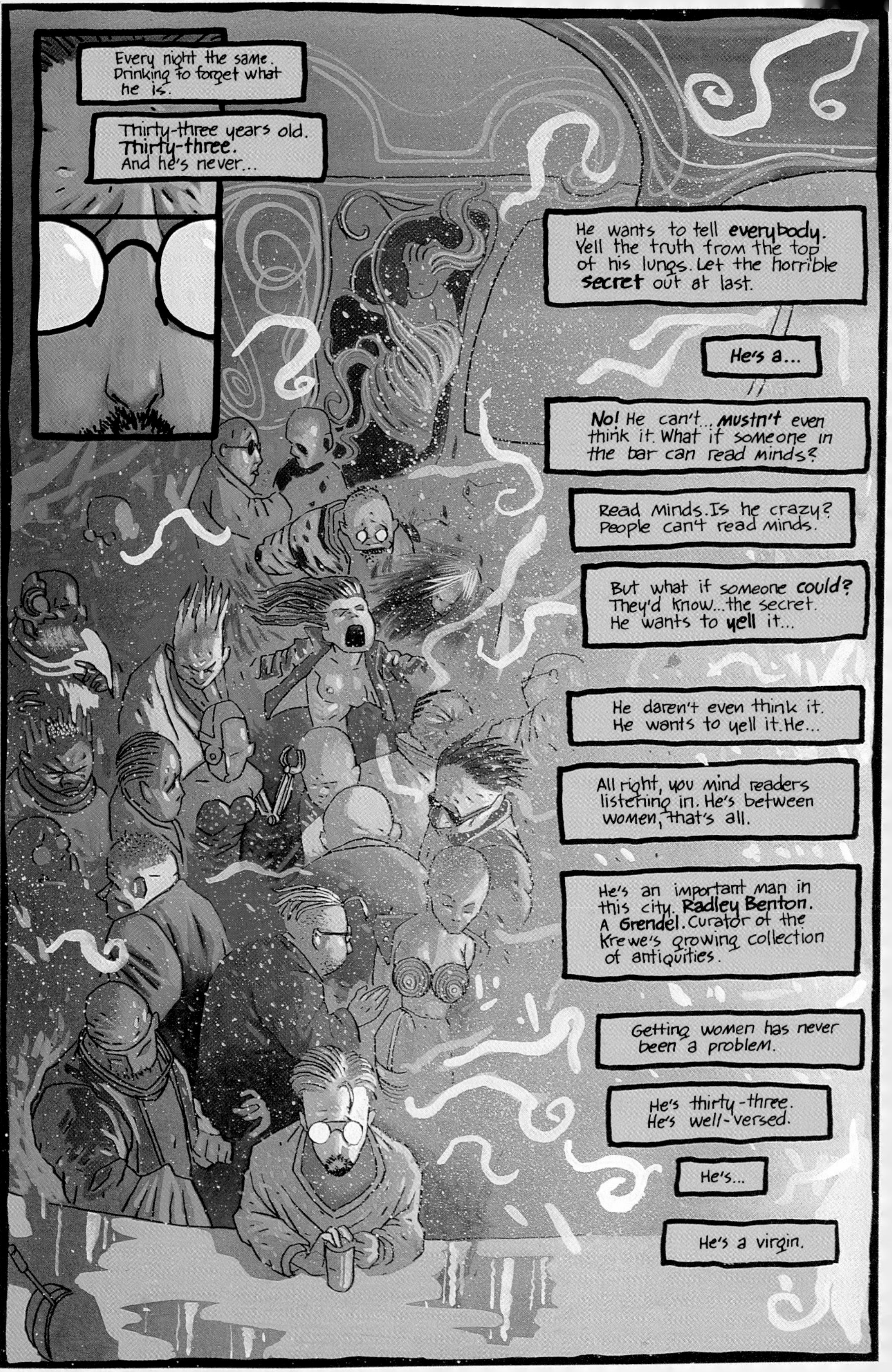

Every night the same. Drinking to forget what he is.
Thirty-three years old. Thirty-three. And he's never...
He wants to tell everybody. Yell the truth from the top of his lungs. Let the horrible secret out at last.
He's a...
No! He can't... mustn't even think it. What if someone in the bar can read minds?
Read minds. Is he crazy? People can't read minds.
But what if someone could? They'd know... the secret. He wants to yell it...
He daren't even think it. He wants to yell it. He...
All right, you mind readers listening in. He's between women, that's all.
He's an important man in this city. Radley Benton. A Grendel. Curator of the Krewe's growing collection of antiquities.
Getting women has never been a problem.
He's thirty-three. He's well-versed.
He's...
He's a virgin.

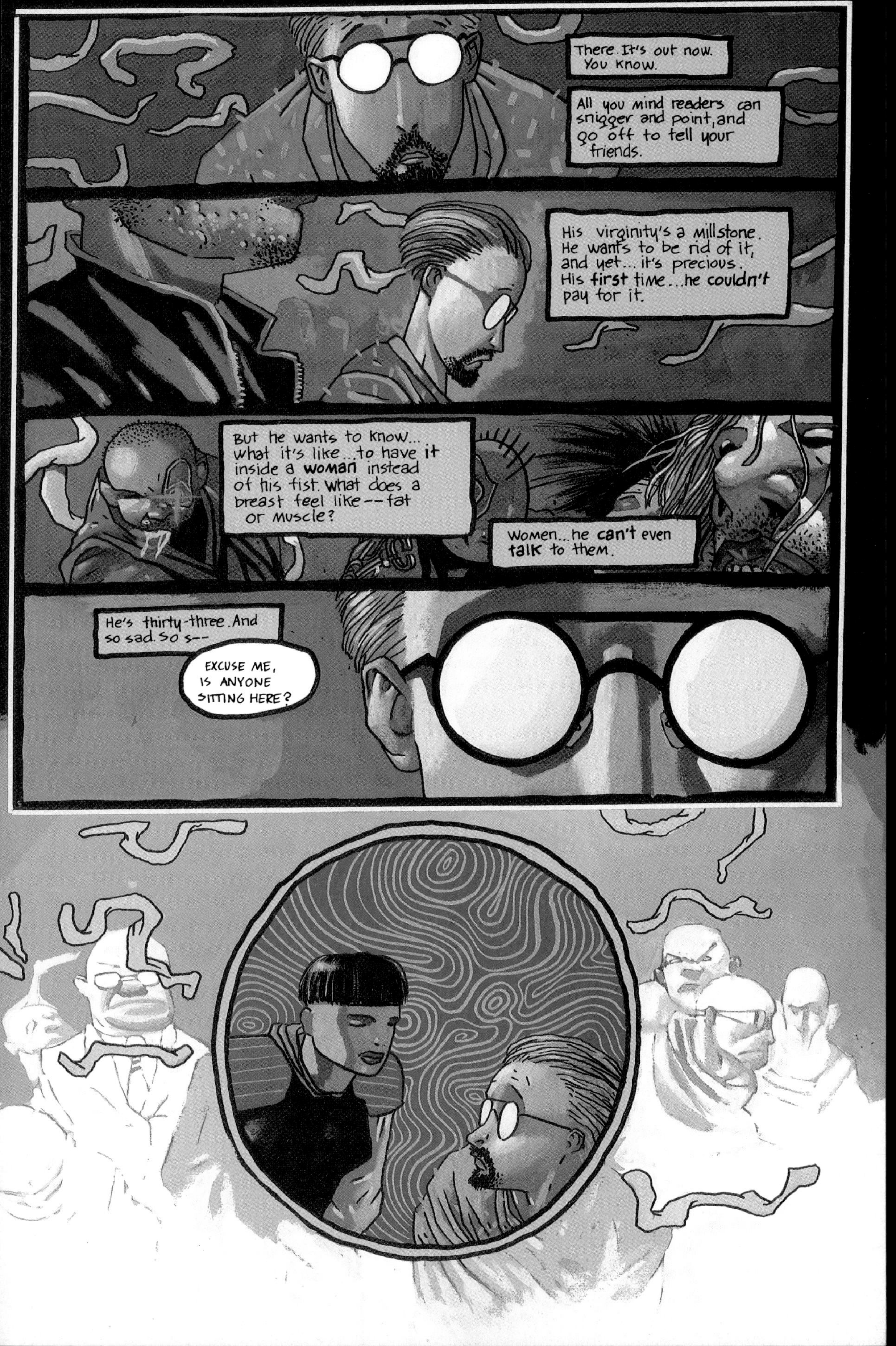
There. It's out now. You know.
All you mind readers can snigger and point, and go off to tell your friends.
His virginity's a millstone. He wants to be rid of it, and yet... it's precious. His first time... he couldn't pay for it.
But he wants to know... what it's like... to have it inside a woman instead of his fist. What does a breast feel like -- fat or muscle?
Women... he can't even talk to them.
He's thirty-three. And so sad. So s--
EXCUSE ME, IS ANYONE SITTING HERE?

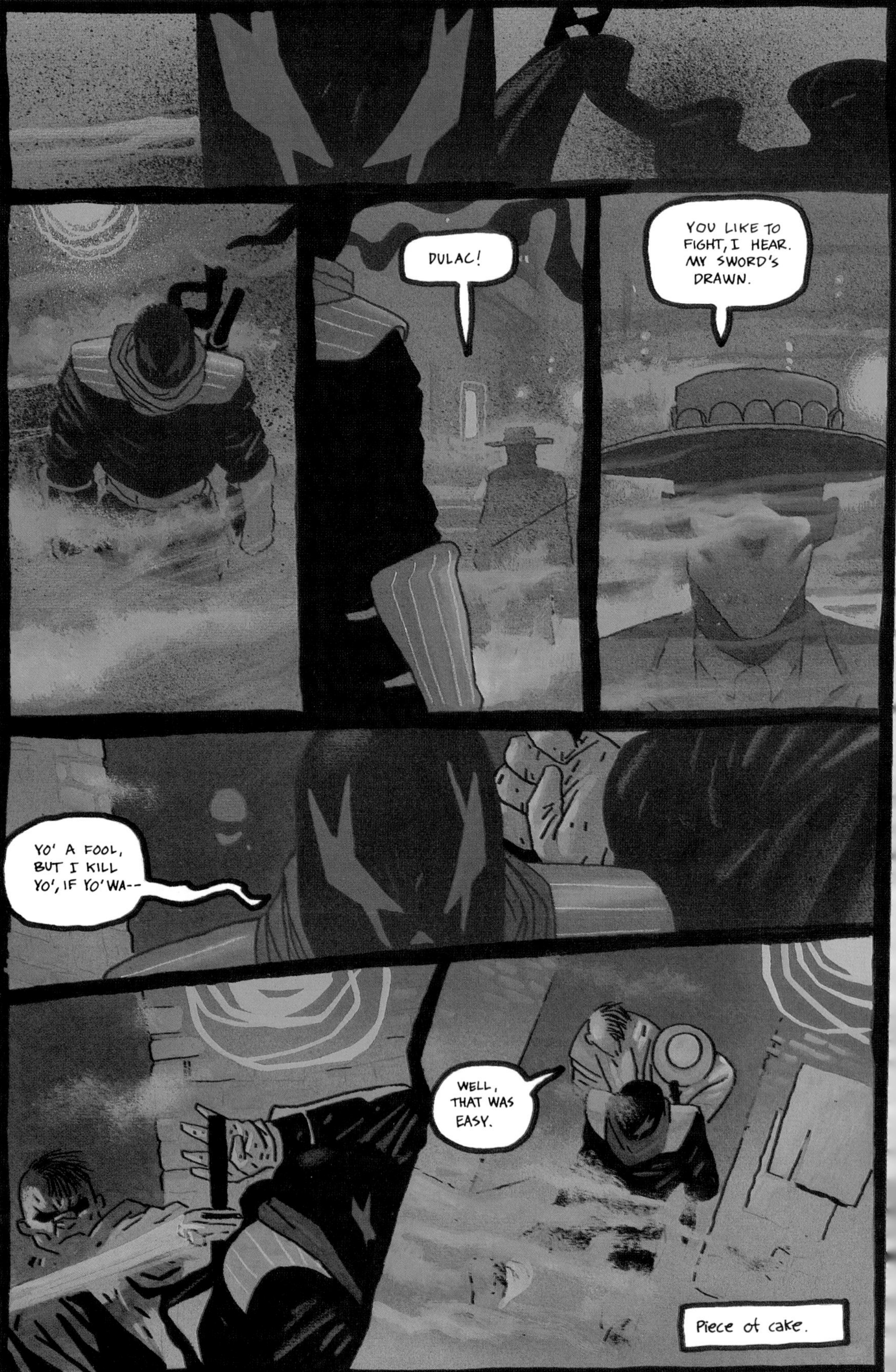
DULAC!
YOU LIKE TO FIGHT, I HEAR. MY SWORD'S DRAWN.
YO' A FOOL, BUT I KILL YO', IF YO' WA--
WELL, THAT WAS EASY.
Piece of cake.

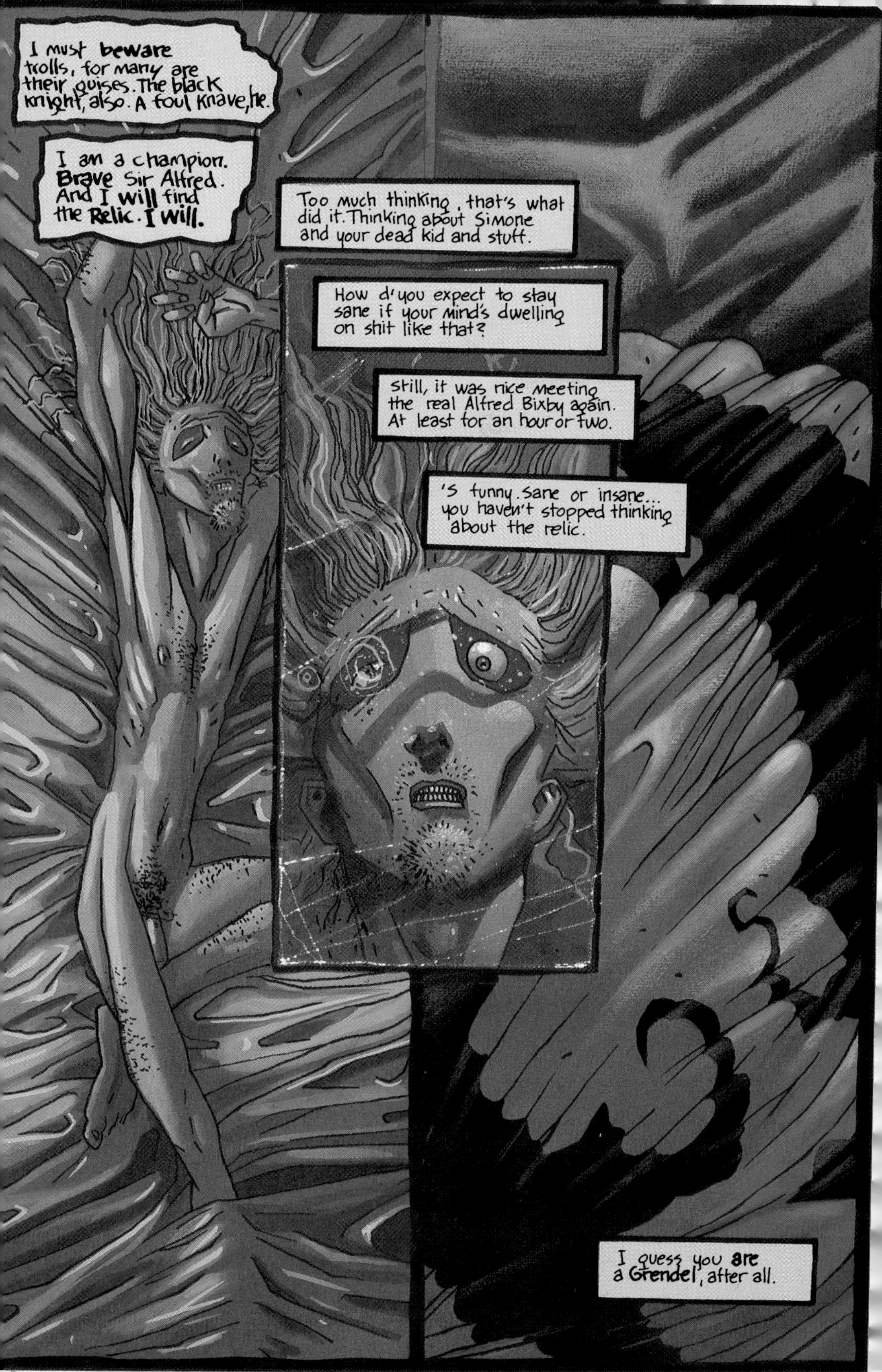
I must beware trolls, for many are their guises. The black knight, also. A foul knave, he.
I am a champion. Brave Sir Alfred. And I will find the Relic. I will.
Too much thinking, that's what did it. Thinking about Simone and your dead kid and stuff.
How d'you expect to stay sane if your mind's dwelling on shit like that?
Still, it was nice meeting the real Alfred Bixby again. At least for an hour or two.
'S funny. Sane or insane... you haven't stopped thinking about the relic.
I guess you are a Grendel, after all.

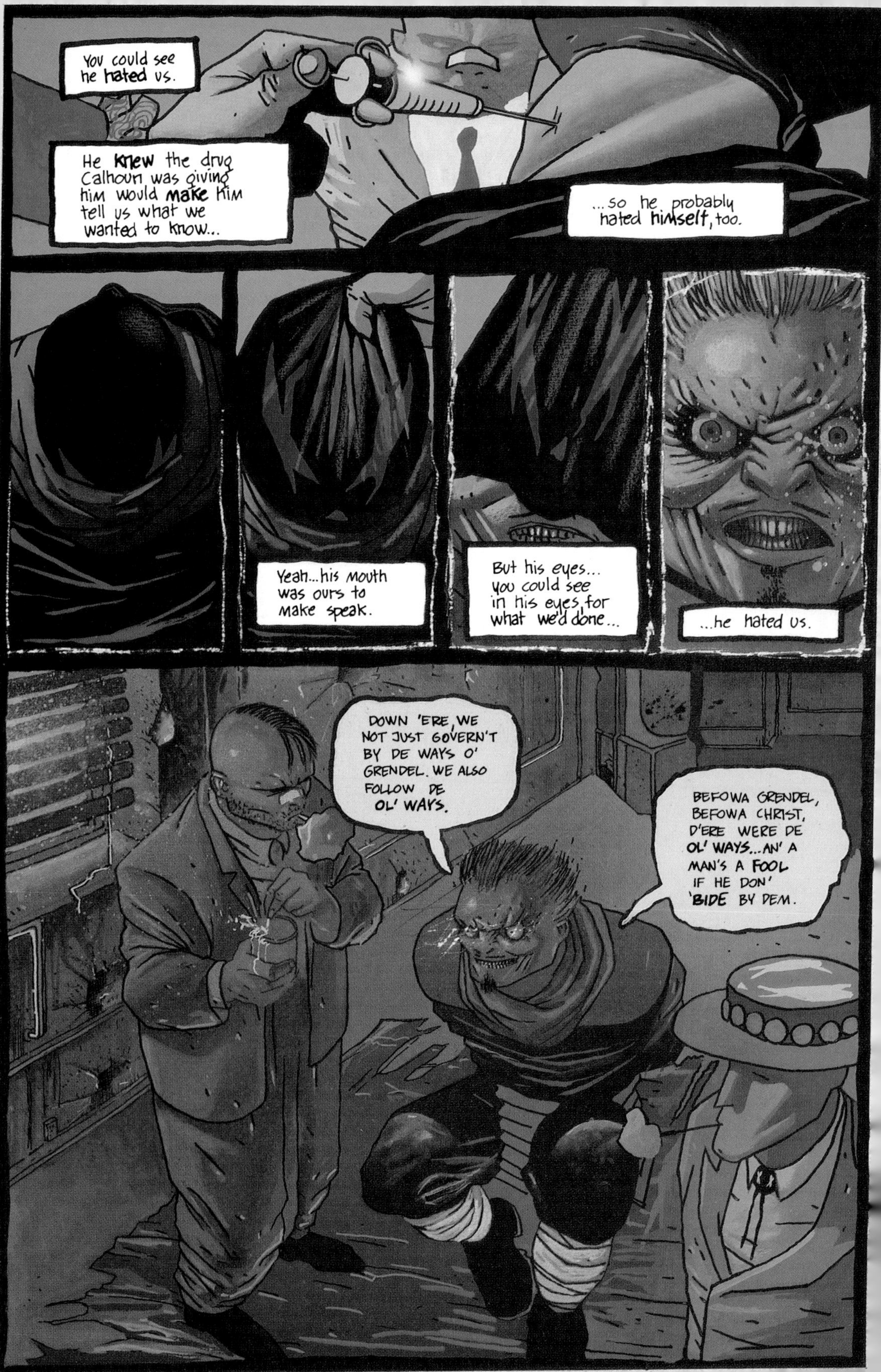
You could see he hated us.
He knew the drug Calhoun was giving him would make him tell us what we wanted to know...
...so he probably hated himself, too.
Yeah...his mouth was ours to make speak.
But his eyes... you could see in his eyes for what we'd done...
...he hated us.
DOWN 'ERE, WE NOT JUST GOVERN'T BY DE WAYS O' GRENDEL. WE ALSO FOLLOW DE OL' WAYS.
BEFOWA GRENDEL, BEFOWA CHRIST, D'ERE WERE DE OL' WAYS...AN' A MAN'S A FOOL IF HE DON' 'BIDE BY DEM.

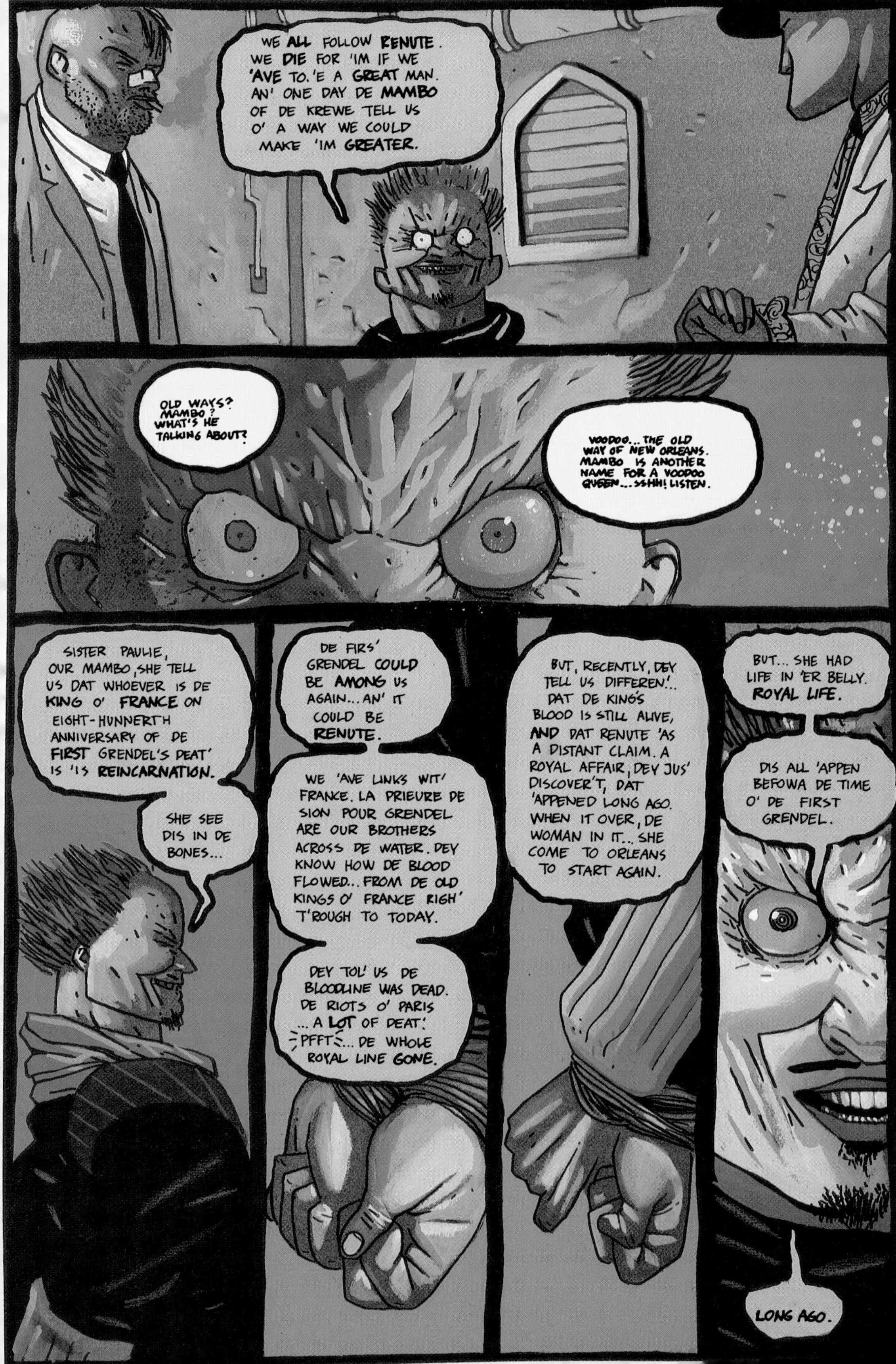
WE ALL FOLLOW RENUTE. WE DIE FOR 'IM IF WE 'AVE TO. 'E A GREAT MAN. AN' ONE DAY DE MAMBO OF DE KREWE TELL US O' A WAY WE COULD MAKE 'IM GREATER.
OLD WAYS? MAMBO? WHAT'S HE TALKING ABOUT?
VOODOO... THE OLD WAY OF NEW ORLEANS. MAMBO IS ANOTHER NAME FOR A VOODOO QUEEN... SSHH! LISTEN.
SISTER PAULIE, OUR MAMBO, SHE TELL US DAT WHOEVER IS DE KING O' FRANCE ON EIGHT-HUNNERTH ANNIVERSARY OF DE FIRST GRENDEL'S DEAT' IS 'IS REINCARNATION.
SHE SEE DIS IN DE BONES...
DE FIRS' GRENDEL COULD BE AMONG US AGAIN... AN' IT COULD BE RENUTE.
WE 'AVE LINKS WIT' FRANCE. LA PRIEURE DE SION POUR GRENDEL ARE OUR BROTHERS ACROSS DE WATER. DEY KNOW HOW DE BLOOD FLOWED... FROM DE OLD KINGS O' FRANCE RIGH' T'ROUGH TO TODAY.
DEY TOL' US DE BLOODLINE WAS DEAD. DE RIOTS O' PARIS ... A LOT OF DEAT'. PFFT... DE WHOLE ROYAL LINE GONE.
BUT, RECENTLY, DEY TELL US DIFFEREN'... DAT DE KING'S BLOOD IS STILL ALIVE, AND DAT RENUTE 'AS A DISTANT CLAIM. A ROYAL AFFAIR, DEY JUS' DISCOVER'T, DAT 'APPENED LONG AGO. WHEN IT OVER, DE WOMAN IN IT... SHE COME TO ORLEANS TO START AGAIN.
BUT... SHE HAD LIFE IN 'ER BELLY. ROYAL LIFE.
DIS ALL 'APPEN BEFOWA DE TIME O' DE FIRST GRENDEL.
LONG AGO.

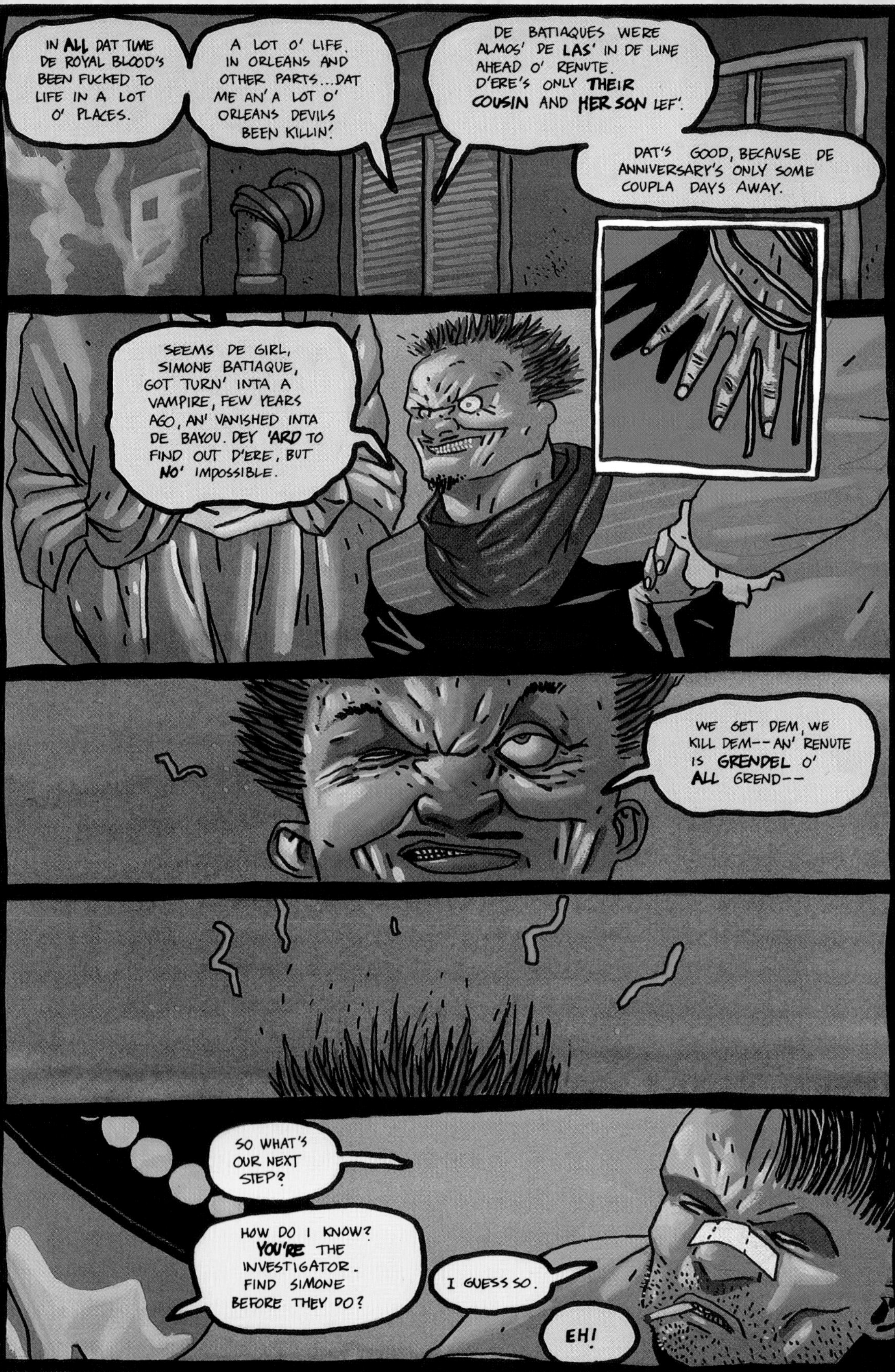
IN ALL DAT TIME DE ROYAL BLOOD'S BEEN FUCKED TO LIFE IN A LOT O' PLACES.
A LOT O' LIFE. IN ORLEANS AND OTHER PARTS...DAT ME AN' A LOT O' ORLEANS DEVILS BEEN KILLIN'.
DE BATIAQUES WERE ALMOS' DE LAS' IN DE LINE AHEAD O' RENUTE. D'ERE'S ONLY THEIR COUSIN AND HER SON LEF'.
DAT'S GOOD, BECAUSE DE ANNIVERSARY'S ONLY SOME COUPLA DAYS AWAY.
SEEMS DE GIRL, SIMONE BATIAQUE, GOT TURN' INTA A VAMPIRE, FEW YEARS AGO, AN' VANISHED INTA DE BAYOU. DEY 'ARD TO FIND OUT D'ERE, BUT NO' IMPOSSIBLE.
WE GET DEM, WE KILL DEM--AN' RENUTE IS GRENDEL O' ALL GREND--
SO WHAT'S OUR NEXT STEP?
HOW DO I KNOW? YOU'RE THE INVESTIGATOR. FIND SIMONE BEFORE THEY DO?
I GUESS SO.
EH!

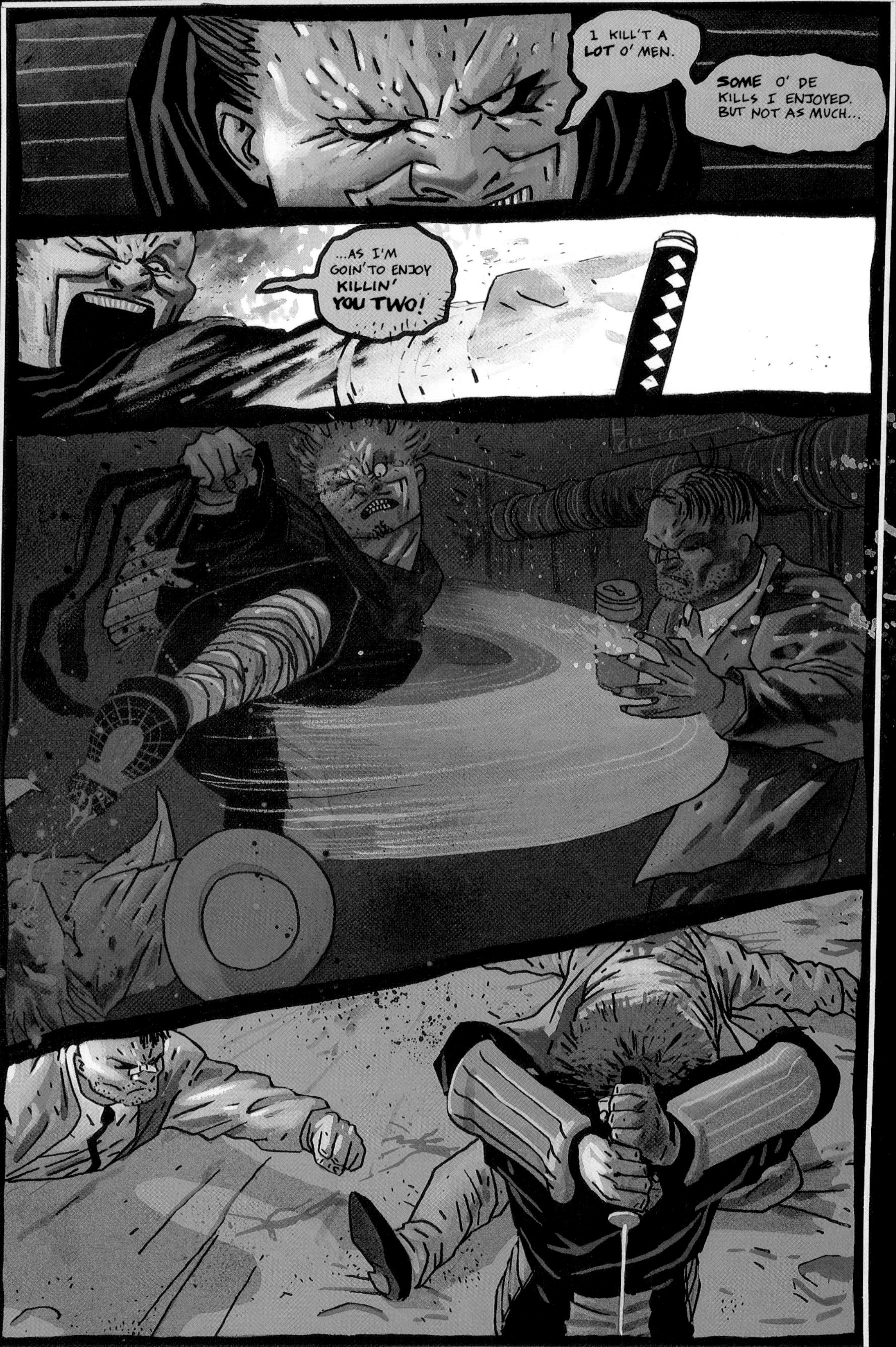
I KILL'T A LOT O' MEN.
SOME O' DE KILLS I ENJOYED. BUT NOT AS MUCH...
...AS I'M GOIN' TO ENJOY KILLIN' YOU TWO!

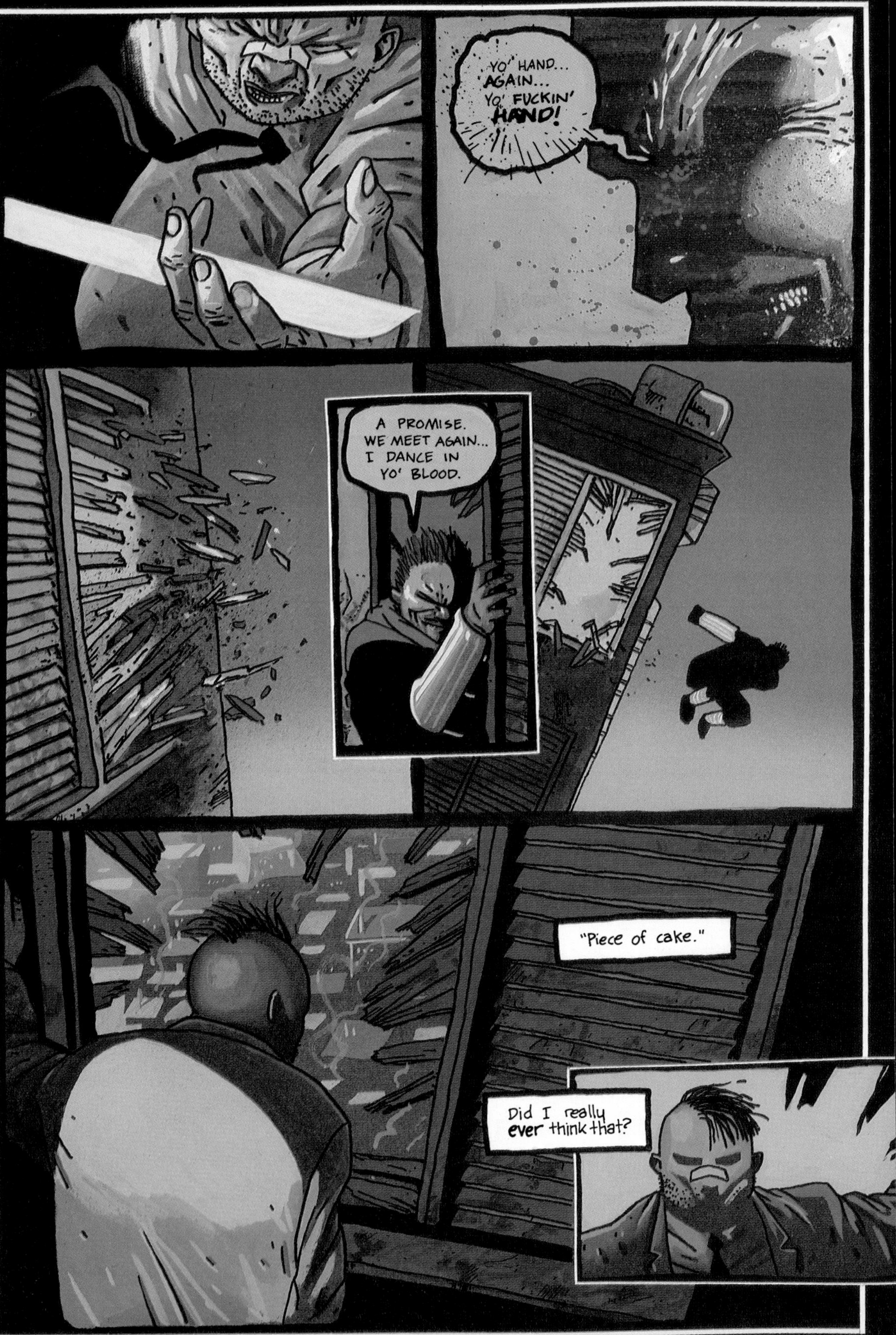

YO' HAND... AGAIN... YO' FUCKIN' HAND!
A PROMISE. WE MEET AGAIN... I DANCE IN YO' BLOOD.
"Piece of cake."
Did I really ever think that?

CHAPTER FOUR

ONE RITE, THREE WRONGS

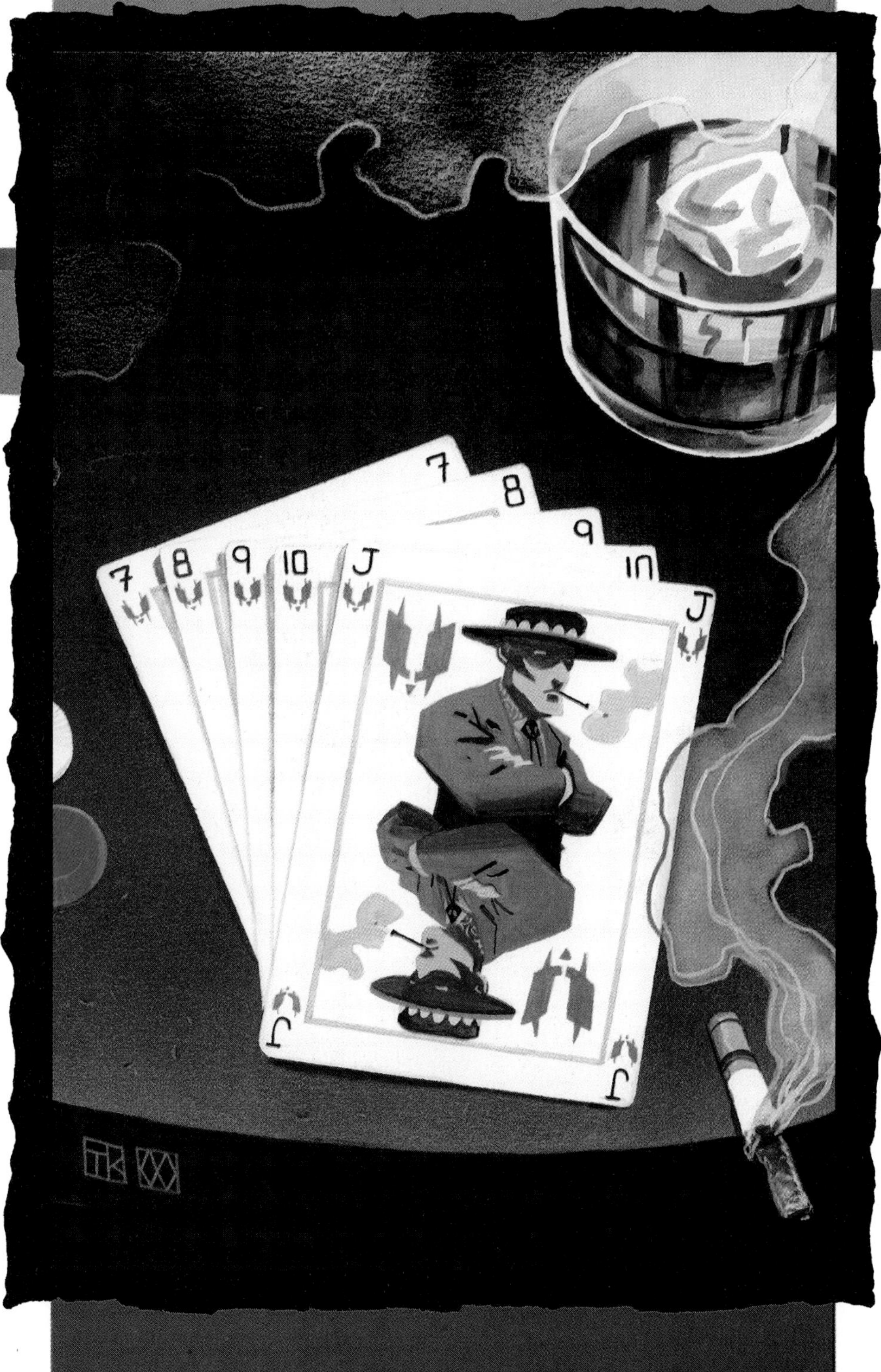

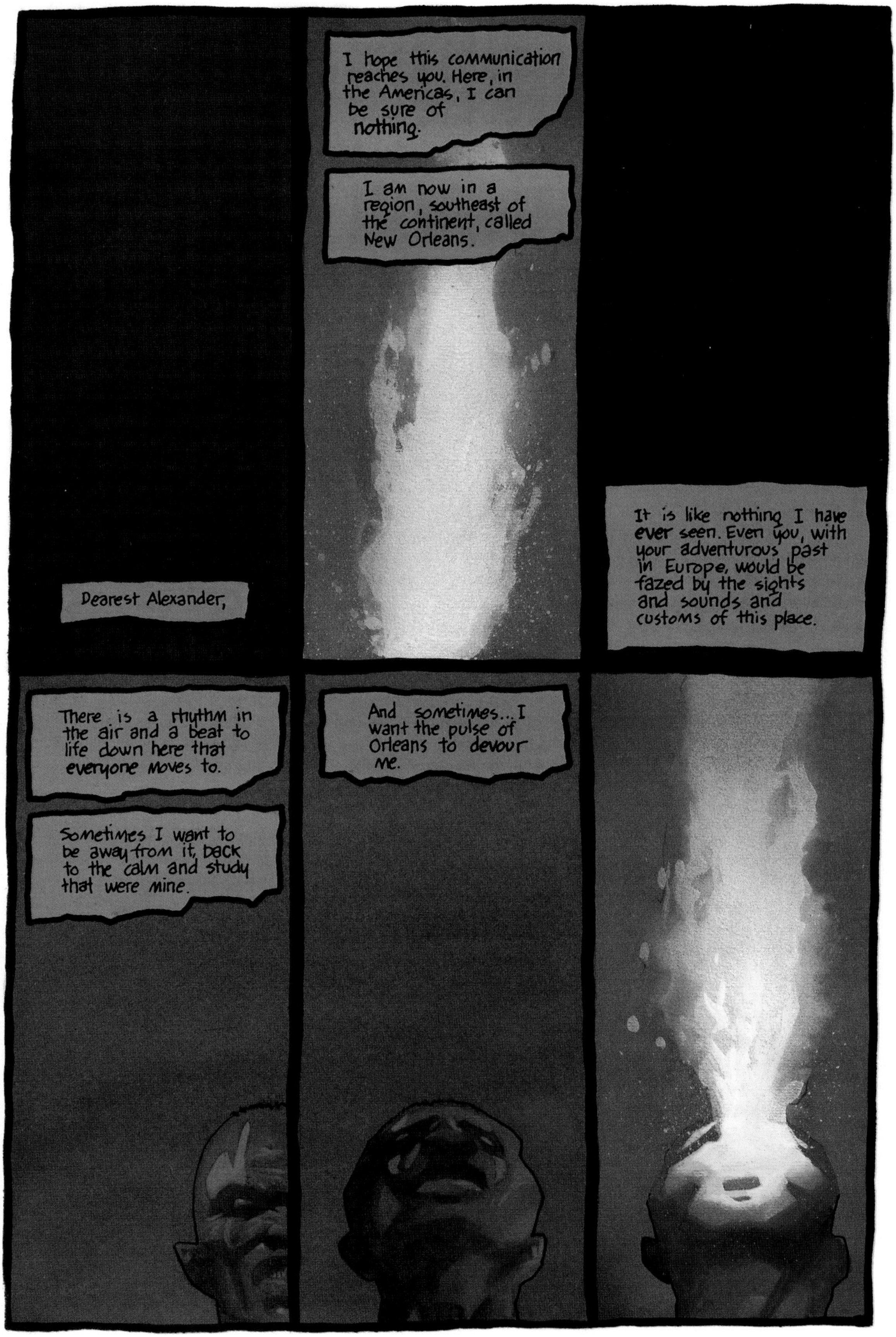
Dearest Alexander,
I hope this communication reaches you. Here, in the Americas, I can be sure of nothing.
I am now in a region, southeast of the continent, called New Orleans.
It is like nothing I have ever seen. Even you, with your adventurous past in Europe, would be fazed by the sights and sounds and customs of this place.
There is a rhythm in the air and a beat to life down here that everyone moves to.
Sometimes I want to be away from it, back to the calm and study that were mine.
And sometimes... I want the pulse of Orleans to devour me.
There is a rhythm in the air and a beat to life down here that everyone moves to.

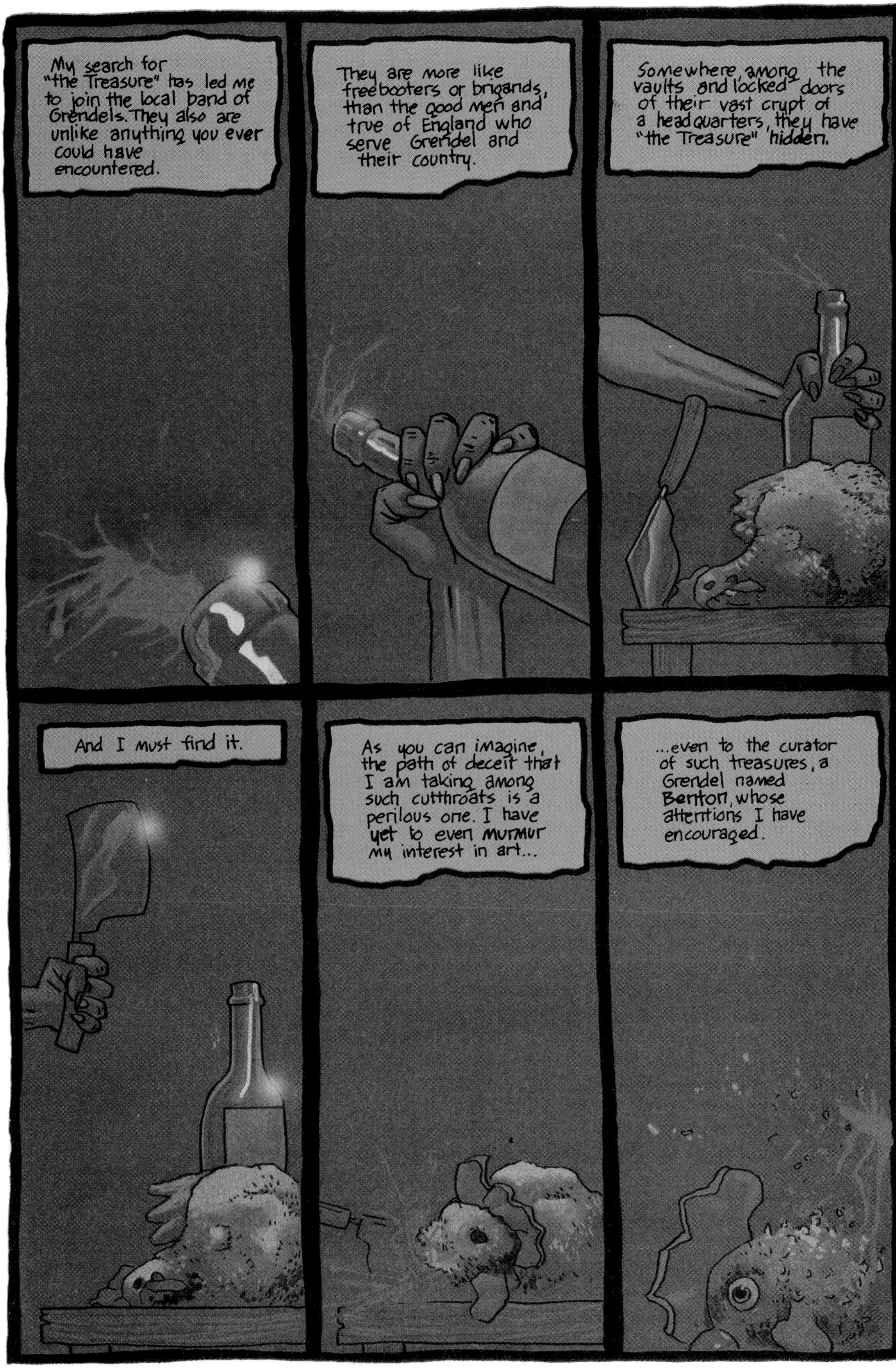
My search for "the Treasure" has led me to join the local band of Grendels. They also are unlike anything you ever could have encountered.
They are more like freebooters or brigands, than the good men and true of England who serve Grendel and their country.
Somewhere, among the vaults and locked doors of their vast crypt of a headquarters, they have "the Treasure" hidden.
And I must find it.
As you can imagine, the path of deceit that I am taking among such cutthroats is a perilous one. I have yet to even murmur my interest in art...
...even to the curator of such treasures, a Grendel named Benton, whose attentions I have encouraged.

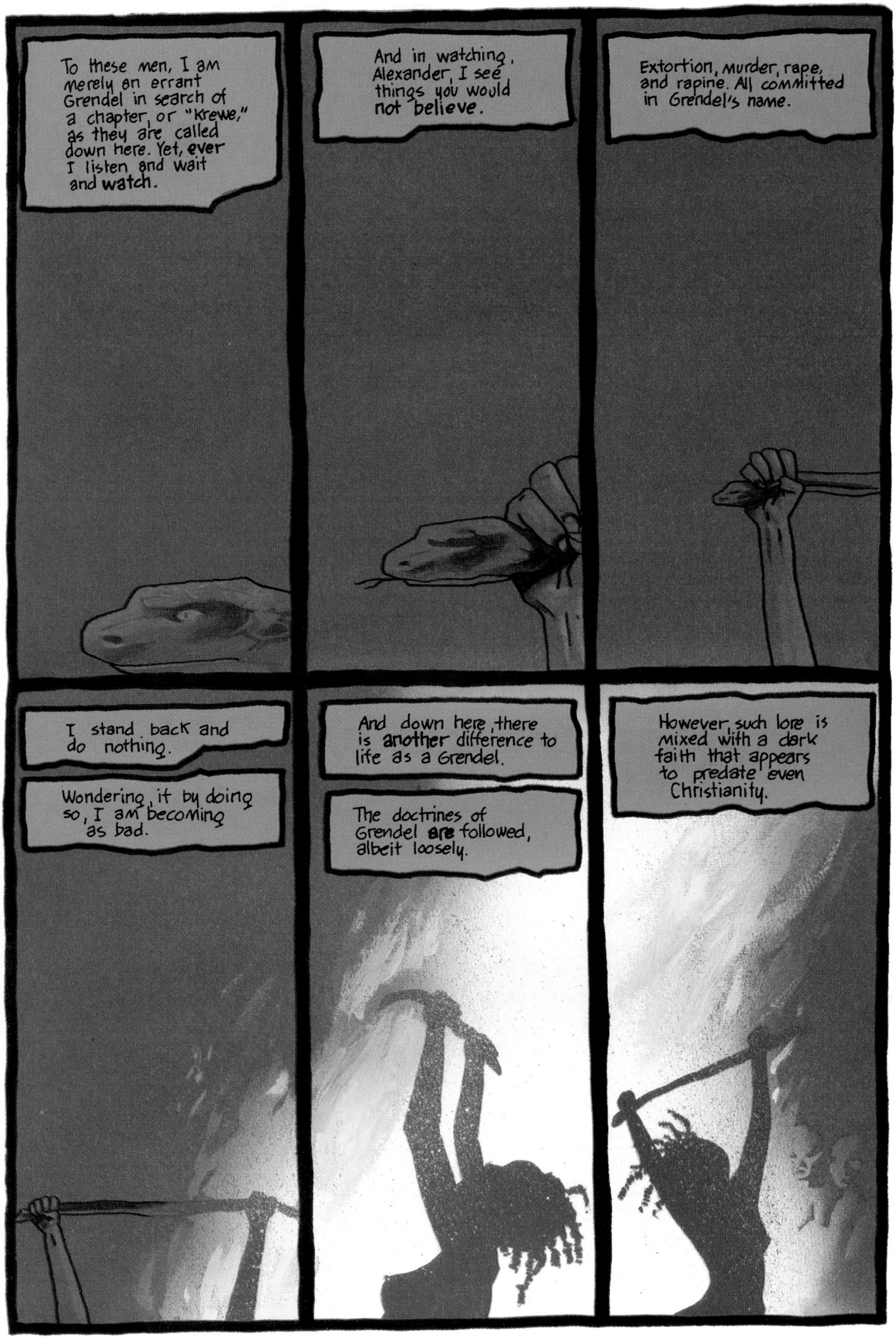

To these men, I am merely an errant Grendel in search of a chapter, or "krewe," as they are called down here. Yet, ever I listen and wait and watch.
And in watching, Alexander, I see things you would not believe.
Extortion, murder, rape, and rapine. All committed in Grendel's name.
I stand back and do nothing.
Wondering if by doing so, I am becoming as bad.
And down here, there is another difference to life as a Grendel.
The doctrines of Grendel are followed, albeit loosely.
However, such lore is mixed with a dark faith that appears to predate even Christianity.

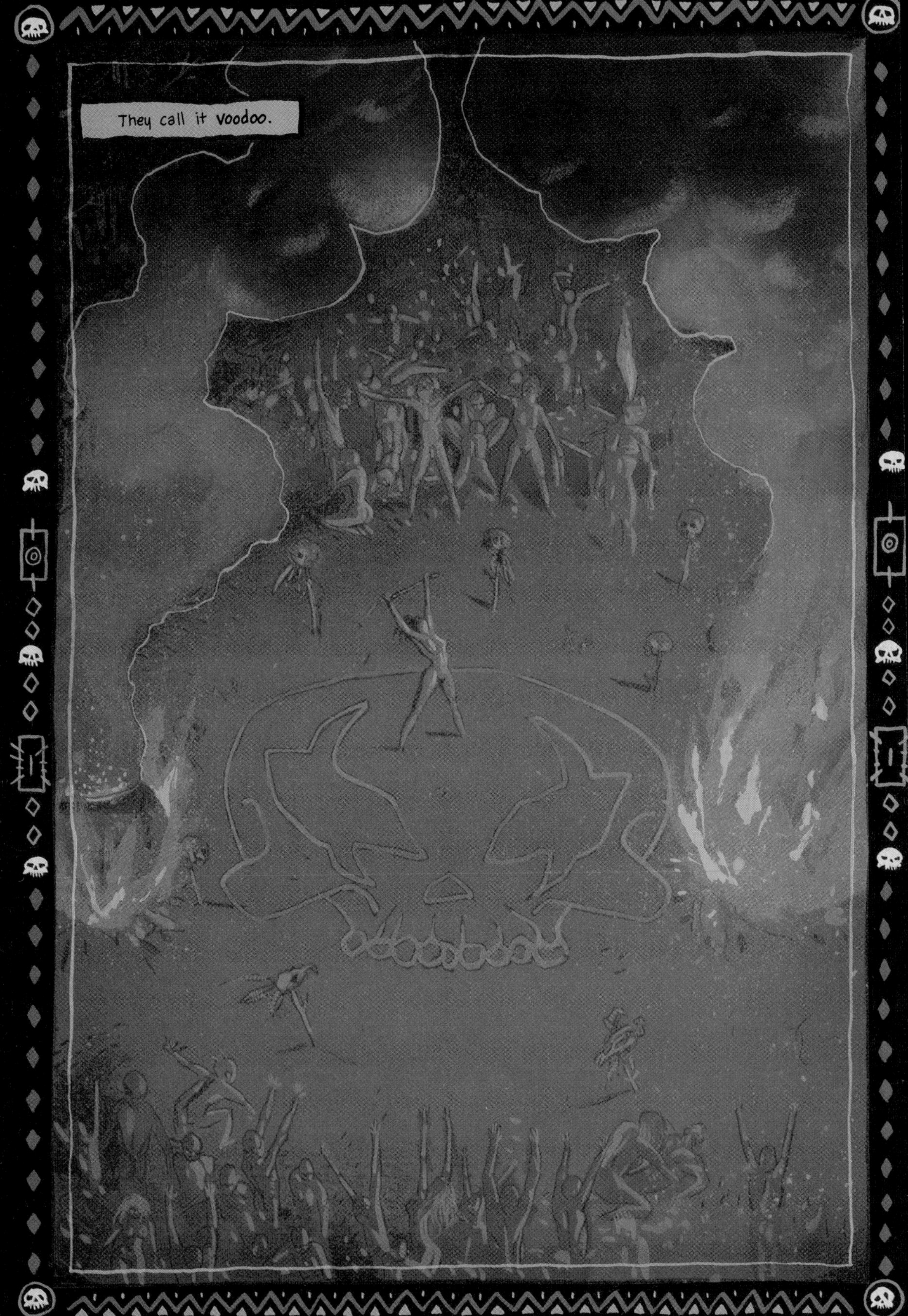
They call it voodoo.

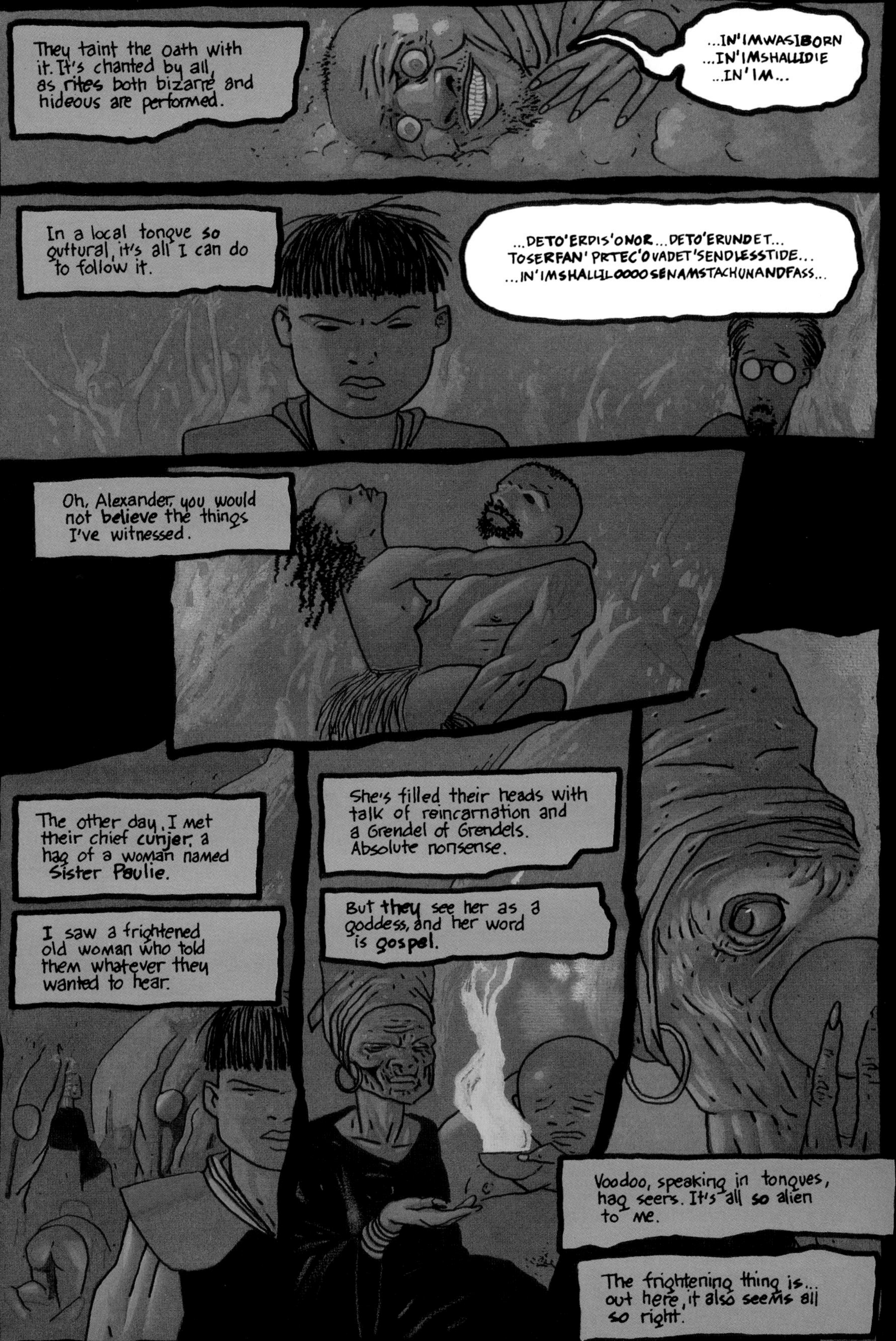
They taint the oath with it. It's chanted by all, as rites both bizarre and hideous are performed.
...IN'IMWASIBORN ...IN'IMSHALLIDIE ...IN'IM...
In a local tongue so guttural, it's all I can do to follow it.
...DETO'ERDIS'ONOR...DETO'ERUNDET... TOSERFAN' PRTEC'OVADET'SENDLESSTIDE... ...IN'IMSHALLLOOOOSENAMSTACHUNANDFASS...
Oh, Alexander, you would not believe the things I've witnessed.
The other day, I met their chief cunjer, a hag of a woman named Sister Paulie.
I saw a frightened old woman who told them whatever they wanted to hear.
She's filled their heads with talk of reincarnation and a Grendel of Grendels. Absolute nonsense.
But they see her as a goddess, and her word is gospel.
Voodoo, speaking in tongues, hag seers. It's all so alien to me.
The frightening thing is... out here, it also seems all so right.

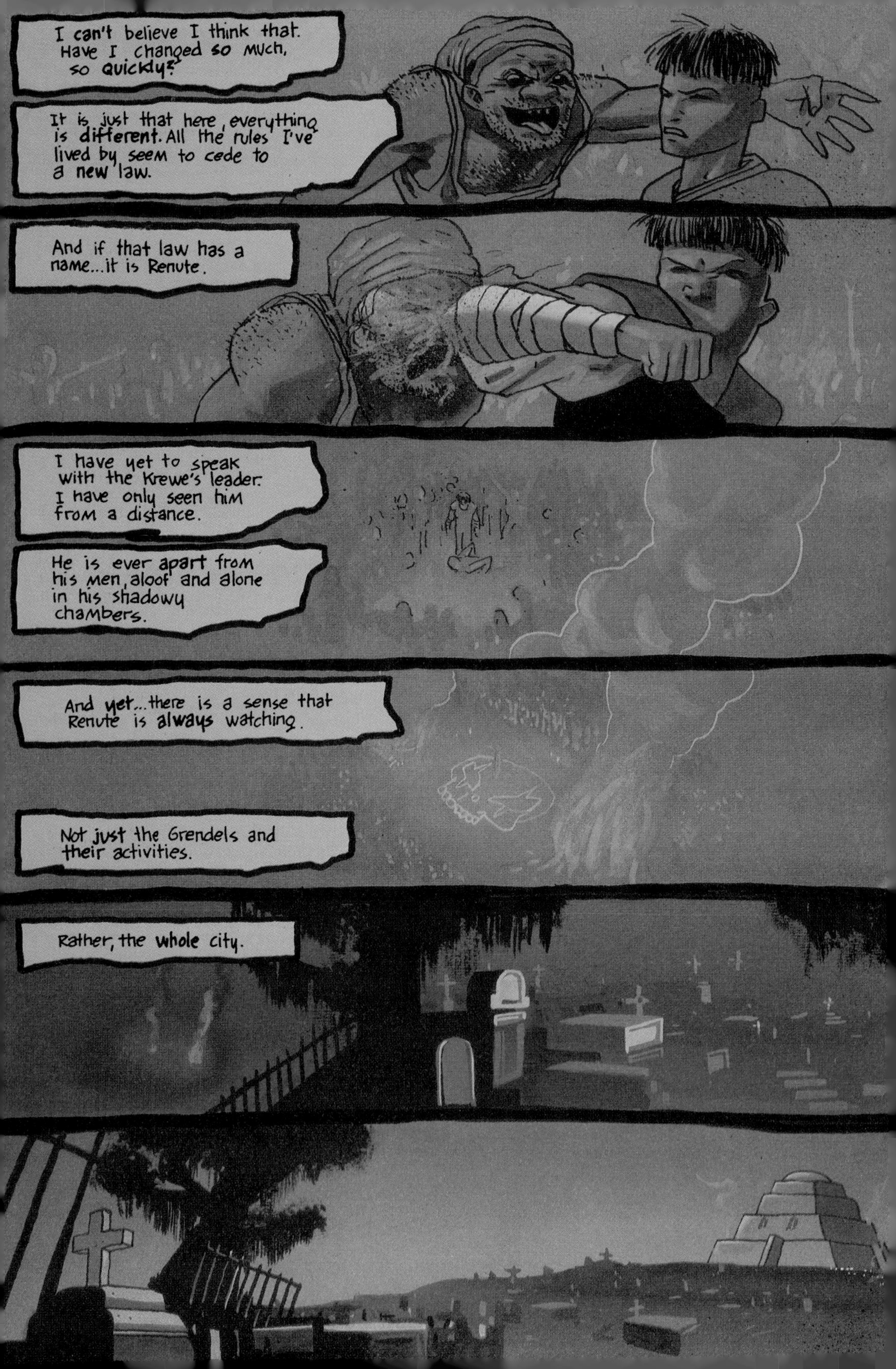
I can't believe I think that. Have I changed so much, so quickly?
It is just that here, everything is different. All the rules I've lived by seem to cede to a new law.
And if that law has a name...it is Renute.
I have yet to speak with the Krewe's leader. I have only seen him from a distance.
He is ever apart from his men, aloof and alone in his shadowy chambers.
And yet...there is a sense that Renute is always watching.
Not just the Grendels and their activities.
Rather, the whole city.

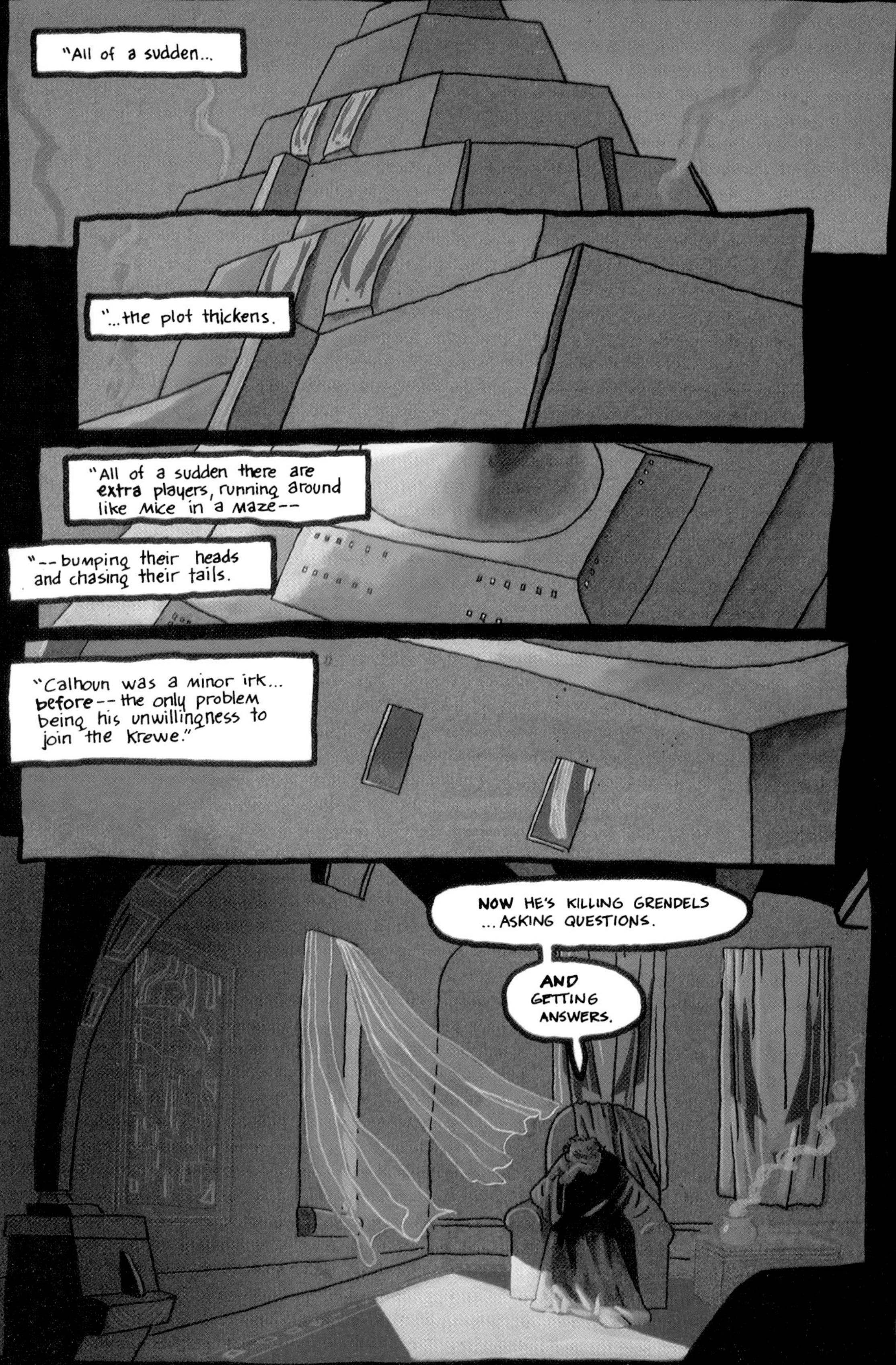
"All of a sudden...
"...the plot thickens.
"All of a sudden there are extra players, running around like mice in a maze--
"--bumping their heads and chasing their tails.
"Calhoun was a minor irk... before--the only problem being his unwillingness to join the krewe."
NOW HE'S KILLING GRENDELS ...ASKING QUESTIONS.
AND GETTING ANSWERS.

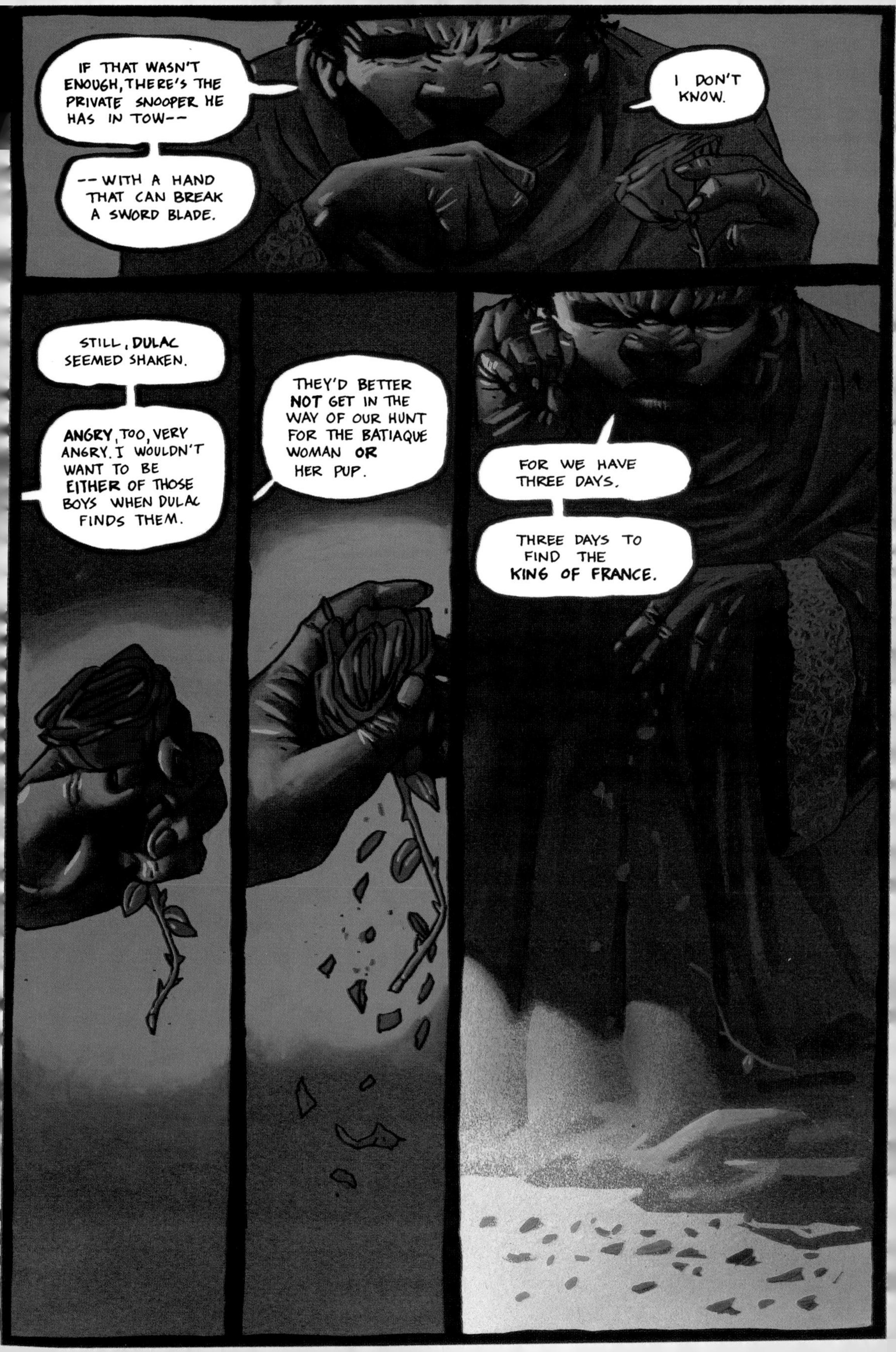
IF THAT WASN'T ENOUGH, THERE'S THE PRIVATE SNOOPER HE HAS IN TOW--
--WITH A HAND THAT CAN BREAK A SWORD BLADE.
I DON'T KNOW.
STILL, DULAC SEEMED SHAKEN.
ANGRY, TOO, VERY ANGRY. I WOULDN'T WANT TO BE EITHER OF THOSE BOYS WHEN DULAC FINDS THEM.
THEY'D BETTER NOT GET IN THE WAY OF OUR HUNT FOR THE BATIAQUE WOMAN OR HER PUP.
FOR WE HAVE THREE DAYS.
THREE DAYS TO FIND THE KING OF FRANCE.

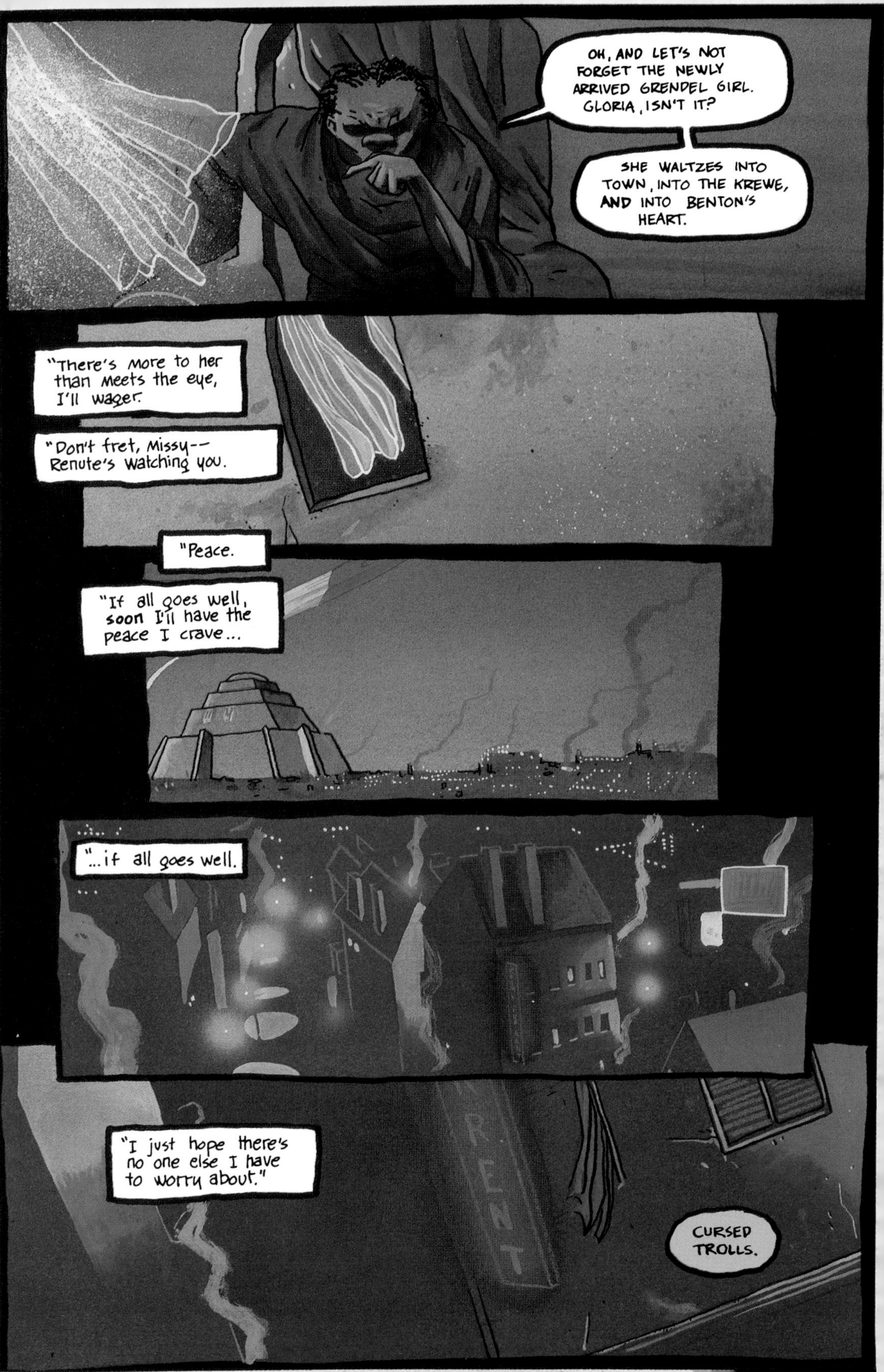
OH, AND LET'S NOT FORGET THE NEWLY ARRIVED GRENDEL GIRL. GLORIA, ISN'T IT?
SHE WALTZES INTO TOWN, INTO THE KREWE, AND INTO BENTON'S HEART.
"There's more to her than meets the eye, I'll wager.
"Don't fret, Missy-- Renute's watching you.
"Peace.
"If all goes well, soon I'll have the peace I crave...
"...if all goes well.
"I just hope there's no one else I have to worry about."
RENT
CURSED TROLLS.

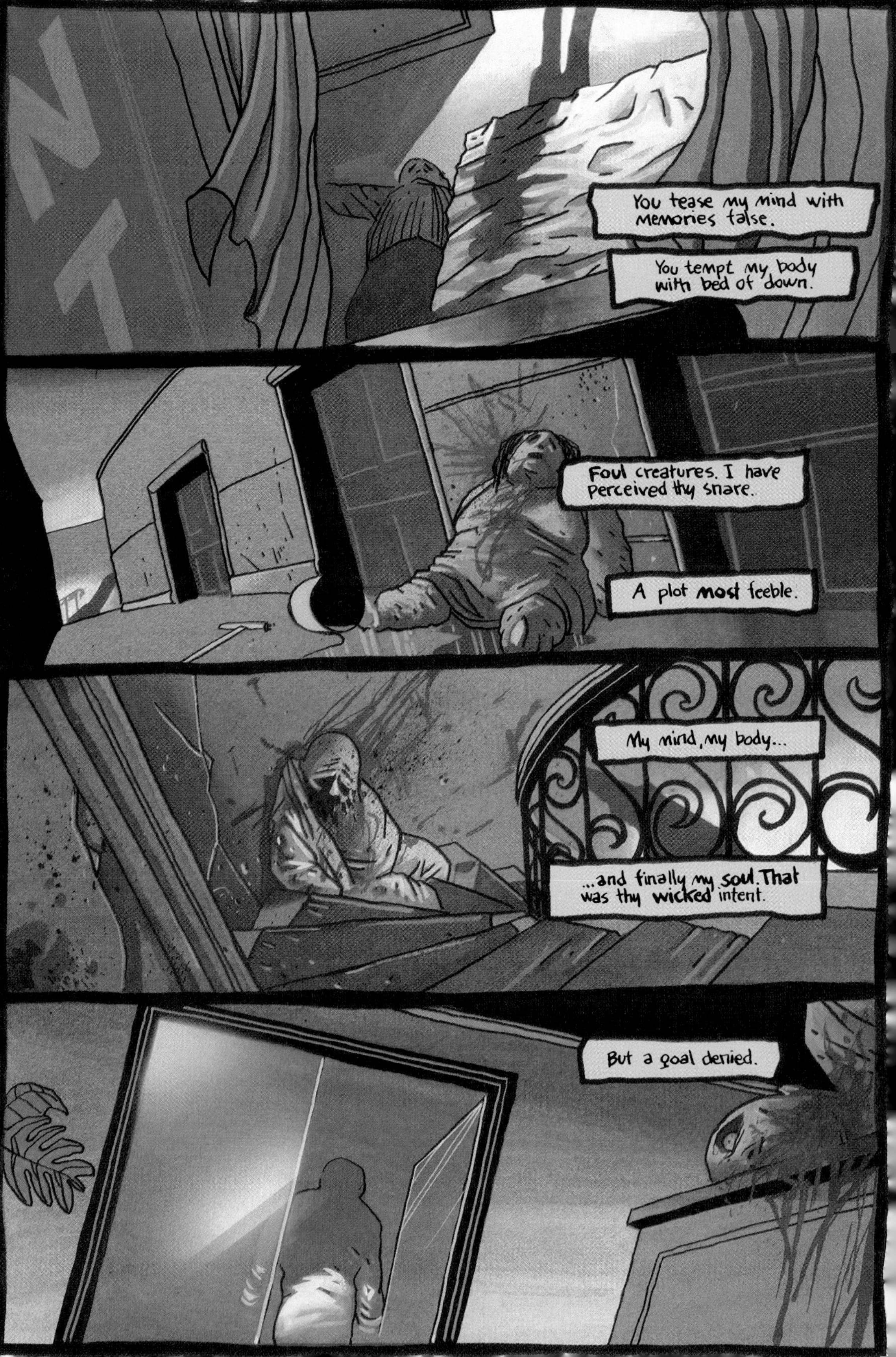
You tease my mind with memories false.
You tempt my body with bed of down.
Foul creatures. I have perceived thy snare.
A plot most feeble.
My mind, my body...
...and finally my soul. That was thy wicked intent.
But a goal denied.

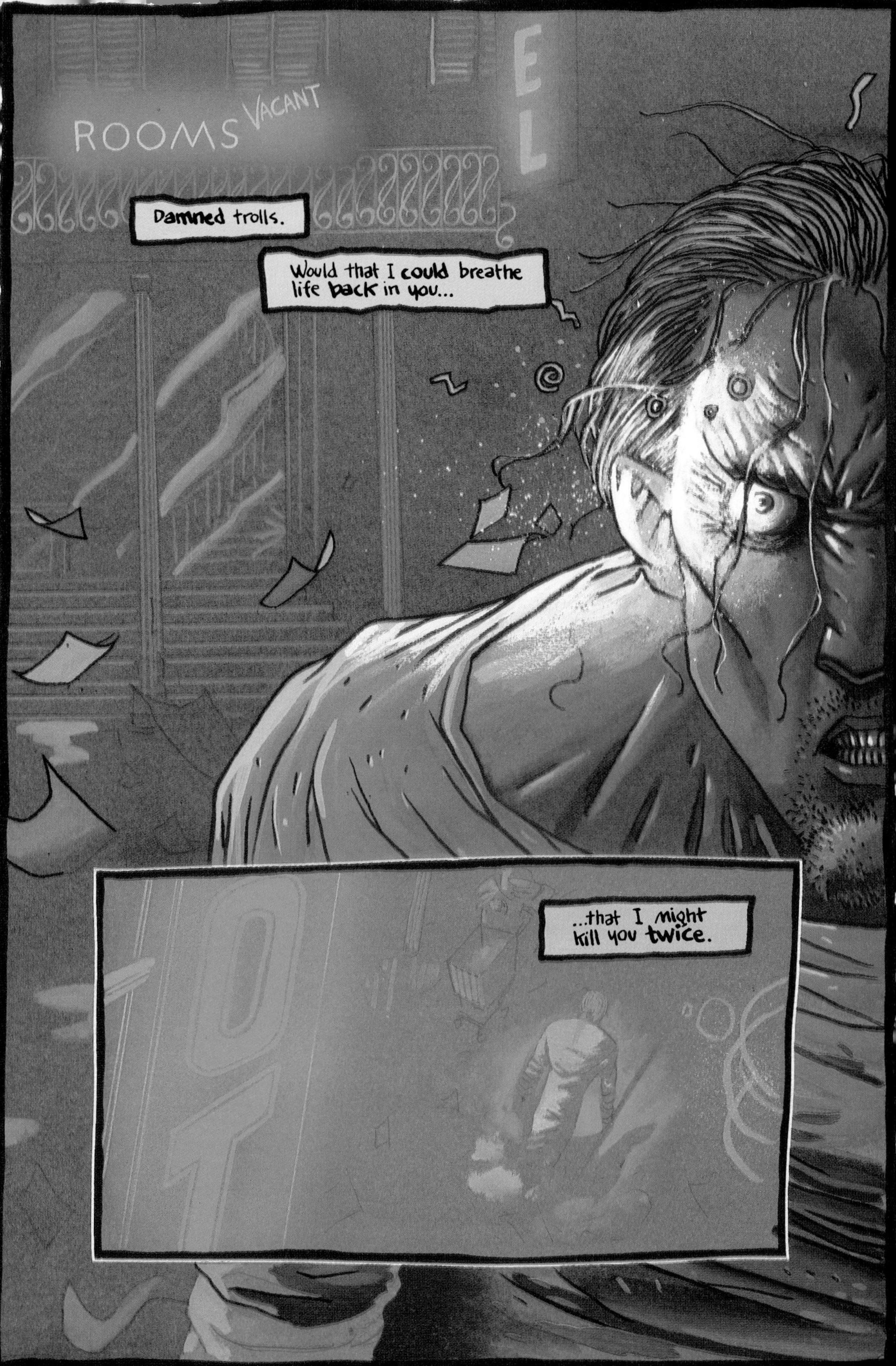
ROOMS VACANT
Damned trolls.
Would that I could breathe life back in you...
...that I might kill you twice.

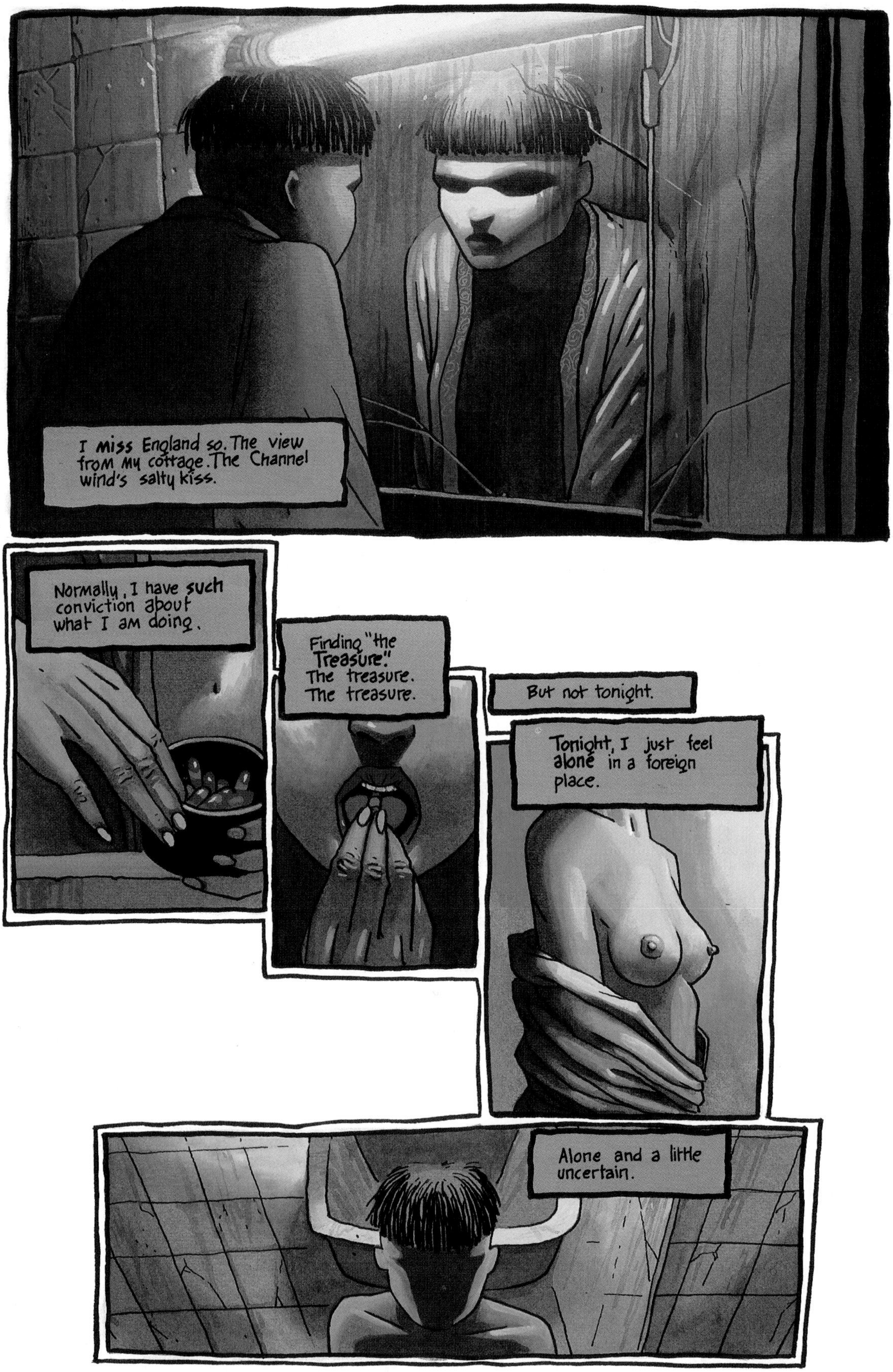
I miss England so. The view from my cottage. The Channel wind's salty kiss.
Normally, I have such conviction about what I am doing.
Finding "the Treasure." The treasure. The treasure.
But not tonight.
Tonight, I just feel alone in a foreign place.
Alone and a little uncertain.

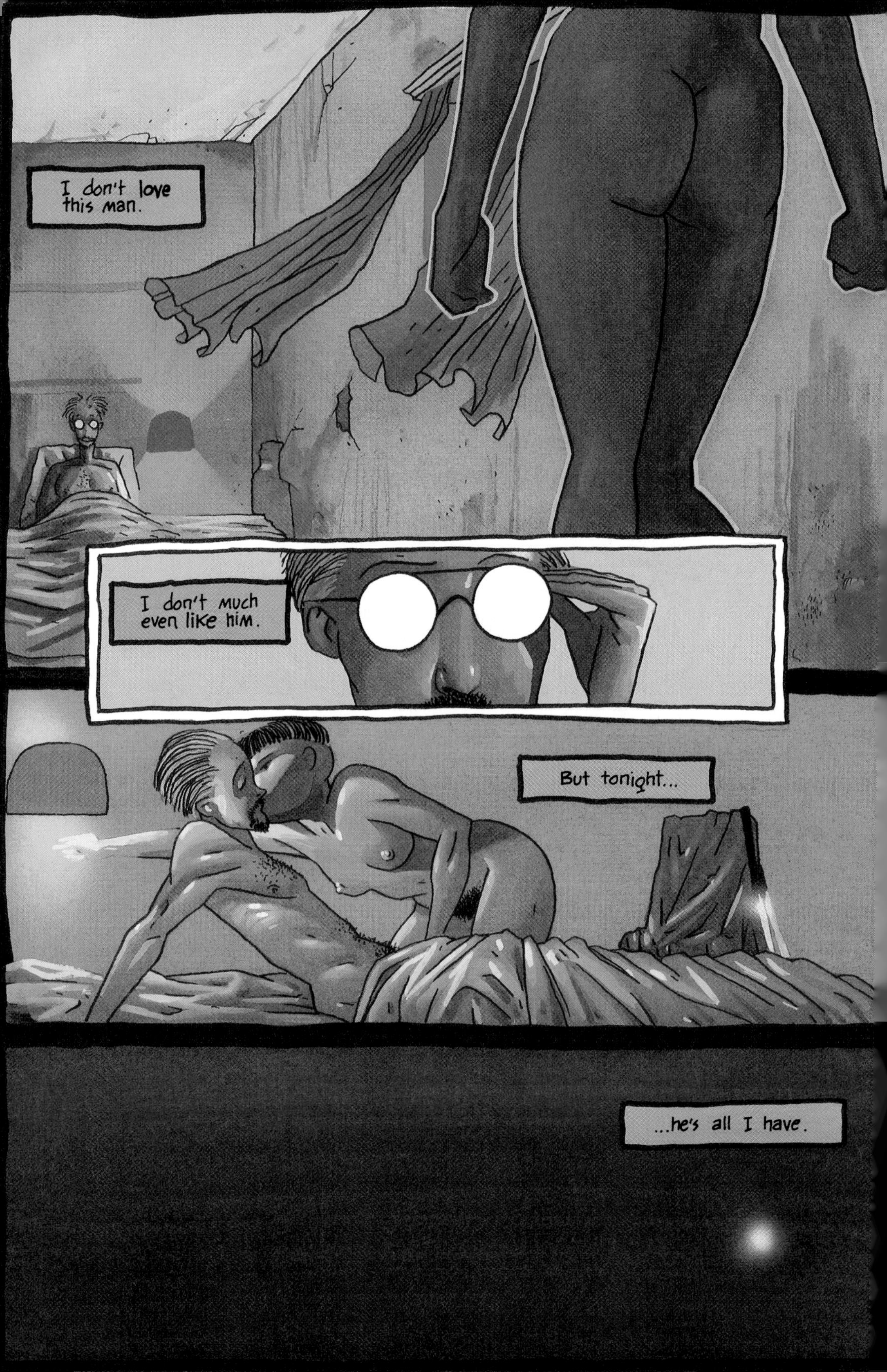
I don't love this man.
I don't much even like him.
But tonight...
...he's all I have.

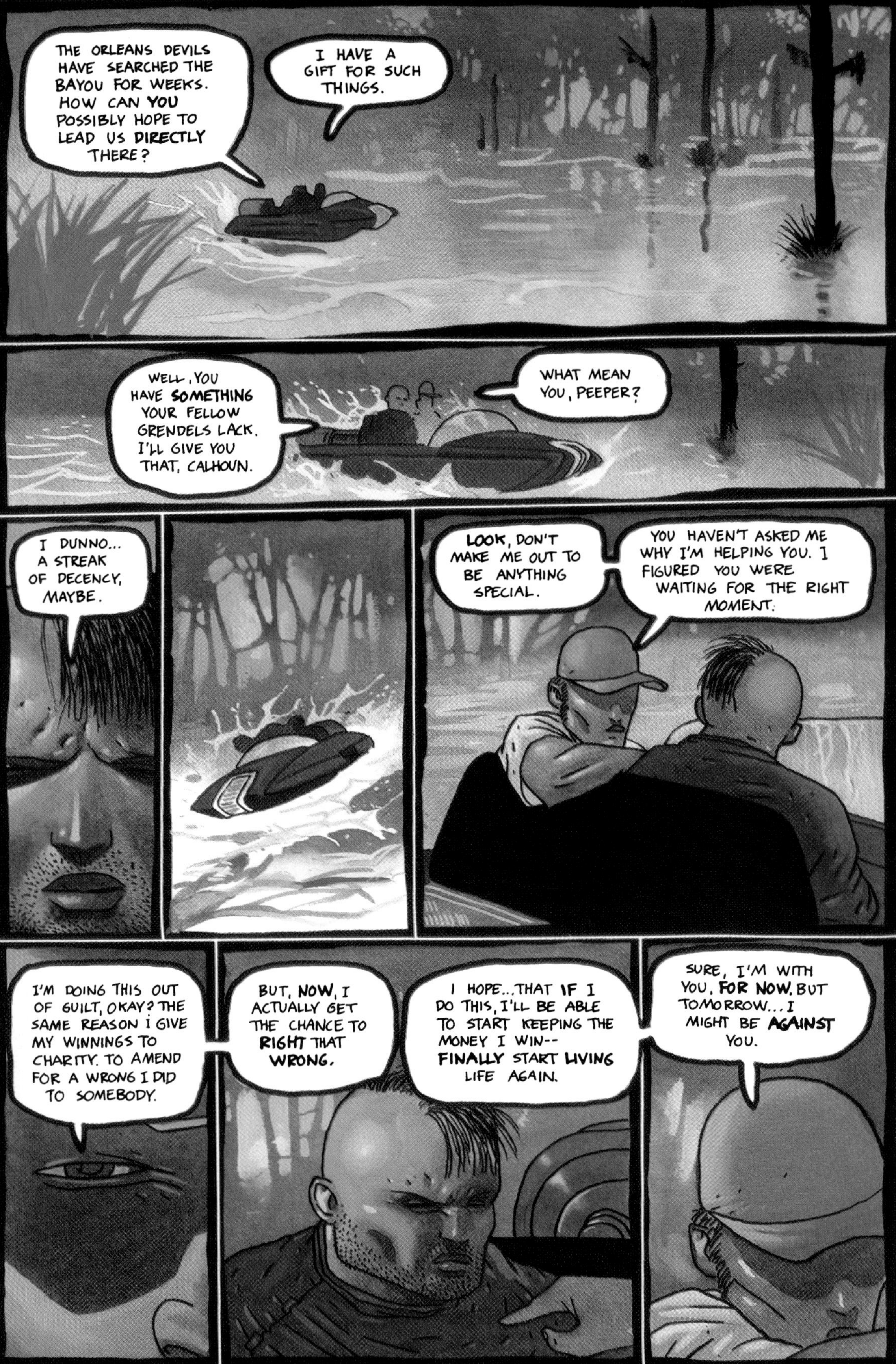
THE ORLEANS DEVILS HAVE SEARCHED THE BAYOU FOR WEEKS. HOW CAN YOU POSSIBLY HOPE TO LEAD US DIRECTLY THERE?
I HAVE A GIFT FOR SUCH THINGS.
WELL, YOU HAVE SOMETHING YOUR FELLOW GRENDELS LACK. I'LL GIVE YOU THAT, CALHOUN.
WHAT MEAN YOU, PEEPER?
I DUNNO... A STREAK OF DECENCY, MAYBE.
LOOK, DON'T MAKE ME OUT TO BE ANYTHING SPECIAL.
YOU HAVEN'T ASKED ME WHY I'M HELPING YOU. I FIGURED YOU WERE WAITING FOR THE RIGHT MOMENT.
I'M DOING THIS OUT OF GUILT, OKAY? THE SAME REASON I GIVE MY WINNINGS TO CHARITY. TO AMEND FOR A WRONG I DID TO SOMEBODY.
BUT, NOW, I ACTUALLY GET THE CHANCE TO RIGHT THAT WRONG.
I HOPE... THAT IF I DO THIS, I'LL BE ABLE TO START KEEPING THE MONEY I WIN-- FINALLY START LIVING LIFE AGAIN.
SURE, I'M WITH YOU, FOR NOW. BUT TOMORROW... I MIGHT BE AGAINST YOU.

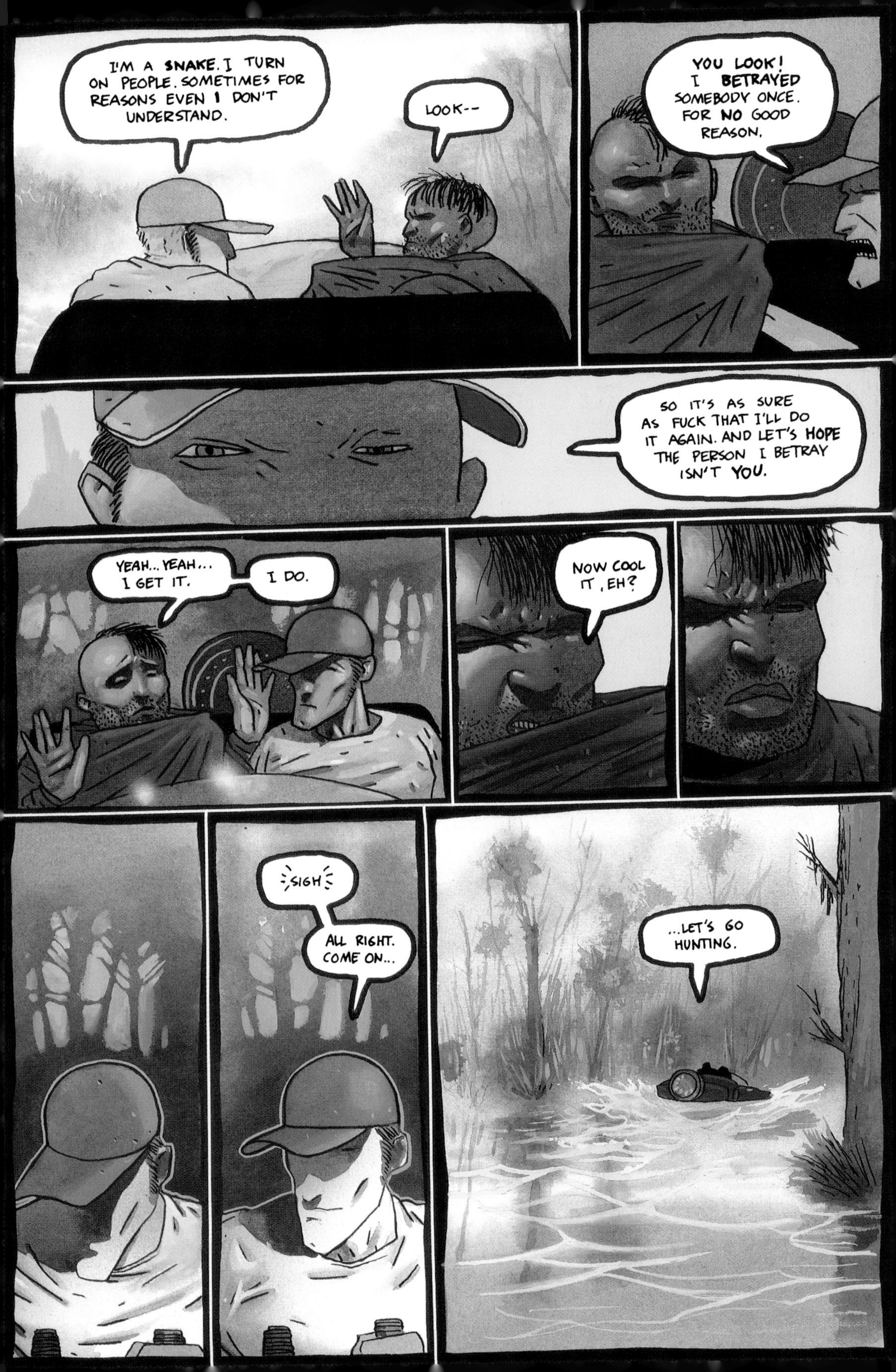
I'M A SNAKE. I TURN ON PEOPLE. SOMETIMES FOR REASONS EVEN I DON'T UNDERSTAND.
LOOK--
YOU LOOK! I BETRAYED SOMEBODY ONCE. FOR NO GOOD REASON.
SO IT'S AS SURE AS FUCK THAT I'LL DO IT AGAIN. AND LET'S HOPE THE PERSON I BETRAY ISN'T YOU.
YEAH... YEAH... I GET IT.
I DO.
NOW COOL IT, EH?
SIGH
ALL RIGHT. COME ON...
...LET'S GO HUNTING.

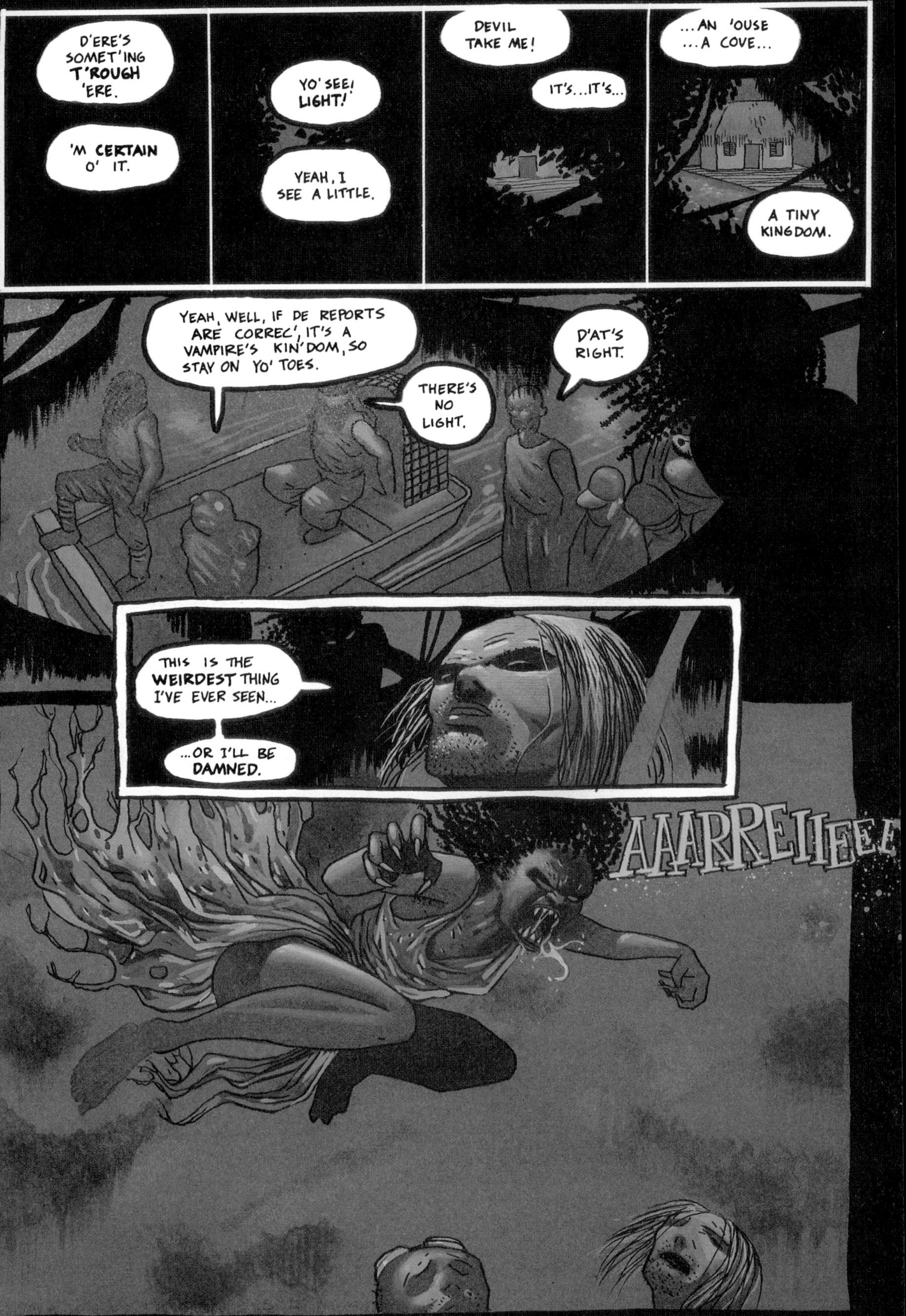

D'ERE'S SOMET'ING T'ROUGH 'ERE.
'M CERTAIN O' IT.
YO' SEE! LIGHT!'
YEAH, I SEE A LITTLE.
DEVIL TAKE ME!
IT'S...IT'S...
...AN 'OUSE ...A COVE...
A TINY KINGDOM.
YEAH, WELL, IF DE REPORTS ARE CORREC', IT'S A VAMPIRE'S KIN'DOM, SO STAY ON YO' TOES.
THERE'S NO LIGHT.
D'AT'S RIGHT.
THIS IS THE WEIRDEST THING I'VE EVER SEEN...
...OR I'LL BE DAMNED.
AAARREIIEEE

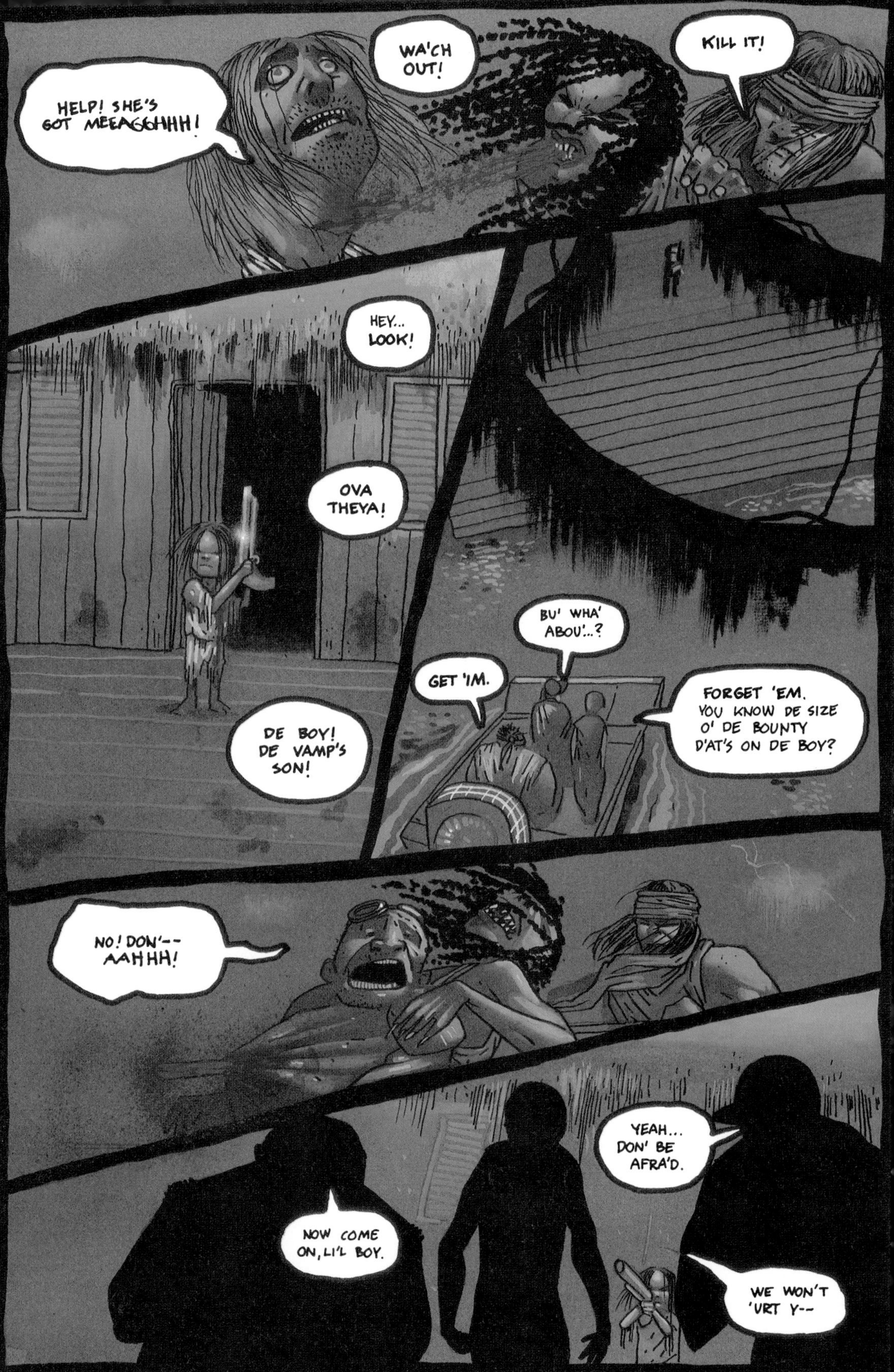
HELP! SHE'S GOT MEEAGGHHH!
WA'CH OUT!
KILL IT!
HEY... LOOK!
OVA THEYA!
DE BOY! DE VAMP'S SON!
BU' WHA' ABOU'...?
GET 'IM.
FORGET 'EM. YOU KNOW DE SIZE O' DE BOUNTY D'AT'S ON DE BOY?
NO! DON'-- AAHHH!
YEAH... DON' BE AFRA'D.
NOW COME ON, LI'L BOY.
WE WON'T 'URT Y--

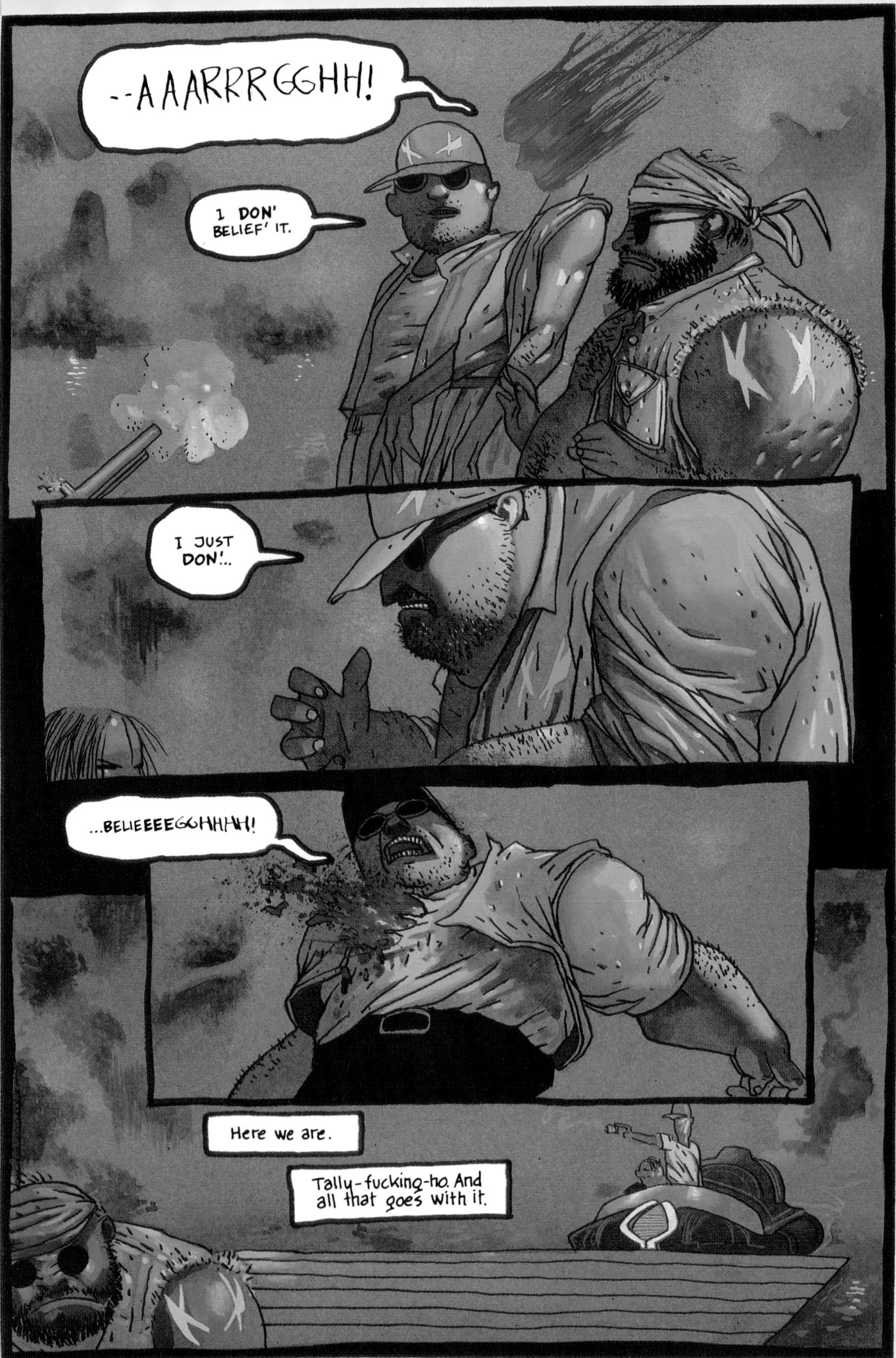
--AAARRRGGHH!
I DON' BELIEF' IT.
I JUST DON'...
...BELIEEEEGGHHHH!
Here we are.
Tally-fucking-ho. And all that goes with it.

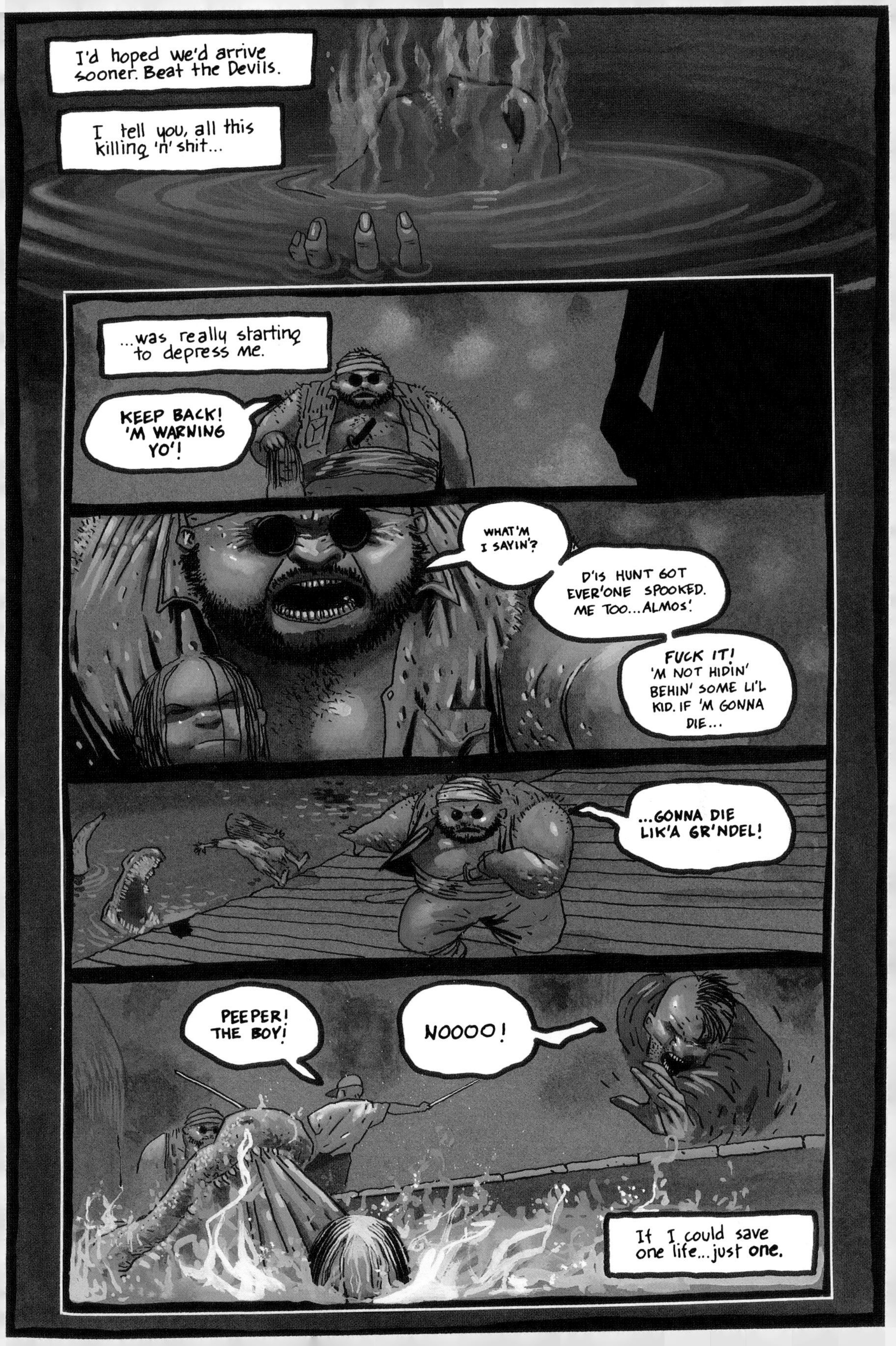
I'd hoped we'd arrive sooner. Beat the Devils.
I tell you, all this killing 'n' shit...
...was really starting to depress me.
KEEP BACK! 'M WARNING YO'!
WHAT'M I SAYIN'?
D'IS HUNT GOT EVER'ONE SPOOKED. ME TOO...ALMOS'.
FUCK IT! 'M NOT HIDIN' BEHIN' SOME LI'L KID. IF 'M GONNA DIE...
...GONNA DIE LIK'A GR'NDEL!
PEEPER! THE BOY!
NOOOO!
If I could save one life...just one.

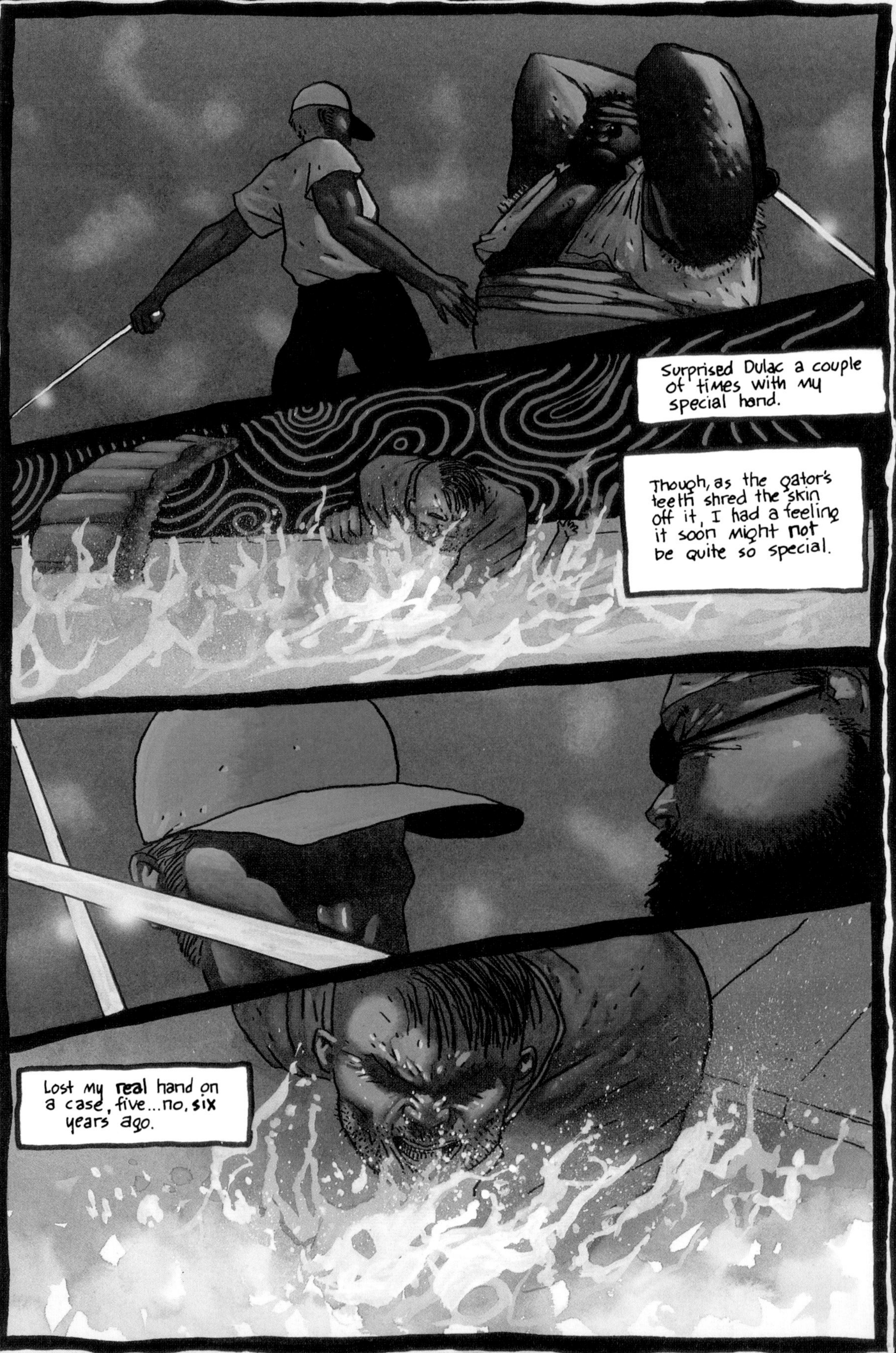
Surprised Dulac a couple of times with my special hand.
Though, as the gator's teeth shred the skin off it, I had a feeling it soon might not be quite so special.
Lost my real hand on a case, five...no, six years ago.

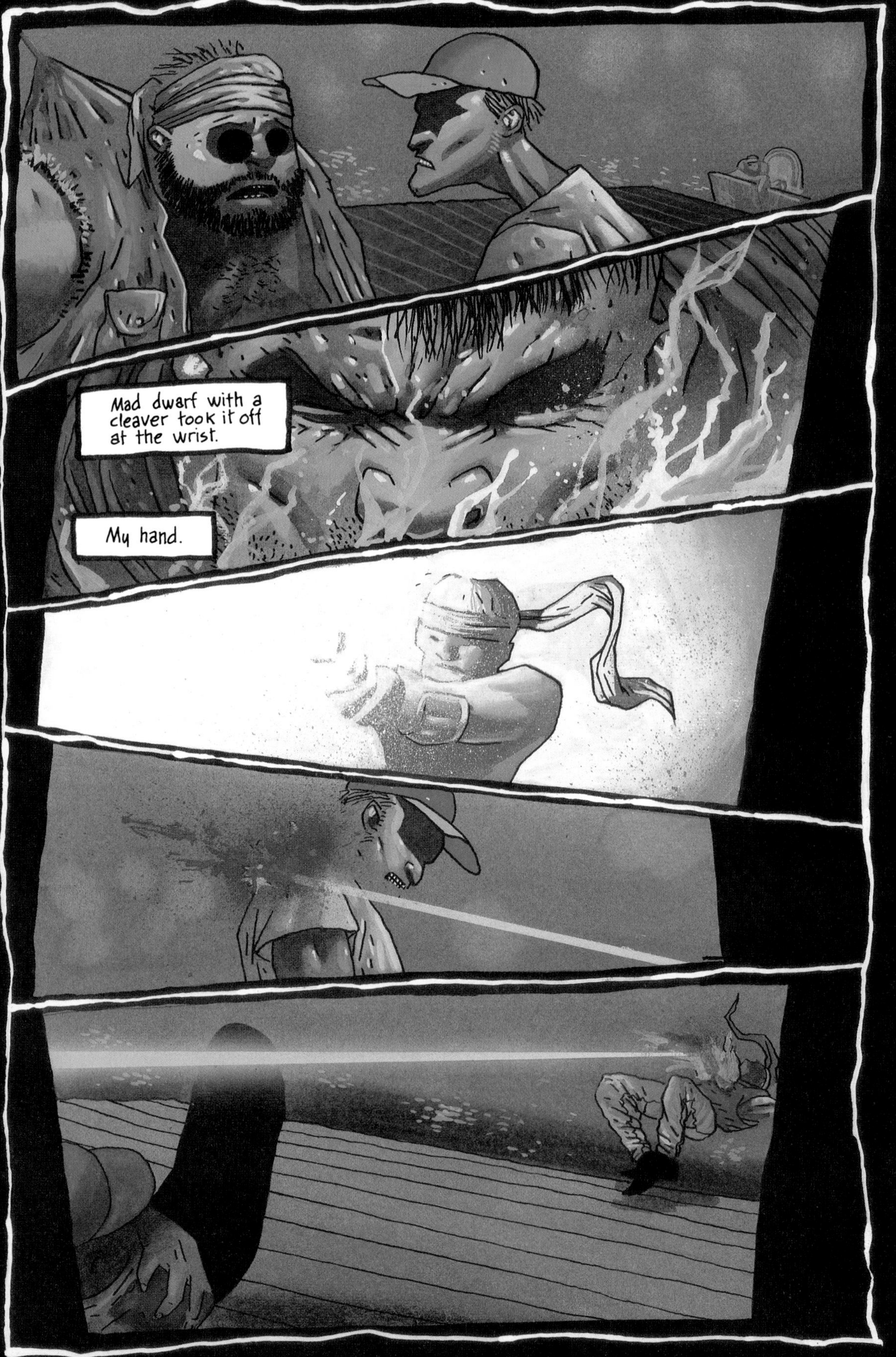
Mad dwarf with a cleaver took it off at the wrist.
My hand.

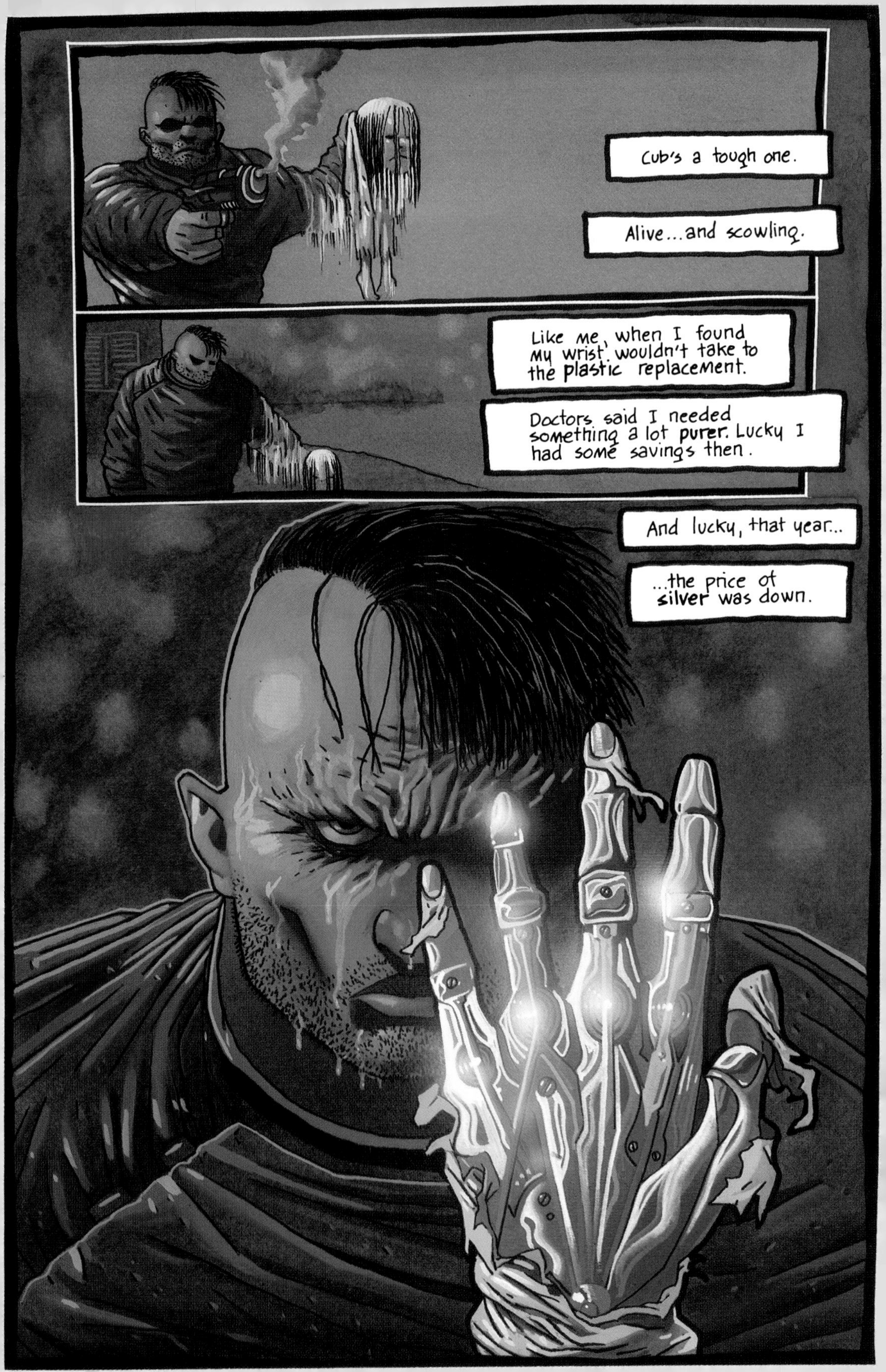
Cub's a tough one.
Alive...and scowling.
Like me, when I found my wrist wouldn't take to the plastic replacement.
Doctors said I needed something a lot purer. Lucky I had some savings then.
And lucky, that year...
...the price of silver was down.

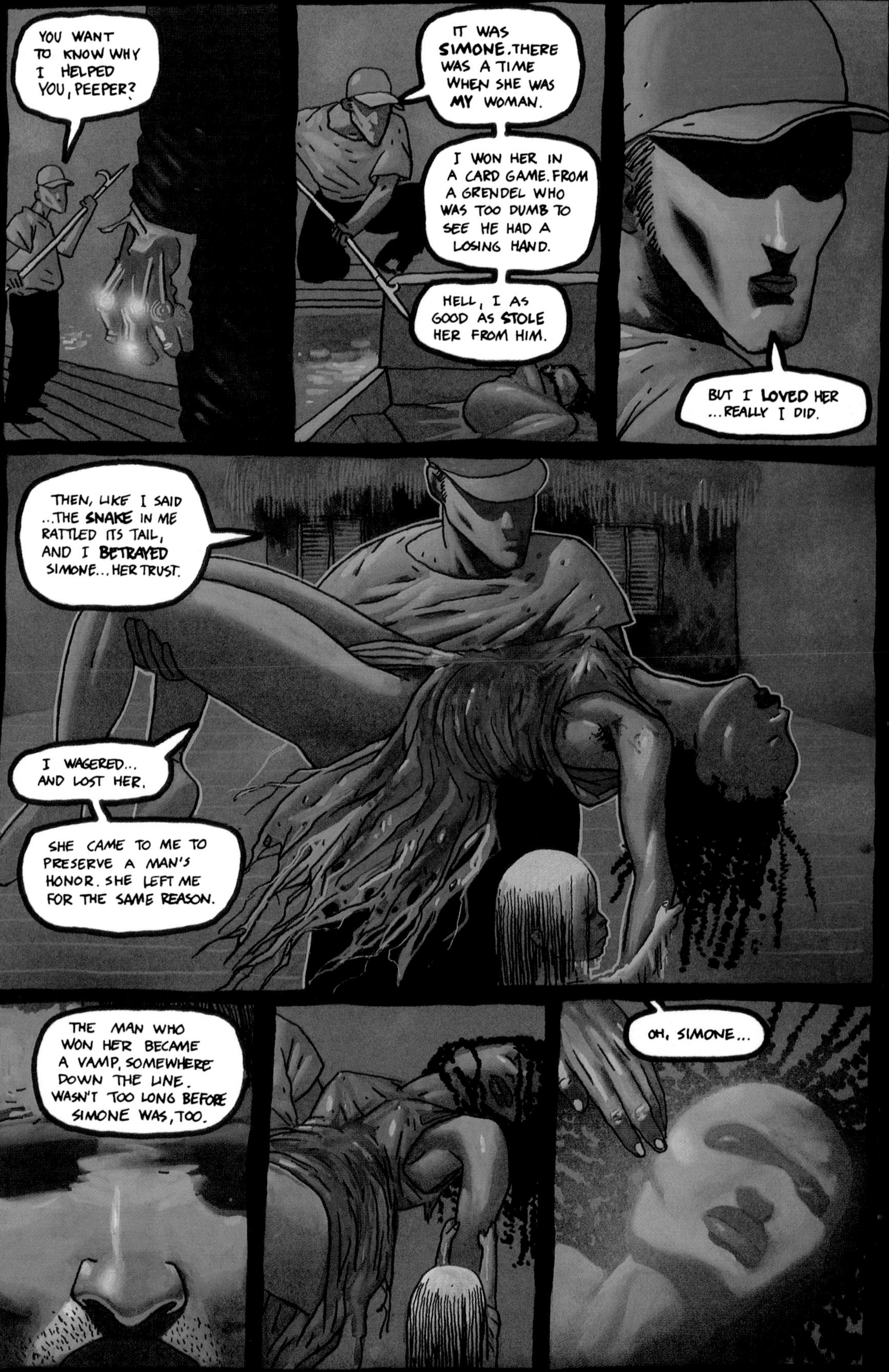
YOU WANT TO KNOW WHY I HELPED YOU, PEEPER?
IT WAS SIMONE. THERE WAS A TIME WHEN SHE WAS MY WOMAN.
I WON HER IN A CARD GAME. FROM A GRENDEL WHO WAS TOO DUMB TO SEE HE HAD A LOSING HAND.
HELL, I AS GOOD AS STOLE HER FROM HIM.
BUT I LOVED HER ...REALLY I DID.
THEN, LIKE I SAID ...THE SNAKE IN ME RATTLED ITS TAIL, AND I BETRAYED SIMONE... HER TRUST.
I WAGERED... AND LOST HER.
SHE CAME TO ME TO PRESERVE A MAN'S HONOR. SHE LEFT ME FOR THE SAME REASON.
THE MAN WHO WON HER BECAME A VAMP, SOMEWHERE DOWN THE LINE. WASN'T TOO LONG BEFORE SIMONE WAS, TOO.
OH, SIMONE...

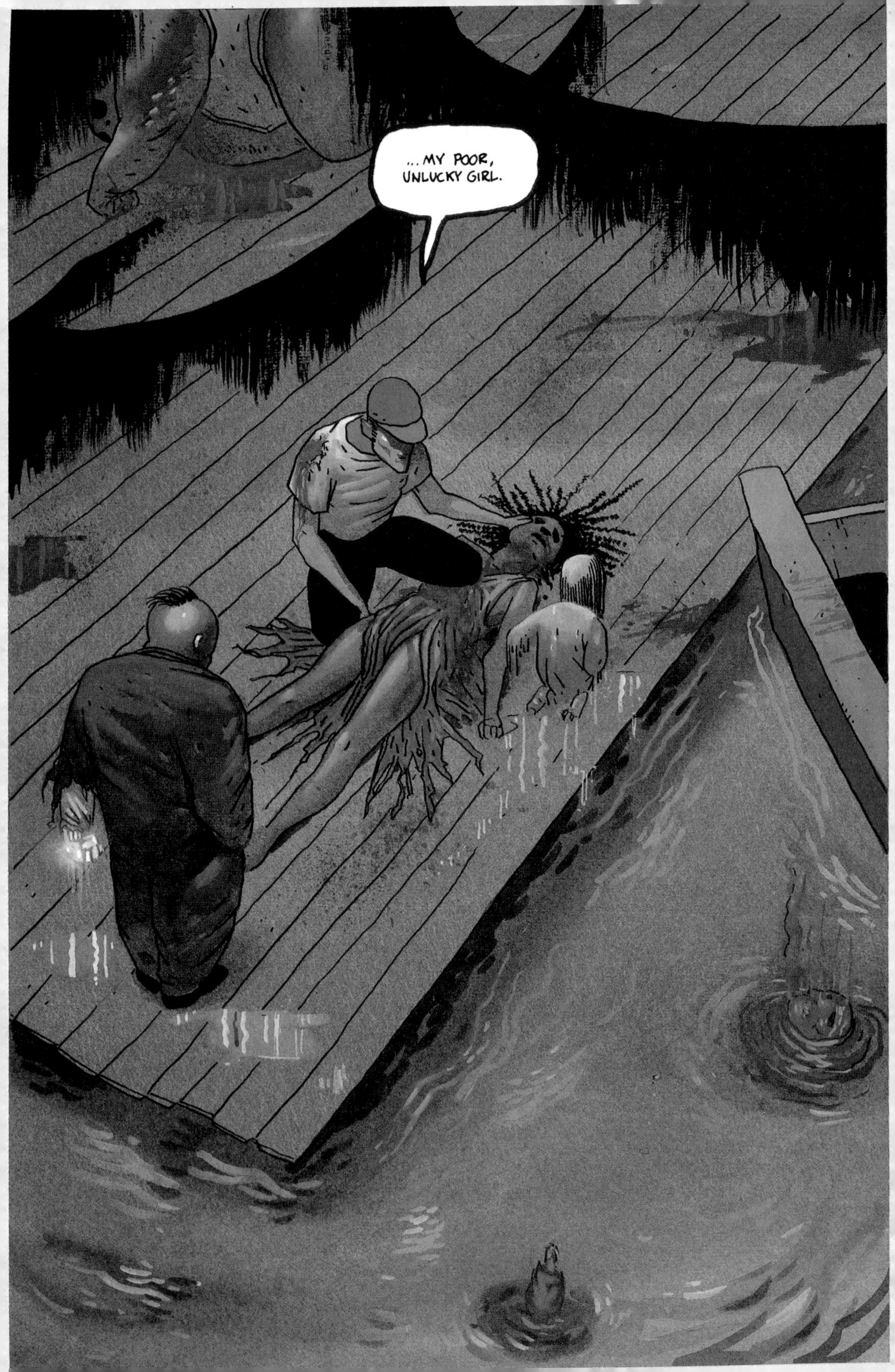
...MY POOR, UNLUCKY GIRL.

CHAPTER FIVE

ONE CARNIVAL, THREE CAPTIVES

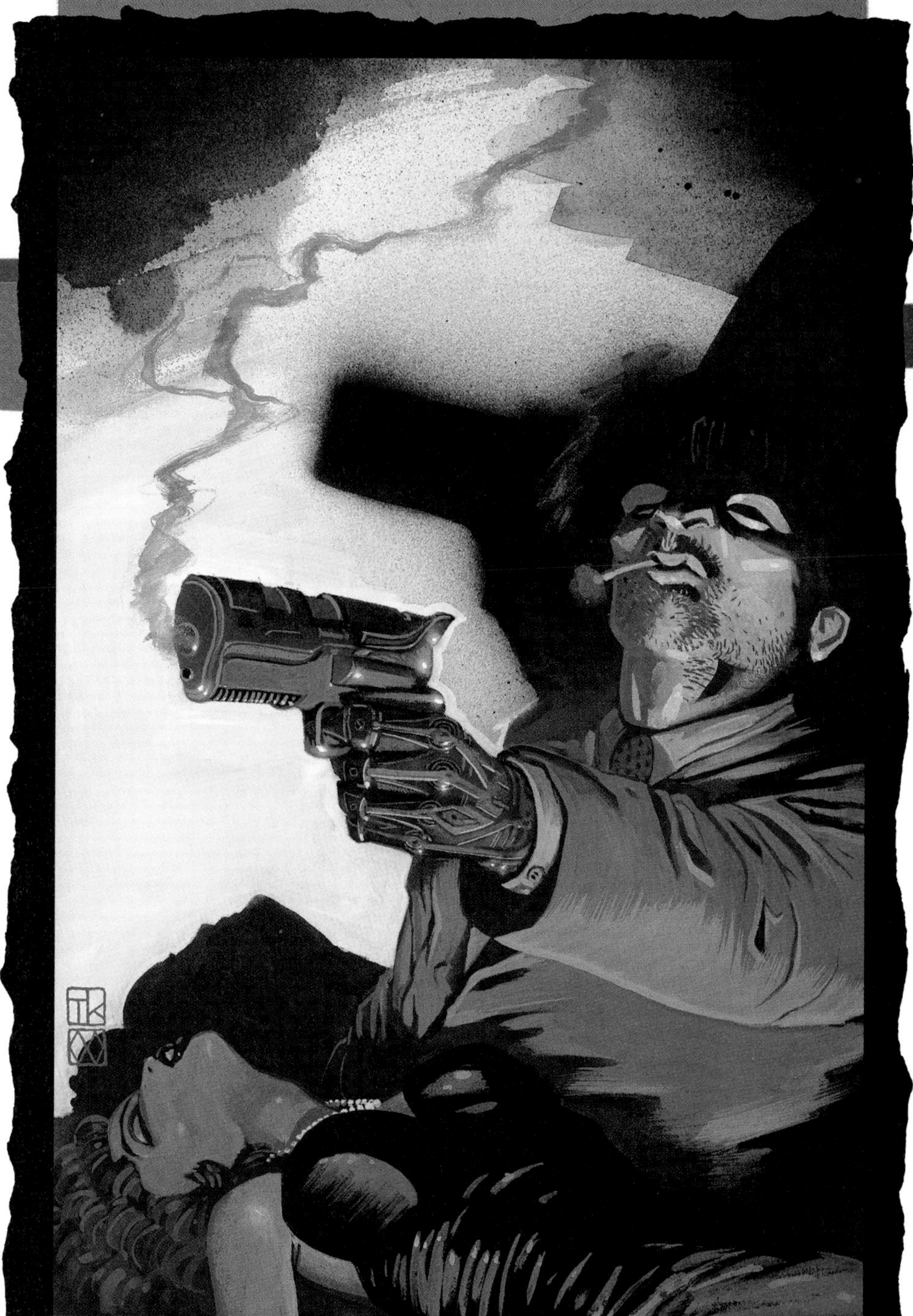

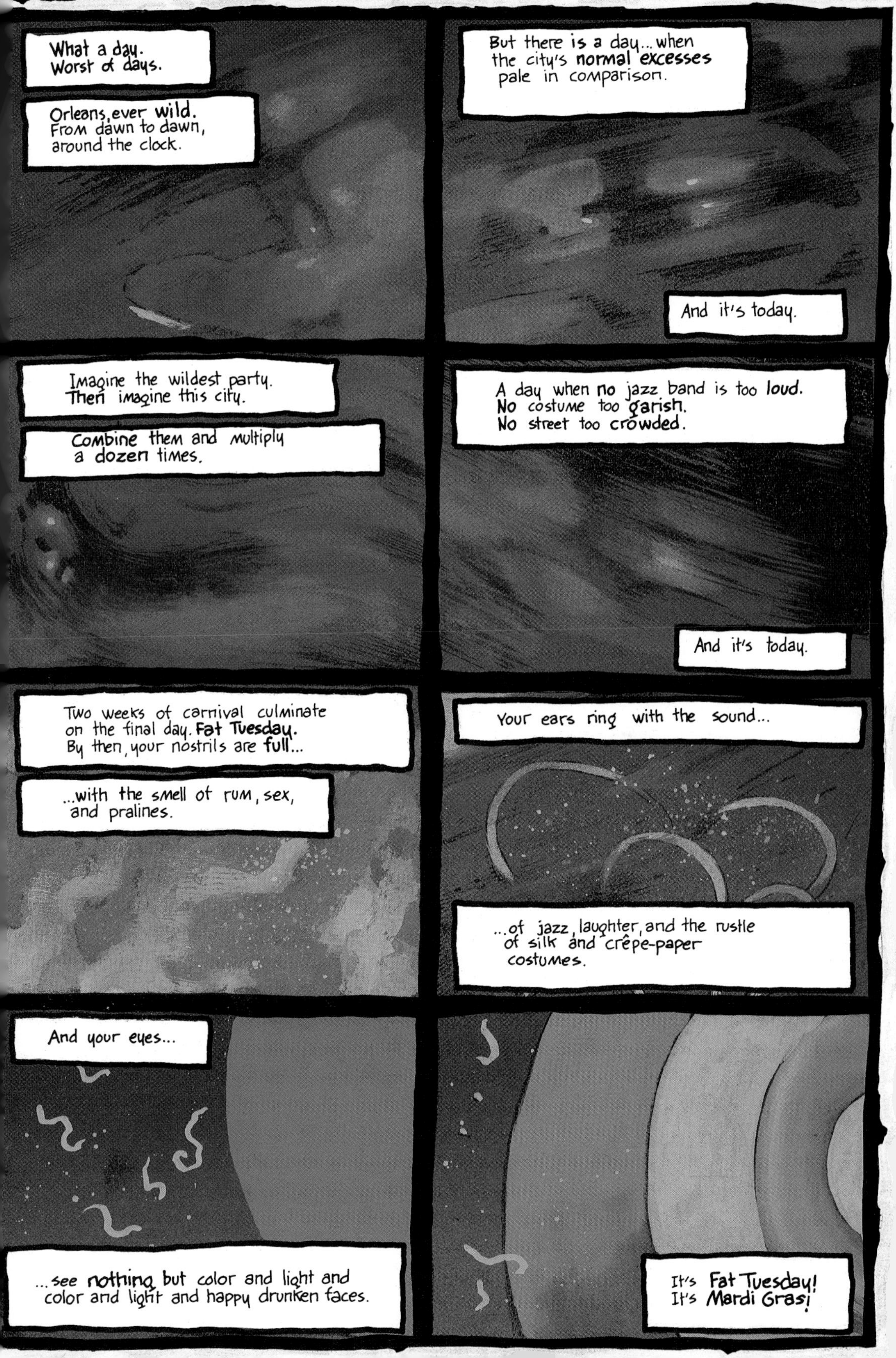
What a day.
Worst of days.
Orleans, ever wild.
From dawn to dawn, around the clock.
But there is a day... when the city's normal excesses pale in comparison.
And it's today.
Imagine the wildest party.
Then imagine this city.
Combine them and multiply a dozen times.
A day when no jazz band is too loud.
No costume too garish.
No street too crowded.
And it's today.
Two weeks of carnival culminate on the final day. Fat Tuesday.
By then, your nostrils are full...
...with the smell of rum, sex, and pralines.
Your ears ring with the sound...
...of jazz, laughter, and the rustle of silk and crêpe-paper costumes.
And your eyes...
...see nothing but color and light and color and light and happy drunken faces.
It's Fat Tuesday!
It's Mardi Gras!

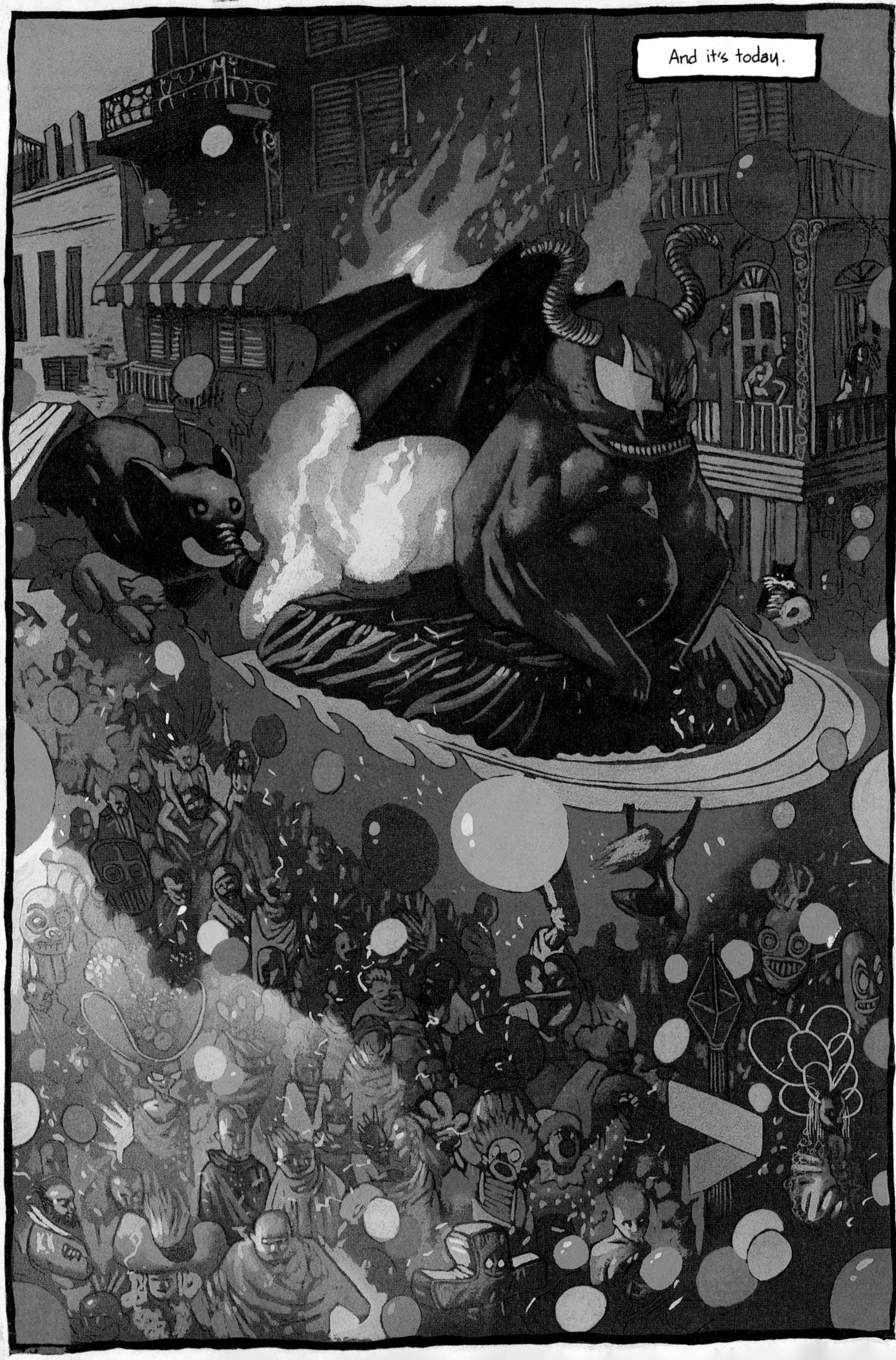
And it's today.

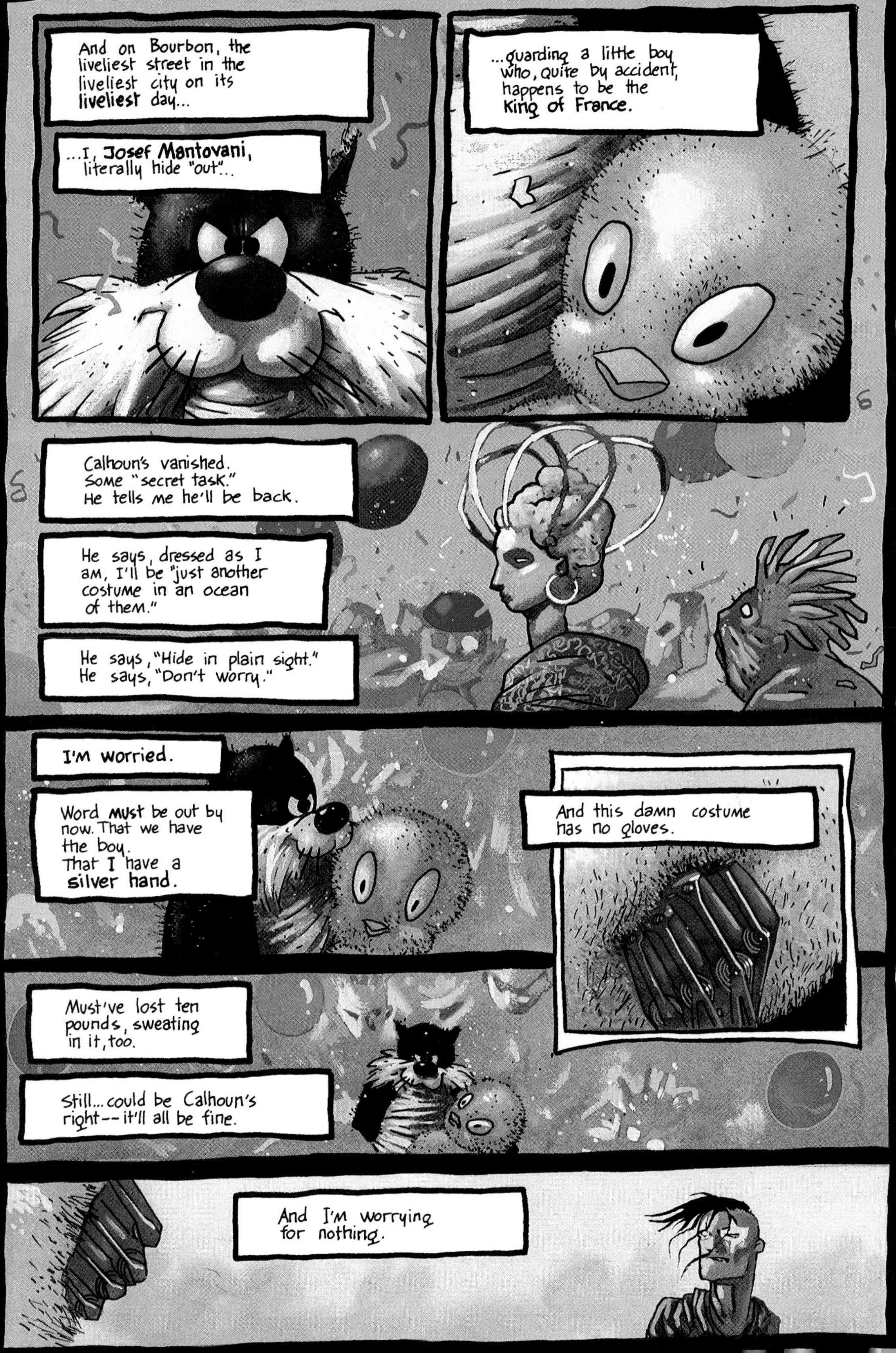
And on Bourbon, the liveliest street in the liveliest city on its liveliest day...
...I, Josef Mantovani, literally hide "out"...
...guarding a little boy who, quite by accident, happens to be the King of France.
Calhoun's vanished. Some "secret task." He tells me he'll be back.
He says, dressed as I am, I'll be "just another costume in an ocean of them."
He says, "Hide in plain sight." He says, "Don't worry."
I'M worried.
Word must be out by now. That we have the boy. That I have a silver hand.
And this damn costume has no gloves.
Must've lost ten pounds, sweating in it, too.
Still... could be Calhoun's right-- it'll all be fine.
And I'm worrying for nothing.

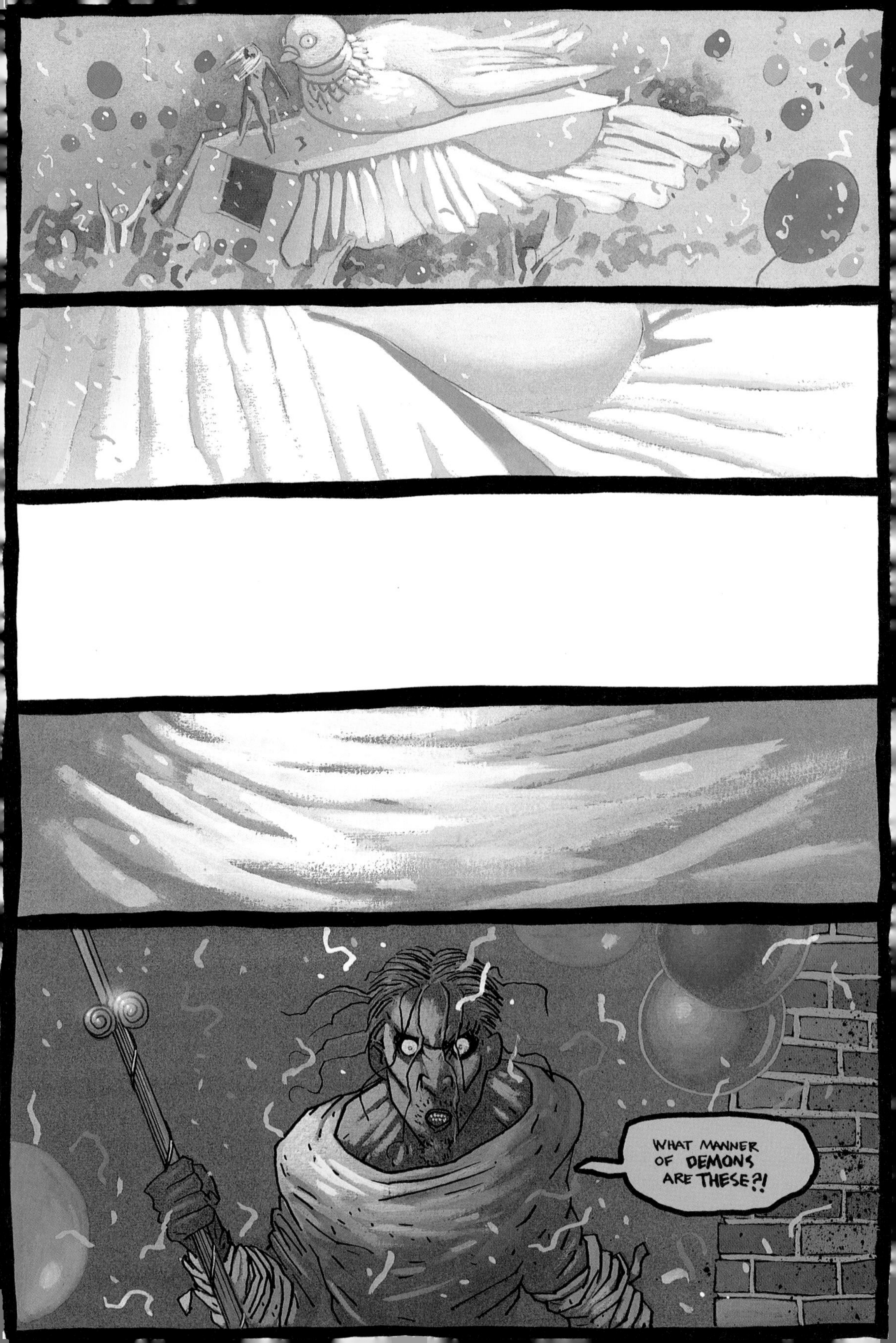
WHAT MANNER OF DEMONS ARE THESE?!

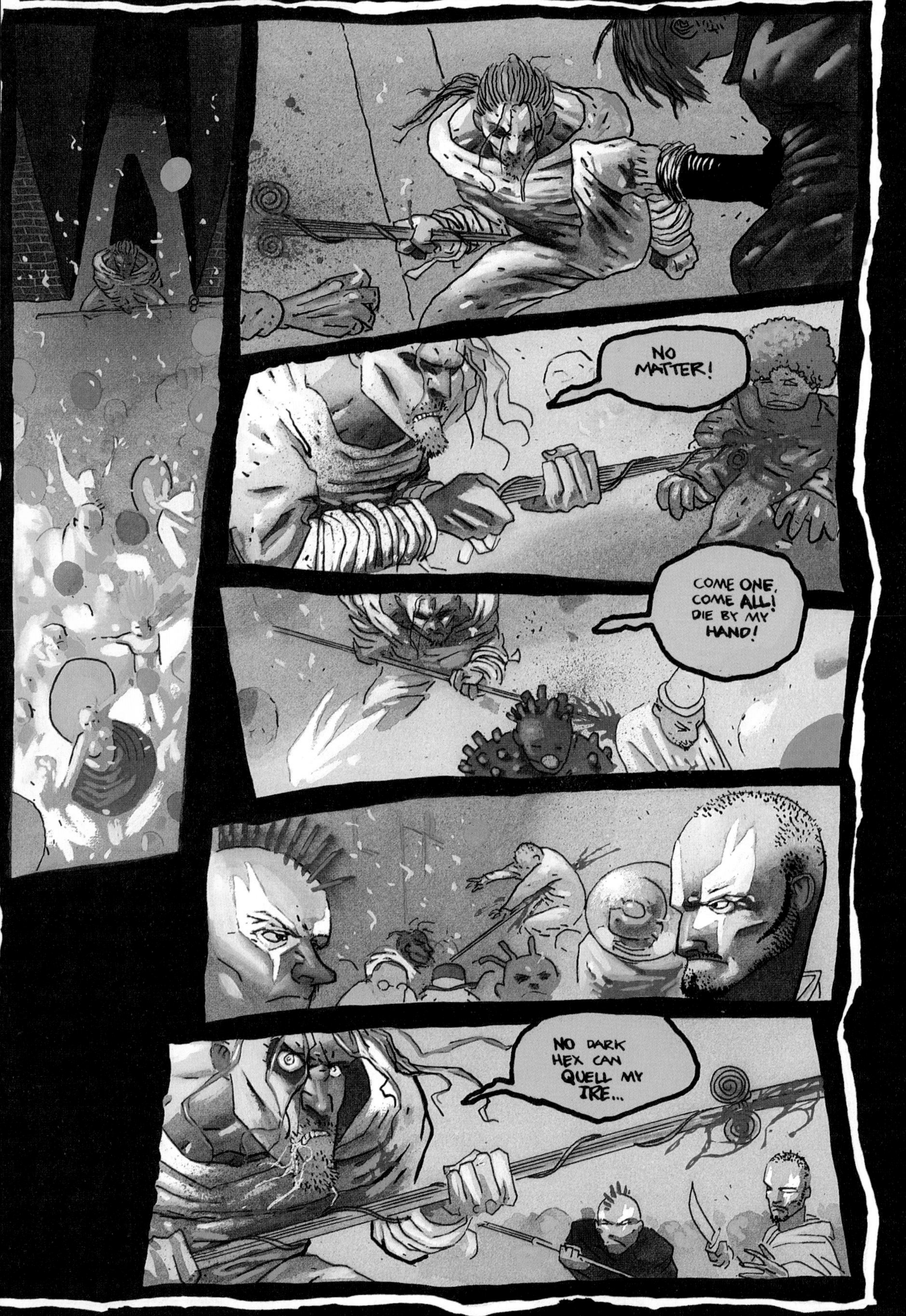
NO MATTER!
COME ONE, COME ALL! DIE BY MY HAND!
NO DARK HEX CAN QUELL MY IRE...

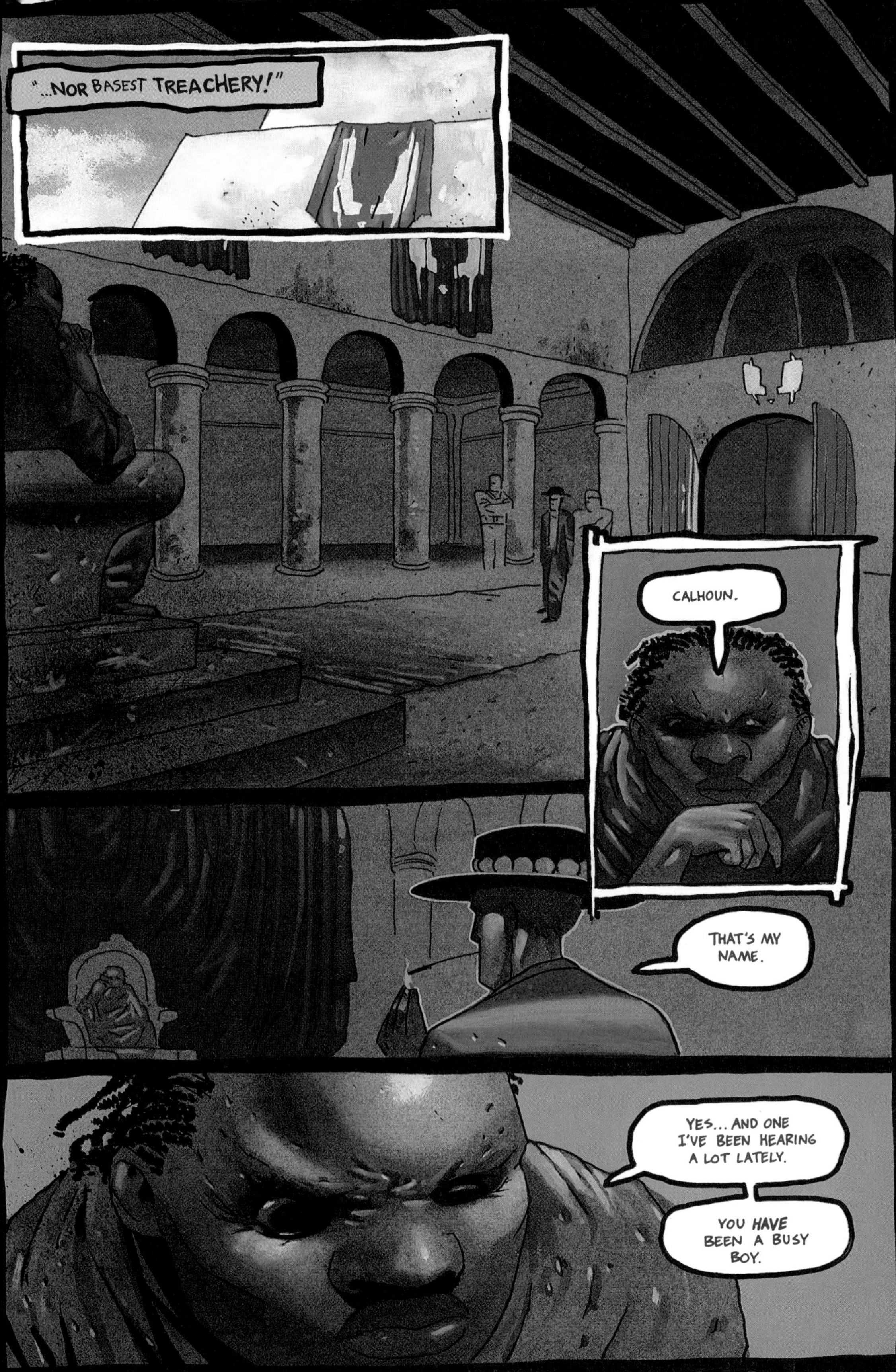
"...NOR BASEST TREACHERY!"
CALHOUN.
THAT'S MY NAME.
YES... AND ONE I'VE BEEN HEARING A LOT LATELY.
YOU HAVE BEEN A BUSY BOY.

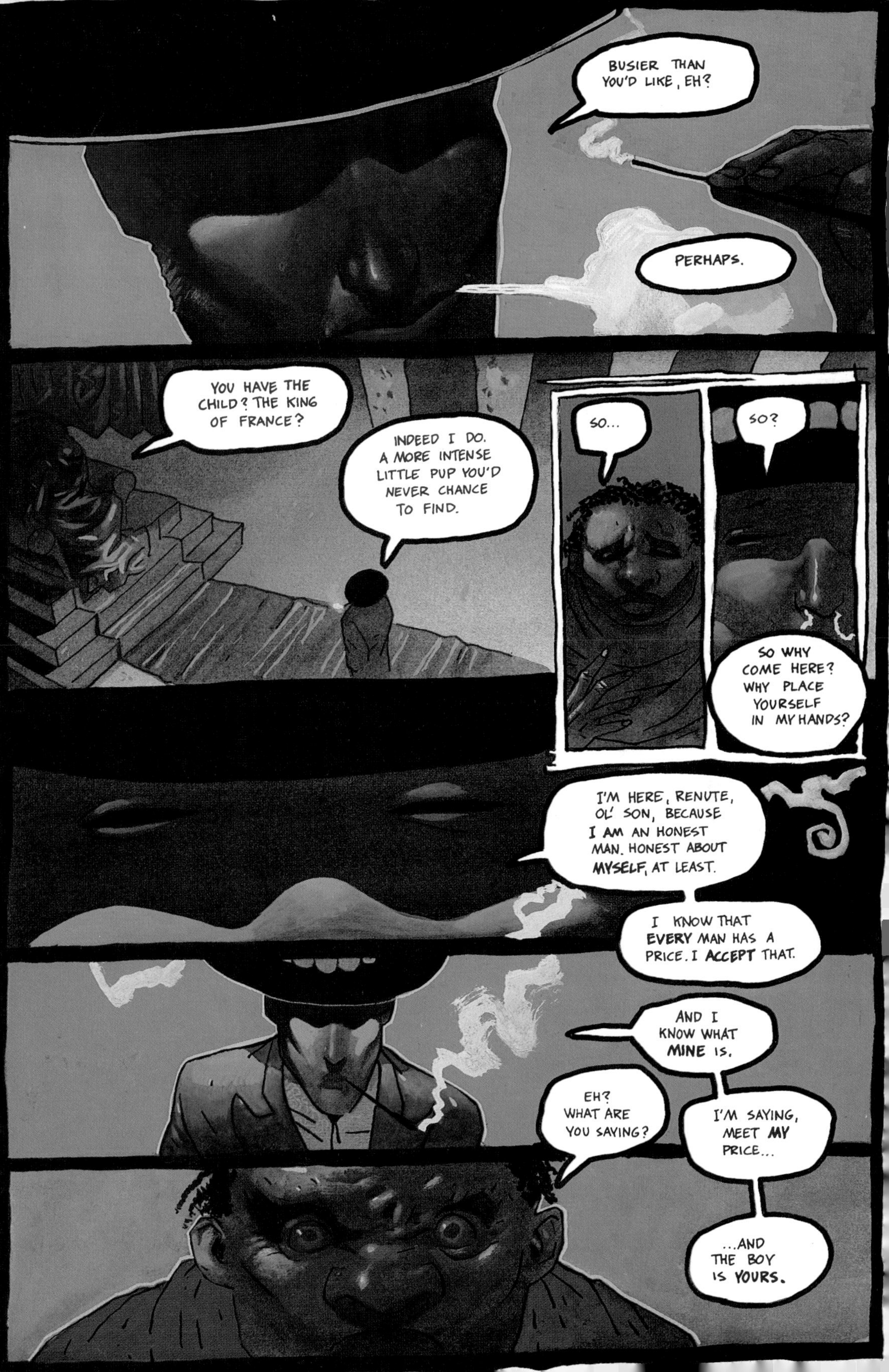
BUSIER THAN YOU'D LIKE, EH?
PERHAPS.
YOU HAVE THE CHILD? THE KING OF FRANCE?
INDEED I DO. A MORE INTENSE LITTLE PUP YOU'D NEVER CHANCE TO FIND.
SO...
SO?
SO WHY COME HERE? WHY PLACE YOURSELF IN MY HANDS?
I'M HERE, RENUTE, OL' SON, BECAUSE I AM AN HONEST MAN. HONEST ABOUT MYSELF, AT LEAST.
I KNOW THAT EVERY MAN HAS A PRICE. I ACCEPT THAT.
AND I KNOW WHAT MINE IS.
EH? WHAT ARE YOU SAYING?
I'M SAYING, MEET MY PRICE...
...AND THE BOY IS YOURS.

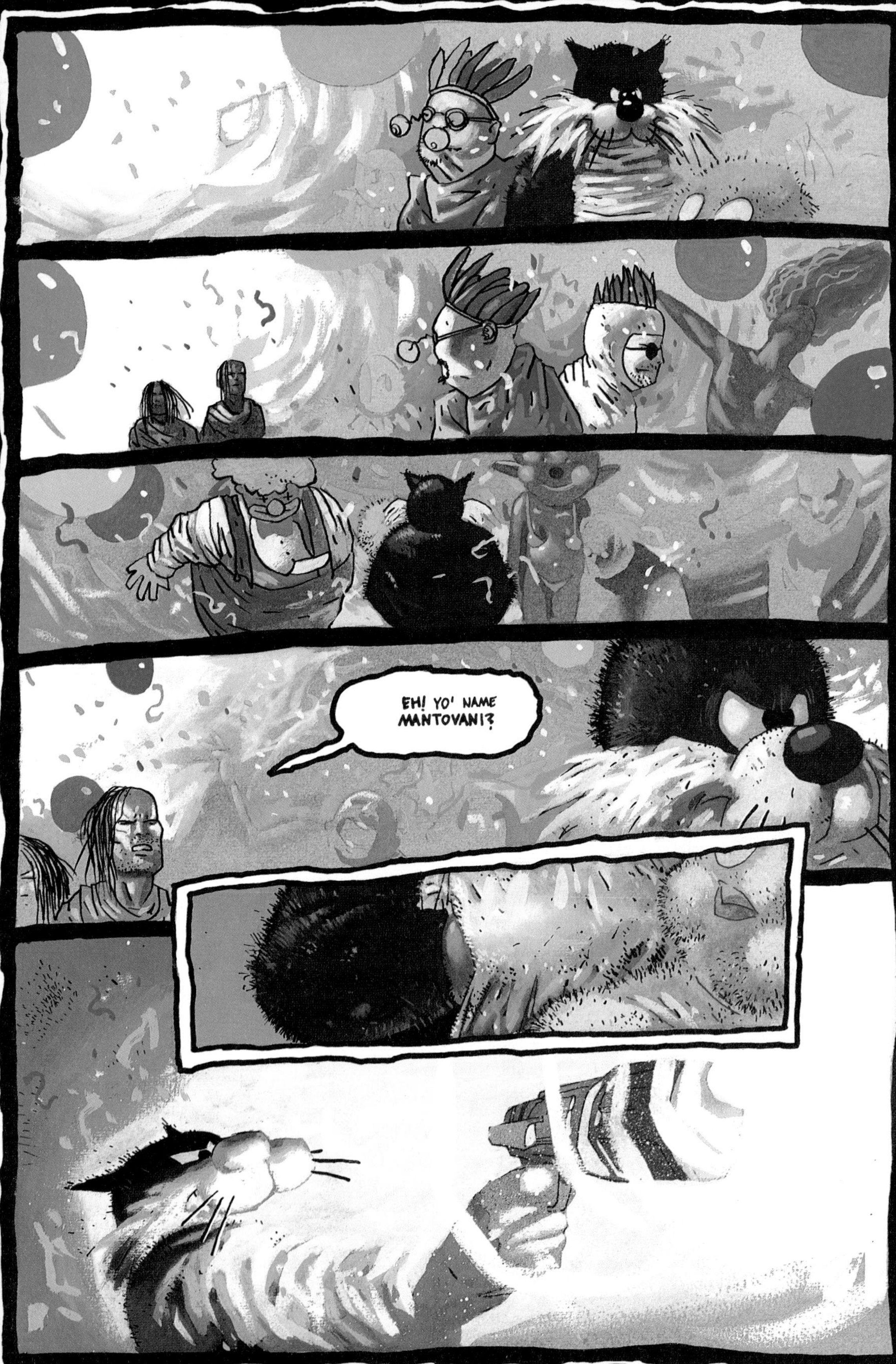
EH! YO' NAME MANTOVANI?

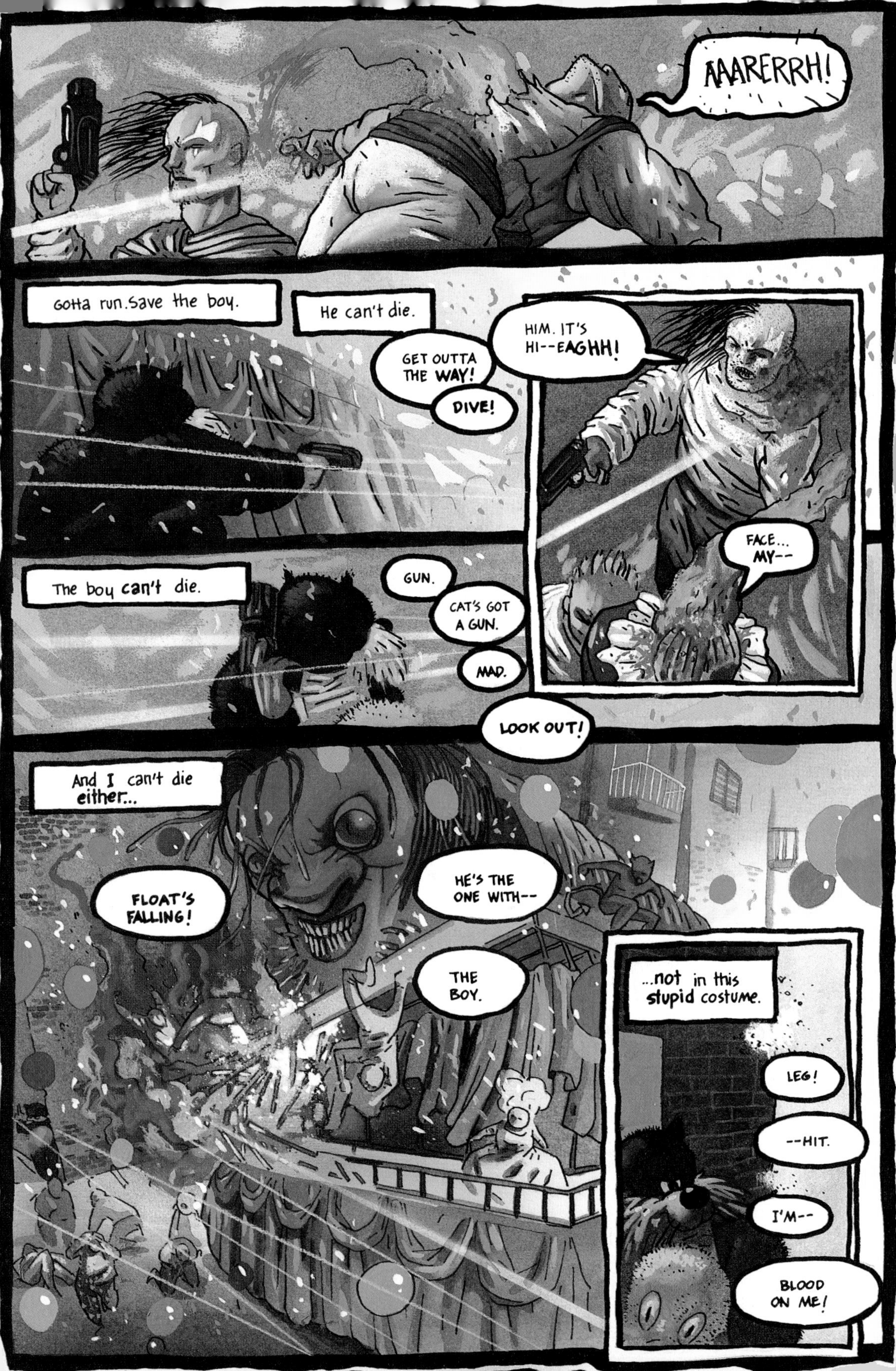
AAARERRH!
Gotta run. Save the boy.
He can't die.
GET OUTTA THE WAY!
DIVE!
HIM. IT'S HI--EAGHH!
The boy can't die.
GUN.
CAT'S GOT A GUN.
MAD.
FACE... MY--
LOOK OUT!
And I can't die either...
FLOAT'S FALLING!
HE'S THE ONE WITH--
THE BOY.
...not in this stupid costume.
LEG!
--HIT.
I'M--
BLOOD ON ME!

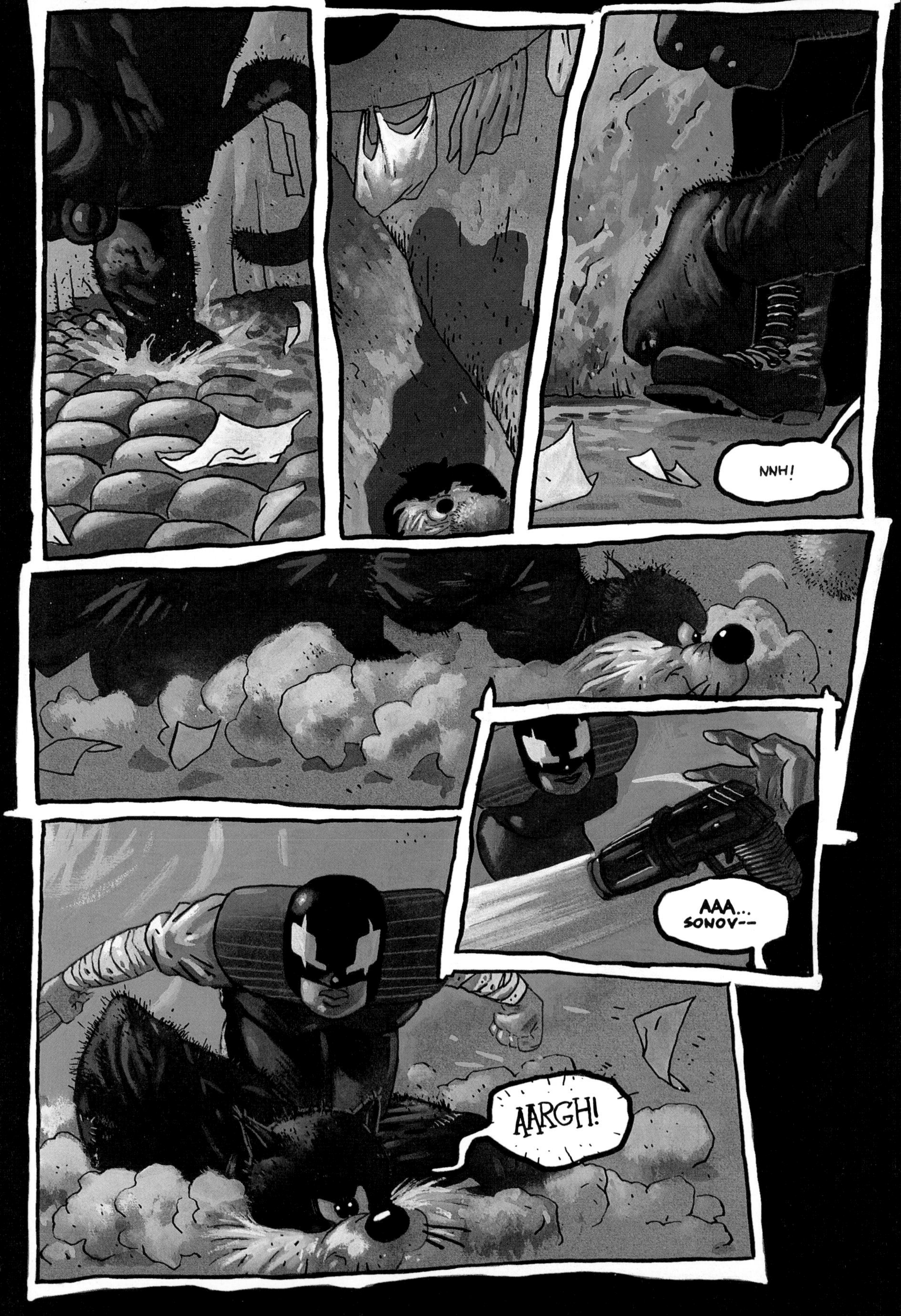
NNH!
AAA... SONOV--
AARGH!

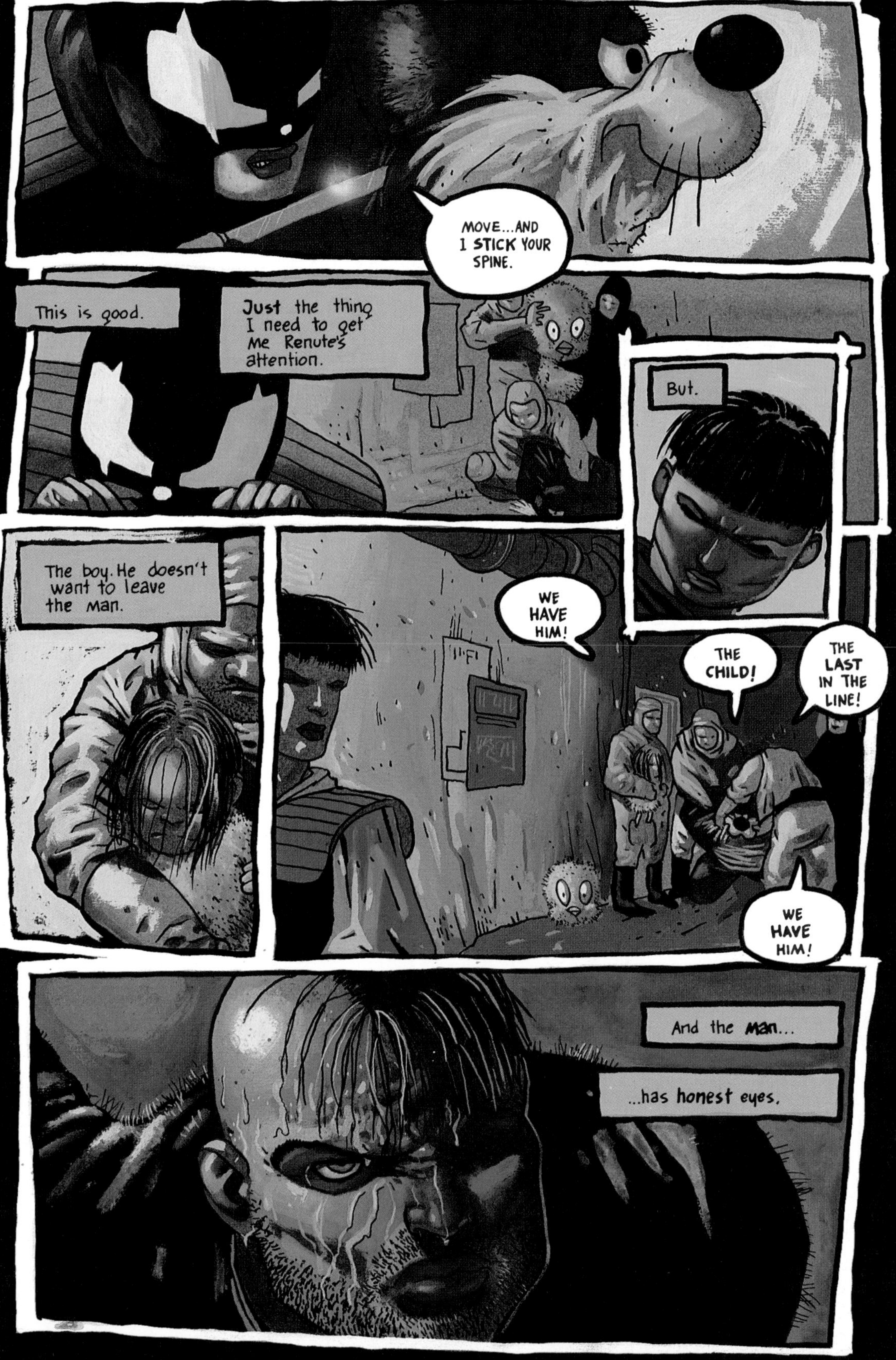
MOVE...AND I STICK YOUR SPINE.
This is good.
Just the thing I need to get Me Renute's attention.
But.
The boy. He doesn't want to leave the man.
WE HAVE HIM!
THE CHILD!
THE LAST IN THE LINE!
WE HAVE HIM!
And the man...
...has honest eyes.

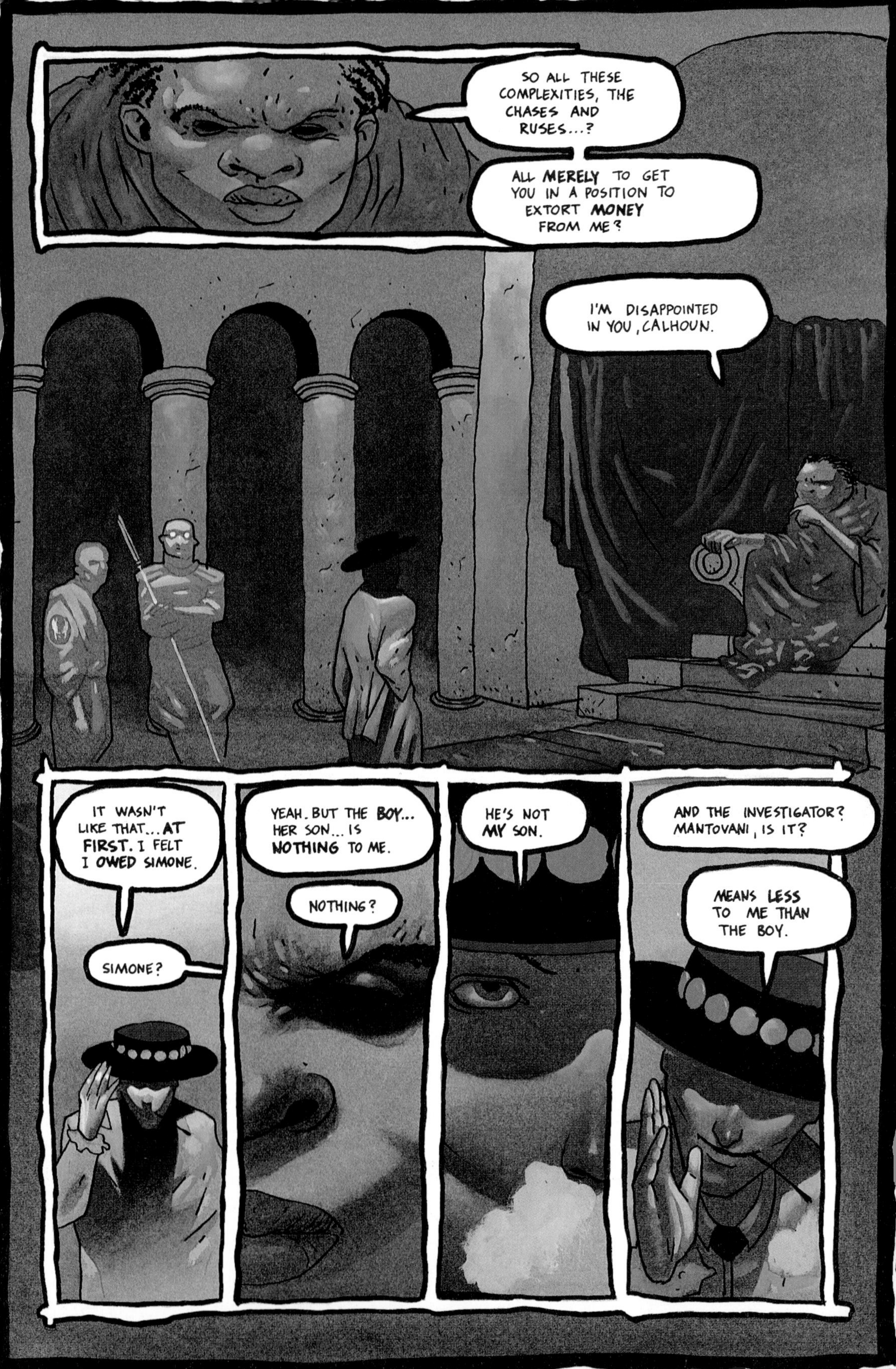
SO ALL THESE COMPLEXITIES, THE CHASES AND RUSES...?
ALL MERELY TO GET YOU IN A POSITION TO EXTORT MONEY FROM ME?
I'M DISAPPOINTED IN YOU, CALHOUN.
IT WASN'T LIKE THAT... AT FIRST. I FELT I OWED SIMONE.
SIMONE?
YEAH. BUT THE BOY... HER SON... IS NOTHING TO ME.
NOTHING?
HE'S NOT MY SON.
AND THE INVESTIGATOR? MANTOVANI, IS IT?
MEANS LESS TO ME THAN THE BOY.

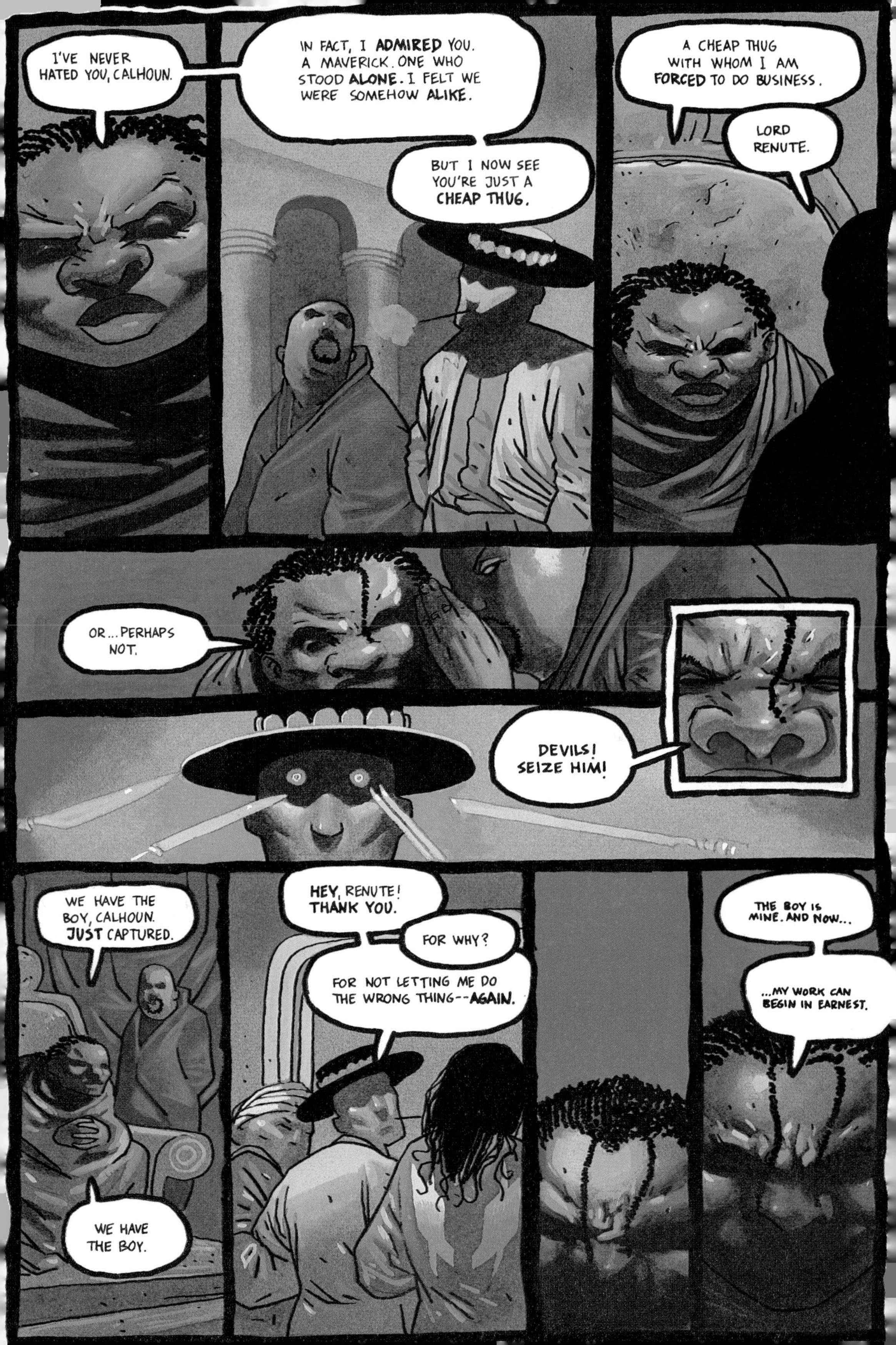
I'VE NEVER HATED YOU, CALHOUN.
IN FACT, I ADMIRED YOU. A MAVERICK. ONE WHO STOOD ALONE. I FELT WE WERE SOMEHOW ALIKE.
BUT I NOW SEE YOU'RE JUST A CHEAP THUG.
A CHEAP THUG WITH WHOM I AM FORCED TO DO BUSINESS.
LORD RENUTE.
OR... PERHAPS NOT.
DEVILS! SEIZE HIM!
WE HAVE THE BOY, CALHOUN. JUST CAPTURED.
WE HAVE THE BOY.
HEY, RENUTE! THANK YOU.
FOR WHY?
FOR NOT LETTING ME DO THE WRONG THING--AGAIN.
THE BOY IS MINE. AND NOW...
...MY WORK CAN BEGIN IN EARNEST.

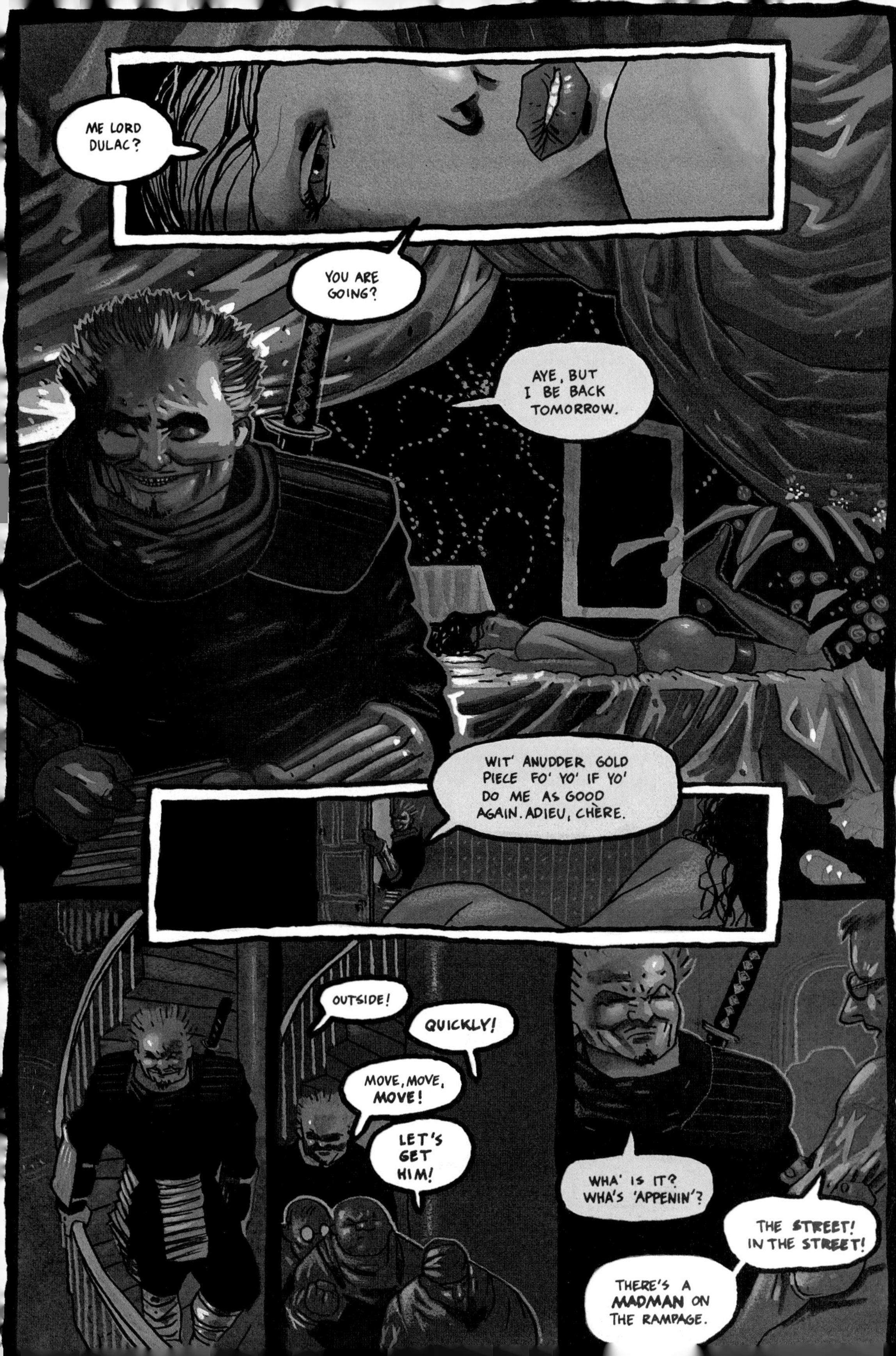

ME LORD DULAC?
YOU ARE GOING?
AYE, BUT I BE BACK TOMORROW.
WIT' ANUDDER GOLD PIECE FO' YO' IF YO' DO ME AS GOOD AGAIN. ADIEU, CHÈRE.
OUTSIDE!
QUICKLY!
MOVE, MOVE, **MOVE**!
LET'S GET HIM!
WHA' IS IT? WHA'S 'APPENIN'?
THE **STREET**! IN THE **STREET**!
THERE'S A **MADMAN** ON THE RAMPAGE.

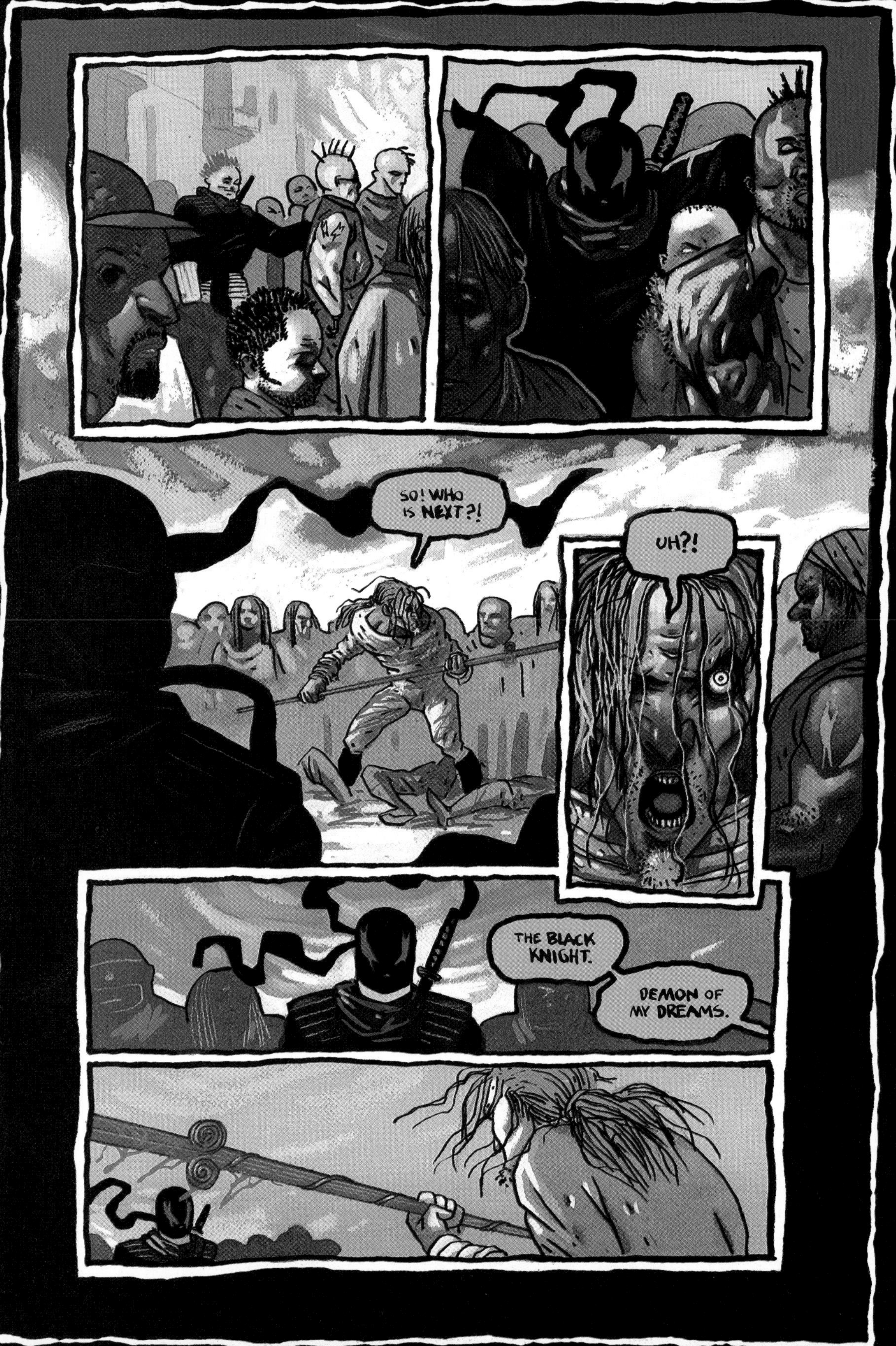
SO! WHO IS NEXT?!
UH?!
THE BLACK KNIGHT.
DEMON OF MY DREAMS.

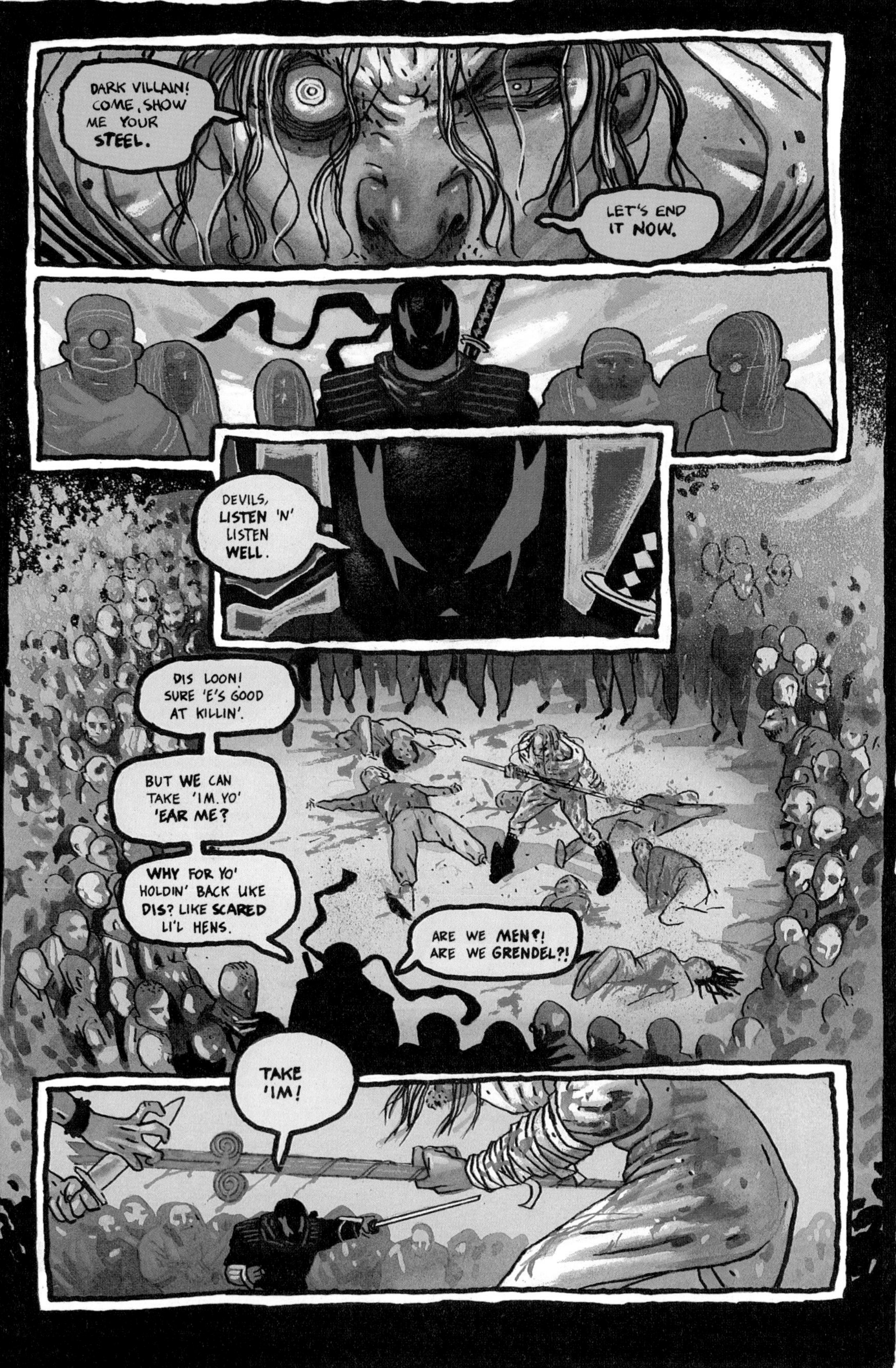
DARK VILLAIN! COME, SHOW ME YOUR STEEL.
LET'S END IT NOW.
DEVILS, LISTEN 'N' LISTEN WELL.
DIS LOON! SURE 'E'S GOOD AT KILLIN'.
BUT WE CAN TAKE 'IM. YO' 'EAR ME?
WHY FOR YO' HOLDIN' BACK LIKE DIS? LIKE SCARED LI'L HENS.
ARE WE MEN?! ARE WE GRENDEL?!
TAKE 'IM!

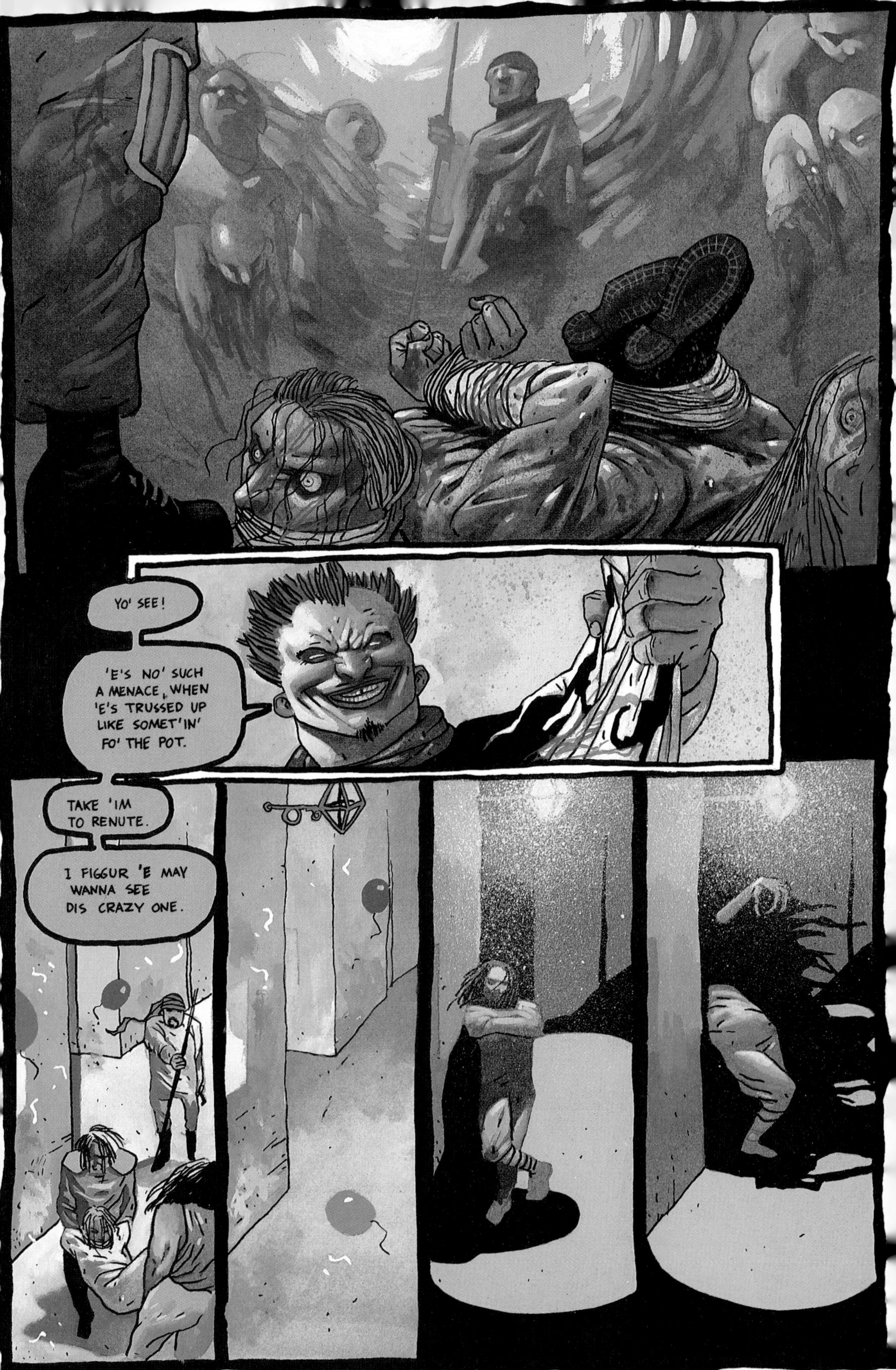
YO' SEE!
'E'S NO' SUCH A MENACE, WHEN 'E'S TRUSSED UP LIKE SOMET'IN' FO' THE POT.
TAKE 'IM TO RENUTE.
I FIGGUR 'E MAY WANNA SEE DIS CRAZY ONE.

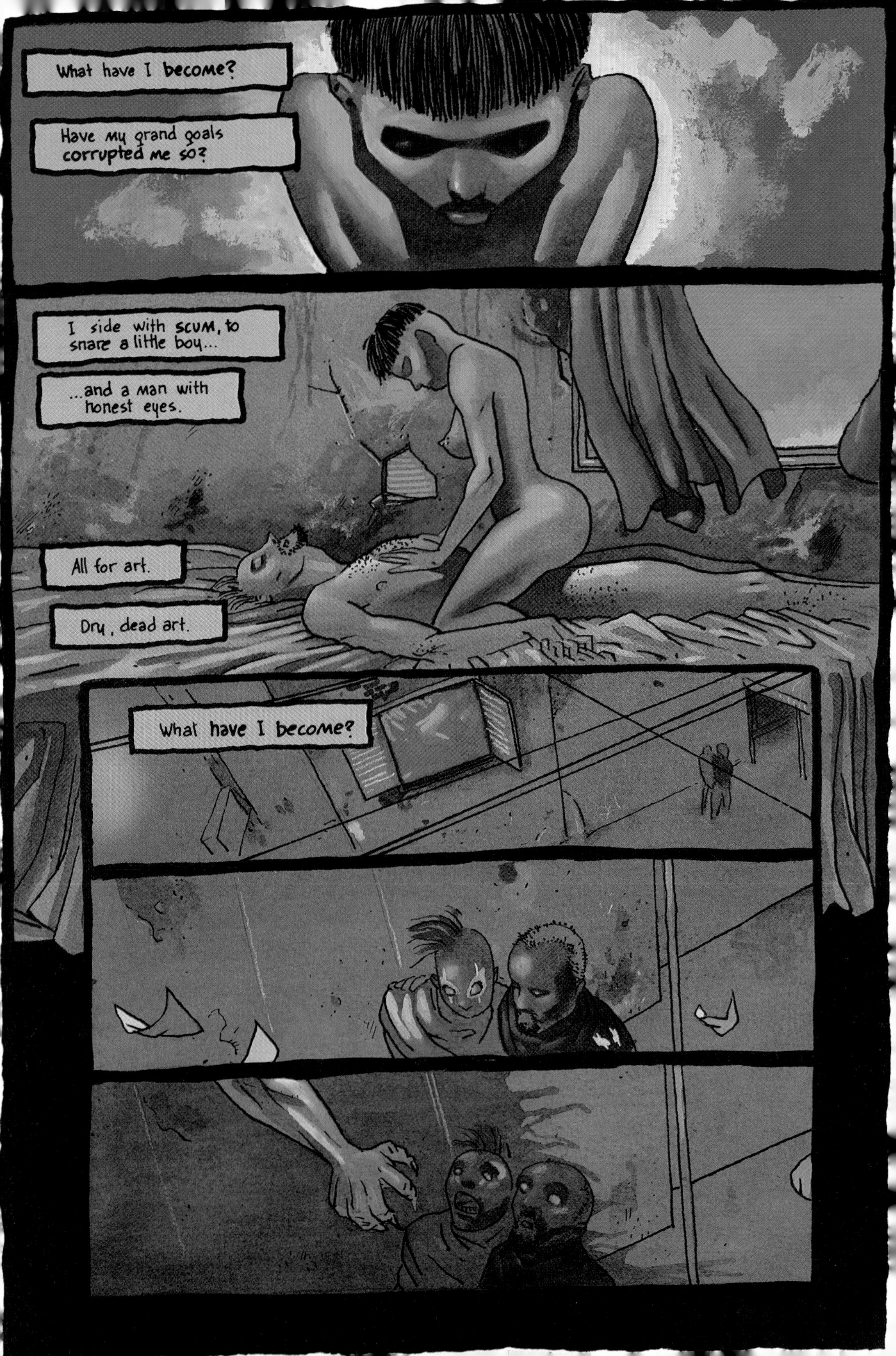
What have I become?
Have my grand goals corrupted me so?
I side with scum, to snare a little boy...
...and a man with honest eyes.
All for art.
Dry, dead art.
What have I become?

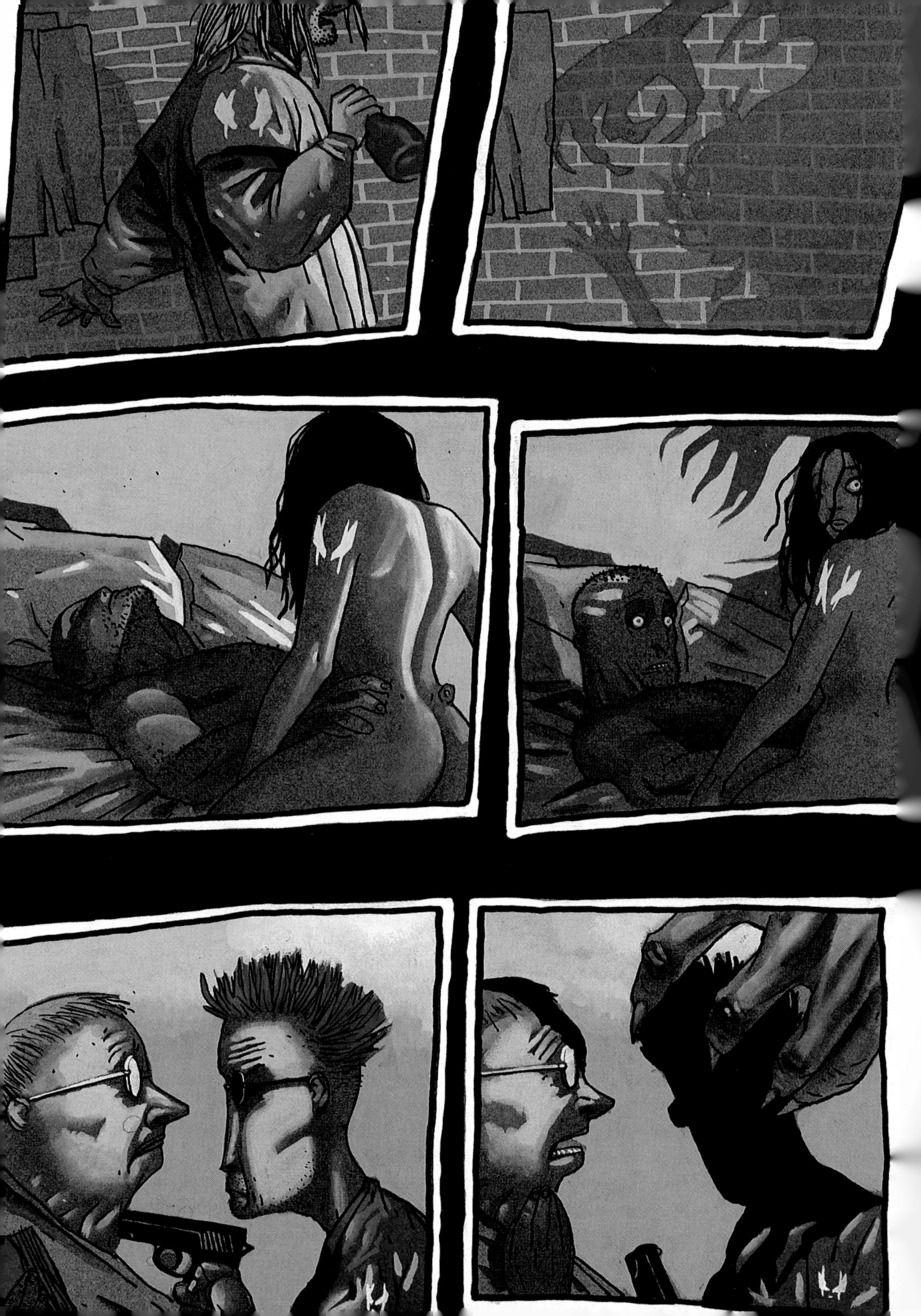

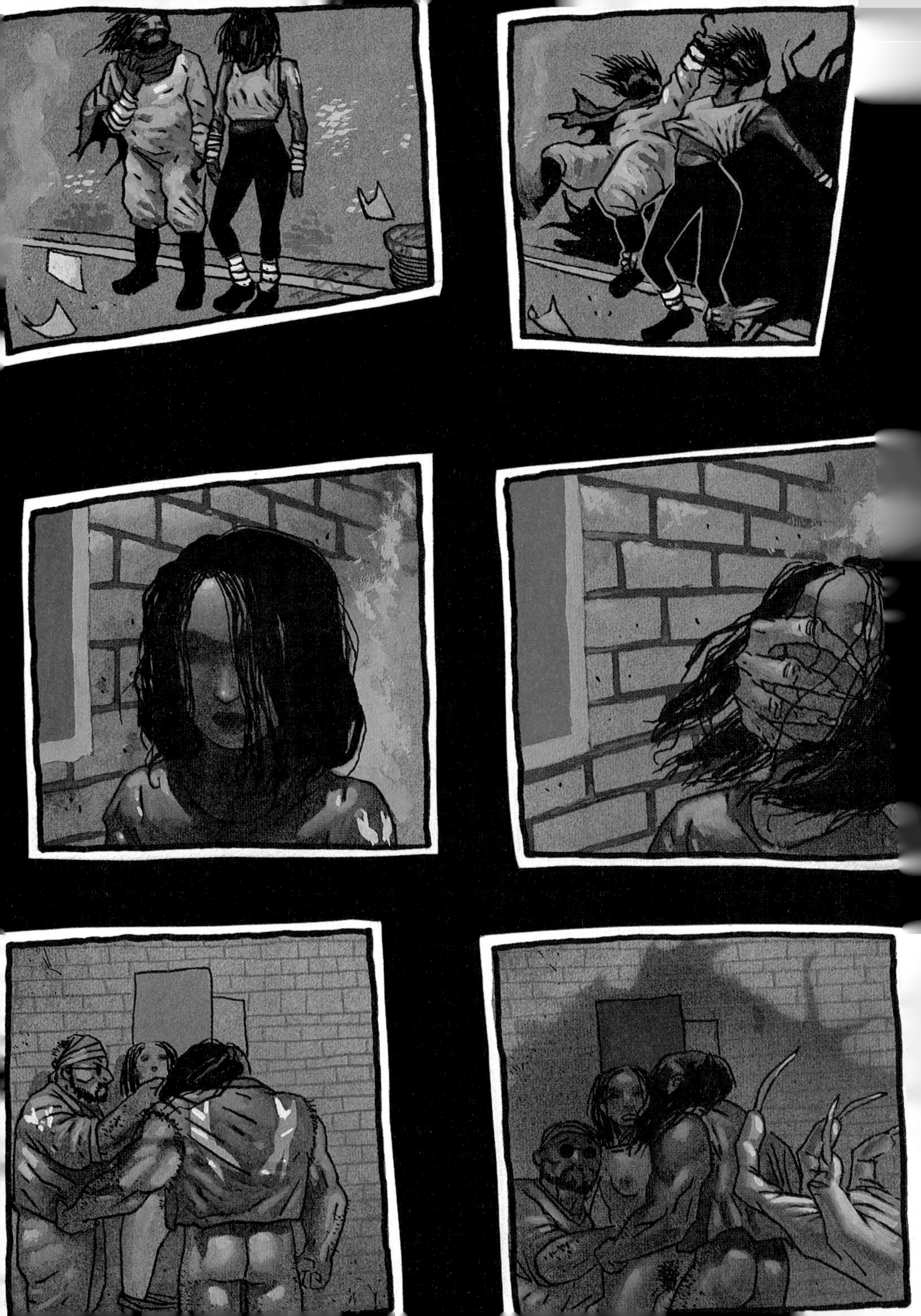

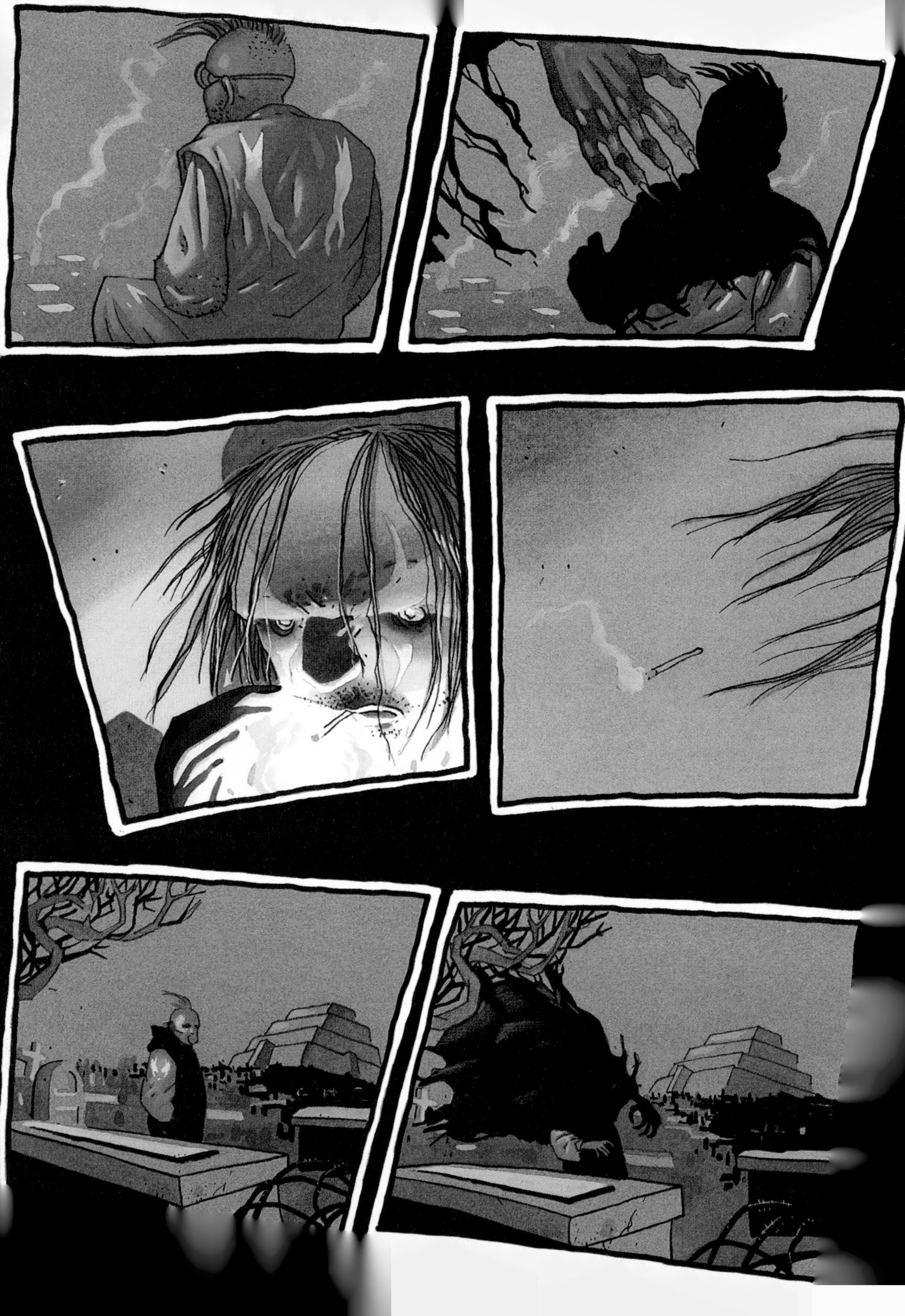

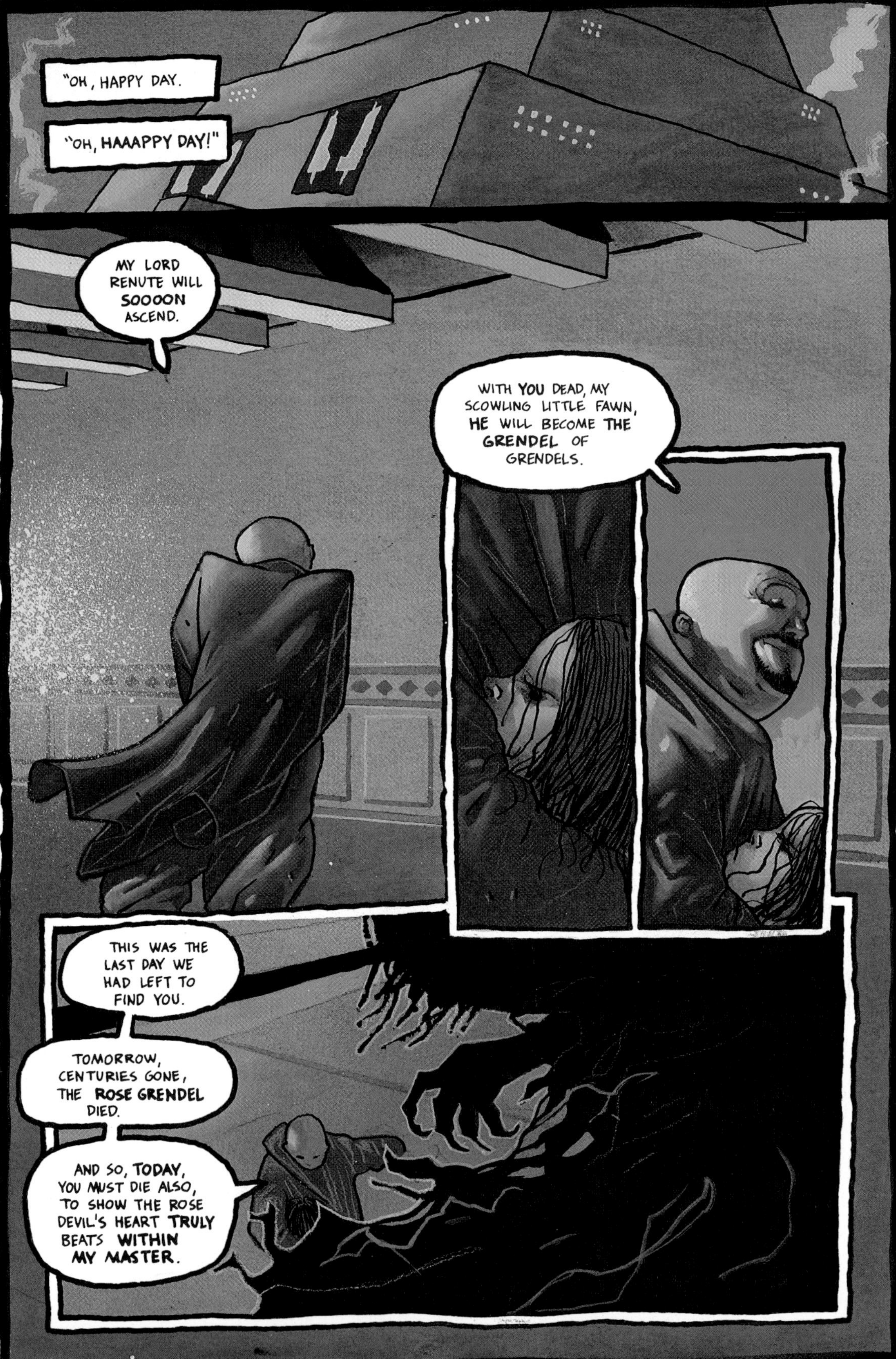
"OH, HAPPY DAY.
"OH, HAAAPPY DAY!"
MY LORD RENUTE WILL SOOOON ASCEND.
WITH YOU DEAD, MY SCOWLING LITTLE FAWN, HE WILL BECOME THE GRENDEL OF GRENDELS.
THIS WAS THE LAST DAY WE HAD LEFT TO FIND YOU.
TOMORROW, CENTURIES GONE, THE ROSE GRENDEL DIED.
AND SO, TODAY, YOU MUST DIE ALSO, TO SHOW THE ROSE DEVIL'S HEART TRULY BEATS WITHIN MY MASTER.

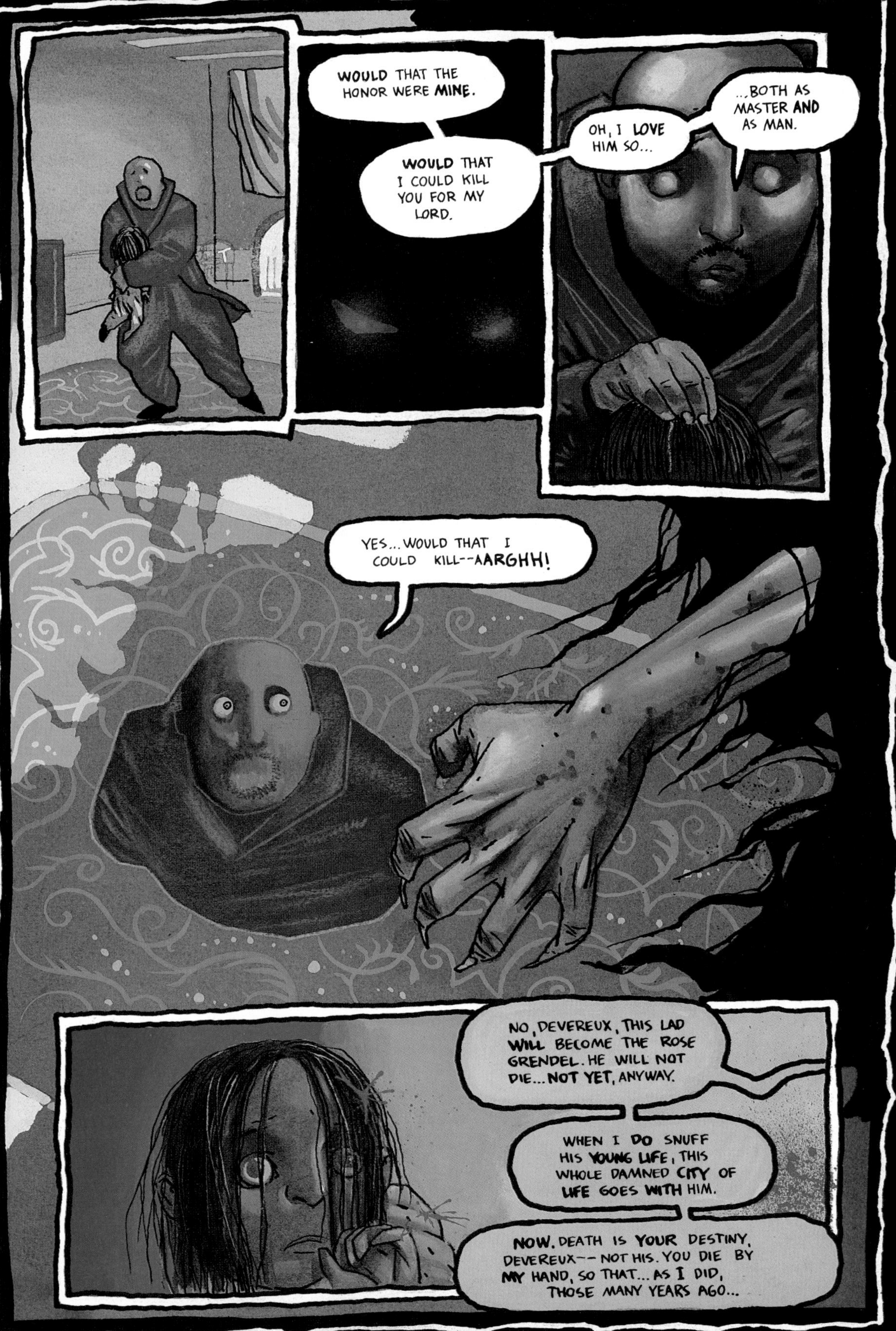

WOULD THAT THE HONOR WERE MINE.
WOULD THAT I COULD KILL YOU FOR MY LORD.
OH, I LOVE HIM SO...
...BOTH AS MASTER AND AS MAN.
YES... WOULD THAT I COULD KILL--AARGHH!
NO, DEVEREUX, THIS LAD WILL BECOME THE ROSE GRENDEL. HE WILL NOT DIE... NOT YET, ANYWAY.
WHEN I DO SNUFF HIS YOUNG LIFE, THIS WHOLE DAMNED CITY OF LIFE GOES WITH HIM.
NOW. DEATH IS YOUR DESTINY, DEVEREUX-- NOT HIS. YOU DIE BY MY HAND, SO THAT... AS I DID, THOSE MANY YEARS AGO...

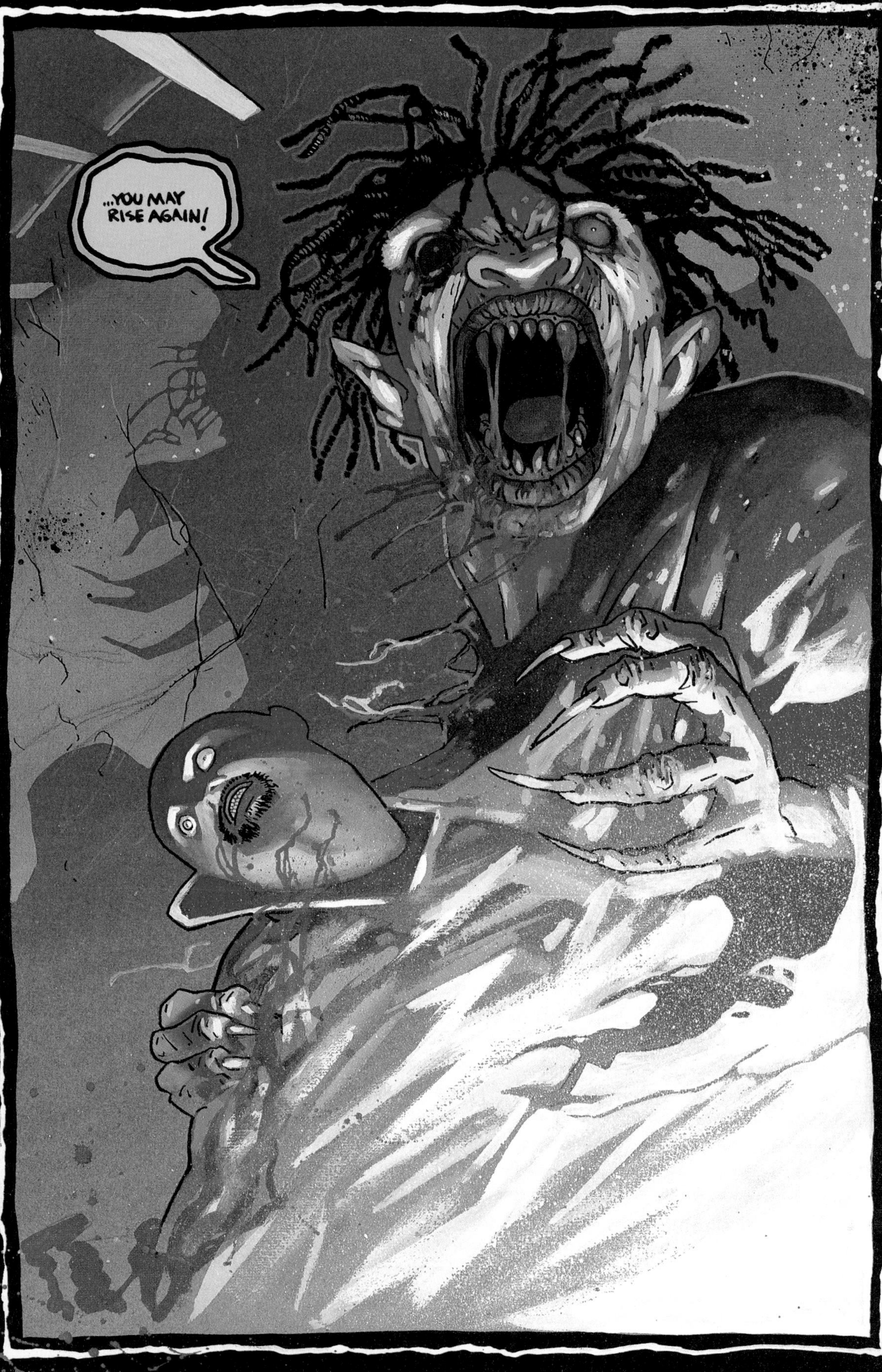
...YOU MAY RISE AGAIN!

CHAPTER SIX

FOUR FATES, ONE FINALE

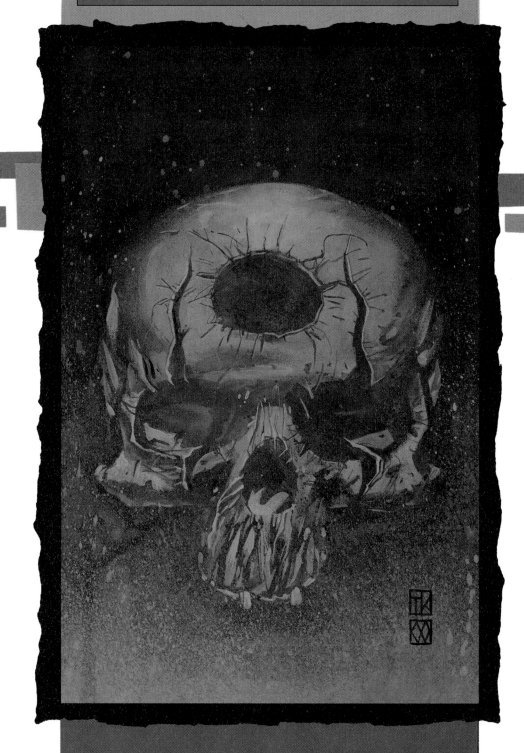

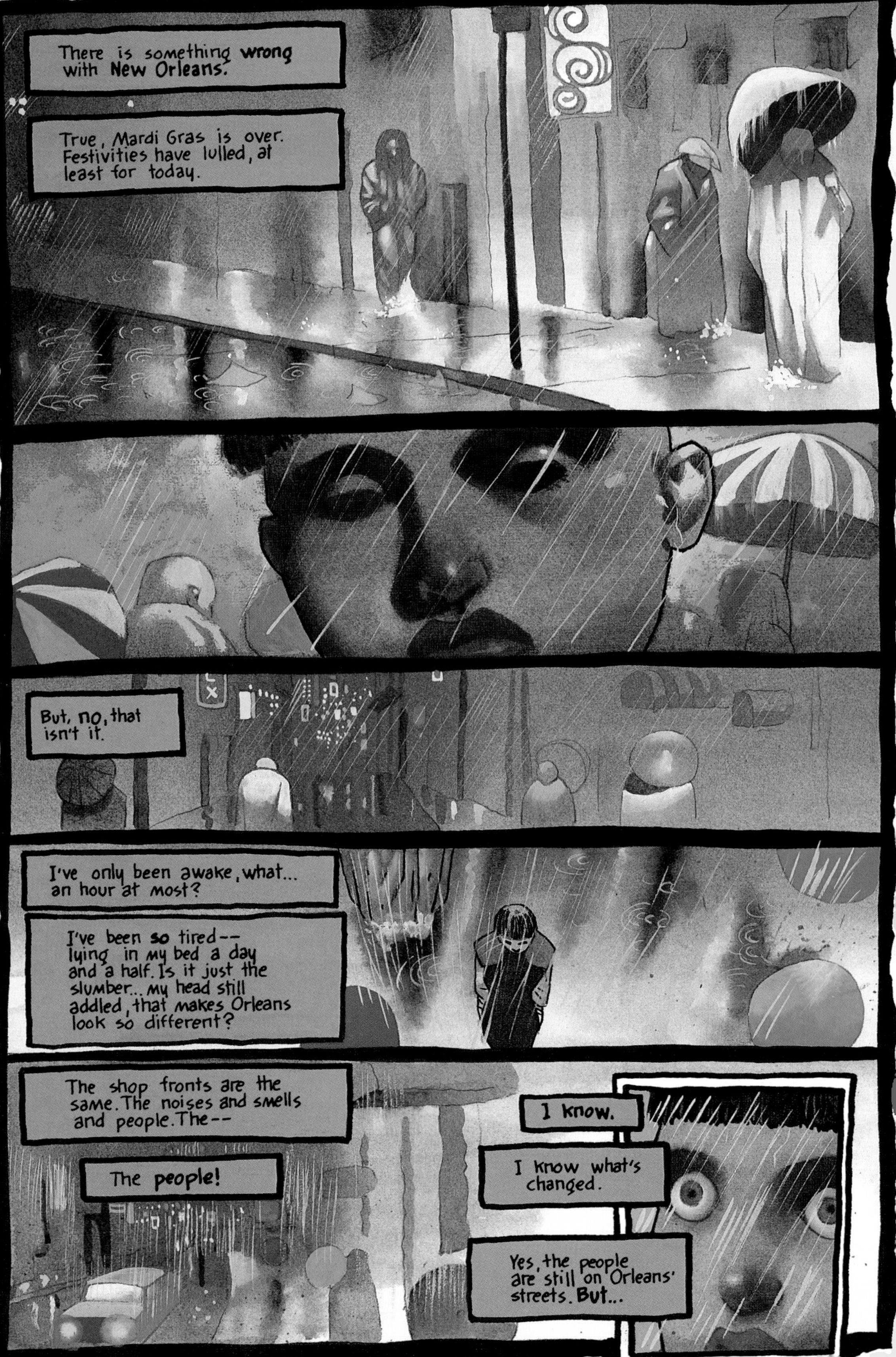

There is something wrong with New Orleans.
True, Mardi Gras is over. Festivities have lulled, at least for today.
But, no, that isn't it.
I've only been awake, what... an hour at most?
I've been so tired-- lying in my bed a day and a half. Is it just the slumber... my head still addled, that makes Orleans look so different?
The shop fronts are the same. The noises and smells and people. The--
The people!
I know.
I know what's changed.
Yes, the people are still on Orleans' streets. But...

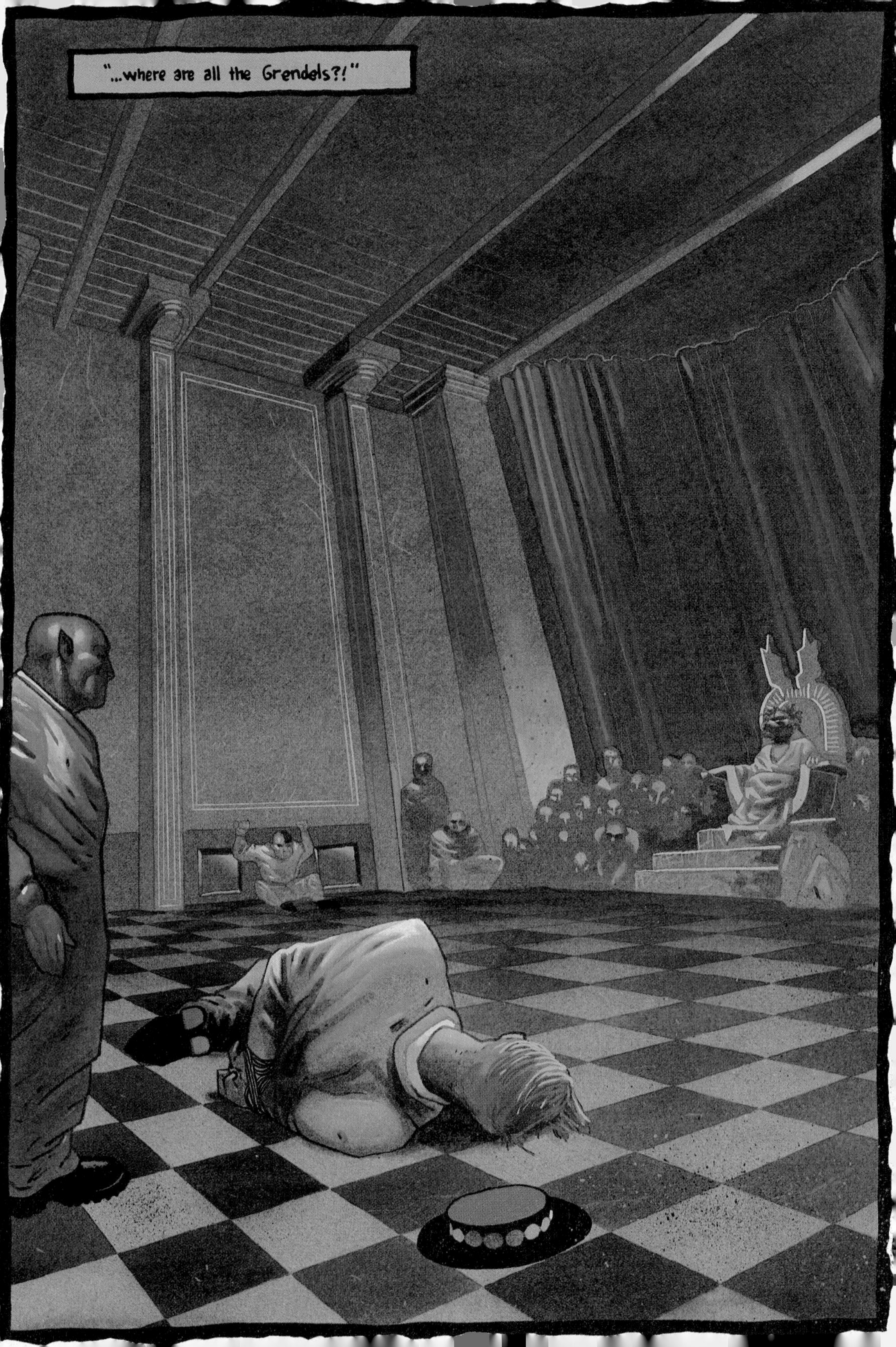
"...where are all the Grendels?!"

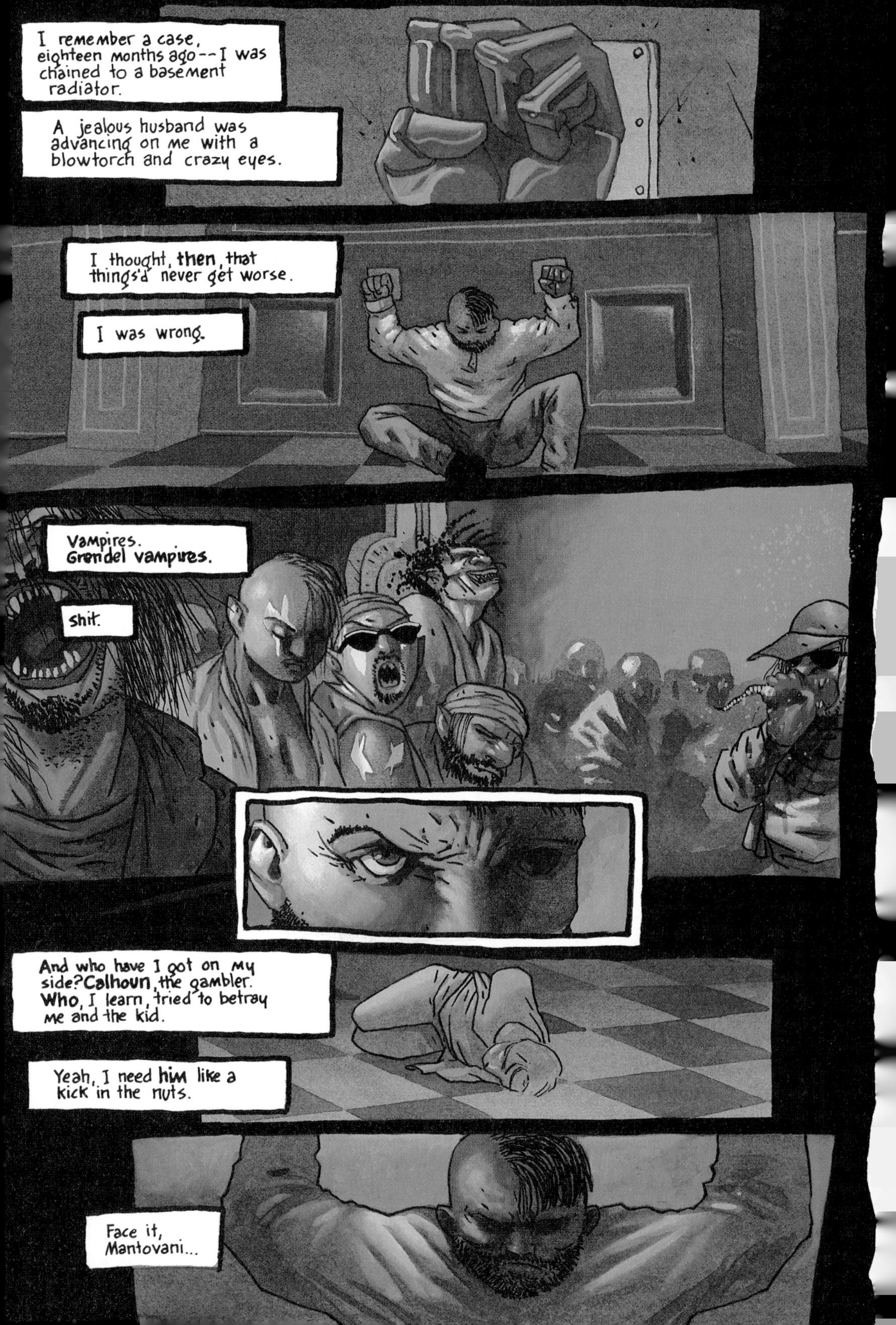
I remember a case, eighteen months ago--I was chained to a basement radiator.
A jealous husband was advancing on me with a blowtorch and crazy eyes.
I thought, **then**, that things'd never get worse.
I was wrong.
Vampires. **Grendel vampires.**
shit.
And who have I got on my side? **Calhoun**, the gambler. **Who**, I learn, tried to betray me and the kid.
Yeah, I need **him** like a kick in the nuts.
Face it, Mantovani...

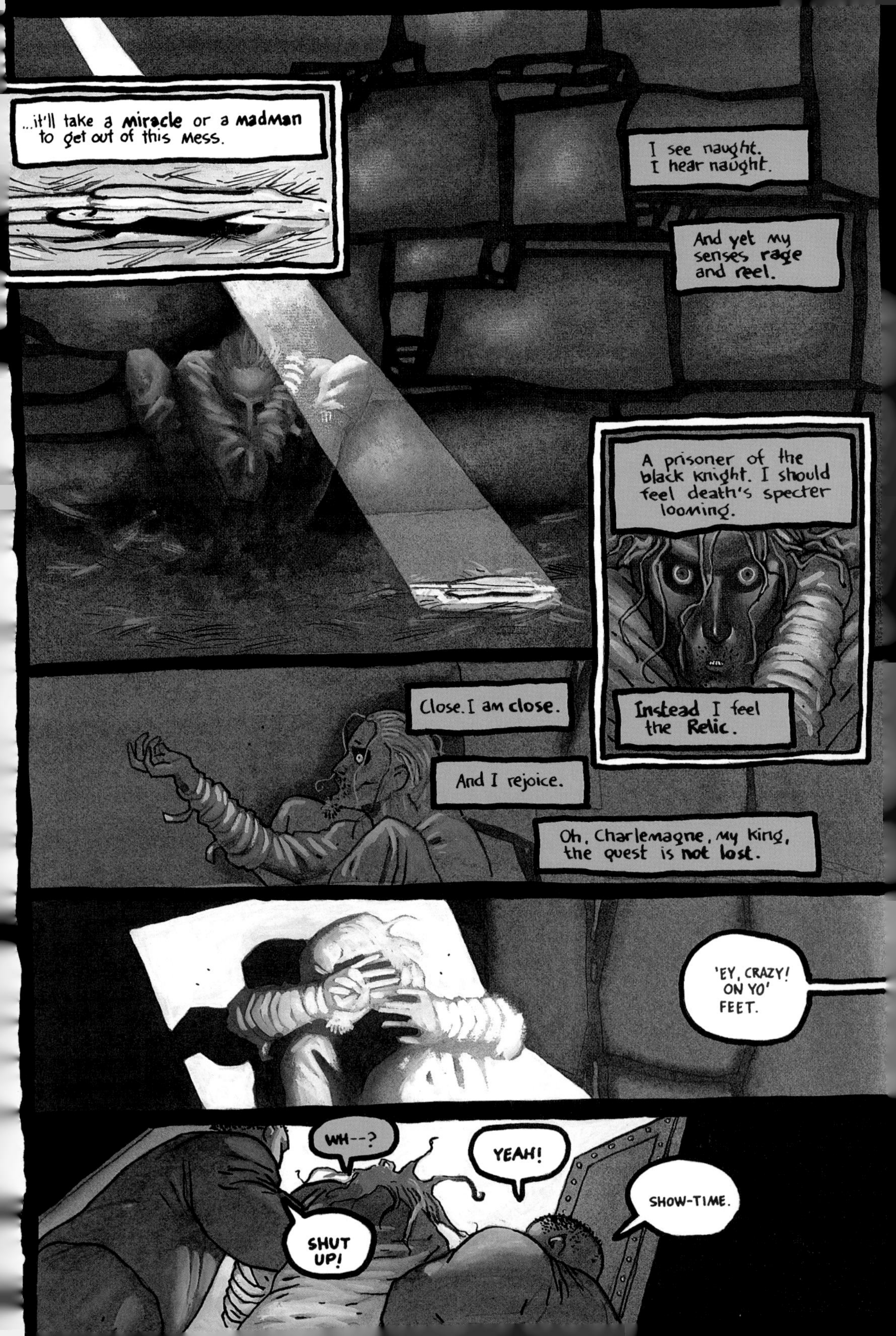

...it'll take a miracle or a madman to get out of this mess.
I see naught. I hear naught.
And yet my senses rage and reel.
A prisoner of the black knight. I should feel death's specter looming.
Instead I feel the Relic.
Close. I am close.
And I rejoice.
Oh, Charlemagne, my king, the quest is not lost.
'EY, CRAZY! ON YO' FEET.
WH--?
SHUT UP!
YEAH!
SHOW-TIME.

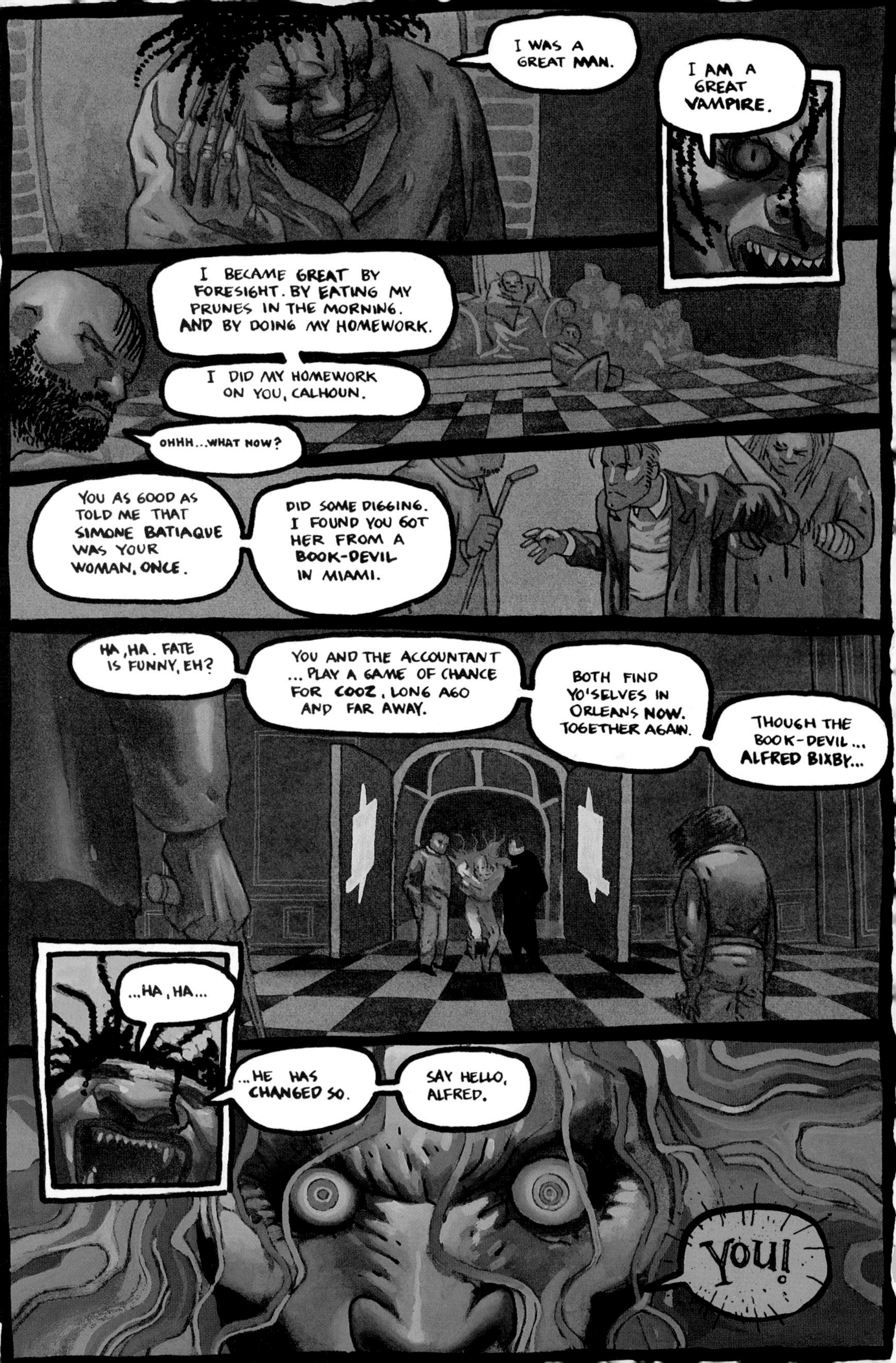

I WAS A GREAT MAN.
I AM A GREAT VAMPIRE.
I BECAME GREAT BY FORESIGHT. BY EATING MY PRUNES IN THE MORNING. AND BY DOING MY HOMEWORK.
I DID MY HOMEWORK ON YOU, CALHOUN.
OHHH...WHAT NOW?
YOU AS GOOD AS TOLD ME THAT SIMONE BATIAQUE WAS YOUR WOMAN, ONCE.
DID SOME DIGGING. I FOUND YOU GOT HER FROM A BOOK-DEVIL IN MIAMI.
HA, HA. FATE IS FUNNY, EH?
YOU AND THE ACCOUNTANT ...PLAY A GAME OF CHANCE FOR COOZ, LONG AGO AND FAR AWAY.
BOTH FIND YO'SELVES IN ORLEANS NOW. TOGETHER AGAIN.
THOUGH THE BOOK-DEVIL... ALFRED BIXBY...
...HA, HA...
...HE HAS CHANGED SO.
SAY HELLO, ALFRED.
YOU!

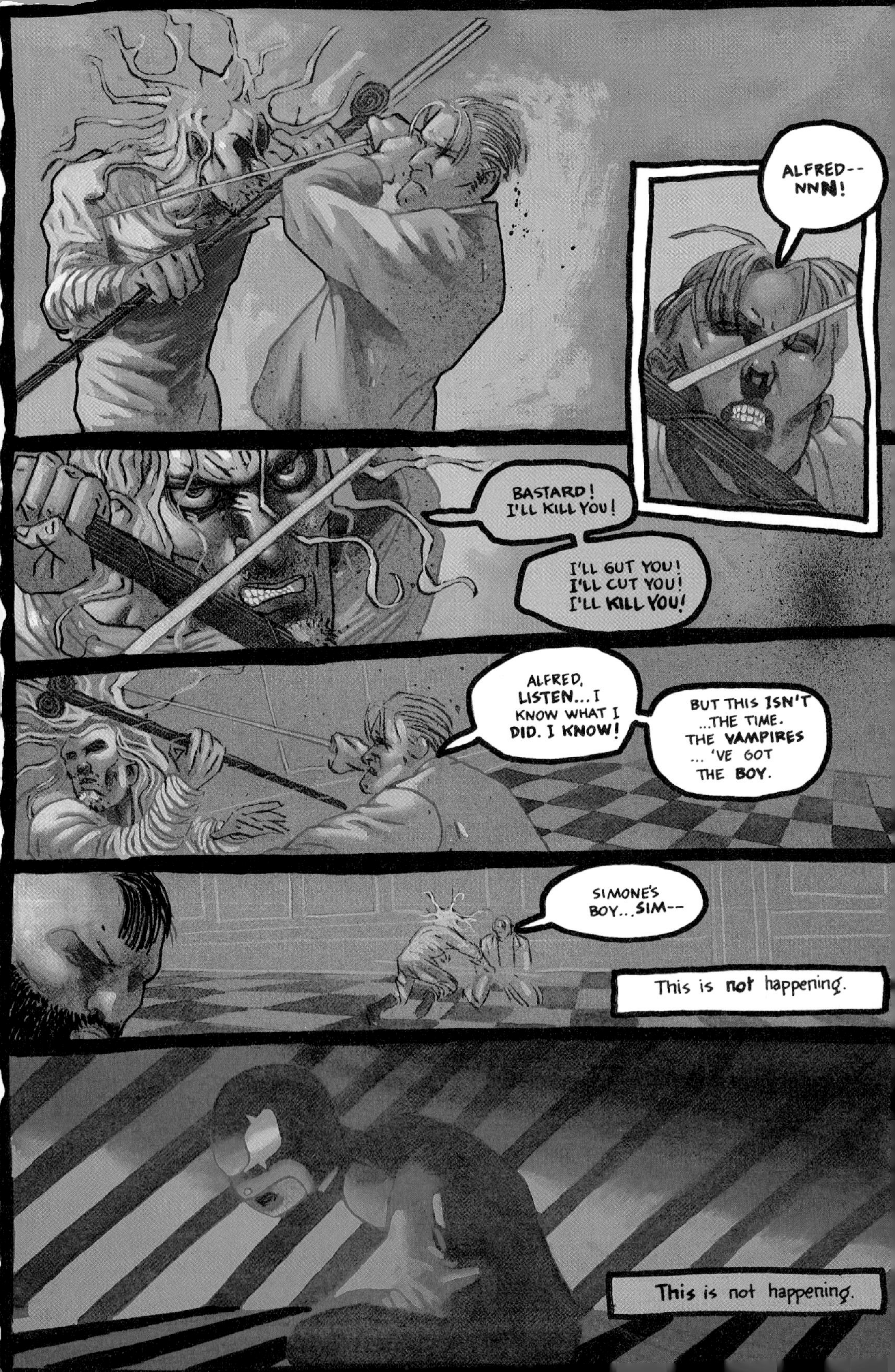
ALFRED--
NNN!
BASTARD! I'LL KILL YOU!
I'LL GUT YOU! I'LL CUT YOU! I'LL KILL YOU!
ALFRED, LISTEN... I KNOW WHAT I DID. I KNOW!
BUT THIS ISN'T ...THE TIME. THE VAMPIRES ... 'VE GOT THE BOY.
SIMONE'S BOY... SIM--
This is not happening.
This is not happening.

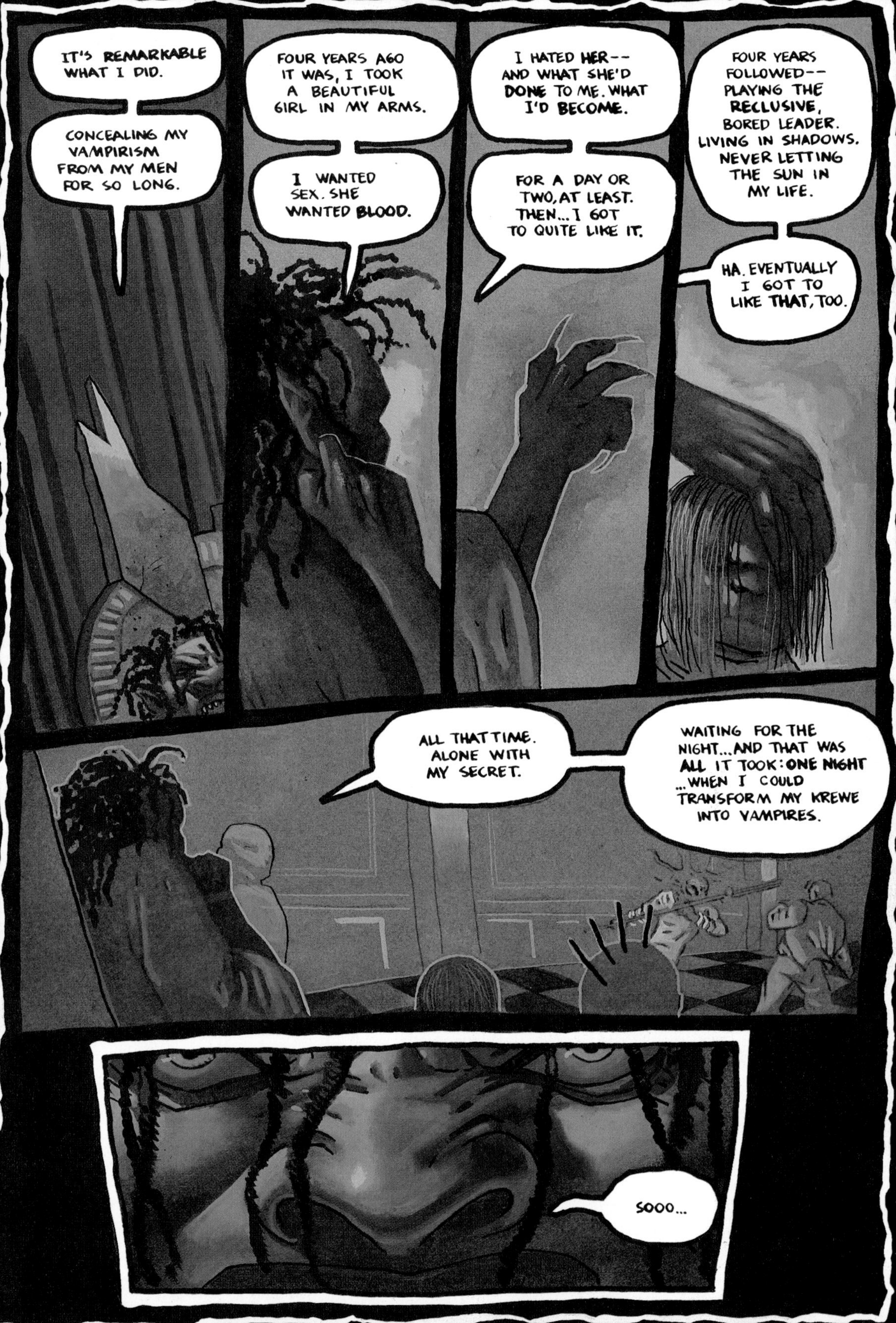

IT'S REMARKABLE WHAT I DID.
CONCEALING MY VAMPIRISM FROM MY MEN FOR SO LONG.
FOUR YEARS AGO IT WAS, I TOOK A BEAUTIFUL GIRL IN MY ARMS.
I WANTED SEX. SHE WANTED BLOOD.
I HATED HER-- AND WHAT SHE'D DONE TO ME. WHAT I'D BECOME.
FOR A DAY OR TWO, AT LEAST. THEN... I GOT TO QUITE LIKE IT.
FOUR YEARS FOLLOWED-- PLAYING THE RECLUSIVE, BORED LEADER. LIVING IN SHADOWS. NEVER LETTING THE SUN IN MY LIFE.
HA. EVENTUALLY I GOT TO LIKE THAT, TOO.
ALL THAT TIME. ALONE WITH MY SECRET.
WAITING FOR THE NIGHT... AND THAT WAS ALL IT TOOK: ONE NIGHT ...WHEN I COULD TRANSFORM MY KREWE INTO VAMPIRES.
SOOO...

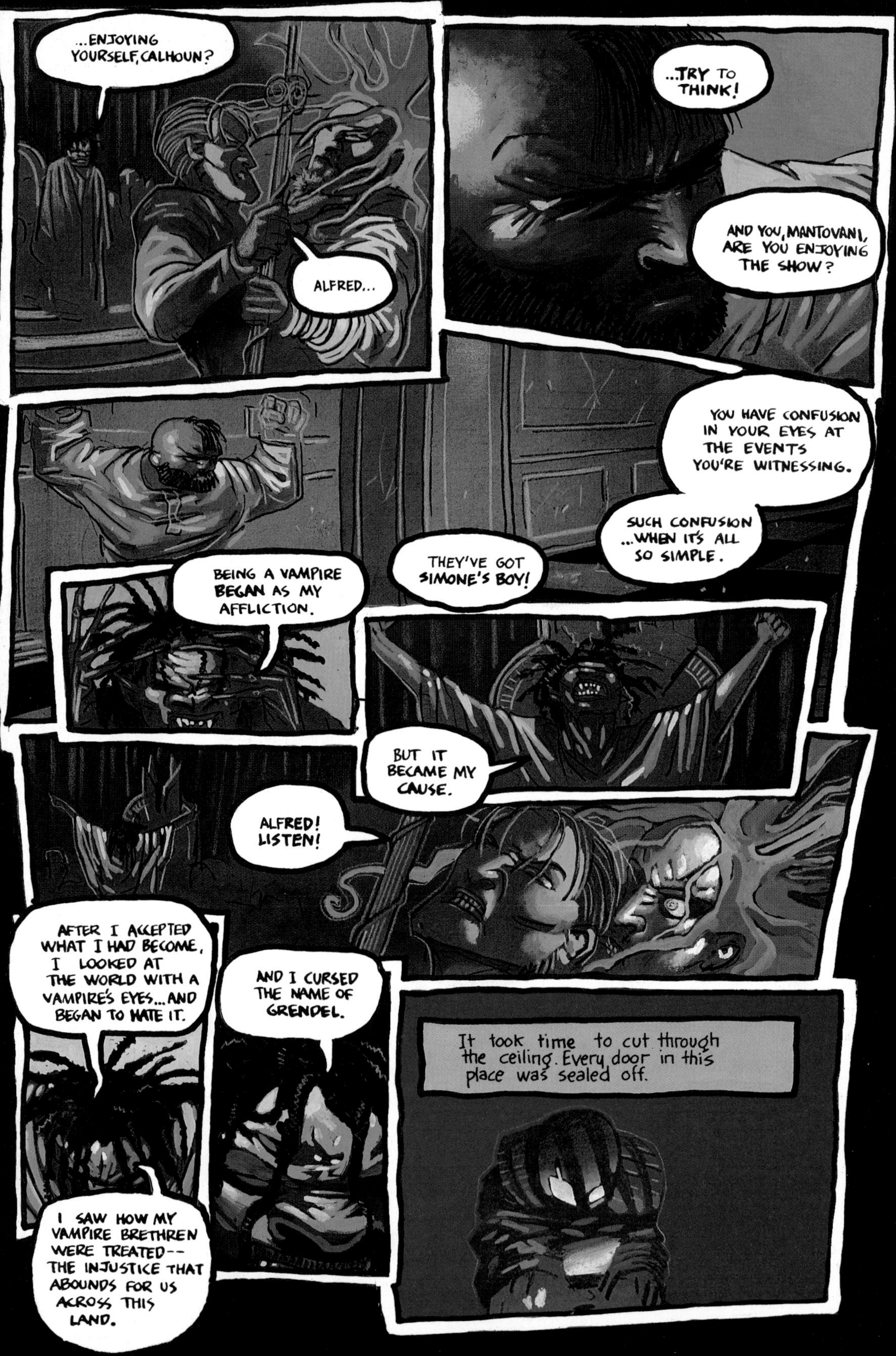
...ENJOYING YOURSELF, CALHOUN?
ALFRED...
...TRY TO THINK!
AND YOU, MANTOVANI, ARE YOU ENJOYING THE SHOW?
YOU HAVE CONFUSION IN YOUR EYES AT THE EVENTS YOU'RE WITNESSING.
SUCH CONFUSION ...WHEN IT'S ALL SO SIMPLE.
THEY'VE GOT SIMONE'S BOY!
BEING A VAMPIRE BEGAN AS MY AFFLICTION.
BUT IT BECAME MY CAUSE.
ALFRED! LISTEN!
AFTER I ACCEPTED WHAT I HAD BECOME, I LOOKED AT THE WORLD WITH A VAMPIRE'S EYES... AND BEGAN TO HATE IT.
I SAW HOW MY VAMPIRE BRETHREN WERE TREATED-- THE INJUSTICE THAT ABOUNDS FOR US ACROSS THIS LAND.
AND I CURSED THE NAME OF GRENDEL.
It took time to cut through the ceiling. Every door in this place was sealed off.

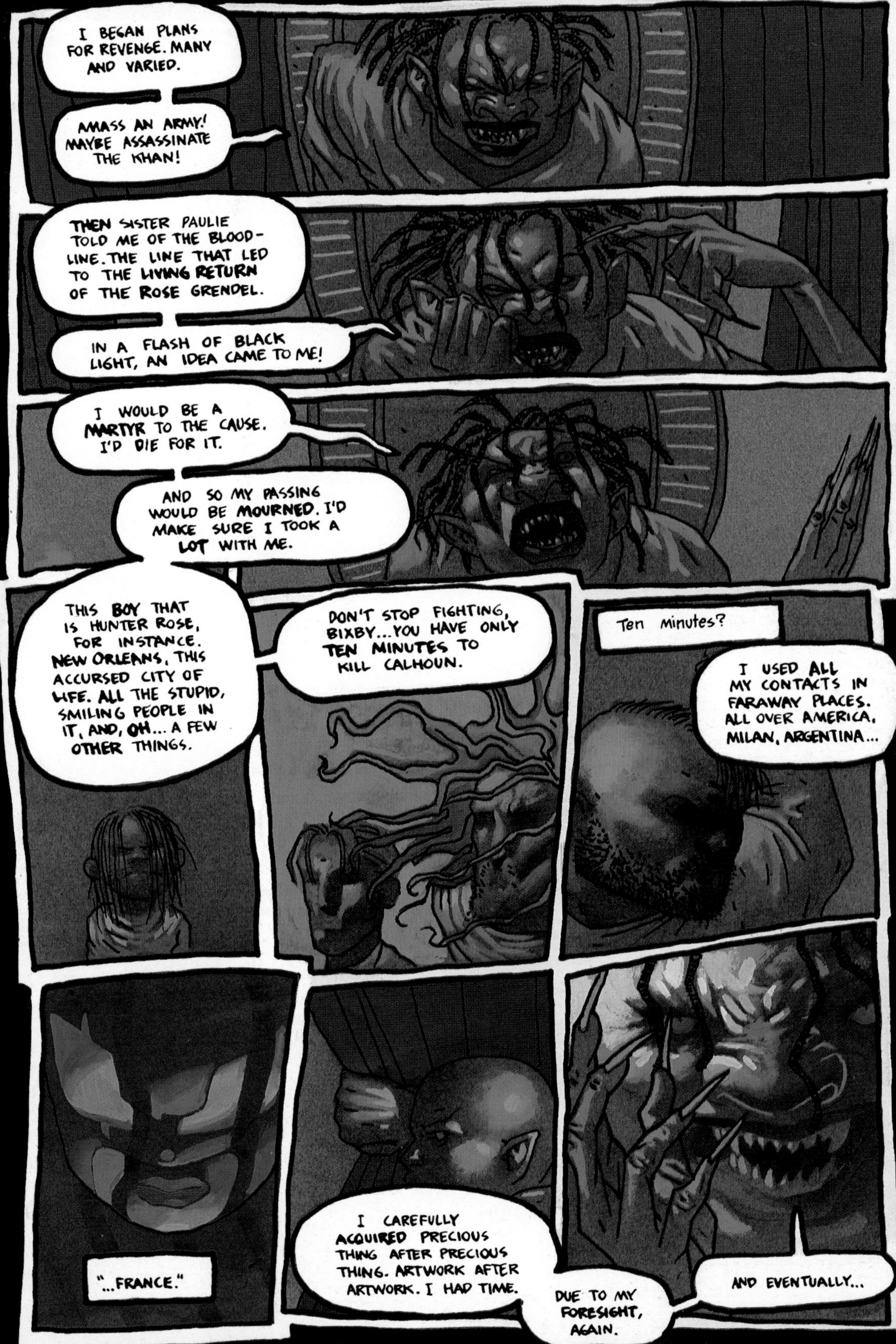
I BEGAN PLANS FOR REVENGE. MANY AND VARIED.
AMASS AN ARMY! MAYBE ASSASSINATE THE KHAN!
THEN SISTER PAULIE TOLD ME OF THE BLOOD-LINE. THE LINE THAT LED TO THE LIVING RETURN OF THE ROSE GRENDEL.
IN A FLASH OF BLACK LIGHT, AN IDEA CAME TO ME!
I WOULD BE A MARTYR TO THE CAUSE. I'D DIE FOR IT.
AND SO MY PASSING WOULD BE MOURNED. I'D MAKE SURE I TOOK A LOT WITH ME.
THIS BOY THAT IS HUNTER ROSE, FOR INSTANCE. NEW ORLEANS, THIS ACCURSED CITY OF LIFE. ALL THE STUPID, SMILING PEOPLE IN IT, AND, OH... A FEW OTHER THINGS.
DON'T STOP FIGHTING, BIXBY... YOU HAVE ONLY TEN MINUTES TO KILL CALHOUN.
Ten minutes?
I USED ALL MY CONTACTS IN FARAWAY PLACES. ALL OVER AMERICA, MILAN, ARGENTINA...
"...FRANCE."
I CAREFULLY ACQUIRED PRECIOUS THING AFTER PRECIOUS THING. ARTWORK AFTER ARTWORK. I HAD TIME.
DUE TO MY FORESIGHT, AGAIN.
AND EVENTUALLY...

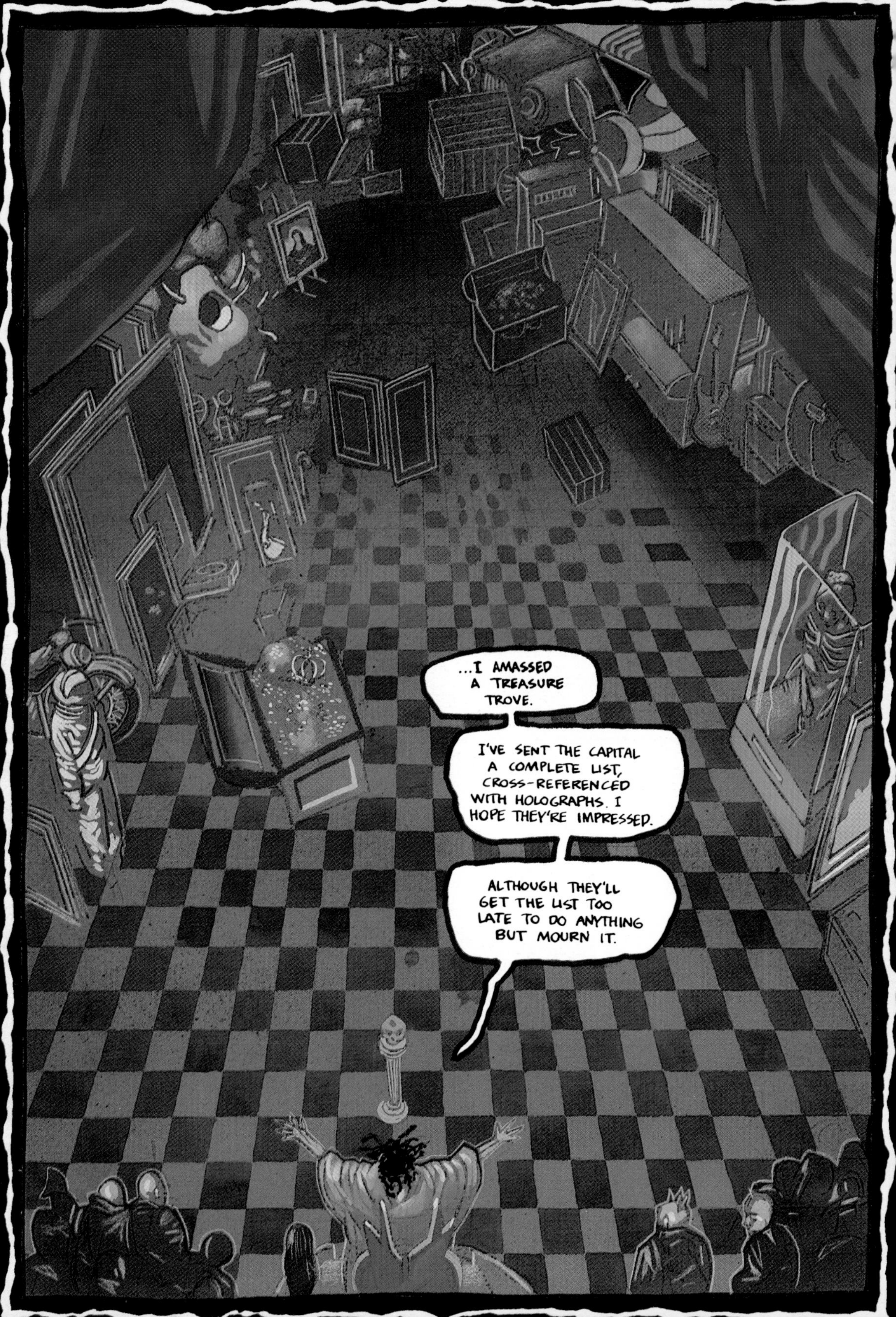
...I AMASSED A TREASURE TROVE.
I'VE SENT THE CAPITAL A COMPLETE LIST, CROSS-REFERENCED WITH HOLOGRAPHS. I HOPE THEY'RE IMPRESSED.
ALTHOUGH THEY'LL GET THE LIST TOO LATE TO DO ANYTHING BUT MOURN IT.

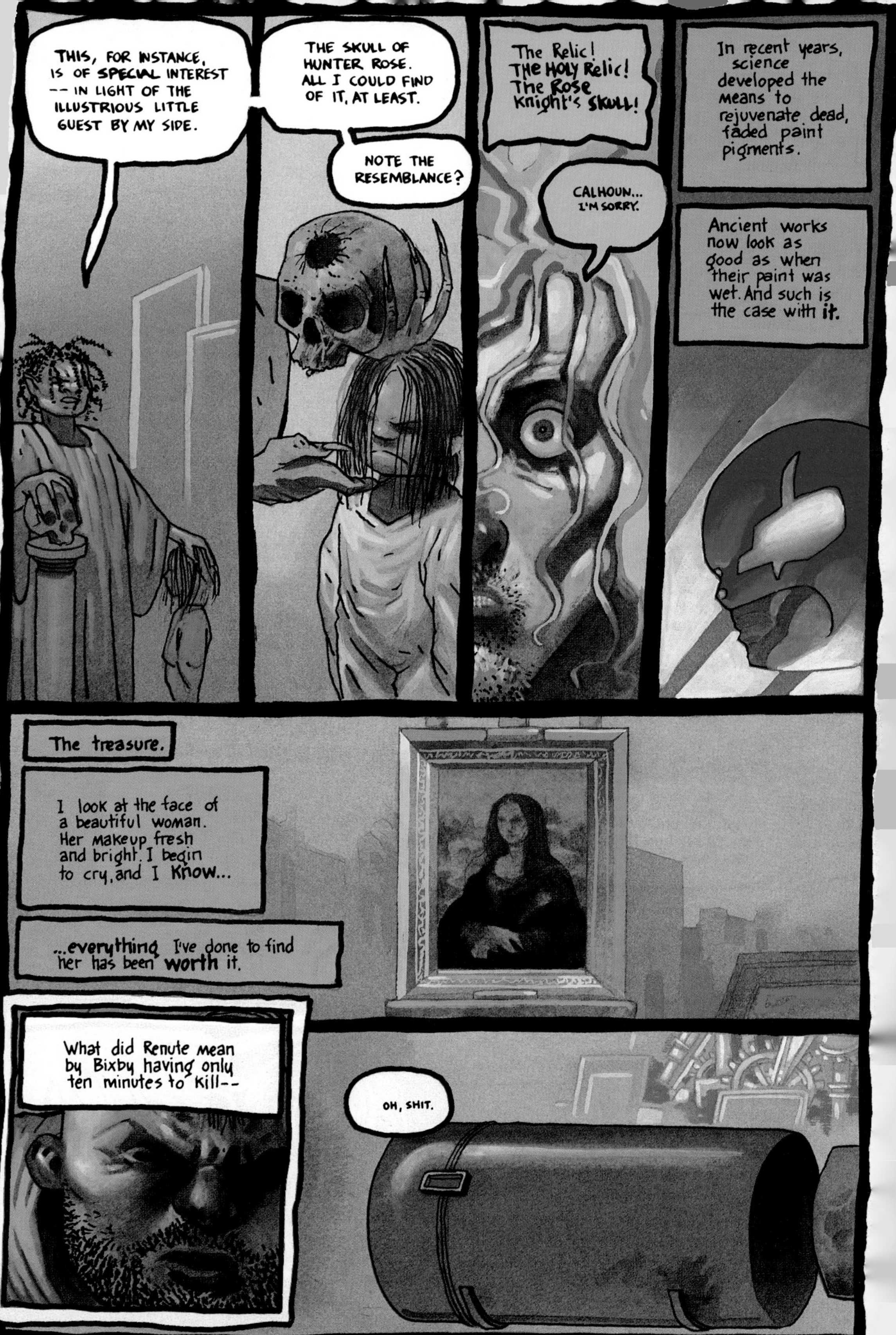
THIS, FOR INSTANCE, IS OF SPECIAL INTEREST -- IN LIGHT OF THE ILLUSTRIOUS LITTLE GUEST BY MY SIDE.
THE SKULL OF HUNTER ROSE. ALL I COULD FIND OF IT, AT LEAST.
NOTE THE RESEMBLANCE?
The Relic! THE HOLY Relic! The Rose Knight's SKULL!
CALHOUN... I'M SORRY.
In recent years, science developed the means to rejuvenate dead, faded paint pigments.
Ancient works now look as good as when their paint was wet. And such is the case with it.
The treasure.
I look at the face of a beautiful woman. Her makeup fresh and bright. I begin to cry, and I Know...
...everything I've done to find her has been worth it.
What did Renute mean by Bixby having only ten minutes to kill--
OH, SHIT.

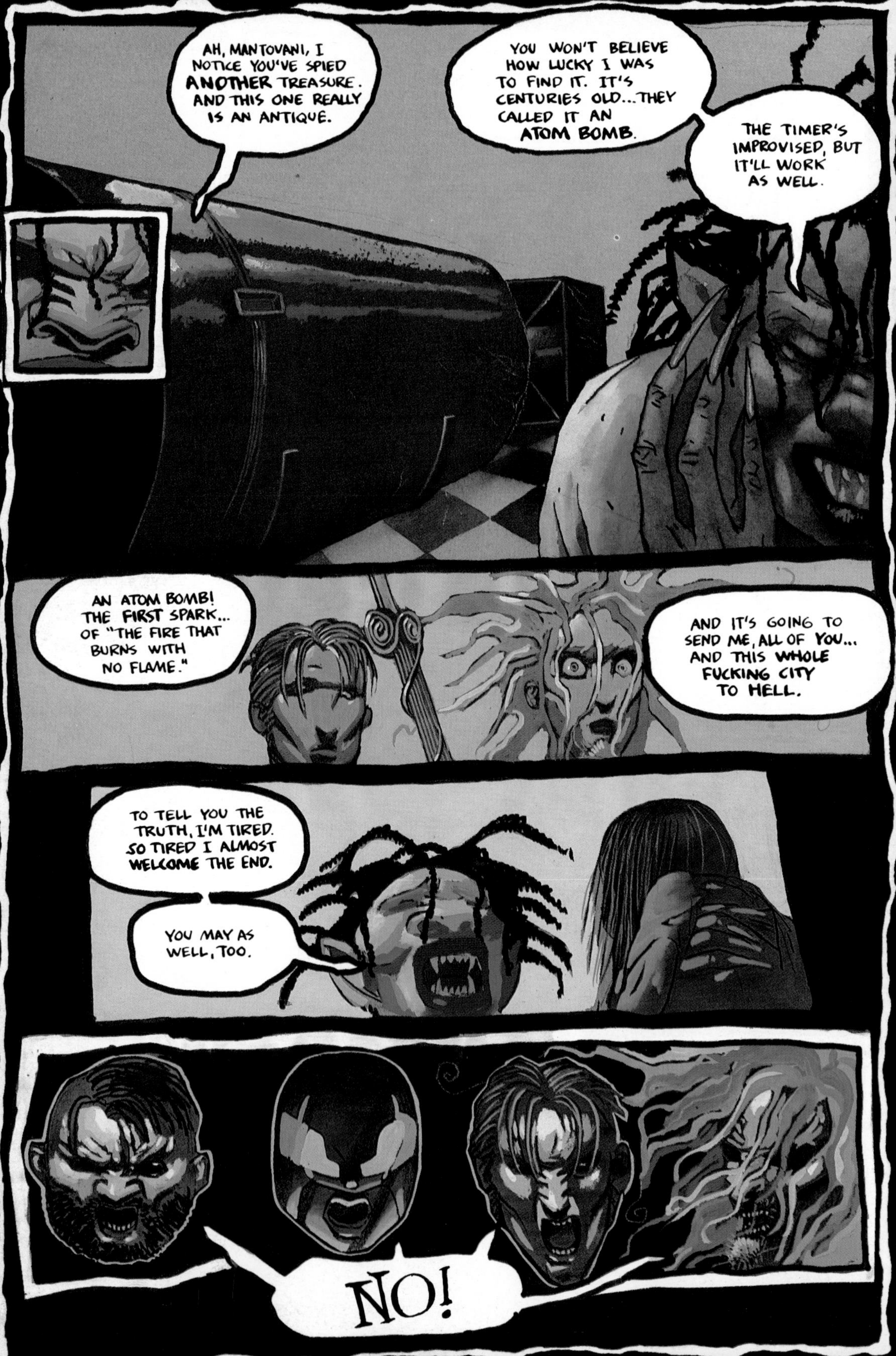
AH, MANTOVANI, I NOTICE YOU'VE SPIED ANOTHER TREASURE. AND THIS ONE REALLY IS AN ANTIQUE.
YOU WON'T BELIEVE HOW LUCKY I WAS TO FIND IT. IT'S CENTURIES OLD... THEY CALLED IT AN ATOM BOMB.
THE TIMER'S IMPROVISED, BUT IT'LL WORK AS WELL.
AN ATOM BOMB! THE FIRST SPARK... OF "THE FIRE THAT BURNS WITH NO FLAME."
AND IT'S GOING TO SEND ME, ALL OF YOU... AND THIS WHOLE FUCKING CITY TO HELL.
TO TELL YOU THE TRUTH, I'M TIRED. SO TIRED I ALMOST WELCOME THE END.
YOU MAY AS WELL, TOO.
NO!

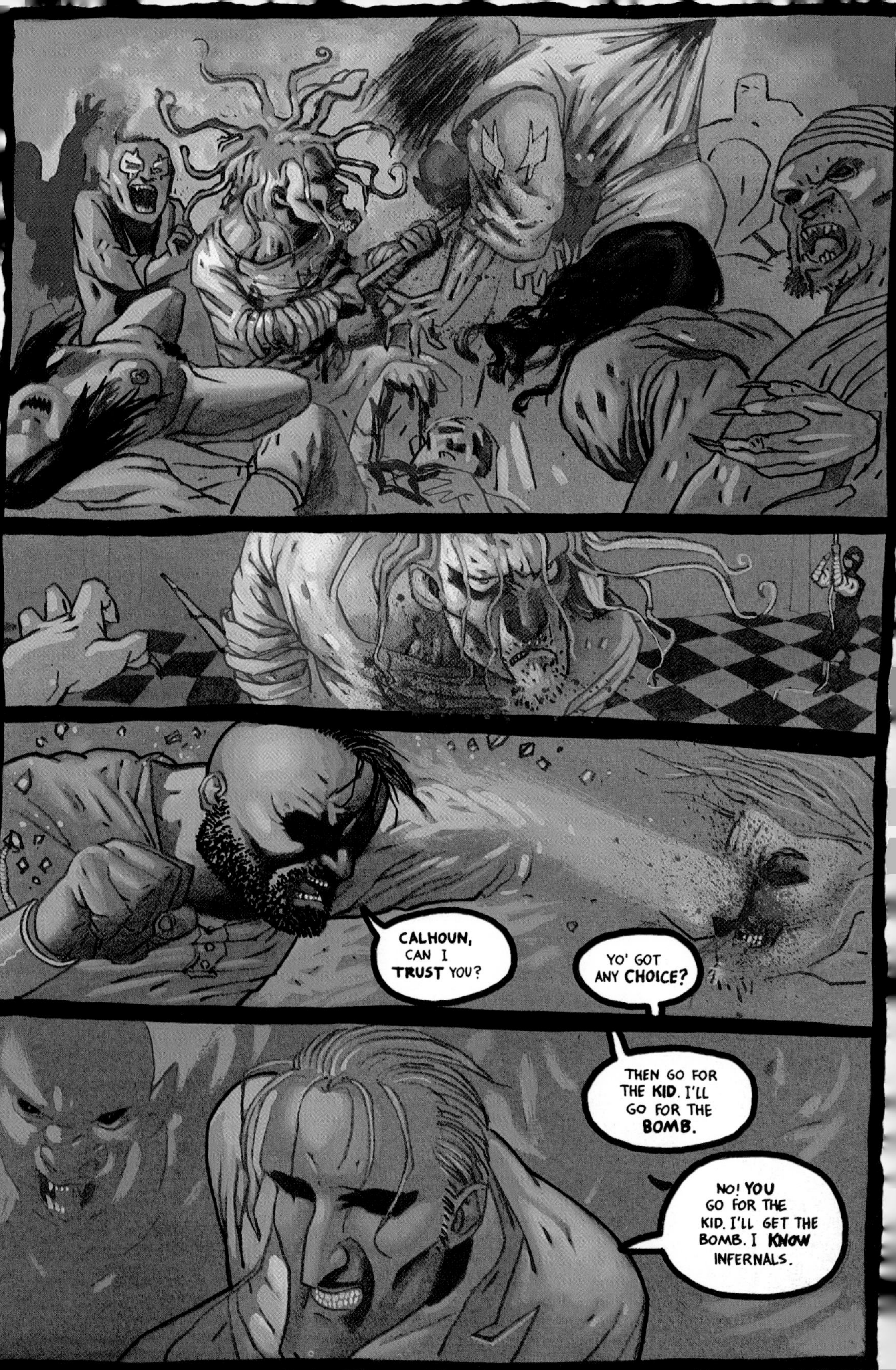

CALHOUN, CAN I TRUST YOU?
YO' GOT ANY CHOICE?
THEN GO FOR THE KID. I'LL GO FOR THE BOMB.
NO! YOU GO FOR THE KID. I'LL GET THE BOMB. I KNOW INFERNALS.

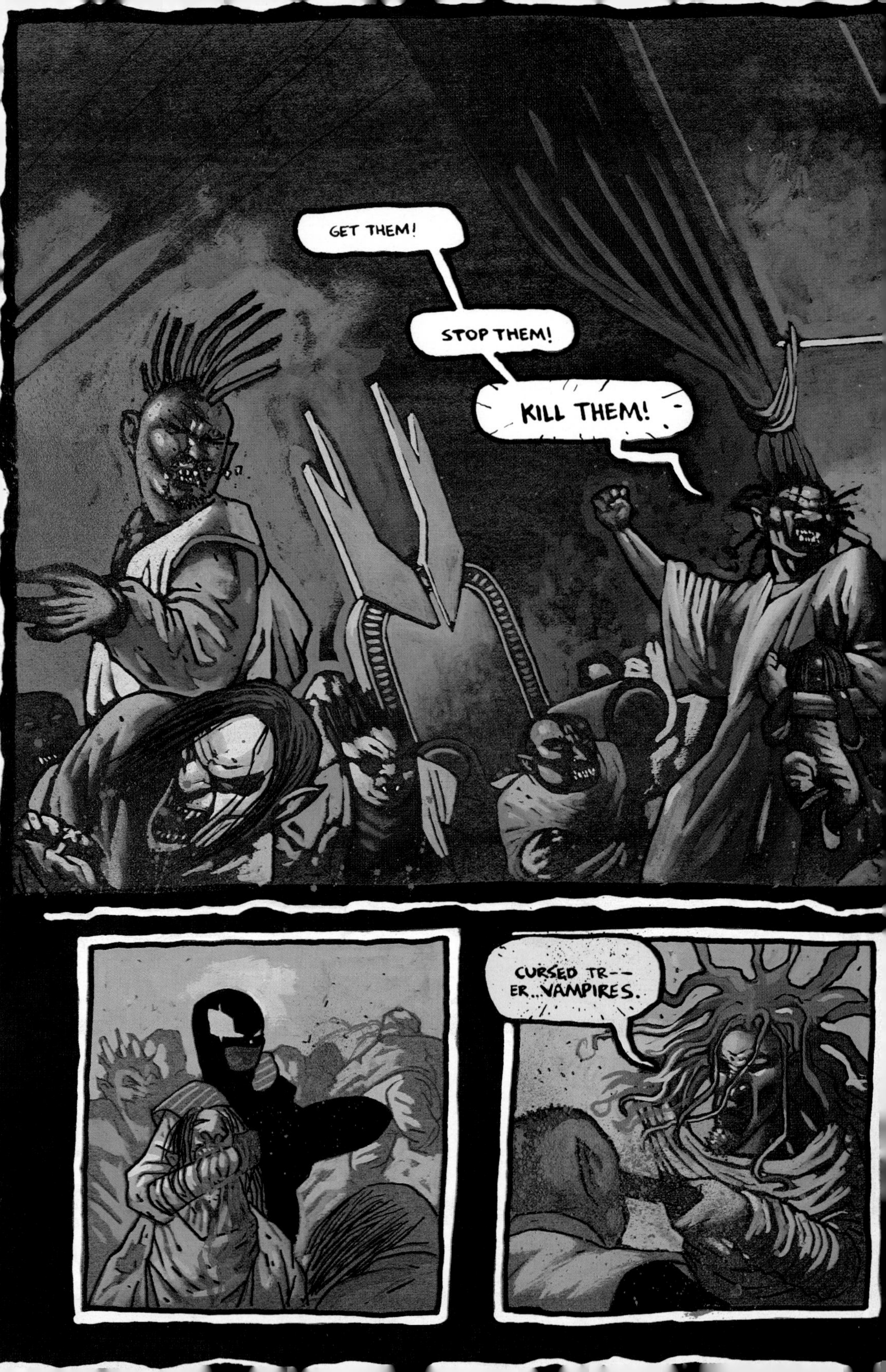
GET THEM!
STOP THEM!
KILL THEM!
CURSED TR--
ER...VAMPIRES.

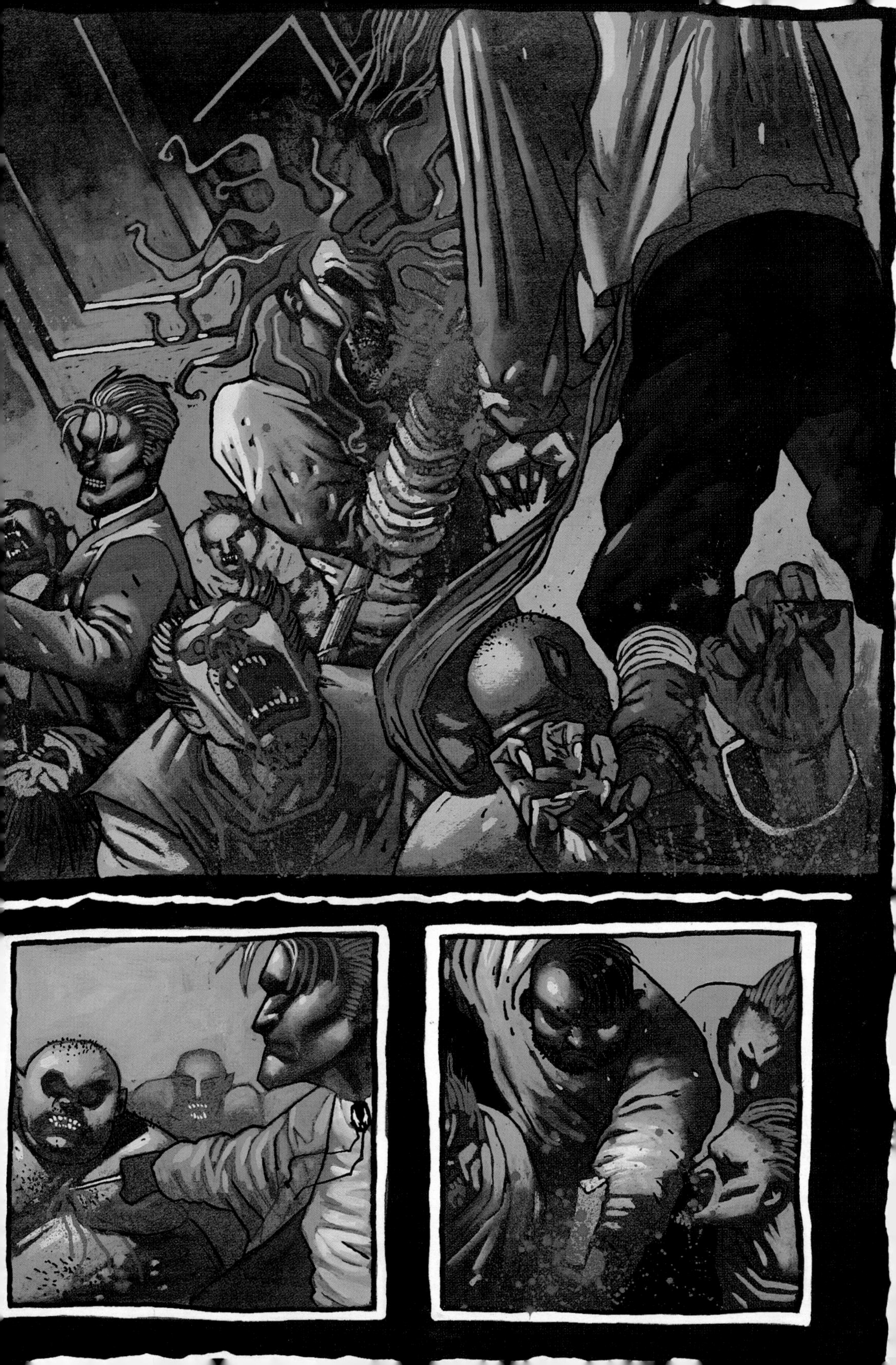

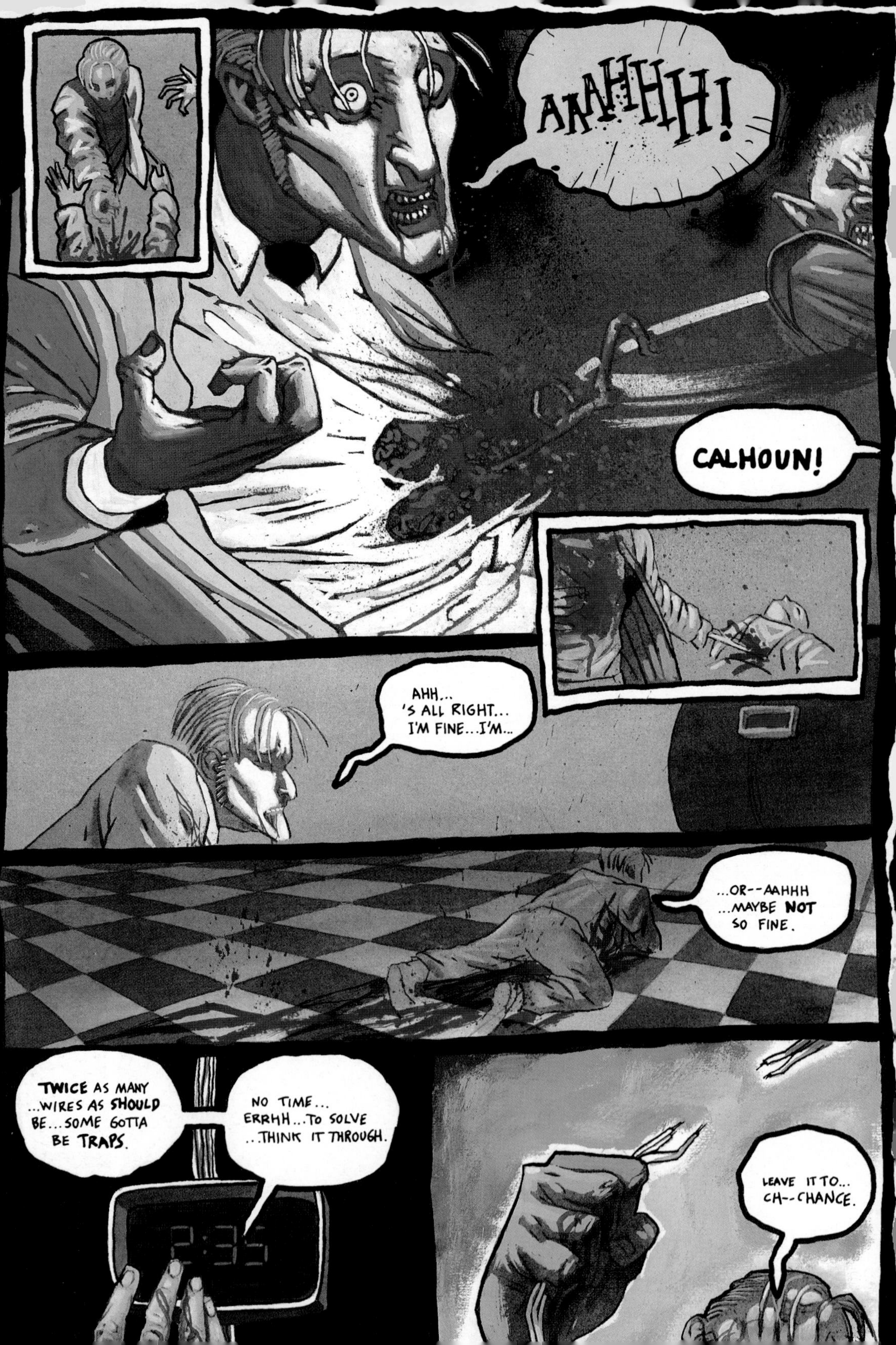
AAAHHHH!
CALHOUN!
AHH...
'S ALL RIGHT...
I'M FINE...I'M...
...OR--AAHHH
...MAYBE NOT
SO FINE.
TWICE AS MANY
...WIRES AS SHOULD
BE...SOME GOTTA
BE TRAPS.
NO TIME...
ERRHH...TO SOLVE
...THINK IT THROUGH.
LEAVE IT TO...
CH--CHANCE.

The Gambler smiled...

...down South...

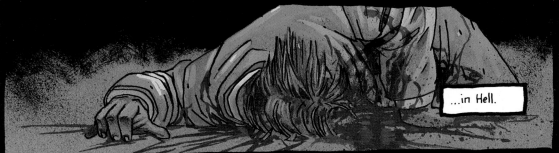

...in Hell.

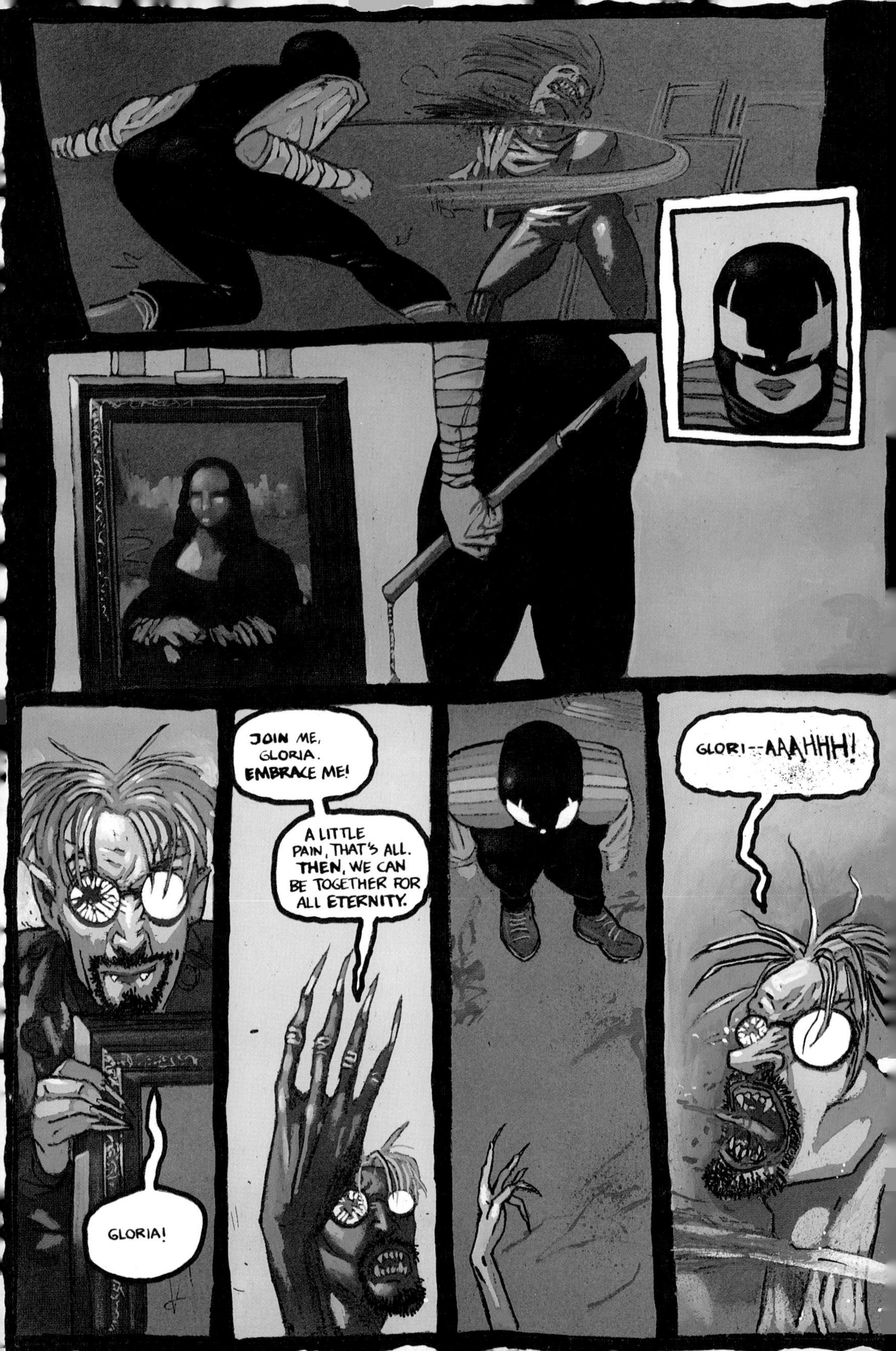
GLORIA!
JOIN ME, GLORIA. EMBRACE ME!
A LITTLE PAIN, THAT'S ALL. THEN, WE CAN BE TOGETHER FOR ALL ETERNITY.
GLORI--AAAHHH!

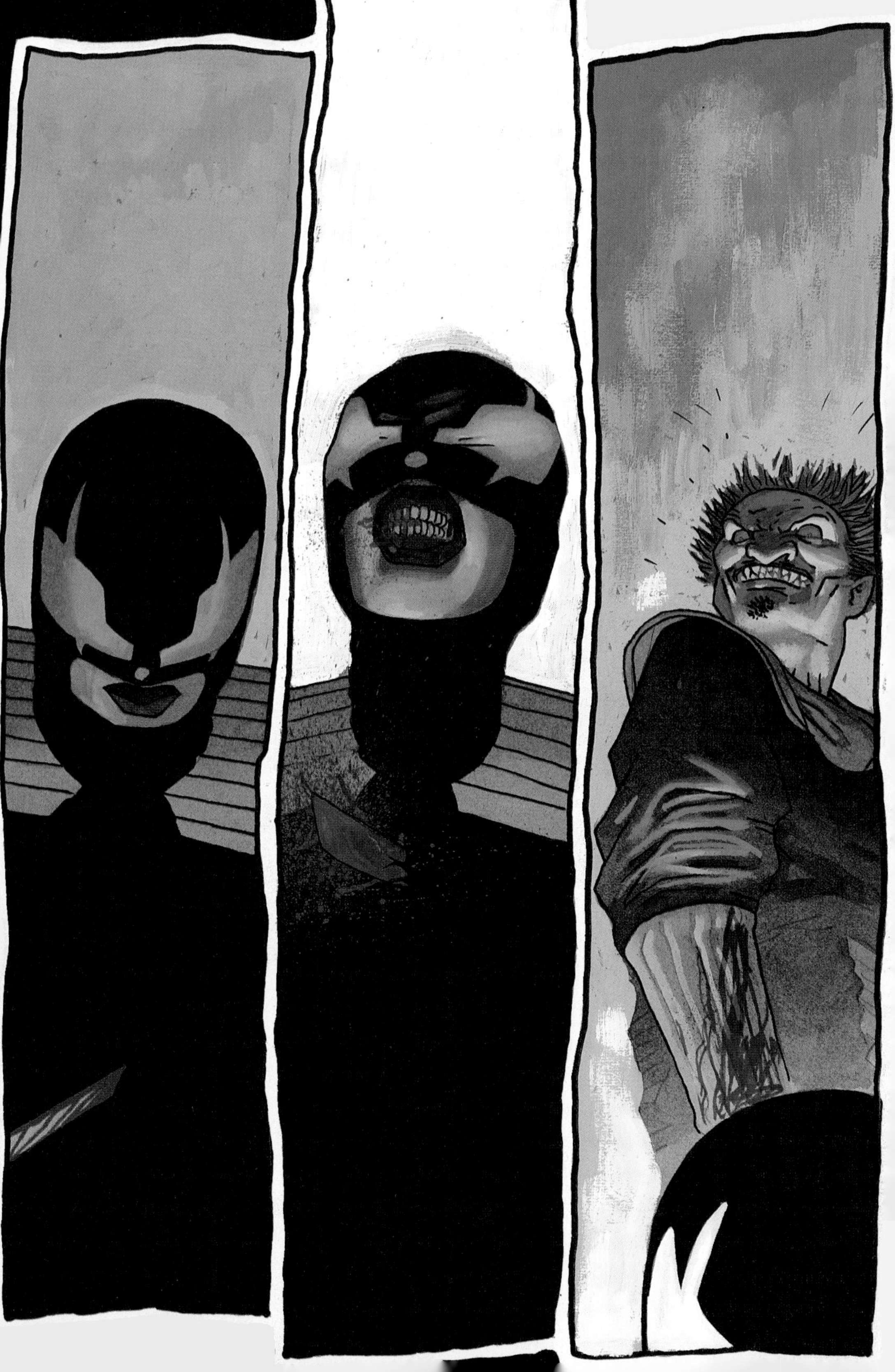

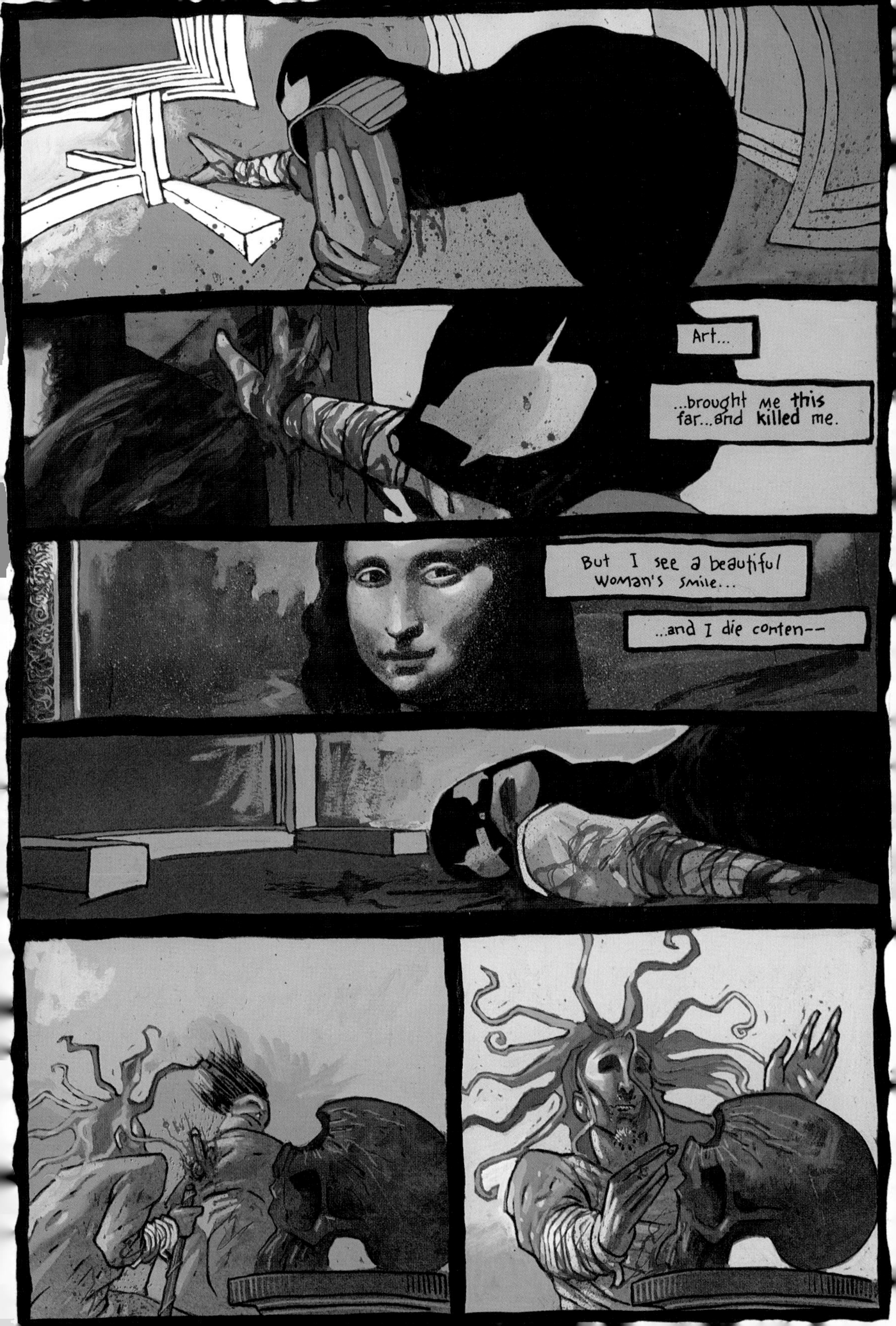
Art...
...brought me this far...and killed me.
But I see a beautiful woman's smile...
...and I die conten--

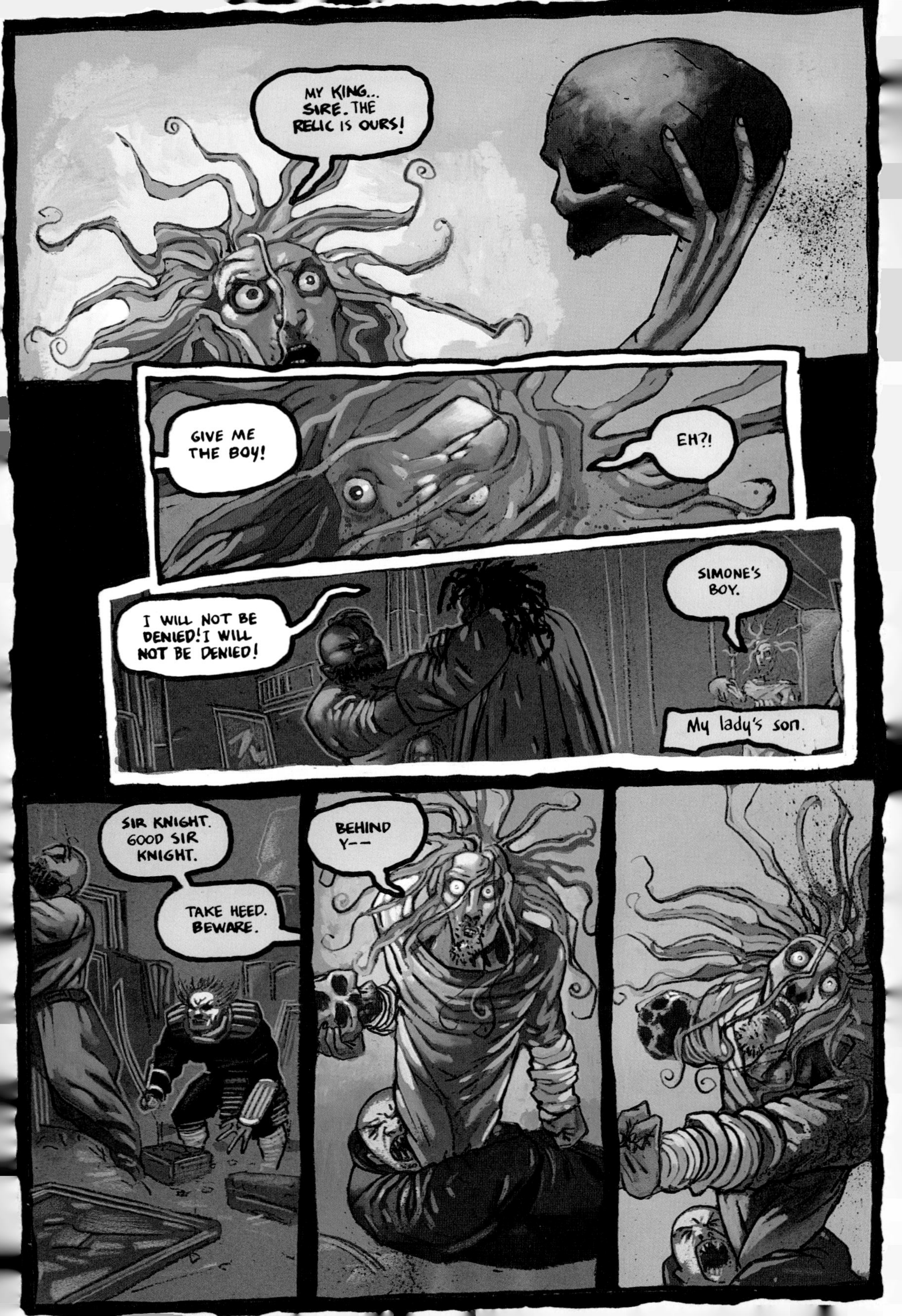

MY KING... SIRE. THE RELIC IS OURS!
GIVE ME THE BOY!
EH?!
I WILL NOT BE DENIED! I WILL NOT BE DENIED!
SIMONE'S BOY.
My lady's son.
SIR KNIGHT. GOOD SIR KNIGHT.
TAKE HEED. BEWARE.
BEHIND Y--

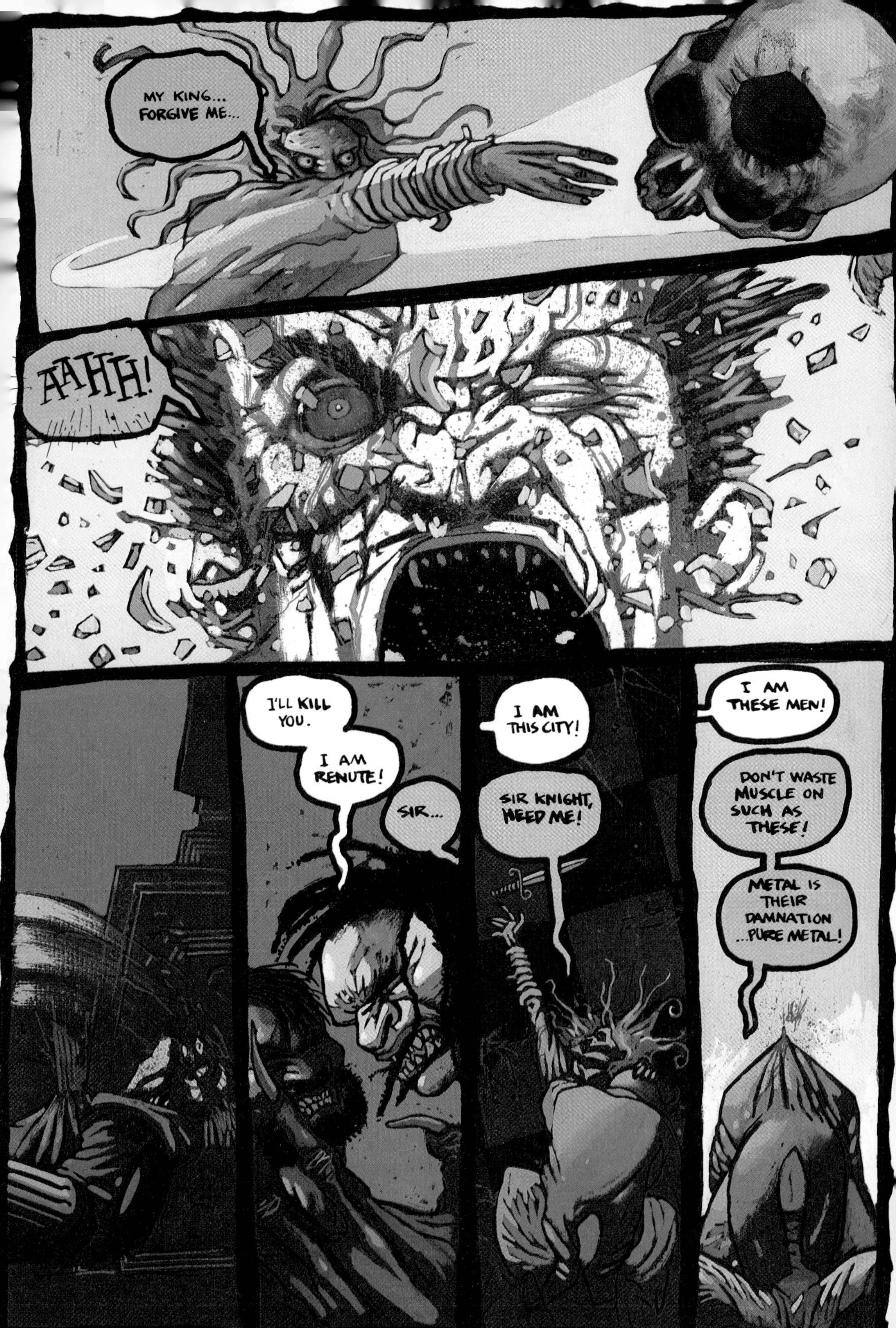
MY KING... FORGIVE ME...
AAHH!
I'LL KILL YOU.
I AM RENUTE!
SIR...
I AM THIS CITY!
SIR KNIGHT, HEED ME!
I AM THESE MEN!
DON'T WASTE MUSCLE ON SUCH AS THESE!
METAL IS THEIR DAMNATION ...PURE METAL!

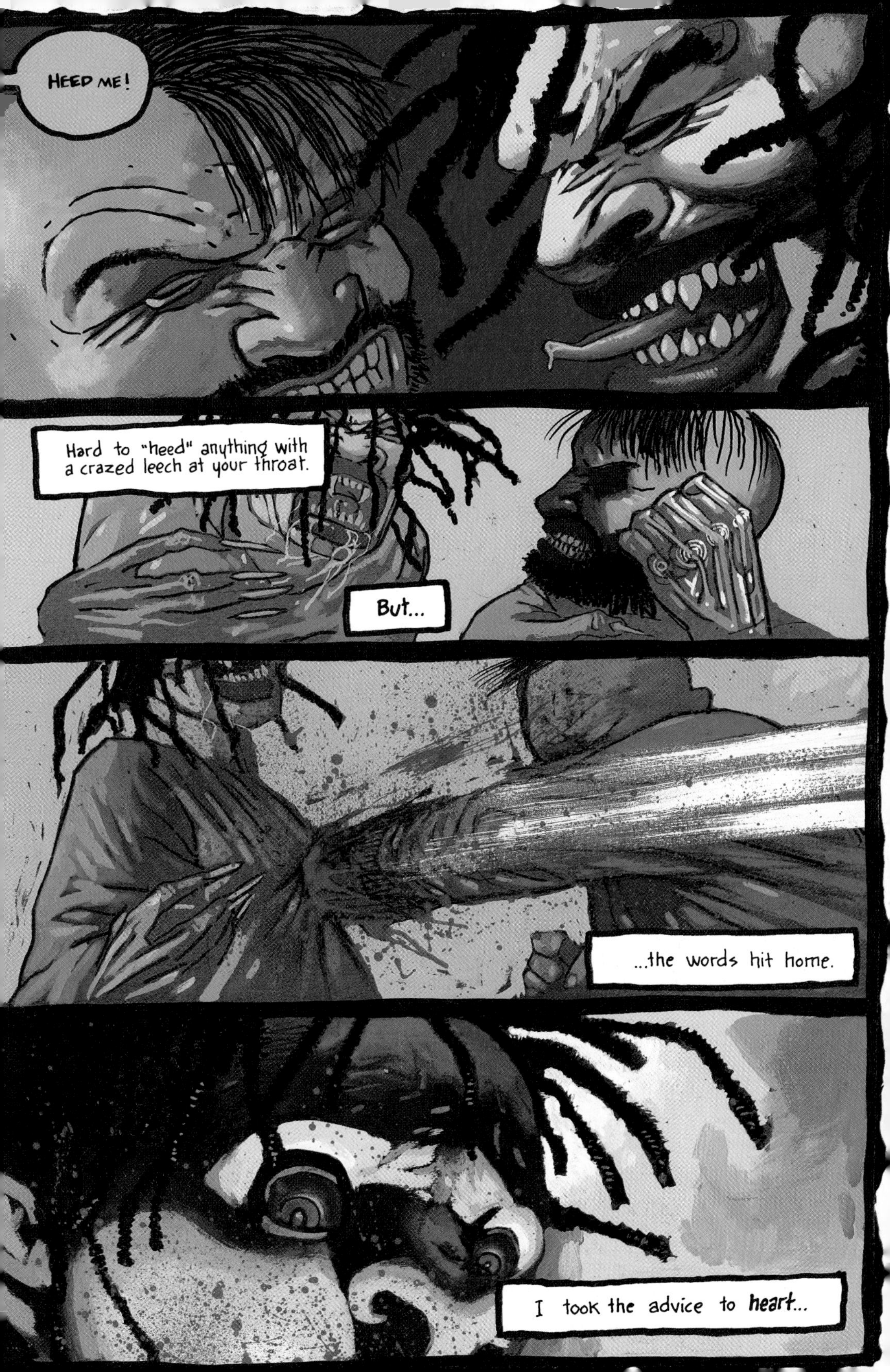
HEED ME!
Hard to "heed" anything with a crazed leech at your throat.
But...
...the words hit home.
I took the advice to heart...

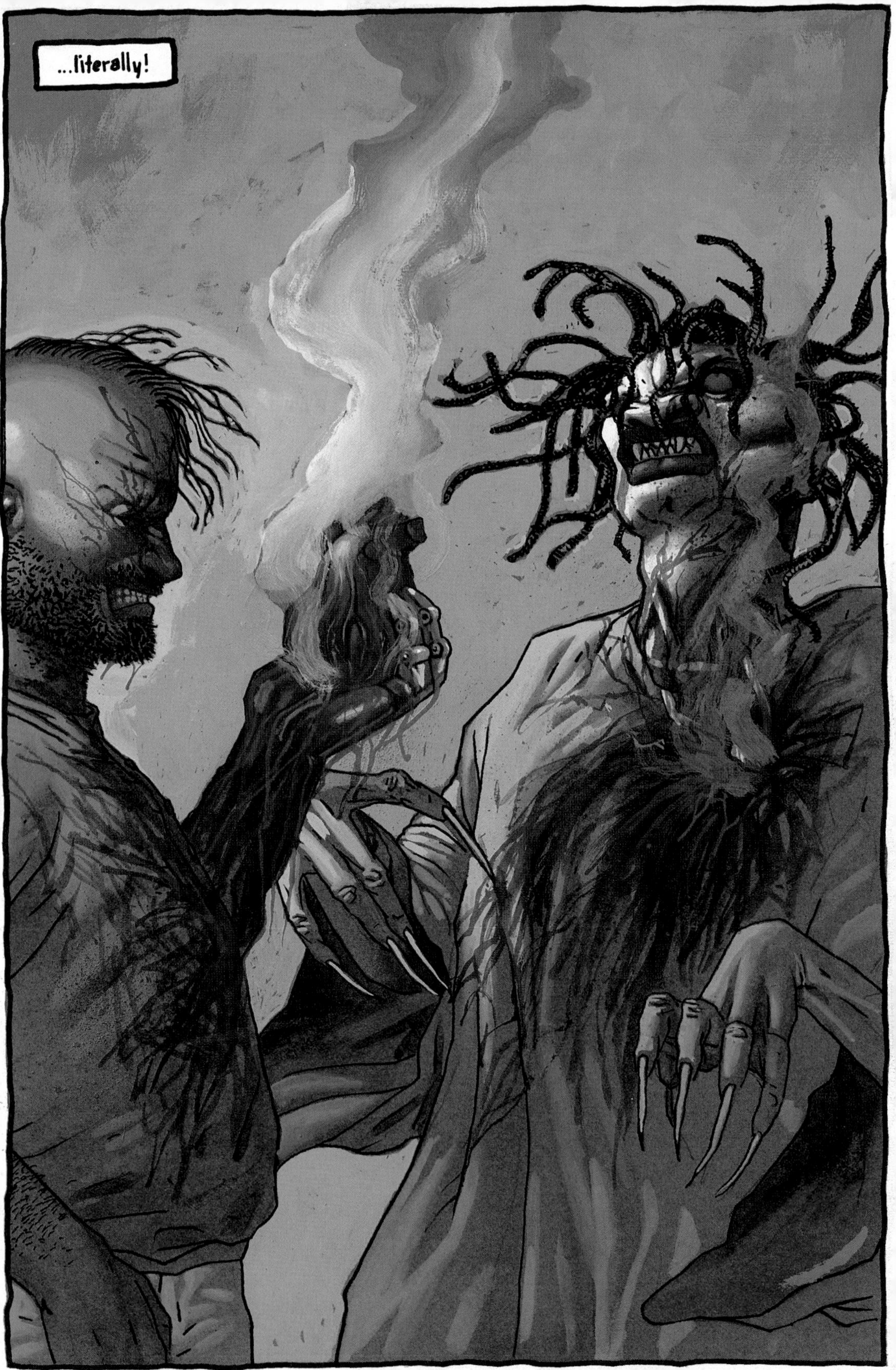
...literally!

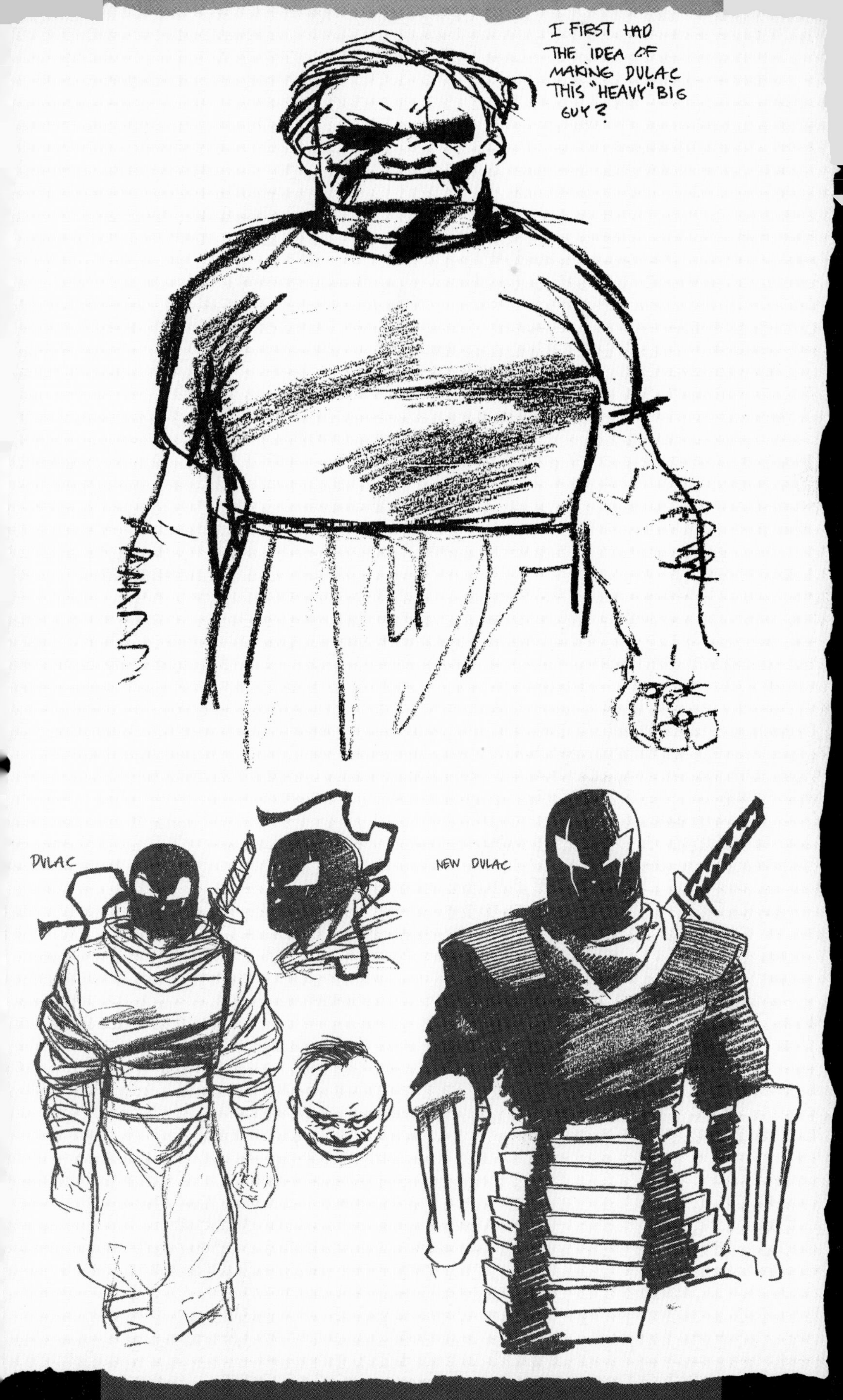
I FIRST HAD THE IDEA OF MAKING DULAC THIS "HEAVY" BIG GUY?
DULAC
NEW DULAC

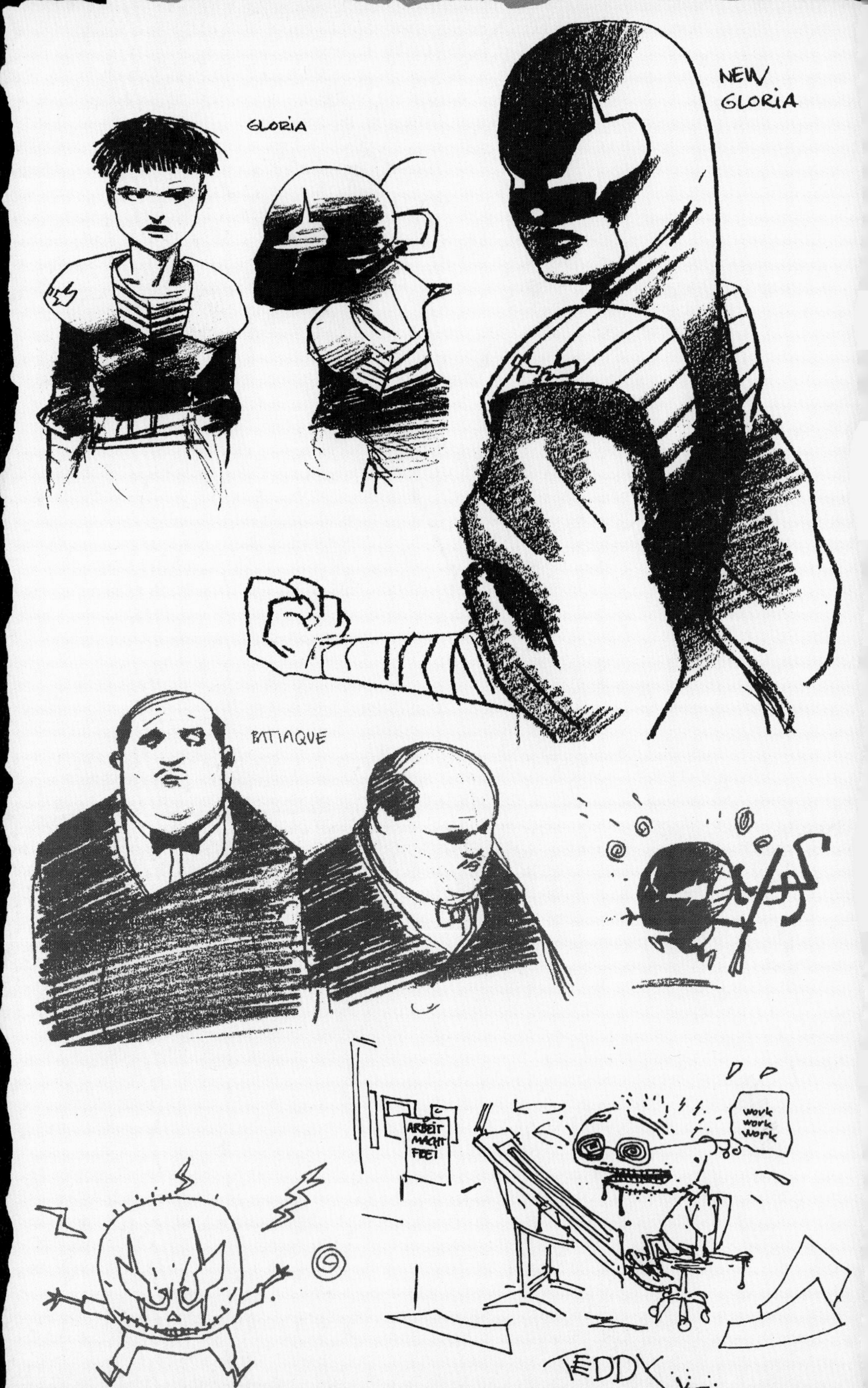
GLORIA
NEW GLORIA
BATTAQUE
ARBEIT MACHT FREI
work work work
TEDDY

AFTERWORD

Although *Four Devils, One Hell* originally appeared in six monthly installments, from August '93 through January '94, the series was actually more than four years in the making. If memory serves, I first read James Robinson's story outline sometime in 1989 and spent a good deal of that summer writing copious notes on each of his six plots. I was living the freelance life in those days, having just moved to southern California, and I remember reading James's weighty tomes (can you say "Alan Moore"?!) while nurturing my year-round tan at the pool.

A year later, everything had changed. I was living in rainy Portland, Oregon, the publication rights to *Grendel* were frozen in bankruptcy court, and all the checks had long dried up. And so . . . we waited. And waited. And waited.

And waited.

By the time Matt Wagner successfully wrested back the rights to his own character, we had lost the original *Four Devils* artist. Enter Teddy Kristiansen, whom I managed to sign up at the 1992 San Diego Con, just before DC Comics got wind of him! Teddy began working on *Grendel Tales* shortly thereafter and didn't stop until about 16 months, 148 pages, a marriage, and a newborn baby later.

One of the great treats of working with artists is that, well, they like to draw. Every Federal Express package and every fax from Teddy would arrive accompanied by caricatures of himself: scribbling furiously, a crazed look in his eyes; or sprawled and sleepless over the drawing board; or Teddy-as-Grendel, a truncated, miniature Grendel, to be sure, but without a doubt one of the cutest devils ever to haunt my desk! The following pages contain some of these caricatures, along with several of Teddy's original character sketches, all of which I saved in the hope of sharing some of the delight I felt upon receiving these "doodles" with you, the reader.

Cheers!

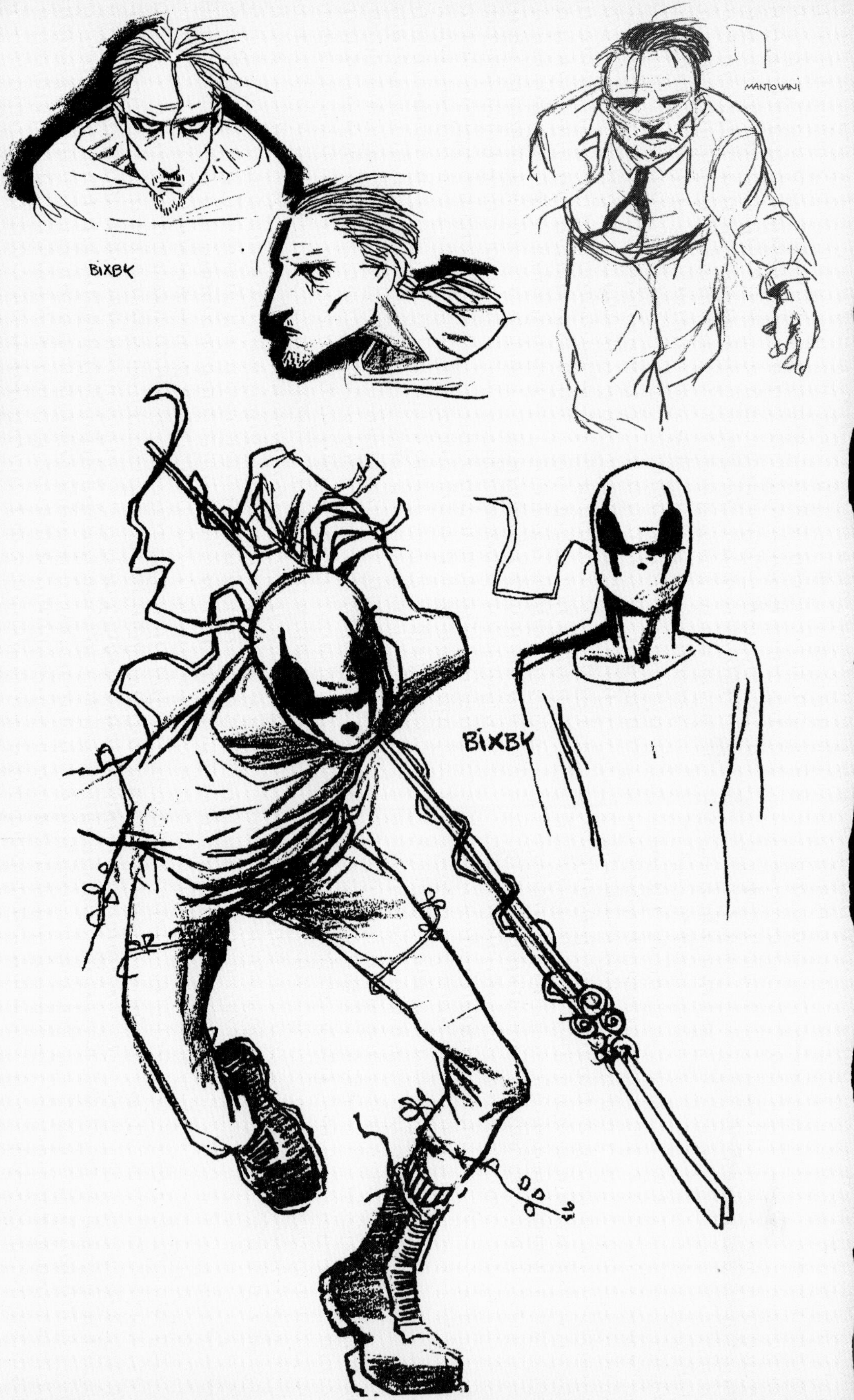
BIXBY
MANTOVANI
BIXBY

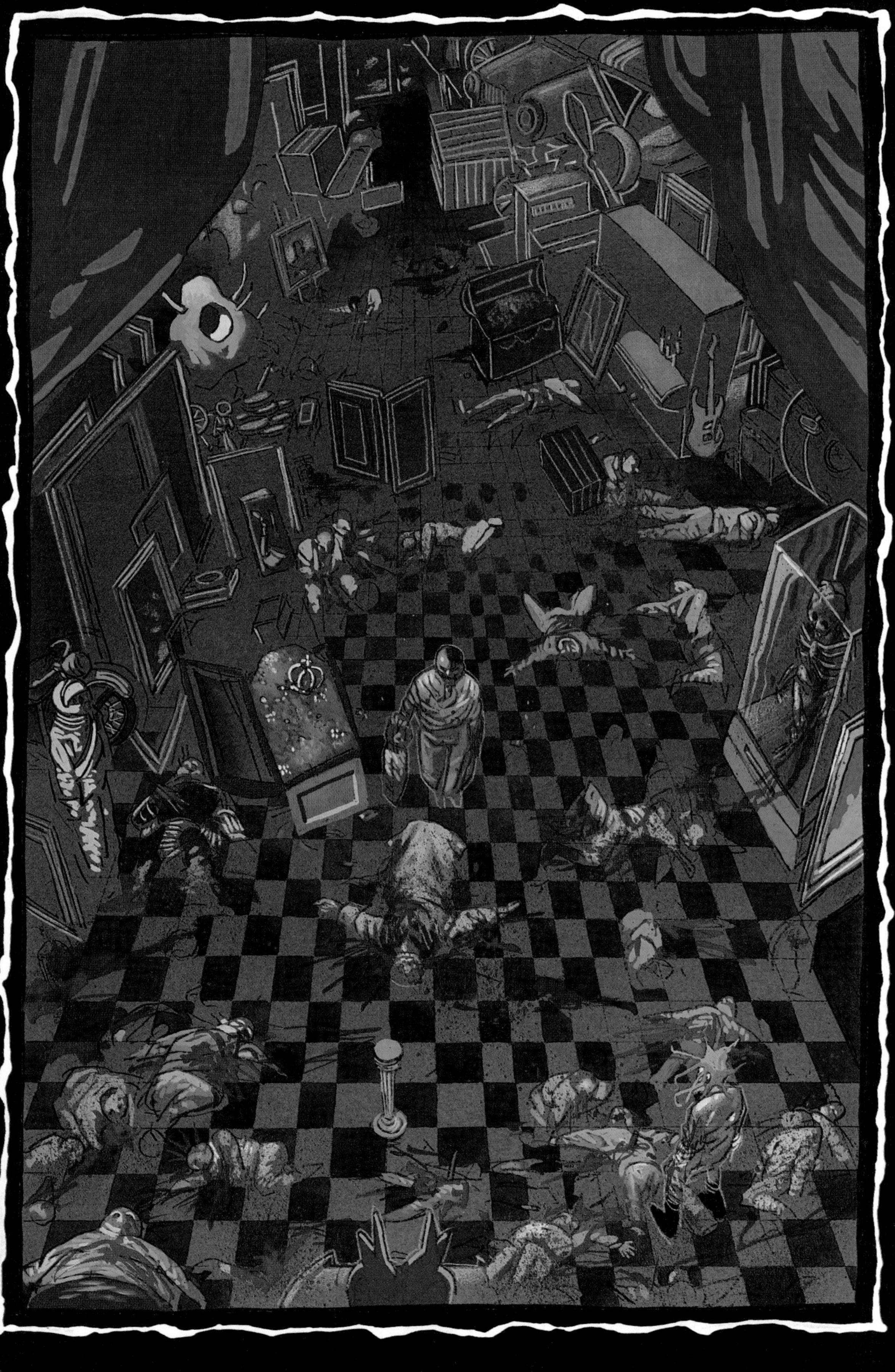

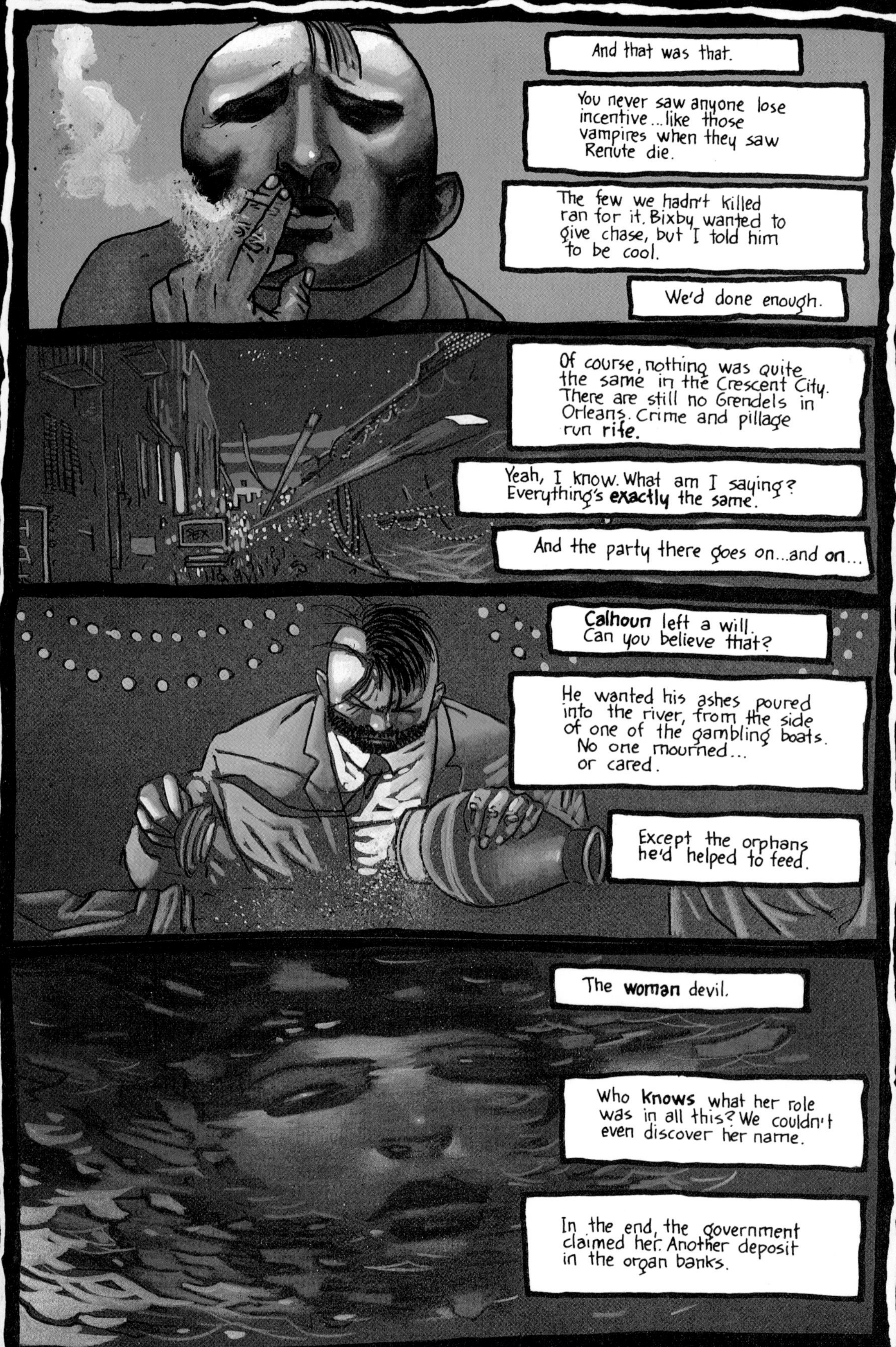

And that was that.
You never saw anyone lose incentive...like those vampires when they saw Renute die.
The few we hadn't killed ran for it. Bixby wanted to give chase, but I told him to be cool.
We'd done enough.
Of course, nothing was quite the same in the Crescent City. There are still no Grendels in Orleans. Crime and pillage run **rife.**
Yeah, I know. What am I saying? Everything's **exactly** the same.
And the party there goes on...and **on**...
SEX
Calhoun left a will. Can you believe that?
He wanted his ashes poured into the river, from the side of one of the gambling boats. No one mourned... or cared.
Except the orphans he'd helped to feed.
The **woman** devil.
Who **knows** what her role was in all this? We couldn't even discover her name.
In the end, the government claimed her. Another deposit in the organ banks.

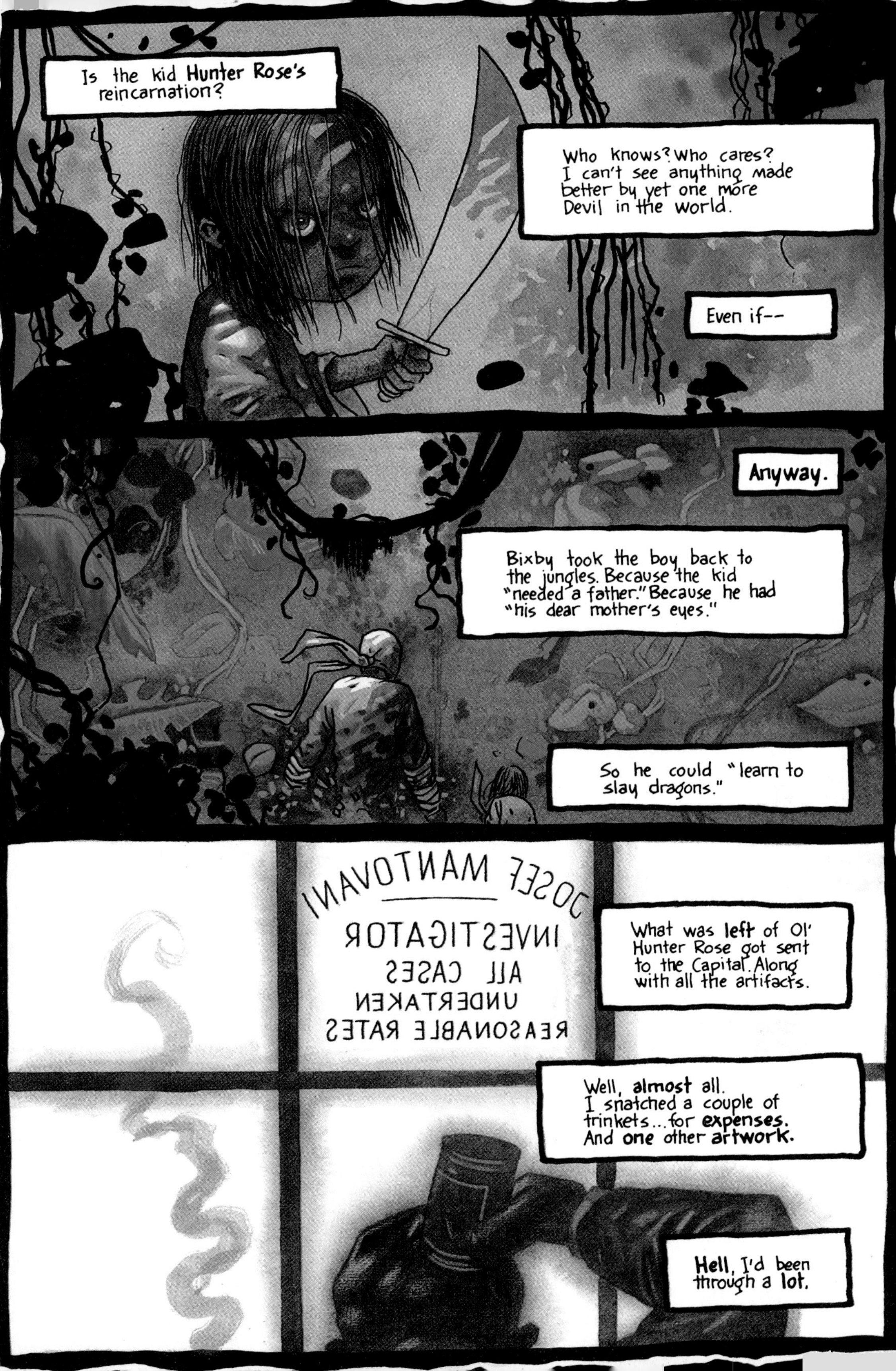
Is the kid Hunter Rose's reincarnation?
Who knows? Who cares? I can't see anything made better by yet one more Devil in the world.
Even if--
Anyway.
Bixby took the boy back to the jungles. Because the kid "needed a father." Because he had "his dear mother's eyes."
So he could "learn to slay dragons."
JOSEF MANTOVANI
INVESTIGATOR
ALL CASES
UNDERTAKEN
REASONABLE RATES
What was left of Ol' Hunter Rose got sent to the Capital. Along with all the artifacts.
Well, almost all. I snatched a couple of trinkets...for expenses. And one other artwork.
Hell, I'd been through a lot.

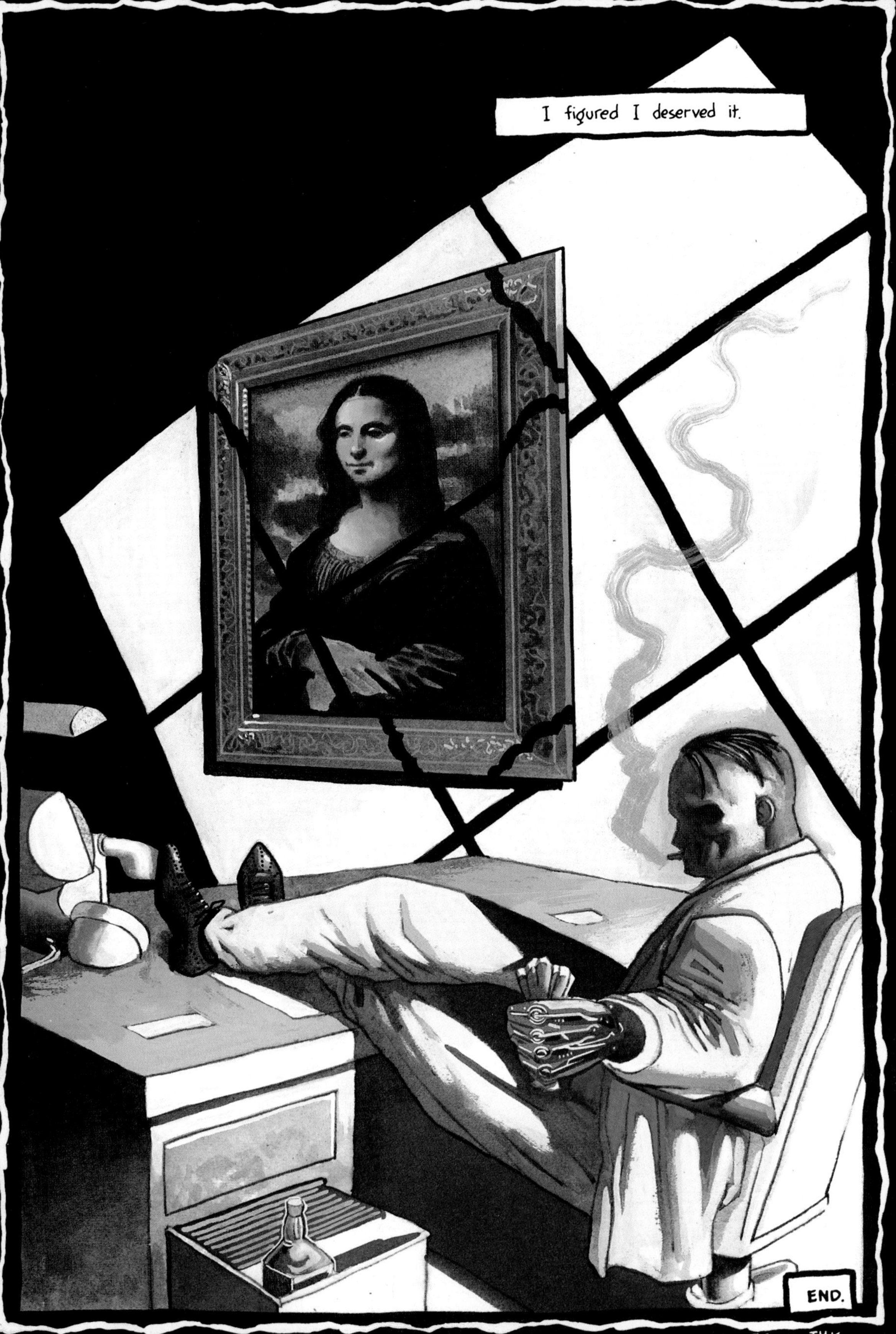
I figured I deserved it.
END.
J.R. T.H.K.